THE COMPANION GUIDE TO TURKEY

VOLUME I
ISTANBUL AND AROUND THE MARMARA·

THE COMPANION GUIDES

*It is the aim of these guides to provide a Companion
in the person of the author; who knows
intimately the places and people of whom he writes, and is able to
communicate this knowledge and affection to his readers.
It is hoped that the text and pictures will aid them
in their preparations and in their travels, and will
help them remember on their return.*

BURGUNDY · THE COUNTRY ROUND PARIS
DEVON · EDINBURGH AND THE BORDER COUNTRY
FLORENCE · GASCONY AND THE DORDOGNE
GREEK ISLANDS · KENT AND SUSSEX
LAKE DISTRICT · LONDON
MADRID AND CENTRAL SPAIN
NEW YORK · PARIS · ROME
SICILY · SOUTH OF SPAIN · VENICE

THE COMPANION GUIDE TO

ISTANBUL

AND AROUND THE MARMARA

JOHN FREELY

COMPANION GUIDES

First published 2000
Companion Guides, Woodbridge

ISBN 1 900639 31 9

*The publishers and author have done their best to ensure
the accuracy and currency of all the information in*
The Companion Guide to Istanbul and around the Marmara.
*However, they can accept no responsibility for any loss, injury,
or inconvenience sustained by any traveller as a result
of information or advice contained in the guide.*

Companion Guides is an imprint of Boydell & Brewer Ltd
PO Box 9, Woodbridge, Suffolk IP12 3DF, UK
and of Boydell & Brewer Inc.
PO Box 41026, Rochester, NY 14604–4126, USA
website: http://www.boydell.co.uk

A catalogue record for this book is available
from the British Library

Printed in Great Britain by
St Edmundsbury Press Ltd, Bury St Edmunds, Suffolk

Contents

II: AROUND THE MARMARA

List of illustrations

Photographs by Tony Baker

List of maps and plans

Introduction

Much of the interest that Turkey has for travellers stems from the fact that it extends into two continents and is thus part of two worlds. Ninety-three percent of Turkey's land mass is in Asia, comprising the subcontinent called Anatolia, which in times past was more generally known as Asia Minor, while the remainder of the country is in Europe, forming the southeasternmost extremity of the Balkan peninsula.

Turkey in Europe, the eastern part of the region known in antiquity as Thrace, is separated from Anatolia by the Bosphorus, the Sea of Marmara and the Dardanelles. Istanbul, Turkey's largest and most historic city, known to the Greeks as Constantinople, stands astride the Bosphorus at the entrance to the strait from the Marmara, where it was founded more than twenty-six centuries ago as the Greek colony of Byzantium. This is the imperial city, capital of the Christian Byzantine Empire for more than a thousand years and then capital of the Muslim Ottoman Empire for nearly five centuries.

The Byzantine and Ottoman empires in their prime extended from southeastern Europe into western Asia and around the eastern Mediterranean into North Africa. The heartland of both empires was the land that now comprises the Republic of Turkey, which Atatürk and his followers created out of the wreckage of the Ottoman Empire in 1923. The Ottoman Empire had itself risen out of the ashes of the Byzantine Empire, the survival of the Roman Empire in its eastern dominions, principally Asia Minor. In Anatolia one finds the ruins and monuments of still earlier empires, kingdoms, city-states and distinctive cultures that stretch back some ten millennia to the Late Stone Age, a palimpsest of civilizations, with each successive one built on and from the ruins of those that have preceded it on this immemorial landscape.

ix

The first two editions of this guide (1979, 1993) covered all of Turkey in a single volume. The present edition will be the first in a three-volume series on Turkey. This first volume describes Istanbul and the region extending around the Sea of Marmara. The second volume will cover the Aegean and Mediterranean coasts from the Dardanelles to the Syrian border, while the third will describe the interior of Anatolia and the Black Sea coast out to the eastern borders of Turkey.

This first volume is divided into two parts. The first part guides the traveller on a series of strolls through Istanbul. The second goes around the Sea of Marmara, first on the European side from Istanbul via Edirne to the Dardanelles, and then on the Asian shore from Çanakkale and Troy via Bursa and Iznik back to the Bosphorus.

A number of appendices are included, some of them of a practical nature and others in the form of background information, to aid the traveller in exploring Turkey and getting to know its people and their way of life, past and present. You could start by reading the first appendix, which explains the spelling and pronunciation of Turkish words, and perhaps before setting out on your journey you might find it useful to study a primer of modern Turkish, although these days most Turks you will come in contact with will know at least some English, particularly in Istanbul.

The present guide has basic maps to follow the strolls in Istanbul and the itineraries around the Sea of Marmara, as well as plans of the more important monuments and archaeological sites. For those who want more detailed maps I recommend the **Euro-City Istanbul** and the **Euro-Atlas Türkiye**.

Northwestern Turkey has a mild climate; the summers are dry and tempered by the prevailing northerly wind; the winters tend to be rainy and it seldom freezes or snows except for the occasional blizzard in Thrace. Late spring and early autumn are also ideal times for a visit to northwestern Turkey, but you can enjoy Istanbul even in the depths of winter, when the Byzantine churches, Ottoman mosques and museums are empty, while the cafes and restaurants are full of locals who will be more than willing to have you join them. 'Hoş geldiniz!' (Welcome) they will say to you in greeting, to which you respond 'Hoş bulduk!' (We are pleased to be here), which will be the truth. So 'Iyi yolculuklar!' – Have a good journey!

Turkish Spelling and Pronunciation

Throughout this book, modern Turkish spelling has been used for Turkish proper names and for things that are specifically Turkish, with a few exceptions for Turkish words that have made their way into English. Modern Turkish is rigorously logical and phonetic, and the few letters that are pronounced differently from English are indicated below. All letters have but a single sound, and none is totally silent. Turkish is very slightly accented, most often on the last syllable, but all syllables should be clearly and almost evenly accented.

Vowels are accentuated as in French or German; i.e., **a** as in father (the rarely used **â** sounds rather like **ay**), **e** as in met, **i** as in machine, **o** as in **oh**, **u** as in mute. In addition there are three other vowels that do not occur in English; these are **ı** (undotted), pronounced as the **u** in but, **ö** as in German or as the **oy** in annoy, **ü** as in German or as the **ul** in suit.

Consonants are pronounced as in English, except the following:

c as **j** in jam; e.g. cami (mosque) = **j**ahmy
ç as **ch** in chat; e.g. çorba (soup) = **ch**orba
g as in get; never as in gem
ğ is almost silent and tends to lengthen the previous vowel
ş as in sugar; e.g. çeşme (fountain) = che**sh**me

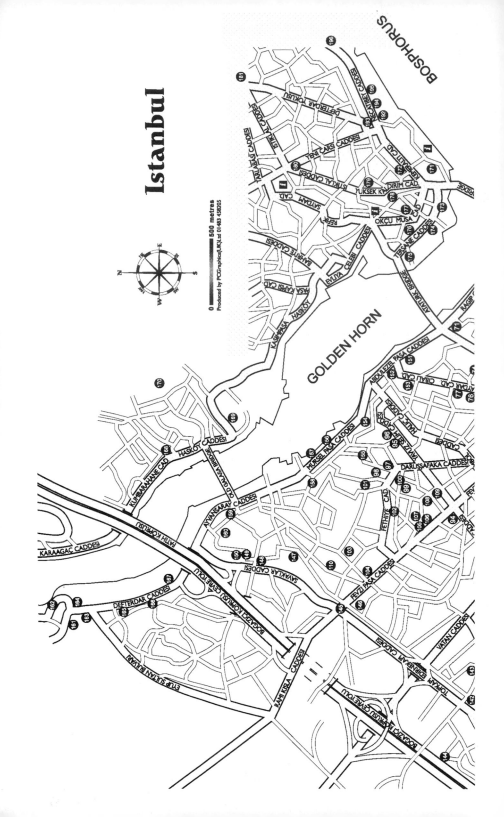

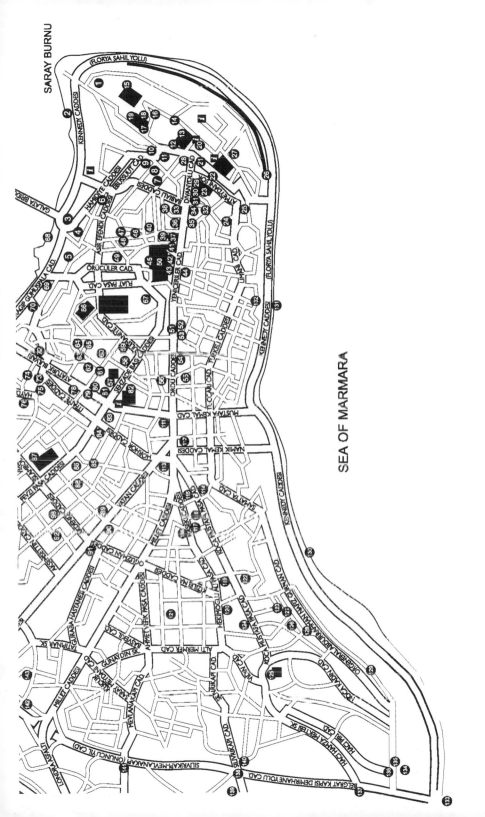

Ortaköy

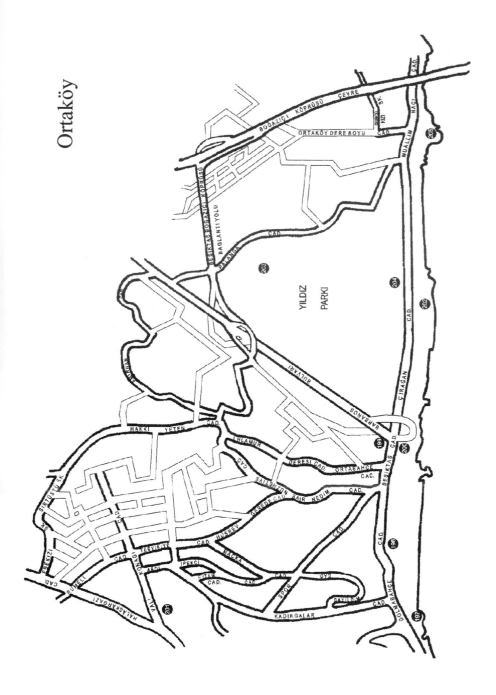

Üsküdar

KEY TO ISTANBUL MAP

1. Goth's Column
2. Sepetçiler Köşku
3. Yeni Cami
4. Spice Bazaar
5. Mosque of Rüstem Pasha
6. Türbe of Abdül Hamit I
7. Cağaloğlu Baths
8. Mosque of Beşir Ağa
9. Sublime Porte
10. Alay Kiosk
11. Mosque of Zeynep Sultan
12. Medrese of Gazanfer Ağa
13. Haghia Sophia
14. Fountain of Ahmet III
15. Topkapî Sarayî
16. Haghia Eirene
17. Museum of the Ancient Orient
18. Archaeological Museum
19. Çinili Köşk
20. Baths of Roxelana
21. Mosque of Sultan Ahmet I
22. Hippodrome
23. Palace of Ibrahim Pasha
24. Mosque of Sokollu Mehmet Pasha
25. Küçük Aya Sofya Camii (Church of SS. Sergius and Bacchus)
26. Palace of Bucoleon
27. Mosaic Museum
28. Yerebatan Saray (Basilica Cistern)
29. Mosque of Firuz Ağa
30. Palaces of Antiochus and Lausus (ruins)
31. Binbirdirek Cistern
32. Theodorus Cistern
33. Türbe of Mahmut II
34. Köprülü Library
35. Köprülü Mosque and Türbe
36. Çemberlitaş Baths
37. Column of Constantine
38. Vezir Hanî
39. Nuruosmaniye Mosque
40. Mosque of Mahmut Pasha
41. Mosque of Atik Ali Pasha
42. Koca Sinan Pasha Külliyesi
43. Çorlulu Ali Pasha Külliyesi
44. Kara Mustafa Pasha Külliyesi
45. Covered Bazaar
46. Mahmut Pasha Baths
47. Kürkçü Hanî
48. Büyük Yeni Han
49. Valide Hanî
50. Sahaflar Çarşîşî
51. Forum of Theodosius (ruins)
52. Şimkeşhane
53. Seyyit Hasan Pasha Hanî
54. Library of Ragîp Pasha
55. Bodrum Cami (Church of the Myrelaion)
56. Laleli Camii
57. Şehzade Camii
58. Külliye of Nevşehirli Ibrahim Pasha
59. Kalenderhane Camii (Church of the Myrelaion)
60. Medrese of Ekmekcizade Ahmet Pasha
61. Primary School of Recai Mehmet Efendi
62. Mosque of Mimar Mehmet Ağa
63. Vefa Camii
64. Library of Atif Efendi
65. Kilise Cami (Church of St.Theodore)
66. The Süleymaniye
67. Beyazit Tower
68. Mosque of Ahi Çelebi
69. Kantarcilar Camii
70. Üç Mirablî Camii
71. Yavuz Ersinan Camii
72. Mosque of Şebsafa Kadîn
73. Primary School of Zenbelli Ali Efendi
74. Zeyrek Camii (Church of the Pantocrator)
75. Şeyh Süleyman Mescidi
76. Eğri Minare Camii
77. Eski Imaret Camii (Church of the Pantepoptes)
78. Çinili Hamam
79. Medrese of Gazanfer Ağa
80. Aqueduct of Valens
81. Burmalî Minare Camii
82. Medrese of Ankaravi Mehmet Efendi
83. Church of St. Polyeuctes (ruins)
84. Külliye of Amcazade Hüseyin Pasha
85. Column of Marcian
86. Medrese of Feyzullah Efendi
87. Fatih Camii (The Mosque of the Conqueror)
88. Mosque of Iskender Pasha
89. Fenari Isa Camii (Monastery of Constantine Lips)
90. Medrese of Selim I
91. Türbe of Şah Huban
92. Türbe of Hüsrev Pasha
93. Mosque of Bali Pasha
94. Mosque of Mesih Pasha
95. Cistern of Aspar
96. Mosque of Selim I
97. Mosque of Ismail Efendi
98. Library of Murat Molla
99. Mosque of Mehmet Ağa
100. Hirami Ahmet Pasha Camii (Church of St. John in Trullo)
101. Fethiye Camii (Church of the Pammakaristos)
102. Draman Camii
103. Kevevi Camii

In memory of my sister Dorothy Lehner

PART I: ISTANBUL

1

The Imperial City

ISTANBUL IS THE only city in the world that stands astride two continents, poised between Asia and Europe, torn between East and West. This is the imperial city – ancient Byzantium, Greek Constantinople, Ottoman Istanbul – now midway through the twenty-seventh century of its tumultuous existence.

The city is at the southern end of the Bosphorus, the 'strait that surpasses all straits', as the French antiquarian Petrus Gyllius wrote in the mid-sixteenth century. The strait is some thirty-five kilometres long, its waters flowing north-south from the Black Sea to the Sea of Marmara, the opposing continental shores only seven hundred metres apart at the narrowest point, between Rumeli Hisarî in Europe and Anadolu Hisarî in Asia.

Near its southern end the Bosphorus is joined by the Golden Horn, a scimitar-shaped inlet fed by two streams once known as the Sweet Waters of Europe. The Golden Horn joins the Bosphorus as they flow together into the Marmara, thus forming what the Byzantine historian Procopius called 'the garland of waters' that entwines itself around the city.

The oldest part of the city, known familiarly as Stamboul, is on the European side of the Bosphorus, a roughly triangular peninsula bounded on the north by the Golden Horn, on the south by the Marmara, and on its western landward side by the late Roman walls of Byzantine Constantinople. It is a city of seven hills, six of them peaking in succession from the ridge that parallels the Golden Horn to the south, the seventh rising above the Marmara shore just inside the land walls.

The first of the seven hills, as numbered by Gyllius, rises above the apex of the triangle where the Golden Horn flows into the Bosphorus, a promontory known as Saray Burnu, or Palace Point. The promontory takes its name from Topkapî Sarayî, the great palace of the Ottoman sultans, which occupies the flat summit of the First Hill. This was the acropolis of ancient Byzantium, a Greek city-state founded by Byzas the Megarian c.658 BC. According to tradition, Byzas had been advised by the oracle at Delphi to settle

3

'opposite the land of the blind'. The oracle was referring to the residents of Chalcedon, a Greek colony that had been founded seventeen years earlier on the Asian shore of the Marmara. The implication is that the Chalcedonians must have been blind not to have seen the much greater advantages of the site on the European side of the Bosphorus.

One of the advantages offered by the site of Byzantium compared to that of Chalcedon was its greater defensibility, for the steep acropolis at the confluence of the Golden Horn and the Bosphorus was protected by the sea on all sides except the west, where a defence wall could be erected. Another advantage was that the Golden Horn provided a superb natural harbour, shielded by the hills that enclose it on all sides except where it opens into the Bosphorus, and there the promontory below the First Hill curves around to shield the inner port. This promontory also acts as a barrier to divert the schools of tunny that swim down the Bosphorus from the Black Sea, forcing them into the port and creating an abundant fishery that became one of the principal sources of income for the people of Byzantium. Other important sources of income were the tolls and harbour fees paid by the ships that passed through the strait, for Byzantium controlled the Bosphorus from the beginning of its history, and this was the principal reason for its rise to greatness. As Gyllius pointed out, 'The Bosphorus is the first creator of Byzantium, greater and more important than Byzas, the first founder of Byzantium.'

The original city of Byzantium comprised only the First Hill, surrounded by a defence wall, with a fortified harbour on the Golden Horn. Byzantium's strategic position at the entrance to the Bosphorus soon made it the most important city in the region, as it acquired considerable territory in Thrace, on the European side of the Marmara, and also in Bithynia, on the Asian side.

Byzantium came under the control of the Persians in 512 BC, when King Darius crossed the Bosphorus on a bridge of boats in his campaign against the Scythians. During the Peloponnesian War the city was occupied first by the Spartans and then by the Athenians, who captured Byzantium in 409 BC after founding the colony of Chrysopolis on the Asian shore opposite the Golden Horn.

Byzantium succeeded in maintaining its independence throughout the Hellenistic period and on through the first two centuries of the Roman imperial era. But then in AD 196, after a two-year siege, Byzantium fell to the Roman emperor Septimius Severus, who totally destroyed the city. A few years later the emperor rebuilt Byzantium, building a new defence wall between the Golden Horn and the Marmara, more than doubling the size of the city, which now extended as far as the Second Hill. The principal public structure that he erected at that time was the Hippodrome, a huge arena for chariot races on the Marmara slope of the First Hill, where its enormous retaining wall can still be seen.

Then in 324 Byzantium was taken by Constantine the Great (324–37) after his victory over Licinius, which made him sole ruler of the Roman Empire. Within two years of his victory Constantine decided to shift the capital of his empire from Rome to Byzantium, rebuilding the old Greek city on a much larger scale to suit its imperial role. The new capital was dedicated on 11 May 330 as Nova Roma Constantinopolitana, 'New Rome, the City of Constantine', but popularly it came to be called Constantinopolis, or in English Constantinople.

Constantinople was five times larger in area than the Byzantium of Septimius Severus. Constantine himself had traced out the boundaries of his new capital, enclosing it on the landward side with a line of defence walls that extended in a great arc of more than two miles from the Golden Horn to the Marmara. Among the public buildings that Constantine founded in Constantinople was the church of the Holy Apostles, a basilica that he erected on the summit of the Fourth Hill together with a huge mausoleum. Constantine was baptized as a Christian a few days before his death on 22 May 337, after which he was buried in the mausoleum of the Holy Apostles.

By then Constantine had taken the first steps toward establishing Christianity as the state religion of the Roman Empire, a process that was completed during the following century by his successors. His son and successor Constantius (337–61) erected a basilica on the First Hill, dedicating it to Haghia Sophia, which in Greek means 'the Divine Wisdom', an attribute of Christ. He also restored the church of Haghia Eirene, dedicated to the Divine Peace, another attribute of Christ. Haghia Eirene had been the principal church of the Christians in Byzantium, but in the reign of Constantius it was supplanted by Haghia Sophia, which became the cathedral of Constantinople. Haghia Sophia also became the seat of the Patriarch of Constantinople, who with the power of the Emperor behind him was the head of the Greek Orthodox Church and the spiritual leader of all other Christians in the empire.

Great changes took place in the Roman Empire during the two

centuries after Constantine. After the death of Theodosius I (379–95) the empire was divided between his two sons, with Honorius (395–423) ruling the West from Rome and Arcadius (395–408) reigning as Emperor of the East in Constantinople. The western part of the empire was overrun by barbarians during the following century, and in 476 the last Emperor of the West was deposed, leaving the Emperor of the East in Constantinople sole ruler of what was left of the Roman Empire. This brought about a profound change in the character of the Roman Empire, for it was now centred in lands populated principally by Greek-speaking Christians. Although Latin remained the official language up until the sixth century, the empire was becoming increasingly Greek and Christian in character, severing its connections with the pagan traditions of Athens and Rome. This gave rise to what in modern times came to be called the Byzantine Empire, the Christian Greek state that evolved from the old pagan Roman Empire during the medieval era, taking its name from the ancient city of Byzantium. As the great churchman Gennadius was to write in the mid-fifteenth century: 'Though I am a Hellene by speech yet I would never say that I was a Hellene, for I do not believe as Hellenes believed. I should like to take my name from my faith, and if anyone asks me what I am, I answer, "A Christian". Though my father dwelt in Thessaly I do not call myself a Thessalian, but a Byzantine, for I am of Byzantium.'

The city grew rapidly in the century after Constantine, spreading beyond the limits defined by its founder. Theodosius II (408–50) built a new line of fortifications nearly a mile farther out into Thrace than the walls of Constantine, which were then demolished. The Theodosian walls extended in a double arc of four miles from the Golden Horn to the Marmara, a powerful defence work that would protect Constantinople from its enemies for more than a thousand years. The new line of walls enclosed seven hills, the same as in Old Rome, a matter of great symbolic importance to the Byzantines. Theodosius organized Constantinople into fourteen regions, again the same as in Rome, with the thirteenth across the Golden Horn in what later came to be called Pera and later still Galata. Theodosius also rebuilt the church of Haghia Sophia, which had been destroyed by fire during the reign of Arcadius.

The Byzantine Empire reached its peak during the reign of Justinian I (527–65). Five years after his accession Justinian was very nearly overthrown in an insurrection of the factions in the Hippodrome, the famous Nika Revolt, which was finally crushed

6

with great loss of life after many of the public buildings on the First Hill had been destroyed, including the Theodosian church of Haghia Sophia. Immediately after the suppression of the revolt Justinian set out to rebuild the city, a task that he completed in five years. The crowning glory of the restored city was the resurrected church of Haghia Sophia, which rose from its ashes to become the symbol of Byzantine Constantinople.

During the course of Justinian's reign his generals succeded in reconquering many of the lost dominions of the empire. But within half a century after his death the empire had collapsed, assaulted from without by the Lombards, Slavs, Avars and Persians, ravaged within by plague, anarchy and revolution. The empire was saved by Heraclius (610–41), who in a series of brilliant campaigns defeated the Persians, the Avars and the Slavs, and succeeded in regaining much of the territory that had been lost in the previous half-century.

Shortly after the death of Heraclius much of the eastern part of the Byzantine Empire was overrun by the Arabs, who on several occasions in the next two centuries besieged Constantinople. But the Byzantines stopped the Arabs and eventually drove them out of all but the southeastern part of Asia Minor. During the ninth and tenth centuries the empire was invaded by the Bulgars, who twice laid siege to Constantinople, but they were eventually crushed by Basil II (976–1025), who was known as Bulgaroctonus, the Bulgar-Slayer.

Despite these numerous wars and serious internal disputes, Byzantium was still strong and basically sound until the middle of the eleventh century, controlling an empire that stretched from the Euphrates to the Adriatic and from the Danube to the southern Mediterranean. But then in 1071 the Byzantines were defeated by the Selcuk Turks at Manzikert, north of Lake Van, after which the victors overran most of Asia Minor. That same year the Normans captured Bari, the last Byzantine possession in Italy, beginning a series of Latin invasions of the empire.

The empire was almost destroyed in 1204, when Constantinople was captured and sacked by the Venetians and the army of the Fourth Crusade, who set up a Latin kingdom that held the city for fifty-seven years. Several fragments of the empire maintained their independence during these years, most notably at Nicaea (Iznik) in northwestern Asia Minor, where the Lascarid dynasty ruled brilliantly for more than half a century. The Lascarid dynasty ended in 1259 when the throne was usurped by Michael VIII Palaeologus (1259–82), who two years later recaptured Constantinople from the

Latins and restored the Byzantine Empire to its ancient capital. Under his successors in the Palaeologus dynasty, who ruled the empire for the last two centuries of its existence, Byzantine culture revived and shared in the early European renaissance.

But the restored empire was much reduced in extent from what it had been in earlier times. The Venetians and other Latins continued to control much of Greece and the Greek islands, including Cyprus and Crete. Most of Asia Minor was held by the Selcuks and various Türkmen tribes who after the battle of Manzikert had overrun Anatolia, or Anadolu, as the sub-continent was known to the Turks, establishing a mosaic of *beyliks,* or emirates. One such *beylik* was that of the Osmanlî Turks, later to be known in the West as the Ottomans, who had been settled by the Selcuks in a tiny emirate near Nicaea in the last quarter of the thirteenth century. The Osmanlî were named for their first leader, Osman Gazi (c.1282–1326) (Gazi means Warrior for the Faith), who invaded the Byzantine domains. In 1326 his son and successor Orhan Gazi (1326–59) captured Prusa, known to the Turks as Bursa, which became the first Ottoman capital.

The Ottomans expanded rapidly, crossing the Dardanelles in the mid-fourteenth century and penetrating into southern Europe. Orhan's son and successor Murat I (1359–89) captured Adrianople, Turkish Edirne, which replaced Bursa as the Ottoman capital. The Byzantines gained a respite in 1402, when Tamerlane defeated Beyazit I (1389–1402) at the battle of Ankara. Beyazit died in captivity soon afterwards and for the next eleven years his sons fought a war of succession that was finally won by Mehmet I (1413–21). Mehmet's son and successor Murat II (1421–51) resumed the Turkish march of conquest, By the middle of the fifteenth century the Ottomans had conquered most of western Anatolia and had penetrated deep into southern Europe, defeating several allied Christian armies that had tried to stop them.

An important factor in the Ottoman success was their elite corps, the Janissaries, who were made up of Christian youths taken into the sultan's service in periodic levies known as the *devşirme.* After induction the recruits became Muslims and were trained for various positons in the army, many of them rising to the highest positions in the empire, including that of grand vezir.

In 1449 Constantine XI Dragases (1449–53) ascended the throne of Byzantium, and two years later the nineteen-year old Mehmet II (1451–81) succeeded his father Murat II as Sultan. The young sultan immediately began preparations for the conquest of Constantinople, which was then entirely surrounded by the domains of the Ottomans. During the summer of 1452 Mehmet built the great fortress of Rumeli Hisarî on the European shore of the Bosphorus at its narrowest stretch, thus cutting off the Byzantines from their grain supplies on the Black Sea. Meanwhile Constantine did what he could to prepare the city for the long-awaited siege, which began early in April of 1453. The siege lasted for seven weeks, as Constantine and his greatly outnumbered forces held off the Turks from the Theodosian walls, which were constantly being battered by the Ottoman artillery. The Turks finally breached the walls early in the morning of Tuesday 29 May, and by noon they had taken full control of the city, with Constantine meeting death in the final moments of the battle. Early in the afternoon Mehmet made his triumphal entry into the city, acclaimed by his troops as Fatih, or the Conqueror. He then turned loose his soldiers to loot Constantinople for three days, as was customary in Islam when a city was taken by storm rather than surrendering, but Mehmet the Conqueror stopped them after a single day, distressed at the damage that was being done. According to his Greek biographer, Kritovoulos of Imbros, Mehmet the Conqueror murmured sadly, 'Allah! What a city have I given over to destruction!'

On that same day Mehmet the Conqueror ordered that Haghia Sophia be converted into a mosque, and the first Muslim service was held there that Friday. Soon afterwards he began to restore the city, which was known to the Turks as Istanbul, a corruption of the Greek *stin poli*, meaning 'in the city' or 'to the city'. Mehmet the Conqueror also repeopled the city, which had lost much of its population in the half-century before the conquest, bringing in Turks, Greeks and Armenians from the provinces of the empire, with Sephardic Jews from Spain arriving in the last decade of the century. Within a year after the conquest Mehmet the Conqueror shifted the seat of his government from Edirne to Istanbul, which thenceforth was the capital of the Ottoman Empire.

Soon after the conquest Mehmet the Conqueror built a palace on the Third Hill. Then a decade or so later he began building a new and much larger residence on the First Hill, the palace that came to be known as Topkapî Sarayî. He also erected on the Fourth Hill a huge edifice known as Fatih Camii, the Mosque of the Conqueror. Fatih Camii was the centre of a *külliye*, a complex of religious and philanthropic institutions, including several theological schools (*medrese*), a public kitchen (*imaret*), a hospital (*daarüşşifa*), a hospice (*tabhane*), an inn for travellers (*kervanserai*), and two tombs (*türbe*), one for Mehmet the Conqueror and the other for his wife Gülbahar, mother of his son and successor, Beyazit II (1481–1512). Mehmet the Conqueror's example was followed by his successors and other notables of the court, who erected numerous mosques and other edifices in the new capital, some of them converting churches into mosques, transforming Byzantine Constantinople into Ottoman Istanbul.

During the century after the conquest, Ottoman armies swept victoriously through the Near East and the Balkans, while the Turkish navy conquered the Aegean islands and the Mediterranean coast of Africa. Selim I (1512–20) conquered eastern Anatolia, Persia, Syria and Egypt, adding the title of Caliph to that of Sultan after his capture of Cairo in 1517.

The Ottoman Empire reached the peak of its power during the reign of Süleyman the Magnificent (1520–66). Süleyman personally led his armies in a dozen victorious campaigns, failing only in his attempt to take Vienna, which thereafter marked the limit of Turkish expansion into Europe. By the end of his reign the Ottoman Empire stretched from Baghdad in the east to Algiers in the west, extending from Egypt to the southern borders of Russia, comparable in extent to the Byzantine Empire in the days of Justinian. The loot from these campaigns, along with the tribute and taxes from the conquered territory, enormously enriched the Ottoman treasury, and much if this wealth was used by Süleyman and his successors to adorn Istanbul and the other cities of the empire with palaces, mosques and other public buildings. The grandest of the edifices erected in Istanbul was the Süleymaniye, the imperial mosque complex built for Süleyman on the Third Hill in the years 1550–57 by his Chief Architect, the great Sinan. Sinan would continue as Chief Architect under Süleyman's immediate successors, his son Selim II (1566–74) and his grandson Murat III (1574–95). He built a magnificent mosque for Selim in Edirne, and for Murat he splendidly restored several rooms in Topkapî Sarayî. Sinan was the architect of the Ottoman golden age, building a total of 321 structures all over the empire in a career that spanned half a century, with 84 of his buildings still standing in Istanbul alone.

The Ottoman sultans succeeded one another father and son for thirteen generations from Osman Gazi through Ahmet I (1603–17), the great-great grandson of Süleyman the Magnificent. During the

10

two generations after Süleyman the successions were followed by mass fratricide, with the new sultan killing off all of his brothers to prevent them from contesting the throne. This Ottoman code of fratricide, which had been practiced occasionally in earlier times by the Osmanlî, was sanctioned by a statement in Islamic tradition that 'death is better than disquiet'. The law of succession was changed after the death in 1617 of Ahmet I, who was succeeded by his brother Mustafa I (1617–18, 1622–23). Thenceforth the succession was to the oldest male in the royal line, and when a new sultan came to the throne his brothers, instead of being killed, were confined to an apartment in Topkapî Sarayî known as the Kafes, or Cage. The consequence was that many of those who succeded to the throne in the latter Ottoman period had been confined to the Cage for most of their life, fifty-one years in the case of Osman III (1754–57), leaving them ill-prepared to rule, one of the causes of the decline of the empire that became increasingly evident in the century after Süleyman.

Many of Sülyman's successors were weak and ineffective rulers, some of them dissolute and a few of them insane, namely Mustafa I, Murat IV (1623–40), and his brother Ibrahim (1640–48), who was deposed and executed. Süleyman's immediate successors were dominated by their women, the power behind the throne usually being the Valide Sultan, or Queen Mother, or in a few cases the Birinci Kadîn, or First Wife, the mother of the heir apparent. The most powerful of these women was the Valide Sultan Kösem, wife of Ahmet I and mother of Murat IV and Ibrahim, who dominated the Harem until she was murdered in 1651 on the orders of her rival Turhan Hadice, mother of Mehmet IV (1648–87).

Another factor in the decline of the empire was the decadence of the Janissary Corps, which ceased to be an effective military force after the time of Süleyman, frequently rebelling against the sultans, two of whom they murdered, namely Osman II (1618–22) and Selim III (1789–1808). The Janissaries were finally put down by Mahmut II (1808–39), who had all of them killed on a single day, 16 June 1826, an historic occasion that contemporary Ottoman chroniclers referred to as Vakayî Hayriye, the Auspicious Incident.

By the mid-nineteenth century the fortunes of the Ottoman Empire had declined to the point where Tsar Nicholas I referred to it as the 'Sick Old Man of Europe'. By that time a reform movement known as the Tanzimat had begun in Turkey, culminating in 1877 with the creation of the first Ottoman parliament. But this apparent

11

triumph of reform was short-lived, for the following year the parliament was dissolved by Abdül Hamit II (1876–1909), who thereafter ruled as a dictator. Abdül Hamit's long and oppressive reign finally ended in 1909, when he was deposed by a liberal party known as the Young Turks, led by Cavit Pasha, Talaat Pasha and Enver Pasha. Abdül Hamit's successor, Mehmet V Reşat (1909–18), was merely a puppet in the hands of the Young Turks, who brought Turkey into the First World War on the side of Germany, which resulted in the final destruction of the Ottoman Empire. Mehmet V died just before the war ended, to be succeeded by his brother Mehmet VI Vahidettin, who became a puppet of the Allies when they occupied Istanbul on 13 October 1918.

After the war, when the victorious Allies prepared to divide up the Ottoman Empire, a movement of national liberation started in Anatolia under the leadership of Mustafa Kemal Pasha, later to be known as Atatürk. Atatürk and his followers defeated an invading Greek army after a three-year war that ended in 1922, by which time the Turkish nationalists had created their own government in Ankara, convening a parliament known as the Grand National Assembly (GNA). On 1 November 1922 the GNA enacted legislation separating the sultanate and the caliphate, the former being abolished and the latter reduced to a purely religious role. Sixteen days later Mehmet VI, the last sultan of the Ottoman Empire, left Istanbul aboard a British warship, never to return, dying in exile in Italy four years later. He was succeeded by his cousin Abdül Mecit Efendi, who held only the title of Caliph, a purely ceremonial office with no political power.

The final articles of the Treaty of Lausanne, signed on 24 July 1923, established the present boundaries of Turkey, except for the province of Hatay in southeastern Anatolia, acquired after a plebescite in 1939. The Allied occupation of Istanbul came to an end on 2 October 1923 of that same year, and four days later a division of the Turkish Nationalist army marched into the city and took control. On 13 October the GNA passed a law making Ankara the capital of Turkey. Then on 29 October the assembly adopted a new constitution that created the Republic of Turkey, with Atatürk as its first president.

On 3 March 1924 the GNA passed a law abolishing the caliphate, thus severing the last tenuous bond that linked the new Republic of Turkey with the old Ottoman Empire. This same law deposed Abdül Mecit Efendi, who was forced to leave Turkey the following day, to

The Imperial City

die an exile in Paris in 1944. Thus the Ottoman Empire came to an end after an existence of more than six centuries, and for the first time in nearly sixteen centuries the ancient city at the confluence of the Bosphorus and the Golden Horn was no longer an imperial capital.

Istanbul has undergone a dramatic transformation since the establishment of the Turkish Republic, as has the rest of Turkey. Much of this change came about through reforms instituted by Atatürk, most notably the disenfranchisement of Islam, as well as the adoption of western dress, the Latin alphabet and the Gregorian calendar, measures intended to make Turkey a more modern and European nation. The more superficial westernizing reforms were lasting, but in recent years Islam has made a dramatic comeback in Turkey, which to a large extent has been caused by the mass migration of poorer Anatolian people into Istanbul and the other major cities. The population of Istanbul, which was somewhat more than a million in 1924, was counted as nearly ten million in the 1998 census, though it is generally believed to be considerably higher. The city now extends for miles along both the European and Asian shores of the Marmara and up the Bosphorus to within sight of the Black Sea. The European and Asian parts of the city were first linked by a bridge across the Bosphorus between Ortaköy and Beylerbey that opened on 29 October 1973, on the fiftieth anniversry of the founding of the Turkish Republic. A second bridge, crossing between Rumeli Hisarî and Anadolu Hisarî, opened in the summer of 1988, exactly 2500 years after Darius built his bridge of boats across the strait at the same place. Such is the antiquity of the imperial city.

The population explosion in recent years has destroyed most of the old wooden houses of Istanbul, which have been replaced by high-rise apartment blocks and commercial buildings, turning picturesque Ottoman neighbourhoods into squalid slums, traffic jamming the streets and poisoning the air, the Golden Horn an open sewer and the once vernal shores of the Bosphorus now part of the urban sprawl of a modern metropolis that is apparently out of control, though those who love Istanbul are doing their utmost to preserve its fading beauty.

The longest-standing renewal programme is that of the Turkish Touring and Automobile Club (TTOK), headed by Çelik Gülersoy. Çelik Bey has restored a number of late Ottoman buildings and converted them into hotels, restaurants, cafés and craft markets, thus preserving and giving new life to venerable edifices that might

13

otherwise have been lost to the city. Atatürk himself instituted a government policy of restoring the Byzantine and Ottoman monuments of the city, most notably Haghia Sophia and Topkapi Sarayî, both of which were converted into museums. Many of the restored Turkish monuments are once again serving the people of Istanbul as they did in times past, with *medreses* housing students; Ottoman libraries open as research centres; the hospitals of imperial mosques serving as clinics; and their *mekteps*, or primary schools, converted into children's libraries.

But beyond all these programmes of restoration, Istanbul refuses to let itself be destroyed, and today it is flourishing in an astonishing renaissance that has given rise to novels and poetry, theatre and music, bars and bookshops, restaurants and cafes, enterprises catering to every intellectual, social and economic level, the city positively throbbing with energy, both creative and destructive, making it a more exciting place to live or visit than it has been in living memory. Istanbul has indeed changed since the days when it was the capital of a great empire, but those who know it best feel that its essential character and spirit have survived the transformation, almost as if it had an immortal soul. Petrus Gyllius sensed this when he wrote his encomium to the imperial city more than four centuries ago: 'It seems to me that while other cities are mortal, this one will remain as long as there are men on earth.'

2

To the Summit of the First Hill

W E WILL BEGIN our first itinerary at the place where the city
itself began, on the promontory at **Saray Burnu**, where the
waters of the Bosphorus join those of the Golden Horn to flow
together into the Sea of Marmara. This is where Byzas the Megarian
and his followers would have landed c.658 BC to found the Greek
city of Byzantium. Directly across the strait from the Golden Horn is
Üsküdar, ancient Chrysopolis, founded in 409 BC by Athenians.
Across the strait farther down along the Asian shore is Kadîköy,
ancient Chalcedon, the place that the Delphic oracle was referring to
when he told Byzas to settle 'opposite the Land of the Blind'.
Üsküdar and Kadîköy are now within the city limits of Istanbul, as is
the former Genoese town of Galata on the northern side of the
Golden Horn.

The area around Saray Burnu is now a park, where one can sit
and enjoy a view of the Bosphorus surging between the continents.
The view extends all the way up the strait to the first Bosphorus
bridge, and up the Golden Horn to the Galata Bridge. The principal
landmark on the northern side of the Golden Horn is the Galata
Tower, the stronghold of Genoese Galata. At the centre of the park
there is a fine bronze statue of Atatürk, founder and first President of
the Turkish Republic, done by the Austrian sculptor Kripple in
1926.

Across the shore highway from Saray Burnu a road leads through
Gülhane Park, which occupies what were once the lower gardens of
Topkapî Sarayî. On the wooded hillside to the east stands one of the
city's oldest monuments, now enclosed within the garden of an
outdoor cafe. This is the **Goth's Column**, a granite monolith 15
metres high surmounted by a Corinthian capital. The name of the
column comes from the laconic inscription in Latin on its base;
FORTUNAE REDUCI OB DEVICTOS GOTHOS, which means:
'To Fortune, who returns by reason of the defeat of the Goths.' The
column has been ascribed to Claudius II Gothicus (268–70) and also
to Constantine the Great, both of whom won notable victories over
the Goths, but there is no firm evidence either way. According to the

Byzantine historian Nicephorus Gregoras, this column was once surmounted by a statue of Byzas the Megarian.

By the side of the park road below the column there is a small archaeological site, with a number of marble columns and some other ancient architectural fragments scattered about on the hillside. This has been identified as the **Orphanage of St Paul**, founded by Justin II (564–78). The orphanage was rebuilt by Alexius I Comnenus (1081–1118); then in the third quarter of the thirteenth century, during the reign of Michael VIII Palaeologus, it was used for a time to house the University of Constantinople.

We now return to Saray Burnu and begin walking up the shore of the Golden Horn, passing the docks of the Turkish Maritime Lines and the railway yards. The only monument along the shore is the **Sepetciler Köşkü**, the Kiosk of the Basket-Weavers, which now serves as the International Press Centre. This is a sea-pavilion built in 1643 for Sultan Ibrahim the Mad, presented to him by the guild of basket-weavers. The sultan used this kiosk whenever he made excursions to his palaces along the Bosphorus and the Golden Horn in one of his *pazar caiques*, or royal barges, which were berthed in the vaults beneath the pavilion.

Beyond the kiosk the shore road passes on its left Sirkeci Station, built in 1889 as the terminus of the Orient Express. Across from Sirkeci the road passes the main *iskele*, or pier, for the ferries of the Turkish Maritime Lines, which leave from here for stations on the Bosphorus, the Asian suburbs of Üsküdar and Kadîkoy, and the Princes Isles, Istanbul's suburban archipelago in the Sea of Marmara.

We now approach the **Galata Bridge**, which crosses the Golden Horn between the quarters of **Eminönü** in Stamboul and Karaköy in Galata. Eminönü is the epicentre of the city's daily life, the quay thronged with commuters rushing to and from the ferries past peddlers hawking their wares and fishermen selling fried-fish sandwiches, loudspeakers blaring out the latest arabesque songs above the din of the traffic along the shore highway and across the bridge. The din is even greater in the subterranean passageways beneath the shore highway, for there the pedestrians have to run the gauntlet of hucksters selling toy helicopter gunships whose racket forces the music shops to turn up their amplifiers to top volume, distorting the adenoidal voices of Anatolian bards singing of unrequited love. This is the very heart of Istanbul, and you feel its energy pulsating through all of your senses as you hurry through to the fresh air and light of day at the far end of the tunnel.

To the Summit of the First Hill

Eminönü is dominated by the great edifice known as **Yeni Cami**, the **New Mosque**. The first mosque on this site was commissioned c.1600 by the Valide Sultan Safiye, mother of Mehmet III (1595–1603). Construction was halted in 1603 when Mehmet III died, for his mother then lost her power in the Harem and was unable to complete her mosque. The half-finished mosque stood desolate on the Golden Horn until 1660, when construction was resumed by Turhan Hadice, mother of Mehmet IV, who appointed Mustafa Ağa as the chief architect. The mosque was dedicated on 6 November 1663, with the Sultan escorting his mother to the royal loge of the building for the first Friday prayers. The French traveller Grelot, who was present at the dedication, wrote that Turhan Hadice was 'one of the greatest and most brilliant ladies who ever entered the Saray', and that it was fitting that she 'should leave to posterity a jewel of Ottoman architecture as an eternal monument to her generous enterprises'.

Yeni Cami is preceded on its western side by a monumental court-yard, the *avlu*. The ceremonial entrance to the *avlu*, now disused, is at its west side, where a broad flight of steps leads up to an ornate entryway. The interior of the courtyard is bordered by a colonnaded portico with six columns on each side, counting corner columns twice, and in the centre there is a pretty octagonal *şadîrvan*, or ablu-tion fountain. But here, as in most other imperial mosques, the *şadîrvan* is no longer used, and the faithful perform their ritual ablu-tions at water taps along the south side of the building. The two minarets rise from the corners where the courtyard joins the mosque, each of them having three *şerefes*, or balconies, with sculptured stalactite parapets. In times past the *müezzins*, or chanters, gave the call to prayer from these balconies, but today a tape recorder is generally used.

At the northeast corner of Yeni Cami is the ***hünkâr kasrî***, or imperial pavilion, through whose centre a great arched portal permits a street to pass behind the mosque. The pavilion is entered by a ramp beside the mosque, to whose royal loge in the upper gallery it is connected by a long corridor. The *hünkâr kasrî* served as a pied-à-terre for the royal family when they attended services, its suite of rooms including a salon, a bedchamber, a toilet, and a kitchen on the lower level.

The central area of the mosque interior, which is a square 41 metres on a side, is defined by the four piers that support the central dome through four great arches, with squinches making the transition from square to circle. At the east end of the mosque is the *mihrab*, the niche that indicates the direction of Mecca, and to its right is the conical-capped *mimber*, or pulpit, from where the *imam*, or preacher, delivers the sermon at the time of the noon prayer on Friday. To the left of the *mihrab*, standing against the main pier on that side, is the *Koran kürsü*, a wooden throne where the *imam* sits when he is reading the Koran to the congregation. The covered marble pew set up against the southwest pier is the *müezzin mahfili*, where the *müezzins* kneel when they chant the responses to the prayers of the *imam*. The women, who take no part in the public prayers, are relegated to the open chambers under the gallery at the rear of the mosque.

The mosque interior is overlooked by an open gallery on both sides and to the rear, with the two side galleries carried on slender marble columns. The *hünkâr mahfili*, or royal loge, is at the north-east corner of the gallery, screened off by a gilded grille for privacy.

Like all of the larger mosques, Yeni Cami is part of an extensive *külliye*. Besides the mosque, Turhan Hadice's *külliye* originally included a *medrese*, hospital, primary school, *türbe*, *çeşme* (foun-tain), *sebil* (fountain-house), *hamam* (public bath), and *çarşî* (market), with the income from the latter two institutions contrib-uting to the support of the rest of the foundation. The hospital, bath and primary school have been destroyed, but the other institutions survive, though only the mosque, *türbe* and market remain open to the public. The market is the handsome L-shaped structure to the south and west of the mosque. It is called the Mîsîr Çarşî, or Egyp-tian Market, because it was once endowed with the Cairo imposts; in English it is more commonly known as the **Spice Bazaar**, because of the spices and herbs that are sold there, though not in quite the volume that they were in Ottoman times, for many other commodi-ties are now on sale there as well in its 88 vaulted rooms. The main entrance to the Spice Bazaar is through the monumental gatehouse near the southwest corner of Yeni Cami, in whose upper chamber there is an excellent restaurant called Pandelis.

From the eleventh century until the Turkish conquest the quarter now known as Eminönü was given over by the Byzantines to traders from several Italian cities, who built docks and warehouses along the Golden Horn. Venice controlled a large strip of territory just above the present Galata Bridge, while the Pisans, Amalfians and Floren-tines had smaller strips successively farther downstream. The Genoese originally had a concession here as well, but later they were given one on the north bank of the Golden Horn which developed into the walled town of Galata, the principal surviving monument of which is the huge conical-topped tower on the heights across the way.

The area where Yeni Cami now stands was for centuries a Jewish quarter, wedged in between the concessions of the Venetians and the Genoese. The Jews who resided here were members of the schismatic Karaite sect, who broke off from the main body of Orthodox Jewry in the eighth century. The Karaites seem to have established themselves on this site as early as the eleventh century, at about the time when the Italians first obtained their concessions here. The Karaites continued living here until 1660, when they were evicted to make room for the final construction of Yeni Cami. They were then resettled some three kilometres up the northern shore of the Golden Horn in the village of Hasköy, where a few of their descendants remain to this day.

Two gateways open out from the angle of the Spice Bazaar's L. The one on the right leads to Hasîrcîlar Caddesi, the Avenue of the Mat Makers, which extends westward parallel to the Golden Horn road. Some 200 metres along Hasîrcîlar Caddesi on the right we come to one of the entryways to Rüstem Pasha Camii. A vaulted stairway leads up to the porticoed courtyard of the mosque, which is built on a high terrace over a complex of shops and warehouses.

Rüstem Pasha Camii is one of the most beautiful of the grand vezirial mosques erected by the great Sinan. The mosque was built in 1561 for Rüstem Pasha, grand vezir under Süleyman and husband of the Sultan's only daughter, the Princess Mihrimah. Rüstem was known in his time as time as Kehle-i-Ikbal, the Louse of Fortune, a nickname that he acquired when he married Mihrimah. It seems that Rüstem's enemies had tried to prevent him from marrying the princess by spreading the rumour that he had leprosy. But when the palace doctors examined Rüstem they discovered that he was infested with lice; consequently they declared that he was not leprous, for accepted medical belief had it that lice never infest lepers. Rüstem was then allowed to marry Mihrimah, and in time Süleyman appointed him grand vezir, after which he became the wealthiest and most powerful of the sultan's subjects. Thus it was that he came to be called Kehle-i-Ikbal, from the old Turkish proverb that says 'When a man has his luck in place even a louse can bring him good fortune.'

The mosque is preceded by a curious double porch; the inner one consisting of a portico of five domed bays, and then, projecting from this, a deep and low-slung penthouse roof, its outer edge resting on a row of columns. The plan of the mosque is an octagon inscribed in a rectangle. The dome is flanked by four small semidomes in the diagonals of the building. The arches of the dome spring from four octagonal pillars, two on the north and two on the south, and from piers projecting from the east and west walls. There are galleries on the north and south supported by pillars and by small marble columns between them.

Rüstem Pasha Camii is renowned for the beautiful tiles that almost cover its walls, not only on the interior but also on the facade of the porch. One should also climb to the galleries to see the tiles there, which are of a different pattern than elsewhere in the mosque. Like all of the very best Turkish tiles, those of Rüstem Pasha come from the kilns of Iznik, the ancient Nicaea, whose ceramic art reached the peak of its perfection in the period c.1555–1620, which was also the great era of Ottoman architecture. The most character-istic element of the Iznik tiles of this period is the tomato-red or 'Armenian bole' pigment. These exquisite tiles, in a wide variety of floral and geometric designs, cover not only the walls, but also the columns, the *mihrab* and the *mimber*, making this one of the most beautiful and striking mosque interiors in the city.

Returning to Yeni Cami, we now walk eastward along the street that passes between the mosque and the Spice Bazaar. The garden within the angle of the Spice Bazaar is the site of a picturesque market, one that specializes in plants, flowers, garden supplies, pets and birds.

The large domed building on the right at the end of the street is the *türbe* of the Yeni Cami complex. Turhan Hadice, foundresss of the mosque, is buried here along with her son Mehmet IV and numerous members of her family and descendants, including five later sultans: Mustafa II (1695–1703), Ahmet III (1703–30), Mahmut I (1730–54), Osman III (1754–57) and Murat V (1876).

The small building to the west of the türbe is the *kütüphane*, or library; this was not part of the original *külliye* of Yeni Cami, but was added later by Turhan Hadice's grandson Ahmet III. Across the street from the *türbe*, at the corner of the wall enclosing the garden of the mosque, there is a tiny polygonal building with a quaintly shaped dome. This is the *muvakithane*, the house and workshop of the *müneccim*, the mosque astronomer. The *müneccim* regulated the times for the five occasions of daily prayer and fixed the exact times of sunrise and sunset during Ramadan, beginning and ending the daily fast that is observed during that month. It was also his duty to determine the day on which each month of the Muslim lunar calendar began, marked by the first appearance of the sickle moon in the western sky just after sunset.

We now continue straight ahead along Bankacîlar Caddesi, which at the first intersection becomes Hamidiye Caddesi. At the near corner on the right is the *sebil* of the Yeni Cami *külliye*, now used for commercial purposes. Originally attendants would have been on duty inside the fountain house, handing out cups of water through the grilled windows to thirsty passersby.

At the near side of the next turning on the right is the famous confectionary of Hacî Bekir, founded here in 1777. Hacî Bekir was Baş Şekerci or Chief Confectioner, during the reign of Abdül Hamit I (1774–89); he is renowned for his creation of *lokum*, or Turkish delight, which was first sold in this shop.

Down the short alley on the right we see at the corner on the left the entrance to the Ticaret Borsasî, or Stock Exchange. This is housed in part of the *medrese* of **Abdül Hamit I**, which takes up the rest of that side of the alleyway and the block beyond it along Hamidiye Caddesi.

The huge building that takes up the entire block on the opposite side of Hamidiye Caddesi is the Fourth Vakîf Hanî, built by the architect Kemalettin Bey in the years 1911–26. This was built on the site of the *imaret*, or public kitchen of Abdül Hamit's *külliye*, standing opposite the sultan's *medrese* and *türbe*.

Continuing along Hamidiye Caddesi, at the first turning on the right we come to the *türbe* of Abdül Hamit I adjoining the northwest corner of his *medrese*. Buried here along with Abdül Hamit I is his son Mustafa IV (1807–08), who was deposed and then executed on 16 November 1808. Abdül Hamit's *külliye*, built by the architect Mehmet Tahir Ağa, also included a *sebil*, this was moved to another site when the road was widened, and we will see it later on this itinerary.

At the end of Hamidiye Caddesi we turn right on Ankara Caddesi, a busy avenue leading up from the Golden Horn to the ridge between the First and Second Hills. On the left side of the avenue we pass the Vilayet, the headquarters of the governor of the Istanbul province. One block beyond the Vilayet we turn left, and then about a hundred metres along on the left we come to the entrance to the men's section of the **Cağaloğlu Hamamî**, one of the most beautiful Turkish baths in the city. (The entrance to the women's section of the hamam is just around the next corner on the left.)

The Cağaloğlu Hamamî was built for Mahmut I in 1741, and it has been in continuous operation ever since. There are over a hundred Ottoman *hamams* in Istanbul, almost all of them still in use, for many of the poorer people in the city in times past did not have baths in their homes (some do not even today), and a weekly visit to the *hamam* is necessary to cleanse oneself properly for the Friday noon prayer.

Turkish *hamams* are the direct descendants of the baths of ancient Rome and are built according to the same general plan. (The men's and women's baths in the Cağaloğlu Hamamî have essentially the same plan except that the rooms are aligned differently.) Ordinarily, a *hamam* has three distinct sections. The first is the *camekan*, the Roman *apoditarium*, which is used as a reception hall and dressing room and as a lounge in which to rest and relax after the bath. This is typically a vast square room covered by a dome, with an elaborate fountain in the centre; round the walls is a raised platform where the patrons undress and leave their clothes. Next comes the *soğukluk*, or *tepidarium*, a chamber of intermediate temperature which serves as an anteroom to the bath, keeping the cold air out on one side and the hot air in on the other; this is almost alway a mere passageway, which contains the lavatories. Finally there is the *hararet*, or steam room, anciently called the *calidarium*; in the centre of this there is a large marble platform, the *göbektaş*, or belly-stone, which is heated from below, with the patrons lying there to sweat or be massaged before bathing at one of the wall fountains in the side chambers. In Cağaloğlu, as in most *hamams*, the most elaborate chamber is the *hararet*. Here this is an open cruciform area, with a central dome supported by a circlet of columns and with domed side-chambers in the arms of the cross. The *hararet* of the Cağaloğlu Hamamî is one of the most beautiful in existence; it has not changed in appearance since Ottoman times, as one can see from the enlarged print on display in the lobby, an engraving done by Thomas Allom c.1834.

At the first intersection beyond the hamam we turn left on to Alay Köşkü Caddesi, which runs downhill as far as the outer defence walls of Topkapî Sarayî. At the first turning on the left we see a small mosque raised on a platform, with an elegant baroque *sebil* at the corner. This mosque and the other elements of the *külliye* were built in 1745 for **Beşir Ağa**, Chief Black Eunuch in the Harem of Topkapî Sarayî during the reign of Mahmut I. Besides the mosque and the *sebil* the *külliye* consisted of a *medrese*, a *tekke*, or dervish monastery, and a complex of shops that occupied the vaults beneath the building. The *tekke* is no longer functioning as such, since all the dervish orders in Turkey were banned in the early years of the Turkish Republic; together with the *medrese* it now serves as a cultural centre for the Turks of Western Thrace, which is now part of Greece.

Continuing down Alay Köşkü Caddesi for another block we come to Alemdar Caddesi, the avenue that here runs past the outer walls of Topkapî Sarayî on its way up to the summit of the First Hill. Just to the left at the intersection there is a large ornamental doorway with a projecting canopy in the Turkish rococo style. This is the famous **Sublime Porte**, which in former days led to the palace and offices of the grand vezir, where from the middle of the nineteenth century onwards most of the business of the Ottoman Empire was transacted. Hence it came to stand for the Ottoman government itself, and ambassadors were accredited to the Sublime Porte, just as in England they present their credentials to the Court of St James. The present gateway dates from 1843; it now leads to the Istanbul Vilayet.

Opposite the Sublime Porte, in an angle of the outer defense-wall of Topkapî Sarayî, we see a large polygonal gazebo in the Turkish baroque style. This is the **Alay Köşkü**, or Review Pavilion, originally constructed c.1565 and rebuilt in 1819 by Mahmut II. The interior consists of a suite of rooms reached by a ramp rising from just inside the gate of Gülhane Park, whose entrance is a short way up Alemdar Caddesi. The sultans used this kiosk as a pied-a-terre to look out upon the passing life of their city, to keep an eye on those calling on the grand vezir at the Sublime Porte, and to review military parades and the occasional public musters known as processions of the guilds. These processions were organized from time-to-time in the earlier Ottoman era, the last being in 1769 during the reign of Mustafa III (1757–89). Some of them were held to celebrate the circumcision rites of young princes, others as celebrations of Ottoman victories, and at least one as a peripatetic census of the trade and commerce of the city, the latter being decreed by Murat IV in 1638, in preparation for his campaign into Iraq. Evliya Çelebi, the seventeenth-century Turkish chronicler, describes the procession of Murat IV at great length and in considerable detail in his *Seyahatname*, or *Chronicle of Travels*. According to Evliya, the procession was organized into 57 sections and consisted of 1,001 guilds, although the number of professions that he describes is just 735. Representatives of each of these guilds paraded in their characteristic garb, exhibiting on floats their various trades, trying to outdo one another in amusing and amazing the Sultan, who looked on with his court from the Alay Kiosk. Evliya tells us that 'the procession began its march at dawn and continued till sunset . . . on account of which all trade and work in Constantinople were disrupted for a period of three days. During this time the riot and confusion filled the town to a degree which is not to be expressed by language, and which I, poor Evliya, only dared to describe.' These are some of the guilds that Evliya describes, evoking the life and spirit of Istanbul in the days of Murat IV:

All these guilds pass in wagons or on foot, with the instruments of their handicraft, and are busy with great noise at their work. The carpenters build wooden houses, the builders raise walls, the woodcutters pass with loads of trees, the sawyers sawing them, the masons crunch chalk and whiten their faces, playing a thousand tricks. . . . The toymakers of Eyüp exhibit on wagons a thousand trifles and toys for children to play with. In their train you see bearded fellows and men of thirty years of age, some dressed as children with hoods and bibs, others as nurses who care for them, while the bearded babies cry after playthings or amuse themselves with spinning tops or sounding little trumpets. . . . The bakers pass working at their trade, some baking and throwing small loaves among the crowd. They also make for this occasion immense loaves the size of the cupola of a hamam, covered with sesame and fennel; these loaves are carried on wagons which are dragged along by seventy to eighty pairs of oxen. No oven being capable of holding loaves of so large a size, they bake them in pits made for that purpose, where the loaf is covered from above with cinders, and from the four sides baked slowly by the fire. It is worth while to see it. . . . The fruit-merchants pass on wagons adorned with all kinds of fruit. They also make artificial trees of apples, apricots, and other kinds of fruit, each carried on poles by eight or ten men. Others make kiosks with fountains playing, the four sides of which are festooned with fruit. Their boys, who are seated in these kiosks, bargain with the spectators and throw fruit to them. Some dress in robes made of chestnuts, reciting verses of the Koran while holding prayer-beads of dried raisins. They also build artificial ships, each ship being towed by a thousand men. The sails, masts, prow and stern of each of these ships are ornamented with fruit kernels. Merchants flock in crowds to enter these fruit-ships to fill their baskets. With the greatest noise and

quarreling from these simulated sales, they pass the Alay Kiosk
This is a faithful representation of what occurs at the port on the
arrival of every fruit-ship, where such noise arises, and many
heads are broken without the injured persons being allowed to ask
for legal satisfaction. . . . These guilds pass before the Alay Kiosk
with a thousand tricks and fits, which it is impossible to describe,
and behind them walk their sheikhs followed by their pages playing the eight-fold Turkish music.

The Alay Kiosk has been restored and is now open to the public
as an exhibition gallery, approached by the ramp on the left inside
the gateway of Gülhane Park. The road on the right inside the park
entrance leads to the three museums in the courtyard below the First
Court of Topkapî Sarayi: the Museum of the Ancient Orient, the
Archaeological Museum, and the Çinili Köşk, or Tiled Pavilion,
which are included in a later itinerary.

Alemdar Caddesi leads upwards to the summit of the First Hill,
curving away to the right as it leaves the outer defence walls of the
Saray. Just around the bend, on the right side of the avenue, we come
to a small baroque mosque, **Zeynep Sultan Camii**. The mosque and
its associated *külliye* were erected in 1769 for Princess Zeynep, a
daughter of Ahmet III; it was designed and built by Mehmet Tahir
Ağa, the greatest and most original of the Turkish baroque architects.
The mosque is a rather pleasant and original example of Turkish
baroque architecture. In form it is merely a small square room
covered by a dome, with a square projecting apse to the east and a
porch with five bays to the west. The mosque look rather like a
Byzantine church, partly from being built in courses of stone and
brick, but more so because of its very Byzantine dome, for the
cornice of the dome undulates to follow the extrados of the round-
arched windows, a pretty arrangement generally used in Byzantine
churches but hardly ever in Turkish mosques. The *külliye* also
included a primary school, which stands at the corner of the street
just below the mosque, and the little cemetery where the foundress
and members of her family and household are buried. The elaborate
rococo *sebil* outside the cemetery gate is not an original part of the
foundation; it was built in 1778 as part of the *külliye* of Abdül Hamit
I, which we saw earlier on the present itinerary, and was moved to its
present location in the 1950s; it too is a work of Mehmet Tahir Ağa.

Just beyond Zeynep Sultan Camii and on the same side of the
avenue we see a short stretch of crenellated wall, almost hidden
behind the building on the street front. This is all that remains of the

25

once-famous Byzantine church of the **Virgin Chalcoprateia**. This church, which is thought to date from the mid-fifth century, was one of the most venerated in Constantinople, since it possessed as a relic the girdle of the Blessed Virgin. It was built on the site of an ancient synagogue which since the time of Constantine had been the property of the Jewish copperworkers, hence the name Chalcoprateia, or Copper Market.

The handsome building midway along the opposite side of Alemdar Caddesi is the recently-restored Soğuk Çeşme Medresesi. The *medrese* takes its name from Soğuk Çeşme Sokağî, the Street of the Cold Fountain, which begins outside the entrance of Gülhane Park and leads uphill beside the outer walls of the Saray. We will approach the entrance to the *medrese* by a roundabout route, first strolling up Soğuk Çeşme Sokağî.

Up until the mid-1980s the old Ottoman houses along Soğuk Çeşme Sokağî had been long abandoned and were in a state of utter ruin, in imminent danger of being demolished. Then in 1986 a renewal programme was begun by the Turkish Touring and Automobile Club (TTOK), directed by Çelik Gülersoy, and within two years all of the old houses along the upper part of the street were restored, most of them converted into a luxurious hotel complex called the Ayasofya Pansionlar. The largest of the old mansions, a *konak* dating from the early nineteenth century, now serves as the **Istanbul Library**, part of the **Çelik Gülersoy Foundation**, housing a rich collection of books, maps, prints and paintings associated with the history of the city. During the course of the reconstruction of Soğuk Çeşme Sokağî an archaeological excavation was made near the lower end of the street, unearthing an ancient cistern with six marble monoliths supporting a vaulted brick ceiling, a structure dated to the late Roman period. The cistern is now the Sarnîç Lokantasî, a deluxe restaurant operated by the TTOK, where one can dine well in a setting of Roman splendour.

We continue along Soğuk Çeşme Sokağî as far as Caferiye Sokağî. Here we turn right and walk down the street as far as a blind alley on the right, where a portal at the end opens into the Soğuk Çeşme Medresesi.

The *medrese* was built by the architect Sinan for **Cafer Ağa**, Chief White Eunuch in the reign of Süleyman the Magnificent. The building was still unfinished when Cafer Ağa died in 1557, but his brother Gazanfer Ağa, who succeeded him as Chief White Eunuch, sponsored the continuation of the project, which Sinan completed in

1559/60. The hillside slopes quite steeply here, so Sinan first erected a vaulted substructure on the west side of the complex, on what is now Alemdar Caddesi, where four lofty shops underlie the *medrese*. This substructure supports the *medrese* and its porticoed courtyard, whose principal axis is north-south; the south end of the court is occupied by the large domed *dershane*, or lecture hall, while the student cells, or *hücre*, are arrayed around the periphery of the cloister, with the kitchen and lavatories on the north. There are 13 domed chambers – seven on the west, three on the east , and two on the north – as well as three vaulted rooms on the latter side, one in the middle and two in the corners, each of them with a fireplace. The *medrese* now serves as a bazaar of Ottoman arts and crafts, such as embroidery, book-binding, and paper marbling, with each speciality housed in one of the chambers around the courtyard. The two rooms at the far right-hand cornrer have been converted into a cafe, a very pleasant place to stop and rest after this walk from Saray Burnu.

We now continue along Caferiye Sokağî, turning left at its end into **Aya Sofya Meydanî**, the great square in front of Haghia Sophia. Here we have reached the summit of the First Hill, the goal of our first itinerary in Istanbul.

3

Haghia Sophia

THE SUMMIT OF the First Hill is dominted by **Haghia Sophia**, known to the Byzantines as Megali Ekklesia, the Great Church, which some consider to be the grandest edifice ever built by the hand of man. Haghia Sophia was erected by the emperor Justinian I, under whom the Byzantine Empire reached its greatest extent and power. Procopius, Justinian's court chronicler, describes the grandeur of the Great Church in his *Edifices*.

The church presents a most glorious spectacle, extraordinary to those who behold it and altogether incredible to those who are told of it. In height it rises to the very heavens and overtops the neighbouring houses like a ship anchored among them, appearing above the city which it adorns and forms a part of. It is distinguished by indescribable beauty, excelling both in its size and the harmonies of its measures.

The present edifice of Haghia Sophia is the third church of that name to stand upon this site. The first church was opened on 15 February 360 by the emperor Constantius. It was destroyed by fire on 9 June 404 in a riot by the supporters of John Chrysostomos, the Patriarch of Constantinople, who had been deposed by the empress Eudoxia, wife of the emperor Arcadius. A new church was built on the same site by Theodosius II, son and successor of Arcadius, who rededicated it on 10 October 415. This edifice, known to archaeologists as the Theodosian church, was destroyed by fire on 15 January 532 during the Nika Revolt.

Shortly after the revolt was crushed Justinian set out to rebuild the church on an even grander scale, bringing in workers and artisans from all over his vast empire. As chief architect he appointed Anthemius of Tralles, the greatest mathematical physicist of late antiquity, and as assistant builder he named Isidorus of Miletus, a renowned geometer who had been director of the Platonic Academy in Athens before it was closed by Justinian in 529. Anthemius died during the first months of the project, whereupon Isidorus was placed in charge, completing the building within five years. The new church was formally opened on 26 December 537, St Stephen's

Eminönu ferry piers, with Topkapî Sarayî in background

Haghia Sophia, the former Church of the Divine Wisdom

Day, when Justinian and and Theodora rededicated it to Haghia Sophia.

During the construction a number of structural crises had occurred, due to the rapidity with which the building had been erected, and also because of the enormous stresses caused by the vast and shallow dome. The structure was then weakened by a series of earthquakes that shook the city between 553 and 557, and on 7 May 558 the eastern part of the dome collapsed, along with the arch and semidome on that side of the building. Isidorus of Miletus was no longer alive, and so Justinian entrusted the task of rebuilding the church to the architect's nephew, Isidorus the Younger. Isidorus decided to change the design of the dome, making it less shallow so as to reduce the lateral stresses. The reconstruction project was completed in five years. The church was rededicated on Christmas Eve 563 by Justinian, who was then eighty-one years old, with less than two years to live, Theodora having passed on twenty-five years before.

Another series of earthquakes in the ninth and tenth centuries damaged the building and caused cracks to appear in the dome. Then in 989 part of the dome and the eastern arch collapsed, so that the church had to be closed. Basil II entrusted the restoration to Trdat, the renowned Armenian architect, and on 13 May 996 the church was reopened.

The church suffered grievously during the Latin occupation of 1204–61, when it was stripped of all of its sacred relics and other valuable objects. During those years it was a Roman Catholic church served by the Venetian clergy, who erected a campanile near the southwest corner of the building.

When the Greeks recaptured Constantinople in 1261 they reconsecrated Haghia Sophia as a Greek Orthodox church, demolishing the campanile and restoring the building. The dome suffered another partial collapse on 19 May 1346, and the church was closed until reconstruction was completed in 1355. During the last century of Byzantine rule the church fell into serious disrepair, sharing in the general decay of the dying city.

On the eve of the day on which Constantinople fell to the Turks, 29 May 1453, the populace of the city flocked to Haghia Sophia, praying to God for deliverance. The Emperor Constantine appeared in the Great Church shortly before midnight, accompanied by his Greek and Italian knights, and he prostrated himself before the high altar. He remained there for some time in silence before he departed to take up his post on the Theodosian walls, where he died fighting against the Turks the following morning. The congregation in Haghia Sophia barred the doors of the church, but later in the morning Turkish soldiers broke in, killing those who resisted them and enslaving the others.

Sultan Mehmet II, now known to the Turks as Mehmet the Conqueror, rode to Haghia Sophia directly after his triumphal entry into the city early in the afternoon of that same day. He dismounted at the door of the church and bent down to take a handful of earth, which he sprinkled over his turban as an act of humility before God. After surveying the church he ordered that it be immediately converted into a mosque, whereupon his engineers hastily erected a wooden minaret outside the building and a *mihrap* and *mimber* within. Three days later, at the time of the Friday noon prayer, Mehmet the Conqueror dedicated the building as Aya Sofya Camii Kabir, the Great Mosque of Haghia Sophia, assisted by his two chief clerics, Akşemsettin and Karaşemsettin. Evliya Çelebi tells the story of Haghia Sophia's conversion into a mosque in his *Seyahatname*:

> Sultan Mehmet II, on surveying more closely the church of Aya Sofya, was astonished at the solidity of its construction, the strength of its foundations, the height of its cupola, and the skill of its builder. He caused the ancient building to be cleared of its idolatrous objects and purified of the blood of the slain, and having refreshed the brains of the victorious Muslims by fumigating it with amber and lion-aloes, converted it that very hour into a mosque.
>
> On the following Friday, the faithful were summoned to prayer by the *muëzzins*, who proclaimed with a loud voice this text of the Koran: 'Verily, God and his angels bless the Prophet.' Akşemşettın and Karaşemsettin then arose, and placing themselves on either side of the sultan, supporting him under his arms; the former placed his turban on the head of the Conqueror, fixing in it the black and white feather of a crane, and putting into his hand a naked sword. Thus conducted to the *mimber* he ascended it, and cried out with a voice as loud as David's, 'Praise be to God, the Lord of all the world', on which the victorious Muslims lifted up their hands and uttered a shout of joy.

Mehmet the Conqueror and his successors continued to keep Haghia Sophia in good repair throughout the Ottoman period, for it held pride of place among the imperial mosques and was always held in great veneration. The last and most thorough restoration in

31

the Ottoman era was commissioned by Sultan Abdul Mecit (1839–61), and was carried out in 1847–49 by the Swiss architects Gaspare and Giuseppe Fossati. During the course of this restoration the surviving figurative mosaics of the church were cleared of the whitewash and plaster with which they had been covered earlier in the Ottoman period. When the restoration was complete the mosaics were covered over once again, in order to protect them from further damage.

Haghia Sophia continued to serve as a mosque until 1932, when it was closed and converted into a museum, which opened two years later. In April 1932 Thomas Whittemore and other members of the Byzantine Institute of America began the task of uncovering and restoring the mosaics, a number of which had disappeared since the Fossati restoration. Restoration of the mosaics was not completed until 1964, when the galleries of Haghia Sophia were for the first time opened to the public.

The entrance to the museum is in the garden to the west of Haghia Sophia, the area that was once the *avli*, or outer courtyard of the church. This was a porticoed arcade that enclosed an area 47.7 metres wide and 32.3 metres deep. The portico has disappeared and what remains of the atrium is roughly its eastern half. The west side and rear of the garden are filled with ancient columns and other architectural fragments, all of which were unearthed in various excavations around the city, most of them on the First Hill.

As we approach the entrance to the museum we see the excavated porch of the **Theodosian church**, discovered in 1935 by the German archaeologist Alfons Maria Schneider. Some blocks of the reliefs remain in the pit, along with part of the front steps of the porch, while other huge architectural fragments have been arrayed farther to the north just beyond the garden cafe. The remaining fragments of the Theodosian basilica show that this was an edifice of monumental proportions, comparable in size and grandeur to Justinian's church. An architectural drawing beside the excavation site shows Schneider's reconstruction of the porch of the Theodosian church.

Before entering the museum we might pause to examine the structure of the building. The main ground plan of Haghia Sophia is a rectangle, some 70 by 75 metres. At the centre of the east wall there is a projecting apse, semicircular within and three-sided on the exterior, while to the west the church is preceded by an inner and outer vestibule, known in Greek as the narthex and exonarthex. The central part of the rectangular area is covered by the great dome, one of the

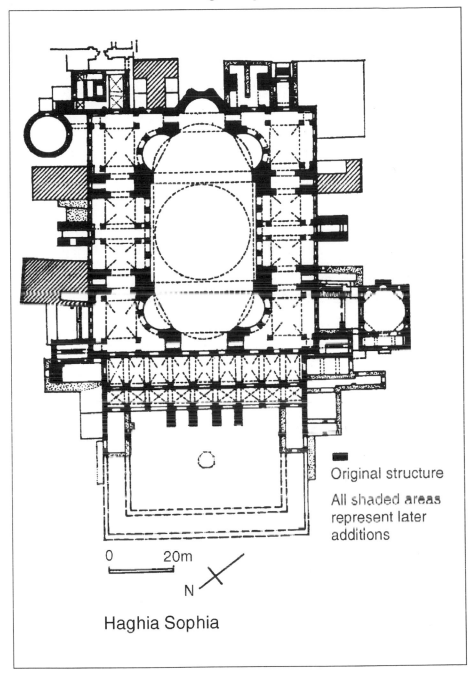

Original structure

All shaded areas represent later additions

0   20m

N

Haghia Sophia

wonders of architecture, with smaller semidomes to east and west and conches over the apse and the four corners. These spherical surfaces cover the central area of the nave, which is flanked by side aisles with galleries above that extend around the sides of the church and also the narthex.

This was the basic form of Justinian's church, but structural crises during the construction and subsequent damage due to earthquakes necessitated the addition of buttresses on all sides of the building. The oldest of these are the two pairs of very tall buttresses against the north and south walls of the church. These were built during Justinian's reign, either in the latter part of the reconstruction of the building or in the rebuilding of the dome in 558–63. The pillar-like outer parts of these buttresses were added in 1317 by Andronicus II Palaeologus (1282–1328) to provide additional support for the building. The four massive flying buttresses against the west gallery were added in the second half of the ninth century. The arch buttresses and retaining walls at the east side of the church were erected by Mehmet the Conqueror soon after the conquest.

Mehmet the Conqueror also built the brick buttress at the south-east corner of the building; this replaced a temporary wooden minaret which had been erected over the southeast buttress when Haghia Sophia was converted into a mosque. Selim II built the stone minaret at the northeast corner in 1574, and the two stone minarets at the northwest and southwest corners were added a year or two later by Murat III. All of these stone minarets are works of Sinan, who also restored the buttresses and the fabric of the building.

In addition, a number of subsidiary structures were erected in the precincts of Haghia Sophia during both the Byzantine and Ottoman periods, most notably the baptistry and the imperial Turkish tombs on the south side of the building; these will be examined after our tour of the museum.

The present entrance to the church is through the central door of the **exonarthex**, which is flanked by the two middle buttresses on the west side of the building. This outer vestibule has nine cross-vaulted bays separated by arches, as does the narthex. Within the bays of the narthex to the right of the entrance there are a number of huge rectangular slabs of mosaic pavements stacked against the walls. These are from the Great Palace of Byzantium, on the Marmara slope of the First Hill. These mosaics were discovered during excavations in the 1930s below the mosque of Ahmet I, where some of the most interesting examples are preserved *in situ* in the Mosaic Museum.

Haghia Sophia

In the last bay on the right there is a huge Byzantine sarcophagus in verd antique. This contained the remains of the empress Eirene, wife of John II Comnenus (1118–43), whose mosaic portrait is preserved in the southeast gallery of Haghia Sophia. Eirene's sarcophagus was originally in the church of the Pantocrator, which she and John erected on the Fourth Hill. The sarcophagus was broken into and looted by the knights of the Fourth Crusade in 1204; in the 1950s it was brought to Haghia Sophia for protection.

Five doors in alternate bays lead from the exonarthex into the **narthex**, which is about twice as wide and high as the outer vestibule. The piers and walls of the narthex are revetted with superb **marble panels**. According to Paul the Silentiary, who wrote a long poem celebrating the rededication of Haghia Sophia by Justinian in 565, these and other marbles within the church came from all over the empire. In order to obtain the elaborate symmetrical patterns of each panel, thin blocks of marble were cut in two, sometimes in four, and opened out like a book so that the natural veining of the stone was duplicated and quadruplicated, giving the unique natural designs that add so much to the beauty of the interior.

Beneath the Turkish painted decoration on the vaults of the narthex we can see here and there portions of the original **mosaic decoration**. A great deal of the Justinianic mosaic decoration survives in the vaults of the narthex and the side aisles of the nave, as well as in the thirteen ribs of the original dome that have never fallen. According to the Silentiary, this mosaic decoration originally covered the great dome, the semidomes, the north and south typanum walls, and the vaults of the narthex, aisles, vestibules and galleries, a total area of more than one and one-half hectacres. This decoration, much of which has survived, consists of large areas of plain gold ground adorned around the edges of architectural forms with bands of geometrical and floral designs in various colours. Simple crosses in outline on the vaults and soffits of arches are constantly repeated, and, according to the Silentiary, there was a cross of this kind on the crown of the great dome. It is clear from the Silentiary's description that in Justinian's time there were no figural mosaics in the church. The figurative mosaics that have survived in Haghia Sophia are all from after the Iconoclastic period (730–843), when icons were banned throughout the Byzantine Empire.

Doors open off from each bay of the narthex into the nave, with the largest one at the centre. This was known as the **Imperial Gate**, since it was reserved for the use of the emperor and his entourage.

35

One of the surviving figurative mosaics is in the lunette above the Imperial Gate. Here Christ is depicted seated upon a jewelled throne, his feet resting upon a stool. He raises his right hand in a gesture of blessing, and in his left hand he holds a book with this inscription in Greek: 'Peace be with you, I am the Light of the World.' At the left a crowned figure prostrates himself before the throne, his hands upraised in supplication. Above, on either side of the throne, there are two roundels, the one on the left containing a bust of the Blessed Virgin and the other an angel carrying a staff or wand. It is believed that the imperial figure is Leo VI (886–912) and thus the mosaic is dated to the period of his reign. If so, it is probable that the emperor is pleading with Christ to forgive him for what Gibbon so aptly called 'the frequency of his nuptials'. The emperor had lost his first three wives without producing a male heir to the throne, and wished to take a fourth wife, ordinarily forbidden by the Orthodox Church. After a long and bitter dispute, the famous scandal of the Tetragamy, Leo finally obtained permission to marry his mistress, Zoe, and legitimized his bastard son, the future Constantine VII Porphyrogenitus (913–59).

Constantine was one of the great chroniclers of medieval Byzantium, his works including the *Book of Ceremonies*, a record of court ritual that is one of the most important sources for Byzantine topography. The *Book of Ceremonies* describes the entry of the emperor and his party through the Imperial Gate: 'The princes remove their crowns, greet the patriarch and proceed to the Imperial Gate. Bearing the candles and bowing thrice, they enter the church after a prayer is pronounced by the patriarch.'

We now pass through the Imperial Gate into the **nave**, an immense contained space pierced by oblique shafts of moted sunlight falling from the circlet of forty windows at the base of the dome. Walking forward, we can now see the whole of the immense interior at once and appreciate its beauty and its grandeur: the fabled dome, which the ancients pictured as being suspended from heaven by a golden chain; its central area flanked by a graceful two-tiered colonnade which Procopius likened to a line of dancers in a chorus, all elements of the vast edifice interrelated in perfect harmony.

The central area of the nave is defined by four enormous and irregularly shaped piers, built of ashlar stone bound together with lead, standing in a square measuring approximately 31 metres on each side. Four great arches rise from the piers, with four pendentives making the transition to the slightly elliptical cornice of the dome, whose diameter measures about 31 metres north-south and 33 metres east-west. The crown of the majestic **dome** is 56 metres above the floor, about the height of a fifteen storey building. The dome has forty ribs which radiate out from the crown, separated at the base by forty windows, of which four toward the west were blocked up during repairs in the tenth century.

Pairs of subsidiary piers to east and west support the main semi-domes, which give the nave its great length, about 80 metres. The central arches to north and south are filled with tympanum walls each pierced by twelve windows, seven in the lower row, five in the upper, of which the three central openings formed a kind of triple arcade. All these windows have in Turkish times been considerably reduced in size, probably by the architect Sinan in the mid-sixteenth century. Between each of the great piers on the north and south four monoliths of verd antique support the galleries, while above six similar columns support the tympana. At the eastern and western ends, to north and south, semicircular exedrae prolong the nave, with two massive columns of porphyry below and six of verd antique above, on which rest smaller semidomes. At the east, beyond the subsidiary piers, a semicircular apse projects beyond the east wall, covered by a conch. Finally, four great buttresses projecting from the north and south walls opposite the central piers help to consolidate the whole fabric.

If the plan is to all intents and purposes that of a basilica, the originality consists in covering it with a dome and two semidomes. For in addition to lengthening the nave, the semidomes make it possible to appreciate from the very threshold the soaring, hovering height, allowing the dome to play its full part in the total effect. Contrast the relative ineffectiveness of the dome of St Peter's in Rome, from which radiate barrel-vaults along the axes of the building. That dome, though higher and somewhat greater in diameter than Haghia Sophia's, is less impressive, for it can only be seen when you are very nearly underneath it, so that you have to crane back your neck to see its crown. How very different here, where from every point of view the dome dominates the whole interior!

Much has been written about the provenance of the various **columns** in the church. The Anonymous of Banduri, the Baron Munchausen among Byzantine writers, is the principal source of various legends that are still repeated about where the great columns of the nave came from: the Temple of the Sun at Heliopolis, some buildings at Rome, the Temple of Artemis at Ephesus, or one of those at Baalbec – the tales differ with the teller. But there seems to be no foundation for these stories and there is every reason to believe that most of the columns, if not all, were specially quarried for Haghia Sophia. From the Silentiary's description, there can be little doubt that the eight monolithic columns of the aisles, the forty columns of the gallery arcade, and all the other verd antique of the building were expressly hewn for Haghia Sophia from the famous quarries in Thessaly near Molossis. But there is a problem about the eight porphyry columns in the exedrae, for there is some evidence that the porphyry mountain at Djebel Dochan near Thebes had ceased to be quarried in the fifth century. If this is true, the eight exedra columns – which, by the way, differ from one another appreciably in height and diameter – must have been taken from some older building. But there is no evidence to connect them to any particular ancient edifice; we simply do not know where they came from.

The only other kind of marble used for columns in the church is that from the island of Proconnesus in the Marmara, known in Turkish as Marmara Adasî. It is a soft white, streaked with grey or black, and is used for the twenty-four aisle columns of the gallery and the eight rectangular pillars at the ends of the ground-floor aisles. The floor of the church, too, the frames of doors and windows, and parts of the wall surfaces are also made of this marble.

A great variety of rare and beautiful marbles was used for the superb revetment of the walls. Besides those already discussed, the Silentiary mentions at least eight different varieties: the deep green porphyry from Mount Taygetus near Sparta, a 'fresh green' from Carystus in the Aegean island of Euboea; the rose-coloured Phrygian marble from Synnada and a variegated one from Hierapolis in Asia Minor; 'Iassian, with slanting veins of blood red on livid white', probably from Lacedaemon; a marble 'of crocus yellow glittering like gold', from Simittu Colonia near Tunis; and one from the Pyrenees, 'the product of the Celtic crags, like milk poured on a flesh of glistening black'; and finally the precious onyx, like alabaster honey-coloured and translucent.

Other types of decorations in rare marbles are also found in the church. The square of *opus Alexandrinum* pavement toward the southeast of the nave has always attracted attention. It is chiefly composed of circles of granite, red and green porphyry, and verd antique. According to Antony, Archbishop of Novgorod, who visited the church in 1200, the Emperor's throne stood upon this square, surrounded by a bronze enclosure.

There are some equally interesting panels above the Imperial Gate: slabs of verd antique alternate with inlaid panels of various marbles. At the top is an elaborate ciborium with drawn curtains revealing a cross on an altar; lower down are other panels with ovals of porphyry, those at the bottom surrounded by pairs of stylized dolphins with foliate tails gobbling up tiny squid with waving tentacles. Finally in the spandrels above the nave and gallery arcades there is a rich and magnificent frieze of sectile work with scrolls of leaves and flowers, and birds 'perched on the twigs'.

The **capitals** of the columns and piers are famous and splendid. There are several different types, but all are alike in having the surface decoration of acanthus and palm foliage deeply undercut so that they produce an effect of white lace on a dark ground; it is possible that they were once gilded. The most common of the capitals – those of the nave and gallery arcades – are generally known as the bowl type: Ionic volutes support a decorated abacus beneath which the bowl-shaped body of the capital is adorned with stylized acanthus leaves, in the centre of which in front and back is a medallion containing a monogram. These monograms are extremely tricky to read, but when deciphered they give the names Justinian and Theodora and the imperial titles Basileus and Augusta. The capitals of the sixteen verd antique columns of the aisles are of similar type but smaller in scale. Those of the eight rectangular pillars at the ends of the aisles are closely related, only here the bowl, instead of becoming circular towards its base, remains square throughout, since the column itself is a square.

The **northwest pillar** in the north aisle is associated by legend with St Gregory the Miracle Worker, who is supposed to have appeared here in the early days of the church and endowed the stone with his healing power. The pillar was encased in brass to protect the stone, but credulous pilgrims have punctured the metal and worn a hole into the pillar itself, for the moisture contained in the cavity has always been considered a cure for eye diseases and a nostrum for fertility.

There are a number of structures in the interior that were added after Haghia Sophia was converted into a mosque, most notably the *mihrap* and *mimber* and the royal loge against the northeast pier, all of which date from the Fossati restorations of 1847–49. The Fossatis were also responsible for the six huge *levhas*, or painted wooden medallions, that hang from the piers at gallery level. These were done by the calligrapher Mustafa Izzet Efendi and record in golden Arabic letters the Sacred Islamic Names, those of Allah, the Prophet Mohammed, and the first four Caliphs: Abu Bekr, Umar, Othman, and Ali. The huge inscription in the dome is also by Mustafa Izzet Efendi; this replaces an earlier inscription with the same text, Surah 24:35 from the Koran: 'In the name of God the Merciful and Pitiful; God is the light of Heaven and Earth. His light is himself, not that which shines through glass or gleams in the morning star or glows in the firebrand.'

Haghia Sophia retains a number of other objects dating from the Ottoman period, all of them gifts of various sultans. Some of these imperial benefactions are described by Evliya Çelebi, who served as a *müezzin* in Aya Sofya Camii during the reign of Murat IV:

> Murat III brought from the island of Marmara two princely basins of white marble, each of them resembling the cupola of a bath. They stand inside the mosque, full of living water, for all the congregation to perform their ablutions and quench their thirst. The same sultan caused the walls of the mosque to be cleaned and smoothed; he increased the number of lamps and built four raised stone platforms for the readers of the Koran, and a lofty pulpit on slender columns for the muezzins. Sultan Murat IV, the Conqueror of Baghdad, raised upon four marble columns a marble throne for the preacher . . . Sultan Murat, who took great delight in this incomparable mosque, erected a wooden enclosure within it near the southern door, and when he went to prayer on Friday he had his attendants hang there cages containing a great number of singing birds, particularly nightingales, so that their sweet notes, mingled with those of the muezzins' voices, filled the mosque with a harmony approaching to that of paradise . . .
>
> Aya Sofya is, in itself, peculiarly the place of God. It is always full of holy men who pass the day there in fasting and the night in prayer. Seventy lectures well pleasing to God are given there daily, so that to the student it is a mine of knowledge, and it never fails to be frequented by multitudes every day.

Except for the wooden enclosure for the nightingales, all of these objects can still be seen in the nave of Haghia Sophia, along with the gifts of later sultans. The two **lustration urns** that Evliya mentions are located in the western exedrae. They are late Hellenistic or early Byzantine urns to which have been added Turkish lids. An English traveller in the seventeenth century reported that they were always kept full of water 'to cool the Mohammedans overheated by their pious gesticulations'. The 'lofty pulpit' for the *müezzins* stands in the north arcade; this is of marble, as are the 'raised platforms' for the readers of the Koran, which stand against the four main piers. The most noteworthy of the later Ottoman additions is the very elegant library, built beyond the south aisle by Mahmut I in 1739. The **library**, endowed by the sultan with the revenues of the Cağaloğlu Hamamî, consists of several domed rooms enclosed with metal grilles. These rooms, housing some five thousand Ottoman books and manuscripts, are revetted with superb Iznik tiles of the sixteenth century, which the sultan found stored in Topkapî Sarayî.

Little now remains of the mosaics that once adorned the nave of Haghia Sophia. The largest and most beautiful of those that have survived is in the conch of the apse. The **mosaic** depicts the **Mother of God with the Christ-Child** on her knees; she is dressed in flowing robes of blue with a small cross on the fold of the mantle over her head and one on each shoulder; her right hand rests on Christ's shoulder and her left upon his knee. The Child is dressed in gold and wears sandals on his feet; his right hand is raised in blessing while his left holds a scroll. The Virgin sits on a simple bench-like throne adorned with jewels; under her are two cushions, the lower green, the upper embroidered with clubs like those on playing cards; beneath her feet is a plinth-like footstool, also bejweled. At the bottom of the arch that frames the apse we see a colossal figure of the Archangel Gabriel; he wears a *divitision*, or undergarment, over which is thrown a *chlamys*, or cloak of white silk; his great wings, reaching nearly to his feet, are of highly-coloured feathers, chiefly blue, green and white. In his right hand he holds a staff, in his left a crystal globe through which can be seen his thumb. Although the upper part of his left side and the top of his wings are lost, he remains a fine and striking figure. Opposite, on the north side of the arch, there are only a few tesserae remaining from a mosaic portrait of the Archangel Michael, the only recognizable fragments being the tips of his great wings.

On the face of the apse conch we see the first three and the last nine letters of an inscription in Greek, of which the whole of the middle part is now missing. The inscription was an iambich distich which once read in full: 'These icons the deceivers once cast down/ the pious emperors have again restored.' The apse mosaic was unveiled by the Patriarch Photius on Easter Sunday 867, a most momentous occasion, for it signified the final triumph of the Orthodox party over the Iconoclasts, marking the permanent restoration of sacred images to the churches of Byzantium. The two pious emperors referred to here are Michael III, the Sot (842–67), and his protégé Basil I, the Macedonian (867–86), who had been made co-emperor on 26 May 866. On the night of 23–24 September 867, after a drunken banquet, Basil had Michael murdered and usurped the throne. Thus began the Macedonian dynasty, which was to rule Byzantium for nearly two centuries.

Three other **mosaic portraits** are located in niches at the base of the north tympanum wall and are visible from the nave. In the first niche on the left is **St Ignatius the Younger**, who was Patriarch of Constantinople from 847–58 and again from 867–77; in the central niche is **St John Chrysostomos**, Patriarch of Contantinople from 398–404; and in the fifth niche **St Ignatius Theophoros** of Antioch. All three of these mosaics are dated to the last quarter of the ninth century.

The only other **mosaics** that are visible from the nave are the **six-winged angels** in the east pendentives. (Those in the west pendentives are imitations in paint done by the Fossatis.) These are the only figurative mosaics that were not covered over during the Ottoman period, although during their restorations the Fossatis did cover the faces of the angels with gold-starred medallions, which are still in place. These mosaics are dated to the mid-fourteenth century, when the east pendentives were restored after the collapse of that side of the dome in 1346. Evliya Çelebi believed that these figures were talismans, albeit moribund ones, as he writes in the *Seyahatname*: 'Before the birth of the Prophet these angels used to speak, and gave notice of all the dangers which threatened the Empire and the city of Istanbul, but since his highness [Mohammed] appeared all talismans have ceased to act.'

All of the other extant figurative mosaics are in the **galleries**, which are approached via a labyrinth leading up from the northern end of the narthex.

Byzantine sources write that the galleries served as the *gynacaeum*, or women's quarters, though the two eastern bays of the south gallery seem to have been reserved for the use of the royal family, and, on occasion, for synods of the Greek Orthodox Church. The throne of the empress stood behind the balustrade at the centre of the west gallery; the spot is marked by a disc of green Thessalian marble set into the pavement, framed by a pair of coupled columns of green marble.

Three of the four surviving mosaics in the galleries are located at the far end of the south aisle, beyond the first bay. That part of the south gallery is partially screened off by two false doors of marble with elaborately ornamented panels, the so-called **Gates of Heaven and Hell**. Between them is the actual doorway, surmounted by a slab of translucent Phrygian marble, above which a wooden beam carved with floral designs in low relief forms a cornice to the whole gateway. This gateway is certainly not an original part of Justinian's church, and seems to have been added to close off the far end of the south gallery as a royal loge and as a meeting-place for church synods.

Turning to the right once inside this portal, we see the most beautiful of all the surviving mosaics in Haghia Sophia, on the east wall of the lateral pier. This is the *Deisis*, an iconographic type in which Christ is shown flanked by the Blessed Virgin and St John the Baptist, who in Greek is known as Prodromos, or the Forerunner. Here John is shown to the right and the Virgin to the left, the opposite of their usual positions in the typical *Deisis;* they lean toward Christ in suppliant attitudes, pleading, so the iconographers tell us, for the salvation of mankind. Christ, holding up his right hand in a gesture of benediction, looks off into space with an expression of sadness in his eyes, appearing here as if he partook more of the nature of man than of God, whatever the medieval theologians may have decided about him. Although two-thirds of the mosaic is now lost, the features of the three figures in the *Deisis* are completely unmarred and it remains a work of great power and beauty. This superb mosaic is dated to the second half of the thirteenth century, when Byzantium was flowering in a renaissance under the Palaeologues, the last dynasty to rule the Empire.

Directly opposite the *Deisis*, below the west face of the next lateral pier, we see set into the floor a **sarcophagus lid** inscribed with the illustrious name of Enrico Dandolo, Doge of Venice. Dandolo, who was almost blind, led the allied force of Venetians and Crusaders that captured Constantinople in 1204. After the conquest of the city he ruled over the Venetian share of Byzantium, which he termed 'a half and a quarter of the Roman Empire', until his death in Constantinople on 16 June 1205, when he was in his ninetieth year. The Venetian clergy buried him here in the gallery of Haghia Sophia, but after the Turkish conquest his tomb was broken open, his armour taken by Mehmet the Conqueror, and his bones thrown to the dogs, or so the story goes.

The two other mosaics in the south gallery, both of them imperial portraits, are on the east wall of the building at the far end of the last bay, flanking a window beside the apse. The **mosaic** to the left of the window depicts a royal couple kneeling on either side of **Christ** enthroned. On the right is the notorious **Empress Zoe**, one of the few women ever to rule Byzantium in her own right, reigning together with her sister Theodora in 1042. On the left is Zoe's third husband, **Constantine IX Monomachus** (1042–55). At the centre of the composition is the enthroned figure of Christ, his right hand raised in a gesture of benediction, his left holding the book of Gospels. On Christ's right stands the emperor holding in his hands the offering of a money-bag, and to his left is the empress holding an inscribed scroll. Above the emperor's head an inscription reads: 'Constantine in Christ the Lord Autocrat, faithful Emperor of the Romans, Monomachus.' Above the head of the empress the inscription reads: 'Zoe, the most pious Augusta.' The scroll in her hand has the same legend as that over the emperor's head, save that the words Autocrat and Monomachus are omitted for want of space.

The curious thing about this mosaic is that all three heads and the two inscriptions concerning Constantine have been altered. A possible explanation for this is furnished by a review of the life and loves of Zoe, daughter of Constantine VIII (1025–28). Zoe and her sister Theodora, a nun, were the last of the Macedonian dynasty, since their father had died without a male heir to the throne. Four emperors in turn ruled after Constantine VIII through their association with Zoe: her first husband Romanus III Argyros (1028–34), her second husband Michael IV (1034–41), her adopted son Michael V (1041–42), and her third husband Constantine IX. The portrait was probably completed in its final form after Zoe's marriage in 1042 to Constantine, whose head and inscription in the mosaic portrait replaced those of one or both of her former husbands. Zoe died at the age of 72 in 1050, mourned by the common people of Constantinople, who called their beloved empress 'Mama'. The court chamberlain Michael Psellus, writing affectionately of Zoe in his *Chronographica*, says that even in her last years, though her hand trembled and her back was bent with age, 'her face had a beauty altogether fresh'.

The **mosaic** to the right of the window shows a royal couple presenting gifts to the **Virgin and Christ Child**, while on the narrow panel of side wall the composition continues to include the portrait of a young prince. These are the figures of **John II Comnenus** and his wife Eirene, daughter of King Ladislaus of Hungary, and their eldest son Alexius, who died in 1122, soon after this portrait was completed. The emperor was known in his time as Kalo Yanis, or John the Good, and Nicetas Choniates wrote of him that 'He was the best of all the emperors, from the family of the Comneni, who ever sat upon the Roman throne.' John and Eirene were full of good works; together they founded the monastery of the Pantocrator, the triple church of which is still one of the principal monuments on the Fourth Hill of the city

There is another imperial portrait in the main bay of the northern gallery, located high on the east face of the northwest pier. This panel represents the emperor Alexander, who came to the throne in May 912, succeeding his elder brother Leo VI. 'Here comes the man of thirteen months,' said Leo with his dying breath, as he saw his despised brother coming to pay his last respects. This cynical prophecy was fulfilled in June of the following year, when Alexander died of apoplexy during a drunken game of polo. Alexander's portrait, the last figurative mosaic to be uncovered during the restoration of 1932–64, is dated to the brief period of his reign, 912–13. The portrait shows him standing full-length in the gorgeous ceremonial costume of a Byzantine emperor. He is crowned with a *camelaucum*, a conical helmet-shaped coronet of gold with pendant pearls; draped in a *loros*, a long, gold-embroidered scarf set with jewels; and shod in gem-studded crimson boots. Four medallions flanking the imperial figure bear this legend: 'Lord help thy servant, the orthodox and faithful Emperor Alexander.'

Before leaving the gallery we should proceed to the last bay on this side, for the balcony there commands a close-up view of the mosaic of the Virgin and Child in the apse and the Archangel Gabriel on the south side of the arch.

We leave the church via the door at the southern end of the narthex. This leads into a hallway known in Byzantine times as the **Vestibule of the Warriors**, since the troops of the imperial bodyguard waited here while the emperor attended services in the church. Looking back here, we see another mosaic portrait in the lunette above the doorway leading from the vestibule into the narthex. The mosaic depicts the Blessed Virgin enthroned in an hieratic pose, holding the Christ-Child in her lap, as she receives two crowned and haloed figures. The figure on the right, identified by an inscription as 'Constantine, the great Emperor among the Saints', offers the Virgin a model of a walled town representing Constantinople. The figure on the left, identified as 'Justinian, the illustrious Emperor', offers her a model church symbolising Haghia Sophia. The mosaic is dated to the last quarter of the tenth century, probably commissioned by Basil II.

There are a number of Ottoman structures in the courtyard of Haghia Sophia, all of them part of the *külliye* of Aya Sofya Camii. In the centre of the courtyard is the *adîrvan* built in the Turkish rococo style for Mahmut I c.1740. The building on the right of the gateway to Ayasofya Meydanî is the *mektep*, a primary school for the children of the mosque's staff, built by Mahmut I in 1740. The little domed structure to the left of the gate is the *muvakithane*, the house and workshop of the mosque astronomer, whose sundial can still be seen on the facade of Haghia Sophia near the southwest corner of the building. The *muvakithane* was built for Abdül Mecit in 1847–49 by the Fossatis.

The four domed buildings in the garden just to the south of Haghia Sophia are all imperial **Ottoman tombs**. The oldest of them is the structure that we pass on the left as we leave the south end of the narthex. This is the former baptistry of Haghia Sophia, an octagonal building with a low dome. The Turks converted it into a mausoleum to bury the mad sultan Mustafa I on 20 January 1639, sixteen years after he had been deposed for the second time. The equally mad sultan Ibrahim was interred here too following his execution on 18 September 1648, ten days after he had been deposed. Evliya Çelebi says that Ibrahim's tomb was much visited by women, 'because he was much addicted to them'.

The three other imperial tombs are in the eastern end of the garden. The earliest in date of these is the one in the centre, that of Selim II, which was completed in 1577. This is a work of Sinan and is one of the finest Ottoman tombs in the city, both the entrance facade and the whole of the interior covered with superb Iznik tiles. The building is square. with an outer dome resting on the exterior walls; within a circlet of columns supports an inner dome. The largest of the catafalques in the tomb covers the grave of Selim II, son and successor of Süleyman the Magnificent. As Evliya Çelebi wrote of him: 'He was an amiable monarch, took much delight in the conversations of poets and learned men, and indulged in wine and gaiety. He was a sweet-natured sovereign but much given to women and wine.' Selim died on 15 December 1574 at the age of fifty-four, after having fallen in his bath in a drunken stupor. Beside Selim's catafalque is that of his favourite wife Nurbanu. Arrayed around them are the tiny catafalques containing the graves of five of Selim's sons, three of his daughters, and thirty-two children of his son and successor, Murat III. Selim's sons were murdered on the night of his death, assassinated according to Ottoman law in order to ensure the peaceful succession of Murat, his eldest son.

The westernmost of the three tombs is that of Murat III. This *türbe* was completed in 1599 by Davut Ağa, who succeeded Sinan as Chief of the Imperial Architects. It is hexagonal in plan, also with a double dome and is adorned with Iznik tiles comparable in quality to those in Selim's *türbe*. The *türbe* contains the remains of Murat III as well as those of his favourite wife, Safiye, four of his lesser concubines, twenty-three of his sons and twenty-five of his daughters. The sultan died on 16 January 1595, in his forty-ninth year. Murat's *türbe* was not finished at the time of his death and so his coffin was temporarily placed under a tent in the garden of Haghia Sophia. The following morning nineteen more coffins were placed there around him, for that night all but one of his surviving sons were executed to ensure the succession of his eldest son, Mehmet III. Most of the other twenty-nine children of Murat III buried here died young, victims of the many epidemics that ravaged the Harem. This was the last use of what Evliya called 'the bloody code of the Ottomans'; thenceforth the younger brothers of a succeeding sultan were spared and instead confined in a prison in Topkapî Sarayî known as the Kafes, or Cage. Built up against Murat's tomb is the little building called the Türbe of the Princes, burial-place of five infant sons of Murat IV who died of the plague.

The tomb at the eastern end of the garden is that of Mehmet III, completed in 1603 by Dalgîç Ahmet Ağa, who succeeded Davut Ağa as Chief Architect. The türbe is octagonal in plan and, like the others, is covered with the finest Iznik tiles. Mehmet died on 22 December 1603 at the age of thirty-six. Nine of Mehmet's children are buried with him, as his favourite wife Handan. Also buried in the türbe are sixteen daughters of Murat III, all of whom died of the plague in 1598.

We now walk around the south and east sides of Haghia Sophia to approach the Imperial Gate of Topkapî Sarayî. As we do so we come on our right to the grandest of all the Ottoman **street-fountains** in the city; this was built in 1728 for Ahmet III, and is a particularly fine example of Turkish rococo architecture. It is a square structure with an overhanging roof surmounted by five small domes. On each of the four sides there is a *çeşme*, or fountain, and at each of the four corners a *sebil*. Each of the fountains is set into a niche framed in an ogival archway. The voussoirs of the arches are in alternating red and pink marble and the facade is richly decorated with floral designs in low relief. The corner *sebils* are semicircular in form, each having three windows framed by engaged marble columns and enclosed with ornate bronze grilles. The curved wall above and below each *sebil* is delicately carved and elaborately decorated with relieved designs and calligraphic inscriptions. Above each of the four *çeşmes* there is a long and beautiful inscription in gold letters on a blue-green ground; the text is by the celebrated poet Seyit Vehbi, who praises the fountain and compares its waters with those of the holy spring Zemzem and of the sacred *selsebils*, or cascade fountains, of Paradise.

On our left, diagonally opposite the Imperial Gate at the upper end of Soğuk Çeşme Sokağî, a large Turkish portal in the rococo style leads to the northeast corner of Haghia Sophia's precincts. The domed structure inside the gate was part of Justinian's church, its *skeuphylakion*, or treasury. All of the precious objects used in the liturgies of Haghia Sophia were stored here, as well as such sacred relics as the Crown of Thorns of Christ's Passion and fragments of the True Cross, which Constantine's mother Helena had brought back from her pilgrimage to Jerusalem. All of these treasures were looted by the knights of the Fourth Crusade and the Venetians when they sacked Constantinople in 1204. The treasury is not open to the public.

Here we might pause to look back on Haghia Sophia, for this is one of the best vantage points for viewing the Great Church, the object of admiration of travellers for more than fourteen centuries. One such encomium was written more than a thousand years ago by an envoy of Prince Vladimir of Kiev, who reported thus after his pilgrimage to Haghia Sophia: 'We know not whether we were in heaven or on earth. For on earth there is no such splendour or such beauty, and we are at a loss how to describe it. We only know that God dwells there among men, and their service is fairer than the ceremonies of other nations. For we cannot forget that beauty.'

4

Topkapî Sarayî

WE NOW APPROACH **Topkapî Sarayî**, the great palace of the Ottoman sultans, whose main entrance is beyond the northeast corner of Haghia Sophia.

After his conquest of Constantinople in 1453, Mehmet the Conqueror found that the former palaces of the Byzantine emperors were in ruins, and so he built a palatial complex for himself on the Third Hill. About six years later he began to create a new and more secluded residence on the acropolis of the First Hill, with gardens laid out on the slopes leading down to the shore. The palace grounds were enclosed on their landward side by a massive defence wall studded with towers, which extended from the Golden Horn to the Marmara, linking up with the ancient Byzantine sea-walls. The main sea-gate in these walls was at Saray Burnu, a portal called Topkapî, the Cannon Gate, because it was flanked by a battery of artillery. The gate, now vanished, soon gave its name to Topkapî Sarayî, the Palace of the Cannon Gate. Mehmet the Conqueror himself called it Dar-üs-Saadet, the House of Felicity. As Evliya Çelebi wrote in his *Seyahatname* describing Topkapî Sarayî: 'Never hath a more delightful residence been erected by the art of man.'

The first phase in the creation of Topkapî Sarayî was completed by about 1465, after which Mehmet the Conqueror made it his principal residence and the centre of his government. His original residence on the Third Hill then came to be called Eski Saray, the Old Palace, which thenceforth was used to house the wives of departed sultans, while the main harem, or women's quarters, was gradually moved to Topkapî Sarayî. The shift was completed and became permanent during the reign of Süleyman the Magnificent, who moved his wife Roxelana into the Harem of Topkapî Sarayî. The women were originally housed in wooden pavilions, with the first brick and stone structures there apparently dating from the reign of Murat III.

Almost the entire plan of the palace as we see it today, with the exception of the Harem and the Fourth Court, belongs largely to the time of Murat III, with extensive reconstructions and additions chiefly under Mehmet IV and Osman III, while the isolated pavilions

Topkapî Sarayî

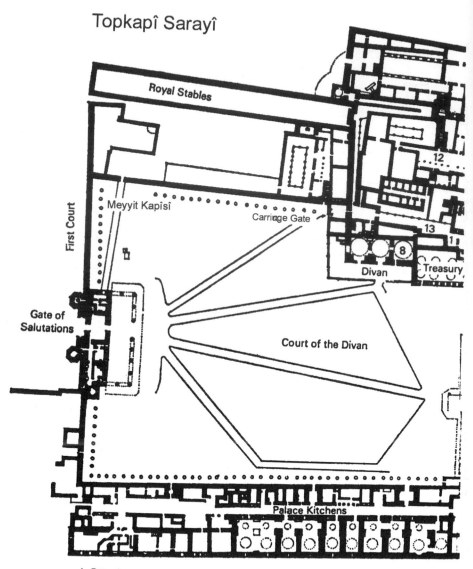

1 Cümle Kapîsî   3 Hall of the Emperor   5 Library of Ahmet I
2 Çeşmeli Oda   4 Salon of Murat III   6 Fruit Room

Topkapı Sarayı

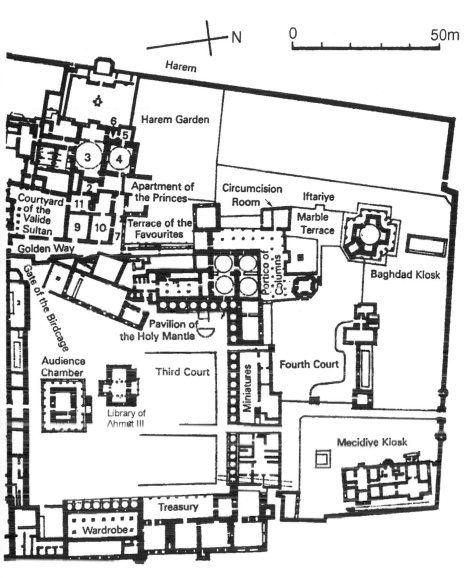

7 Place of Consultation of the Jinns
8 Grand Vezir's Office
9, 10 Suites of the First and Second Kadins

11 Ocakli Oda
12 Courtyard of the Cariyeler (Women Slaves)
13 Hall of Black Eunuchs

51

of the Fourth Court date from various periods. On three occasions, in 1574, 1665 and 1856, very serious fires devastated large sections of the palace, so that while the three main courts have preserved essentially the arrangement given them by Mehmet the Conqueror, many of the buildings have either disappeared or have been reconstructed in later periods.

Topkapî remained the imperial residence up until 1856, when Abdül Mecit abandoned it in favour of the new palace of Dolmabahçe on the Bosphorus. Thereafter Topkapî Sarayî was used to house the women of departed sultans and their servants. Then, in 1909, when Abdül Hamit II was deposed, the imperial harem was officially disbanded, and most of those who were still living in Topkapî Sarayî were forced to leave. After that the old palace on the First Hill remained virtually unused until 1924, when Atatürk decided to convert it into a museum. Since then Topkapî has undergone a continuous process of restoration, with additional rooms being opened to the public from time to time.

The main entrance to Topkapî Sarayî is **Bab-î-Hümayün**, the **Imperial Gate**. The monumental gatehouse dates from the last years of Mehmet the Conqueror's reign; originally there was a second storey, but this was demolished in 1867 when Abdül Aziz (1861–76) revetted the gate in marble. The rooms in the gateway housed the Kapîcîs, or guards, of whom as many as fifty were on watch at all hours of the day and night. The older part of the arch contains four beautiful caligraphic inscriptions, one recording the erection of the gate by Mehmet the Conqueror in 1478 and the other three quoting passages from the Koran. The *tuğra*, or imperial monogram, is that of Mahmut II, the last sultan to live out his reign in Topkapî Sarayî, and other calligraphic inscriptions record the reconstruction of the gateway by Abdül Aziz.

Passing through the Imperial Gate, we enter the **First Court** of the Saray. This was also known as the Courtyard of the Janissaries, for the elite corps of the Ottoman army mustered here when they were on duty in the Saray, up until their annihilation in 1826 by Mahmut II. The First Court, which was open to the public, was the service area of the palace. It contained a hospital, a bakery, an arsenal, the Mint and Outer Treasury, storehouses for firewood and other things, and dormitories for guards and domestics of the Outer Services of the Saray, those whose duties did not ordinarily bring them into Inner Palace, the private residential area inhabited by the sultan and his court. All of the buildings that housed these services have vanished except for the **Darphane**, or **Mint**, the complex of building on the left side of the courtyard. The road beside it leads down to Gülhane Park and the museums on the terrace below the First Court, which we will visit after our tour of the palace. The road on the right side of the courtyard leads down to the parking area, which originally was used for the palace menagerie, while below that was the area where the palace pages played *cirit*, a game in which horsemen hurled darts at one another.

As we walk through the First Court we come on our left to the Byzantine church of **Haghia Eirene**, which we will also visit on our next tour.

At the far end of the First Court we come to **Bab-üs-Selam**, the **Gate of Salutations**, better known as **Orta Kapî**, the **Middle Gate**. This was the entrance to the Inner Palace where everyone had to dismount, for no one but the Sultan was allowed to ride beyond this point. This impressive entryway, flanked by a pair of conical-capped octagonal towers connected by a crenellated parapet, also dates from Mehmet the Conqueror's time. The double-arched doorway is closed by two pairs of splendid doors, the outer one of which bears the date 1524/25. Above the gateway is the *tuğra* of Süleyman the Magnificent and a calligraphic inscription of the Islamic creed: 'There is no God but Allah and Mohammed is his Prophet.'

The gateway is now the entrance to the **Topkapî Sarayî Museum**. The suite of rooms to the right of the gateway was formerly the residence of the Chief Gatekeeper of the Saray. The watchmen of lower rank lived in rooms to the left of the central chamber, where there was a small suite of rooms that housed the Chief Executioner of the Saray, a post that was held by the Chief Gardener. One of the chambers akso served as a waiting-room for foreign ambassadors who had an audience with the Grand Vezier or the Sultan, the latter being a very rare occurrence.

The inner side of Bab-üs Selam has an elaborate but oddly irregular portico of ten columns with a widely-overhanging roof, unfortunately badly repainted in the nineteenth century. To the right of the gate there are two display cases with topographical models, one showing the entire area of Topkapî Sarayî and the other the Inner Palace.

We now enter the **Second Court of the Saray**, a vast area 130 metres long and 110 metres wide. The courtyard, still very much as it was when Mehmet the Conqueror laid it out, is a tranquil cloister of imposing proportions, planted with venerable cypress trees; several fountains once adorned it and mild-eyed gazelles pastured on the glebe.

This was known as the **Court of the Divan**. It took its name from the **Divan**, or **Imperial Council**, which met in the domed chambers at the far left corner of the courtyard. On the first four days of every week the Grand Vizier and other high officials of the realm met here to settle all of the civil affairs of the Ottoman state. Mehmet the Conqueror presided over meetings of the Divan in the early years after the conquest, but later in his reign he ceased to attend directly, merely looking on from his adjacent loge through a grilled window over the Grand Vizier's seat, a practice followed by his successors. On the days of Divan meetings the whole courtyard was filled with a vast throng of officials along with the corps of palace guards and Janissaries, at least 5,000 people on ordinary days, but more than twice that number on special occasions.

From the Middle Gate paths radiate to various parts of the courtyard. The diagonal path on the left leads to the Divan and its associated chambers, dominated by the conical-roofed tower that is the principal landmark of the Saray when viewed from the Golden Horn. This complex dates in its essentials from Mehmet the Conqueror's time, though much altered in later periods. The tower was lower in Mehmet the Conqueror's day and had a pyramidal roof, the present structure with its Corinthian columns having been added by Mahmut II in 1820.

The Divan complex consists of three domed chambers that project from the northwest corner of the courtyard under the tower, their outer periphery shaded by a colonnaded portico with overhanging eaves. The first room on the left is the Divan proper, the meeeting place of the Imperial Council; the one in the centre was the Public Records Office, and the one on the right was the Office of the Grand Vizier. The first two rooms, both of which are square and covered by a dome, open widely into one another under a great arch. The lower walls are revetted with Iznik tiles of the best period; the upper parts of the walls, as well as the vaults and the domes, have been redecorated in recent years. Around three sides of the first room there is a low couch covered with Turkish carpets, the divan from which the Council took its name. Here sat the members of the Council, the Grand Vizier in the centre opposite the door, the other viziers on either side of him in strict order of rank. Over the Grand Vizier's seat there is a grilled window known as the Eye of the Sultan, used by Mehmet the Conqueror and his successors whenever they wanted to observe the proceedings in the Divan.

Adjacent to the three rooms of the Divan complex is the **Inner Treasury**, a long chamber with eight domes in four pairs supported internally by three massive piers. This building dates from the late fifteenth or early sixteenth century. Here, and in the vaults below, were stored the tax receipts and tribute money as they arrived from all over the Empire. These funds were kept here until the quarterly pay days for the use of the Council in meeting the expenses of government, and at the end of each quarter what remained unspent was transferred to the Imperial Treasury in the Third Court. The Inner Treasury is now used to display the Saray's **Collection of Arms and Armour**, most of it Turkish, including many objects that belonged to the sultans.

Around the corner from the Divan, under the south side of the **Divan Tower**, is the **Carriage Gate**, the main entrance to the Harem. Guided tours of the Harem start here, but we will delay our visit until we have seen the rest of the palace.

The remainder of the west side of the Second Court is occupied by a long portico, at the south end of which there is a portal known as **Meyyit Kapîsî**, the **Gate of the Dead**, because those who died in the palace were carried through it for burial outside. This gateway leads down to the area of the Royal Stables, where the imperial carriages and harnesses are preserved, though these buildings are now temporarily closed. Some of the ornate carriages from the stables are occasionally on view under the portico to the right of the Middle Gate as you enter.

Returning to the Middle Gate, we now take the right-hand diagonal path towards the kitchens. On the way we pass an enormous Byzantine capital unearthed here in the mid 1960s, along with a similar one that is now inside the kitchen area. Both capitals appear to date fom the fifth or six century, and probably bore statues.

Most of the east side of the Second Court is taken up with the **palace kitchens** and the quarters of the culinary department of the Inner Service, those who served in the Inner Palace. The kitchens themselves comprise a series of ten spacious chambers along the sheer eastern wall of the Inner Palace, their lofty domes and tall conical chimneys making them distinctive landmarks when seen from the Marmara shore. The two southernmost domes date back to Mehmet the Conqueror's time, the other eight to that of Beyazit II, while the chimneys in front of them are additions by Sinan, who reconstructed much of this part of the Saray after a fire in 1574. Parallel to the kitchens and facing them across a narrow alley are the domed chambers that once housed the kitchen staff. Today the kitchens and staff chambers are used to display the Saray's incomparable **collection of Chinese porcelain** and other china, glassware and silverware. The collection of Chinese porcelain is said to be the third richest and most varied in the world, surpassed only by those at Taipei (formerly at Beijing) and Dresden. Begun by Beyazit II, augmented by Selim I and above all by Süleyman the Magnificent, the pieces date from the wonderful celadons of the Sung and Yuan collections (960–1368) to the later Ming of the seventeenth century. The European specimens, Limoges, Sèvres, Meissen, and others, are less impressive. There is also an interesting display of the utensils that were once used in the Saray kitchens, most notably the great *kazans*, or bronze cauldrons. The rooms at the north end of the courtyard are used to display the Saray's collection of **Istanbul glass and porcelain**, while the chambers on the west side are used to exhibit **silver objects** that once belonged to the sultans, along with a display of European porcelain.

At the far end of the Second Court we come to **Bab-üs-Saadet**, the **Gate of Felicity**. This is the entryway to the **Third Court**, the central area of the **Inner Palace**, the actual **House of Felicity**, the strictly private and residential area of the Saray. The gateway itself dates from Mehmet the Conqueror's time, though it was reconstructed in the sixteenth century and thoroughly redecorated in the rococo style in the eighteenth century. When a new sultan began his reign he sat before the Gate of Felicity in his gold and emerald Bayram Throne, receiving the homage of all the dignitaries in the civil and religious hierarchies of the Empire in turn, beginning with the descendants of the Prophet Mohammed. The Sultan also received his subjects here on the eve of the two most festive Moslem holidays, Şeker Bayramî and Kurban Bayramî.

Immediately inside the Gate of Felicity is the **Arz Odasî**, or **Audience Chamber**. Although in the Third Court, it belongs by function rather to the Second, for it was the setting for the last act of the ceremonies connected with meetings of the Divan. Here, at the end of each session of the council, the Grand Vizier and the other high functionaries waited on the Sultan and reported to him upon the business transacted and the decisions taken, which could not be considered final until they had received the royal assent. Here also the ambassadors of foreign powers were presented at their arrival and leave-taking.

The Audience Chamber occupies a small building with widespreading eaves supported by an arcade of ancient marble columns.

The foundation and plan are from Mehmet the Conqueror's time, but most of the building dates from the reign of Selim I, with inscriptions recording restorations by Ahmet III and Mahmut II. The room was restored again after a fire in 1856, which destroyed most of its furnishings and decorations. The building is divided into a small anteroom on the right and the audience chamber proper on the left, where the Sultan sat enthroned. The magnificent canopy of the throne, dated by an inscription to 1596, and the gilt-bronze *ocak*, or chimney-piece, are the only parts of the decoration that survived the fire.

The Third Court was the centre of the Inner Service of the Saray, which included the royal pages, the students in the **Palace School**, and the servants and officials in the various departments of the Sultan's household staff. The Palace School was designed to train young men for important positions in the civil, religious and military hierarchies of the Empire. The pages who attended the school entered at various ages from twelve to eighteen, most of them taken in the *devşirme*, the annual levy of Christian youths in the provinces of the Empire. The school was organized in six divisions, or Halls, which were housed around the periphery of the Third Court. Here also were housed the White Eunuchs and their Ağas, who were in charge of the administration and discipline at the school. The large building jutting out into the courtyard to the left is **Ağalar Camii**, the **Mosque of the Ağas**, which was used by the pages, the students and faculty at the school, and the White Eunuchs. Ağalar Camii now serves as one of the libraries of the Topkapî Sarayî Museum, along with the building in the middle of the court, a library founded by Ahmet III in 1719. The latter is an elegant little building of Proconnesian marble consisting of a domed area flanked by three loggias with sofas and cupboards for books.

The structure at the beginning of the right side of the court is the former **Campaign Hall**, the branch of the Palace School that trained pages who would accompany the Sultan on campaign. This is preceded by a domed colonnade supported by a row of very handsome Byzantine columns in verd-antique. The hall is one of the largest chambers in the Saray, a long room divided into three aisles by two rows of pillars supporting barrel vaults. This is now used to house the **Imperial Wardrobe**, a fascinating collection of costumes of the sultans. All of the older ones are of the *kaftan* type, a long robe reaching to the feet made of silk, satin or velvet brocade in brilliant colours and bold design, often lined or trimmed with fur; many are of outstanding beauty and nearly all are in perfect conndition.

The rest of the east side of the Court beyond the Campaign Hall is taken up with the **Treasury**. This was a pavilion originally built by Mehmet the Conqueror as the **Selamlîk**, a suite of reception rooms used by the Sultan, the royal princes, and the palace pages. The vaults below were used as the Privy Treasury, and gradually the chambers above became storehouses for precious objects, so that in later times the Selamlîk was shifted to another part of the Saray. These rooms have now been restored as the Treasury of the Topkapî Sarayî Museum, an astonishing collection of precious objects formerly owned by the sultans. The most prominent exhibits are four great thrones encrusted with precious stones, of which the huge golden one studded with chrysolites was used on *bayrams* and other state occasions right down to the end of the empire. Other exhibits include bejeweled swords and daggers, objects of jade and other semi-precious stones often mounted in gold, caskets overflowing with uncut emeralds and rubies, and hundreds of other precious objects of gold and jewels, altogether an astonishing collection, admirably mounted and displayed.

The two buildings on the north side of the court formerly housed the **Hall of the Treasury** (left) and the **Hall of the Commissariat** (right). The Hall of the Commissariat now serves as offices for the director of the museum. The Hall of the Treasury houses the Saray's collections of **calligraphy** and of **Turkish and Persian miniatures**. From an artistic point of view the collection of miniatures is perhaps the supreme treasure of the Saray, a total of some thirteen thousand pictures, most of them in albums, of which only a very few can be exhibited at any time. The oldest miniatures in the collection are in the so-called Mehmet the Conqueror Album; tentatively ascribed to Mohammed Siyah Kalem ('of the black pen'), they are from Iran and have been dated variously from earlier than the thirteenth century to the second half of the fifteenth century. The oldest Ottoman works are by Matrakci Nasuh, court-painter of Süleyman the Magnificent, the most interesting of which is a detailed map of Istanbul, including Galata. Other miniatures are in three albums commissioned by Murat III, one of the books illustrating a procession of the guilds held in 1583 to celebrate the circumcision of the future Mehmet III, which lasted for fifty-seven days. The latest in date of the imperial albums was composed in 1720 to commemorate the circumcision of four sons of Ahmet III; here the miniatures are by Levni, one of the two greatest Ottoman painters. The other is Nigari, whose finest work is a portrait of Süleyman in his last years. The gallery at the rear is now used to display the Saray's wonderful collection of Karagöz figures, the Turkish shadow puppets. The gallery on the upper floor is hung with portraits of all the sultans of the the Ottoman dynasty, known in Turkish as the Osmanlî.

In the last building on the north side of the courtyard there is a chamber known as the **Treasury of the Sword-Bearer**, which is now used to exhibit some of the Saray's **Clock Collection**.

At the northwest corner of the courtyard is **Hîrka-i-Saadet Dairesi**, the chambers where the relics of the Prophet Mohammed are kept. These relics, of which the Prophet's mantle is the most sacred, were brought from Egypt by Selim I following his capture of Cairo in 1517, after which he and his successors assumed the title of Caliph. The pavilion itself consists of four domed rooms forming a square, with a fifth opening off to the left of the southwest chamber. The foundation and plan of these rooms date to Mehmet the Conqueror's reign, though they were partly reconstructed and refurnished by Murat III.

One enters the pavilion into a room with a pretty fountain under the dome, which opens by a huge arch into the second room. Here are displayed the bow of the Prophet Mohammed and the swords of the first four Caliphs; farther on is one of the doors of the great mosque at Mecca. In the room to the left are some beautiful ancient Korans; the solid gold covering for the Hacer-i Esved, the meteoritic stone which is built into the Kaaba at Mecca; also water-gutters from Mecca of chased and moulded silver-gilt, and other precious objects. Returning to the room with the fountain, we pass into another chamber where are preserved the more precious relics of the Prophet: hairs from his beard, one of his teeth, his footprint, his seal, and so on. (Many of these objects were brought to Istanbul after the victorious campaign of Selim I in 1517.) Through an opening here one looks into (one cannot enter) the room where the Holy Mantle of the Prophet is preserved in a golden coffer under a magnificent golden baldachino, and in another coffer is the Holy Standard, which in times past was unfurled when a holy war was proclaimed against the infidel. An *imam* now kneels in this room and chants the Koran throughout the day, the sound of his voice resonating throughout the Pavilion of the Holy Mantle.

We continue on into the **Fourth Court**, which is really a garden on several levels with a number of pavilions. We begin at the highest level in the southwest corner of the court, where a flight of steps leads up to the Portico of Columns, an L-shaped colonnaded area that borders the Pavilion of the Holy Mantle. Here we come to a marble pool flanked by two handsome imperial kiosks. The one at the northeast corner of the portico is the **Rivan Köşkü**, built by Murat IV in 1636 to commemorate his capture of Rivan (modern Erivan) in the Caucasus. It is a cruciform room entirely revetted in beautiful Iznik tiles, while the outside has a polychrome revetment of marble.

During the latter years of his reign Murat was hopelessly addicted to drink, and when he was drunk he became a homicidal maniac. Demetrius Cantemir, Prince of Moldavia, describes Murat's insane behaviour in his history of the Ottoman Empire.

> Very often at midnight he stole out of the women's quarters through the private gate of the palace with his drawn sword, and running through the streets barefooted with only a loose gown around him, like a madman, killed whoever came his way. Frequently from the windows of the higher rooms, where he used to drink and divert himself, he shot with arrows such as accidentally passed by. In the day time he ran up and down in disguise, and did not return until he had killed some unfortunate wretch for little or no cause.

The kiosk at the northwest corner is the **Sünnet Odasî**, or **Circumcision Room**. This was built for Sultan Ibrahim in 1642 to celebrate the circumcision rites of his first son, the future Mehmet IV. The kiosk is rectangular in plan and is entirely revetted in Iznik tiles, both inside and out. The Sünnet Odasî stands at the south end of a broad marble terrace, which on its west side is bordered by a white marble balustrade looking out over the lower gardens of the palace to the Golden Horn. At the centre of the balustrade there is a charming little balcony covered by a domed canopy in gilded bronze carried on four slim bronze pillars. An inscription on the canopy records that the balcony is called **Iftariye** and that it was made for Sultan Ibrahim in 1640, the first year of his reign. The balcony takes its name from Iftar, the festive meal taken just after sunset in the holy month of Ramadan, ending the daily fast. According to palace tradition, Ibrahim always took his Iftar on this balcony, and miniatures in the Saray's collection depict him seated there, throwing handfuls of coins to his pages.

When Ibrahim succeeded to the throne, after having been locked up in the Cage throughout the reign of his brother Murat IV, it was thought at first that he was impotent. Since Ibrahim was the only male left in the Ottoman line his mother Kösem did what she could to remedy this, having a quacksalver dose him with aphrodisiacs while she supplied him with beautiful women from the Istanbul slave market. Her treatment worked, and on 6 January Ibrahim's concubine Turhan Hadice bore him a son, the future Mehmet IV, and in the next fourteen months he sired two more sons, the future sultans Süleyman II (1687–91) and Ahmet II (1691–95). By that time he had developed a prodiguous sexual appetite, as Cantemir writes, contrasting Ibrahim's lust with Murat's alcoholism.

As Murat was wholly addicted to wine, so was Ibrahim to lust. They say he spent all his time in sensual pleasure, and when nature was exhausted with the frequent repitition of venereal delights he endeavoured to restore it with potions or commanded a beautiful virgin richly habited to be brought to him by his mother. . . . In the palace gardens he frequently assembled all the virgins, made them strip themselves naked, and neighing like a stallion ran amongst them and as it were ravished one or the other, kicking or struggling by his order. Happening once to see the private parts of a wild heifer, he sent the shape of them in gold all over the empire with orders to make enquiry whether a woman made in just that manner could be found for his lust. At last such a one was found and received into the women's quarters. [She was an Armenian girl named Şeker Para, or Piece of Sugar, a giantess who apparently weighed more than three hundred pounds.] He made a collection of great and voluminous books expressing the various ways of coition, whence he even invented some new and previously unknown postures.

A third pavilion stands at the north end of the terrace. This is the **Bagdat Köşkü**, built by Murat IV in 1638 to commemorate his capture of Baghdad. The kiosk is cruciform in plan and its wide overhanging eaves are carried by an arcade of marble columns. The columns are crowned with lotus capitals, and the voussoirs of the arches are in alternating white and coloured marble with serrated edges. The walls inside and out are sheathed in ceramic tiles, chiefly blue and white, and the interior is beautifully furnished, its dome decorated with elaborate arabesques on a crimson ground, painted on leather.

At the centre of the garden in the main area of the Fourth Court there is a charming pavilion known as the **Sofa Köşkü**. This was built early in the eighteenth century for Ahmet III, probably as a kiosk for his use during the famous tulip festivals that he held here in the gardens of the Fourth Court. He was known in the West as the Tulip King, and in Turkish the period of his reign is called Lale Devri, the Tulip Period. In 1752 the bulding was redecorated in the rococo style by Mahmut I. At the far end of the court is the **Mecidiye Köşkü**, an ornate pavilion of European appearance standing on a marble terrace at the northeastern corner of the acropolis-hill. The pavilion takes its name from Abdül Mecit, for whom it was built c.1840. The kiosk now houses an excellent restaurant named Konyalî, which commands a panoramic view of the lower Bosphorus.

We now return to the Carriage Gate in the Second Court to begin a tour of the **Harem**. The gate took its name from the fact that the Harem ladies entered their carriages here when they went on an outing. Above the gateway is an inscription giving the date of its construction, 1588.

The gateway opens into a vestibule called **Dolaplî Kubbe**, the **Domed Cupboard**. and from there we go on into a guardroom revetted with fine tiles. The Black Eunuchs were stationed here, guarding the approach to **Altîn Yolu**, the Golden Way, a walkway paved with pebble mosaics extending along the eastern side of the Harem.

At the beginning of the Golden Way on its left we pass a portico bordered by ten marble columns with lotus capitals, surmounted by wrought-iron lamps that once lighted the way to the Carriage Gate. The tiled building to the rear of the porch was the **dormitory of the Black Eunuchs**, dated to 1668–69. A passageway leads to the central courtyard of the dormitory, which has about a dozen little rooms on each side of its three floors. We cannot enter the courtyard, but we can look into the rooms on its east side through the windows under the portico. The last room on the north has been restored with two wax figures representing Black Eunuchs dressed in their characteristic costumes.

Since there were several hundred Black Eunuchs in the palace, they must have served in watches and slept here in relays when they were not on duty. Generally, the Black Eunuchs guarded the Harem, while the older ones dominated the Inner Service under their Chief, whose title was Kîzlar Ağasî, Ağa of the Girls. The **apartment of the Kîzlar Ağasî** was the building at the left side of the Golden Way just beyond the portico. The young princes in the Harem received their primary education from the Chief Black Eunuch on the second floor of his apartment; after they reached the age of puberty they moved to the *selamlîk* and attended the Palace School along with the pages.

The apartment of the Chief Black Eunuch commanded the approach to **Cümle Kapîsî**, the main entrance to the Harem proper. Beyond Cümle Kapîsî is another guardroom, strategically situated at the Harem's main intersection. On the right a corridor leads to **Kuşhane Kapîsî**, the **Aviary Gate**, which gives access to the Third Court; on the left a long and narrow passageway leads down to the **Courtyard of the Cariyeler**, the women servants in the Harem. On the east side of this courtyard there are three suites of rooms for the chief women officials of the Harem: the Head Stewardess, the Treasure, and the Head Laundress. The domed and tiled rooms are very attractive, particularly as they overlook the lower gardens of the Saray. The long staircase just beyond the three suites leads down to a large courtyard on a much lower level, once the site of the Harem hospital.

Returning to Cümle Kapîsî, we now pass through a portal and turn left off the Golden Way into the **Courtyard of the Valide Sultan**. The apartments of the Valide Sultan occupy most of the west side of the courtyard on two levels, while those of the First and Second Kadîns, the highest-ranking of the Sultan's four official wives, were on the north side.

At the northwest corner of the courtyard there is a mounting block used by the Sultan when he rode to and from the Inner Palace along the Golden Way; behind it a portal leads into **Ocaklî Oda**, the **Room with a Hearth**, a beautifully tiled chamber dominated by a splendid bronze chimney-piece. On the right a door leads to the suites of the First and Second Kadîns. On the left a door opens into a smaller chamber called **Çeşmeli Oda**, the **Room with a Fountain**, whose pretty fountain bears the date 1665/66, as does the inscription on the door leading to the next room. These rooms served as antechambers between the Harem and the Sultan's suite.

A passageway at the southwest corner of the courtyard leads into the **Salon of the Valide Sultan**. The Valide's chambers also included an adjoining reception room, an interior court, a sitting-room, a prayer-room, and a smaller suite on the upper floor, altogether a vast apartment considering the cramped confines of the Harem, where even the First and Second Kadîns had just two rooms each. At the far end of the salon there is an alcove that has been restored with wax figures representing the Valide and her ladies in waiting, all dressed in the costumes they would have worn in the Harem.

We leave the Valide's apartment along a corridor paved in marble. A doorway on the left, now closed, leads into what were once the **apartments of Sultan Abdül Hamit I**. Farther along on the right a door leads into the **private baths of the Sultan**, where he bathed after visiting his favourites in the Harem. Selim II died in these baths on 15 December 1574, after falling while in a drunken stupor and hitting his head on the marble pavement.

Evliya Çelebi, who served Murat IV as a page in the mid 1630s, writes in his *Seyahatname* of a dizzying encounter that he had with the sultan outside these baths.

> One day the Sultan came out covered with perspiration from his *hamam* near the throne room, saluted those present and said, 'Now I have had my bath.' 'May it be to your health,' was the general reply. I said, 'My Sultan, you are now clean and comfortable, do not therefore oil yourself for wrestling today, especially since you have already exercised with others and your strength must be considerably reduced.' 'Now have I no strength left?' said he. 'Let me see,' upon which he seized me like an eagle, raised me over his head and whirled me about as children do a top. I exclaimed, 'Do not let me fall, my Sultan, hold me fast!' He said, 'Hold fast yourself!' and continued to swing me about, until I cried out, 'For God's sake, my Sultan, cease, for I am quite giddy!' He then began to laugh, released me, and gave me forty-eight pieces of gold for the amusement which I had offered him.

At the end of the corridor beyond the baths we come to the largest chamber of the Inner Palace – **Hünkâr Odasî** – the **Hall of the Emperor.** The room is divided by a great arch into two unequal sections; the larger part is domed, the smaller, slightly raised, has a balcony where the women musicians of the Harem played. This splendid hall is believed to date from the reign of Murat III, and is almost certainly a work of Sinan. The upper part of the room – domes, pendentives and arches – has been restored to its original appearance, but the lower zone retains the baroque decorations, including the blue and white Dutch tiles, added by Osman III. At the southeastern corner there is a small chamber that was used by the Sultan as a private sitting-room.

Evliya Çelebi writes of the weekly schedule of audiences that Murat IV held in this room, during the time that he himself was serving the Sultan as a page.

> During the winter he regulated his audiences as follows: On Friday he assembled all the divines, sheikhs and the readers of the Koran, and with them he disputed till morning on scientific subjects. Saturday morning was devoted to the singers who sang the Ilahi, the Na't, and other spiritual tunes. Sunday evening was ap-

propriated to poets and reciters of romances. On Monday evening he had the dancing boys and the Egyptian musicians. The assembly sat until daybreak and resembled the musical feast of Hüseyin Bukhara. On Tuesday evening he received the old experienced men who were upwards of seventy and with them he used to converse in the most familiar manner. On Wednesday he gave audience to the pious saints, and on Thursday to the dervishes. In such a manner did he watch over the affairs of the Ottoman state, that not even a bird could fly over it without his knowledge. But were we to describe all of his excellent qualities we could fill another volume.

Through the windows on the outer side of the room we see the **courtyard and kiosk of Osman III**, a large pavilion in the baroque style that projects over the retaining wall of Topkapî Sarayî above Gülhane Park.

A door at the northeast corner of Hünkâr Odasî opens into a small but lavishly tiled **anteroom** that was probably built by Sinan. We then enter the **Salon of Murat III**, a magnificent chamber only slightly smaller than Hünkâr Odasî but far more beautiful since it has retained the whole of its original decoration. The walls are sheathed in beautiful Iznik tiles; the panel of plum blossoms surrounding the elegant bronze chimney-piece being among the most noteworthy, along with the calligraphic frieze that extends around the room. Opposite the fireplace there is a pretty three-tiered *selsebil*, a cascade fountain of carved polychrome marble set in a marble embrasure. The beauty of the decoration and the perfect and harmonious form of the room identify it as a work of Sinan.

Murat III was the most prolific of the Ottoman sultans. The palace archives credit him with having fathered fifty-six children, including twenty-four sons and thirty-two daughters, a record for the Osmanlî dynasty. The record is all the more impressive in that fifty-four of these children were born in the last twelve years of Murat's life, when he greatly expanded his harem, whereas in the first nine years of his reign he had remained faithful to his wife Safiye, mother of his son and successor Mehmet III. Gianfrancesco Morosini, Venetian ambassador to the Sublime Porte during the reign of Mehmet III, writes in one of his reports of the sultan's heightened sexual activity and of the increased bathing that this required.

He tried out many beautiful young girls, whom everyone brought to him, and in this way began the life he now leads. This is very different from his old ways; he is now not satisfied with one or two but has relations with more than twenty. Every night he sleeps with two, and often with three. Since their religious laws require a man who has been with one woman to wash before going to another, he often bathes two or three times a night. This is a real danger to his life because his health is weak, and he suffers from epilepsy; he could easily drop dead without warning.

Opening off the west side of the salon there is a small chamber that Ahmet I converted into a **library and sitting-room** in 1608. This is one of the most delightful rooms in the Saray, with carved marble bookshelves and cabinets inlaid with sea-tortoise shell and mother-of-pearl, its walls revetted with green and blue tiles almost as beautiful as those in the salon. The library is lighted by windows on both its north and south sides, with views of the Marmara, the Bosphorus, and the Golden Horn. A marble door in the south wall of the library leads into another delightful chamber, the **Dining Room of Ahmet III**, created for the Tulip King in 1705. This is also known as Yemiş Odasî, the Fruit Room, because of the bowls of fruit and vases of flowers depicted on the brightly-painted panels of lacquered wood with which its walls are decorated. These decorations are characteristic of the Tulip Period, the first half of the eighteenth century, when European rococo art and architecture made their first appearance in Istanbul.

Returning through the Salon of Murat III and its anteroom, we now come to a pair of beautiful rooms known as the **Apartments of the Princes**. Up until recently this was thought to be the infamous Kafes, or Cage, the place where the younger brothers of the Sultan were confined to prevent them from contesting the throne. But the Kafes has now been identified as a congeries of small and dark rooms farther down the corridor that leads past the Apartments of the Princes, a hallway known for some forgotten reason as the **Consultation Place of the Jinns**. The Apartments of the Princes have been dated to the late sixteenth century or the early seventeenth; this is principally because of their very beautiful Iznik tiles, which are of the greatest period. The first room has a dome magnificently painted on canvas; the ceiling of the inner room is flat but also superbly painted. The inner chamber has a splendid brass-gilt chimney-piece, on each side of which, above, are two of the most gorgeous tile panels in existence.

The Consultation Place of the Jinns leads to **Gözdeler Taşlîgî**, the **Terrace of the Favourites**, a large courtyard overlooking the lower gardens of the Saray and a large swimming-pool once used by the women in the Harem. This is named for the long building in two storeys that forms the eastern side of the courtyard, a dormitory that once housed the Sultan's favourite women, who were known as Gözde, or 'in the eye'. The Sultan had a suite of rooms on the ground floor of the dormitory at its northeast corner. Sultan Ibrahim the Mad was confined to this apartment after he was deposed on 8 September 1668, and ten days later he was strangled there by the Chief Executioner, Black Ali.

Guided tours of the Harem end here, and one is led back along the Golden Way to the exit from the Harem. Enroute we pass on our left the stairway to the upper level of the Harem, where in 1808 the future Mahmut II fled from the assassins who had been sent to kill him by his brother Mustafa IV. Then at the end of the corridor we come to the Aviary Gate, where in 1651 the Chief Black Eunuch and his men murdered the Valide Sultan Kösem, mother of sultans Murat IV and Ibrahim, who was making a desperate effort to flee from the Harem. Here we leave the Harem and enter the Third Court, having completed our tour of the House of Felicity.

5

Haghia Eirene and the Museums

WE NOW RETURN to the First Court of Topkapî Sarayî to visit **Haghia Eirene**, which we bypassed on our last tour.

Haghia Eirene is the second largest Byzantine church in the city, surpassed in size only by Haghia Sophia. It is dedicated to the Divine Peace (*eirene*, in Greek), another attribute of Christ. The original church of Haghia Eirene apparently predated the first Haghia Sophia, because it was always called Palaia Ekklesia, the Old Church. At the time of the Nika Revolt in 532 Haghia Eirene was destroyed by fire along with Haghia Sophia. The two churches were rebuilt by Justinian, and the present Haghia Eirene was probably redicated at the same time as Haghia Sophia in 537. The new churches of the Divine Wisdom and the Divine Peace were thenceforth closely linked and formed two parts of what were essentially one religious establishment, both of them administered by the Patriarchate and served by the same clergy.

Haghia Eirene was almost destroyed in 564, when a fire ruined the atrium and part of the narthex, but it was immediately restored by Justinian, then in the last year of his life. The church was severely damaged by an earthquake in October 740; it was restored by either Leo III (717–41) or his son and successor Constantine V (741–75). It appears that no other major catastrophes have befallen the church, therefore the building we see today dates from Justinian's reign with the exception of eighth-century repairs and minor Turkish additions. After the Turkish conquest Haghia Eirene was enclosed within the outer walls of Topkapî Sarayî, serving as an arsenal for the Janissaries. In the late nineteenth century the building became a storehouse for antiquities, particularly old Ottoman armaments. The building was restored in the 1980s and is now used for exhibitions and concerts.

The church is rectangular in plan, 42.2 metres long and 35.7 metres wide on the exterior, with a five-sided apse projecting from the east wall, and to the west a narthex preceded by an atrium. The central area of the nave is covered by a dome carried on a high drum, with peaked roofs to the north, east and south, and a low domical vault to the west. The ancient architectural fragments arrayed around the building are from excavations on the First Hill. The ground around the church has risen some five metres above its original level. The present entry is through a Turkish porch and outbuildings outside the northwest corner of the church, from where a ramp leads down to the level of the interior.

The church is a basilica in form, but of a very unusual type. The central nave is flanked by a pair of side aisles, above which there is a gallery which also surmounts the narthex. The central area of the nave is surmounted by the dome, some 15.5 metres in diameter. The dome is supported primarily by four huge piers standing on the corners of a square. Between these piers there are four round arches, with pendentives curving between them and the circular cornice of the drum that carries the dome. Barrel vaults open off from these arches to north, east and south, with a conch covering the apse. Another pair of piers at the west end of the nave supports an elliptical domical vault, from which barrel vaults open off to the north and south.

The wide **nave** is separated from the side aisles by a colonnade, with four pairs of monoliths between the main piers and another pair between the west piers and the supports of the rear gallery. Around the periphery of the circular apse there is a *synthronon*, the only one in the city that has survived from the Byzantine period. This has six tiers of seats for the clergy, with doors on either side leading to an ambulatory beneath the fourth tier.

In the conch of the apse a **mosaic cross** in black outline stands on a pedestal of three steps against a gold ground with a geometric border. The inscription here is from Psalm lxv. 4 and 5; that on the bema arch is from Amos ix. 6, with alterations. In both cases parts of the mosaic have fallen away and letters have been painted in by someone who was indifferent to both grammar and sense. There is some difference of opinion concerning the dating of these mosaics; one theory is that they date from the reconstruction after the earthquake of 740, the other that they are from Justinian's reign. The decorative mosaics in the narthex, which are similar to those in Haghia Sophia, are almost certainly from Justinian's time.

At the west end of the nave a modern wooden staircase leads to the galleries. At the west end of the nave five doors lead from the church into the narthex, a vestibule of five bays, the central bay and those on the two ends cross-vaulted and the other two groin-vaulted. From the narthex five doors originally led into the atrium, but three of these have been blocked off.

The **atrium** has been rather drastically altered; the whole of the inner peristyle is Turkish, as well as a good many bays of the outer, with only parts of the outer walls remaining from the Byzantine period. The two huge porphyry sarcophagi in the atrium date from the early Byzantine period, belonging to emperors prior to the sixth century. They were originally in the imperial mausoleum at the church of the Holy Apostles on the Fourth Hill, looted by the Latins in 1204. They were brought here during the period when Haghia Eirene was used as a storage place for antiquities; four other similar porphyry sarcophagi are arrayed outside the Archaeological Museum.

Beyond Haghia Eirene on the west side of the First Court is the **Darphane**, the **Imperial Mint**, which has now been restored and is used to house temporary exhibitions. The Darphane was first built here in Mehmet the Conqueror's time, but the present buildings range in date from 1727 up to the early twentieth century. Beyond the Darphane we pass through Kîz Bekçiler Kapîsî to go down to the terrace below the west side of the Saray. We then come to the entrance to the terrace and its three museums.

Entering the terrace, on the left we see the Museum of the Ancient Orient, on the right the Archaeological Museum, which takes up the whole of the east and north side of the courtyard, and farther on along the west side the Çinili Köşk, or Tiled Pavilion. We will visit the Archaeological Museum first, after which we will go on in turn to the Çinili Köşk and the Museum of the Ancient Orient. The latter two have very limited openings hours, and on any given day some of the galleries of the Archaeological Museum may be closed, so one should check at the entrance booth to see which museums and galleries are open. (All three museums are closed on Monday.)

The **Archaeological Museum** was founded in 1856, and in 1881 the present bulding was completed by Osman Hamdi Bey, the first Turkish archaeologist of international stature. In 1991, on the hundredth anniversary of the opening of the museum, a new wing was dedicated behind the central section of the old building.

When we enter the museum we are confronted by a colossal statue of **Bes**, the **Cypriot Hercules**, holding up a headless lioness by her hind paws. Apparently the head of the lioness was removed when the statue was converted into a fountain, the water pouring forth from the god's loins through a gigantic phallus. The statue is dated to the sixth century BC.

We now turn left from the entrance, passing on our left the museum shops and on our right the entrance to the new wing, to which we will return after seeing the other galleries that are open on the ground floor of the old museum.

We now come to the first of two galleries devoted to the Royal Necropolis at Sidon in Lebanon. The sarcophagi exhibited in these two galleries were unearthed by Osman Hamdi Bey in 1887; they belonged to a succession of kings who ruled in Phoenicia from the mid-fifth century BC to the latter half of the fourth century BC. Just inside the doorway of the first room is the **Tabnit Sarcophagus**, the earliest of the sarcophagi found at Sidon. This is a so-called anthropoid sarcophagus, i.e., in the form of a mummy-case, in this case of diorite The Egyptian hieroglyphic inscription on the lid records that the sarcophagus originally belonged to an Egyptian commander named Peneptah. Below this another inscription, in the Phoenician alphabet, states that the second owner of the sarcophagus was Tabnit, King of Sidon, whose mummy is displayed in the glass case just beyond.

Beyond the Tabnit Sarcophagus we come in turn to the **Lycian Sarcophagus** and the **Satrap Sarcophagus**. The first of these is from Lycia in southern Turkey and dates from the end of the fifth century BC. Its shape is patterned on the lodges of the ancient Lycians, its lid shaped like the inverted keel of a ship. The reliefs on the sides of the sarcophagus depict a lion-hunt and a boar-hunt, while those on the end show sphinxes and a fight between centaurs. The second sarcophagus, which dates from the latter half of the fifth century BC, is decorated with scenes from the life of the deceased, who is believed to have been a satrap, or oriental potentate.

The next room beyond, from which a stairway leads to the upper floors, is a memorial to Osman Hamdi Bey (1842–1910), who besides being an archaeologist was also an outstanding painter.

The next room is the second of two galleries devoted to the Royal Necropolis at Sidon. On entering we first see three undecorated sarcophagi of Pentelic marble in the shape of classical Greek temples, all dating from the fourth century BC. Beyond them we come to the most famous work of art in the museum, the so-called **Alexander Sarcophagus**, dating from the late fourth century BC. The sarcophagus was originally believed to have been that of Alexander the Great, for it is adorned with sculptures in deep, almost round relif, showing the Emperor in scenes of hunting and battle. But Alexander is known to have been buried in Egypt, and the sarcophagus has now been identified as that of Abdalonymos, who became King of Sidon in 333 BC after Alexander defeated the Persians at the battle of Issus, one of the scenes depicted in the reliefs.

At the far end of the gallery is the so-called **Sarcophagus of the Mourners**, dating from the mid-fourth century BC. This sarcophagus, which is in the form of an Ionic temple, takes its name from the figures of the mourning women standing between the columns, three at each end and six on each of the sides. Other mourning women are shown in the triangular pediments, while above the architrave on each of the long sides there is a funeral cortege with mounted men and two four-horse carriages, the latter one carrying the sarcophagus of the deceased. The sarcophagus is believed to be that of King Straton of Sidon, who ruled in the years 374–358 BC.

The galleries beyond are not presently open to the public, and so we now return to the entrance lobby and continue on into the southern half of the museum, which is devoted to Graeco-Roman sculpture.

The first gallery has sculptures of the archaic period. The free-standing statues are of the type known as a *kouros*, an idealized figure of a young man personifying Apollo, or of a *kore*, a young woman representing Artemis. The most notable are the head of a *kouros* from Samos and another from Cyzicus, both of the sixth century BC, the face in both cases wreathed in the hauting archaic smile characteristic of this period. Other sculptures are in the form of reliefs on stelae used as funerary monuments, the finest being one from Cyzicus of the sixth century BC, showing a long-haired youth driving a chariot.

The next hall contains sculpture from the period of Persian rule in Anatolia. The two best examples are funerary stelae of the fifth century BC from Daskylion, both showing funeral processions in which mourners are following a cart carrying a sarcophagus.

The following gallery is devoted to Attic grave stelae with reliefs as well as other sculptures of the classical period, the most notable representing a young athlete from the Aegean isle of Nisyros, dated c.480–460 BC. The finest sculpture in the round is the head of a horse dating from the second half of the fifth century BC, provenance unknown.

The gallery beyond has sculpture of the Hellenistic period, the most famous being a **head of Alexander the Great** from Pergamum, a copy made in the second century AD after the original of the fourth century BC by Lysippos, which may have been done from life. Alexander is here represented in the classic pose which became the archetype of all later representations: shown with what Plutarch called his 'swimming eye' and lion's mane of hair, his mouth slightly open and his head inclined to the left, a strange lost look on his handsome face. Near the head is a statue of Alexander in which he is show as a young Hercules, another archetypal representation of the young god-king, an original work from Magnesia ad Sipylum of the mid-third century BC.

The next gallery features sculpture from Tralles and Magnesia on the Maeander. The best-known work here is the **Ephebos of Tralles**, dating from c. AD 100. This life-size statue represents an *ephebe*, or youth in military training; he is shown standing in a relaxed attitude after exercise, with a cape draped over his shoulders, smiling wistfully.

We now enter the first hall of the south wing, which is devoted to Hellenistic and Roman sculpture. Beside the door on the left is a Herm, an idealized statue of Hermes in which only his head and genitals are represented on a stele, a work of the second century AD from Pergamum. An inscription on the stele states that it is a copy of the famous Herm by Alkamenes, which stood just outside the Propylon on the Athenian acropolis. In the centre of the room there is a colossal head of a young woman traditionally identified as the poetess Sappho, found in Izmir (Smyrna) a Roman copy of a Hellenistic original. The left side of the hall has portrait heads of Roman emperors ranging in date from Augustus to Constantine the Great, as well as the empresses Agrippina the Elder and Faustina the Younger. Among the works in the right side of the room there is a relief honouring Euripides, found in Izmir and dating to the beginning of the Christian era.

The next galley has sculptures from Ephesus, Miletus and Aphrodisias. The principal work from Ephesus is in the centre of the room, a large reclining statue of the sea-god Oceanus, dated second century AD. The works from Miletus, on the left side of the gallery, include statues of Apollo Kitharados and five Muses, all dated second century AD. The sculptures from Aphrodisias are in the right side of the room, an area dedicated to the memory of the Turkish archaeologist Kenan Eren (1929–91), who devoted his life to the excavations there. These include statues ranging in date from the second century AD to the late fifth, including representations of a young matron, a Roman judge, and the Emperor Valentinian II, and a relief of a Gigantomachia, or battle between the Olympian gods and the Giants.

The last hall in this wing is devoted to sculpture of the Roman imperial period. To the left of the doorway is a colossal statue of

Tyche, the Greek Goddess of Fortune (in Latin she is called Fortuna), who is shown holding the child Plutos, the God of Wealth; behind him is the Cornucopia, the Horn of Plenty, symbolizing the fertility of the earth. This sculpture, which still retains traces of its original colours, was found in Prusias ad Hypium and is dated tentatively to the second century AD.

At the centre of the wall opposite the door is a colossal statue of Zeus from Gaza, dated second century AD. Other noteworthy sculptures in this gallery, all of them dating from the second or third century AD, are: a group of statuettes of Erotes in a cock-fight, from Tarsus; a statue of the lady Cornelia Antonina, from Antioch in Pisidia; a statue of Dionysus, from Synnada; a statuette of Pan, from Tirnova in Bulgaria; and a statue of Artemis, from Cyrene in Libya.

We now return past the entrance lobby and enter the new wing of the museum. Here we see the small Children's Museum, which opened in the summer of 1996, the most prominent exhibit being a large model of the Trojan Horse.

Beyond the stairway we see a full-scale reproduction of the front of the **Temple of Athena at Assos**. Completed c.530 BC, this is the only Doric temple known to have been constructed in Asia Minor during the archaic period. The temple was first excavated in 1881–83 by J. T. Clarke and F. H. Bacon of the Antiquarian Society of Boston. The reliefs that they found are now in the Boston Museum of Fine Arts, represented here in this model by casts, along with a few of the original sculptures. The chart to the right shows which of the reliefs are originals and which are copies.

Beyond the reconstructed temple front we see two pairs of early capitals of the Aeolic order from the northern Aegean coast of Asia Minor. One pair is from Neandria in the Troad, and the second is from Larissa in Aeolia, both of them dating from the late sixth century BC.

The rest of the ground floor of the new wing is devoted to **Thrace, Bithynia and Byzantium**, a gallery that opened on 5 August 1998. Thrace and Bithynia are the regions that bordered Byzantium on the European and Asian sides of the Sea of Marmara, respectively, and we will be exploring them after our tour of Istanbul.

The hallway leading into the Thrace, Bithynia and Byzantium galleries has on its left side three sarcophagi of the early Byzantine period, fourth to sixth century, and on the end wall there is a colossal masque of Oceanus from Nicomedeia (Iznik), dating from the second century AD.

The first gallery generally has exhibits from Thrace on the right side and from Bithynia on the left. The exhibits are arranged chronologically, covering a time span from the archaic period to the end of the Roman era. A number of the exhibits are from tumuli, huge earth mounds covering burial chambers, including those at Inceğîz-Maltepe, Karakoç-Eriklece, Marmara Ereğlisi, the Tersiye Tumulus, the Hîdîrsîhler Tumulus, the Aytazî Tumulus, and the Vize Tumulus. The most distinctive of the objects found in these tombs are the reliefs of the Heroic Horseman Cult, represented by a mounted warrior, probably a deified chieftain. One particularly striking object, found in the Vize Tumulus, is a superb bronze head of a warrior, with a tightly-fitted helmet and cheek-protectors elaborately carved in relief, belonging to a prince who died in 46 BC. Besides the tumuli, there are also exhibits from the ancient cities of Selymbria, Perinthos and Eleonte in Thrace, and Chalcedon, Nicomedeia, and Claudiopolis (Bolu) in Bithynia. Most of the sculptures exhibited in the gallery are marble funerary reliefs, portrait busts and statues, the most striking exception being a life size bronze figure of a boar, a work of the fifth century BC found near Edirne. There are also a number of fine bronzes, particularly a plate of the third century AD with a Medusa head.

The inner gallery is devoted to works from the Byzantine period, most of them from Constantinople. This gallery is built up against the wall of a Byzantine structure of the fifth century AD, discovered when the new wing of the museum was being erected; this has been left exposed so that one can see its brick and limestone construction.

The exhibits in the gallery include a large part of the architrave of the Baths of Constantine, now vanished, a statue of Valentinian III; four statuettes of the 'Good Shepherd'; a relief showing Jonah being swallowed by the whale; a parapet slab showing the labarum, or Christogram; several early Byzantine sarcophagi, some with reliefs; two monuments to the famous charioteer Porphyrios, with reliefs showing him and his four-horse chariot in the Hippodrome; a huge mosaic pavement from Jerusalem with Orpheus as the central figure; a two-sided relief showing the comic actor Kefalos wearing a masque in the form of a wolf's head; the ambo of the church of Haghia Sophia in Thessalonica; several capitals with lavish relief decorations, including some with pagan themes; bronze liturgical objects; silver plates with reliefs of religious scenes; a pair of reliefs with figures of a fabulous beast called the Simurg, with the head of a wolf, the body of a lion, and the tail of a peacock; a marble icon of the Virgin Hodegitria, the protectress of Byzantium; an icon of Haghia (Saint) Eudokia in coloured stone inlay on marble; two slabs of a parapet with reliefs of peacocks, the Byzantine symbol of eternal life; the bust of an evangelist; and an almost perfectly preserved fresco portrait of Haghios Mercurios from the now vanished Byzantine church known as Odalar Camii, dating from the fourteenth century.

We now ascend the stairway to the mezzanine, which is devoted to an exhibition area called **Istanbul Through the Ages**. The exhibits here range from the prehistoric era through those of the Greek city-state of Byzantine and Byzantine Constantinople, ending with the Turkish conquest of 1453.

The first exhibits show the very earliest sites of human habitation in the environs of Istanbul. The most notable site is the Yarîmburgaz Cave on the European shore of the Marmara, where archaeologists have unearthed evidence of settlement dating back some 300,000 years to the Palaeolithic era. A glass case contains the complete skeleton of a man from Pendik, on the Asian shore of the Marmara, dated to the sixth millennium BC. The oldest object found in Istanbul itself is a large baked clay jar, also of the sixth millennium BC, unearthed below the Hippodrome.

The next section of the gallery is devoted to objects from ancient Byzantium, the earliest of them dated to the seventh century BC. These include pottery and other artefacts, as well as a large number of tombstones from the early cemeteries of the city, with reliefs showing the deceased and their family and belongings.

The area at the end of the first corridor is devoted to the region around the upper reaches of the Golden Horn. The most striking exhibit here has sculptures fron a nymphaion, or monumental fountain, of the second century AD, representing a Gigantomachia. The Olympians, who include Artemis, Apollo and Selene, goddess of the Moon, are done in white marble, while the Giants, of whom only fragments survive, are in dark grey limestone. Above are three marble busts, a man flanked by two woman, probably representing the donors.

The other exhibition areas are dedicated to Byzantine Constantinople. The displays are arranged topographically, with each area devoted to one or more of the Byzantine monuments, sections of the city, or its public works. The first of these is concerned with ancient Chalcedon, now the suburb of Kadîköy, on the Asian shore of the Marmara. The displays that follow include the harbours of

Constantinople; hydraulic works and cisterns; the Theodosian walls; the sea walls along the Golden Horn; the sea walls along the Marmara; the Augustaeum; the churches of Haghia Sophia; Haghia Eirene, and SS. Sergius and Bacchus; the Hippodrome; the palaces of Antiochus and Lausus; the Great Palace of Byzantium; the ancient structures within the walls of Topkapî Sarayî; the Forum of Theodosius; Kalenderhane Camii, the former church of the Kyriotissa (incorectly identified here as St Saviour Akataleptos), with a fresco of the Latin period and a pre-iconoclastic mosaic; the imperial palaces at the Hebdomon (Bakîrköy) and Rhegium (Küçükçekmece); the forum and column of Arcadius; the church of St John of Studios; the church of St Polyeuktos; the column of Marcian; the palace of Blachernae; the church of the Holy Apostles; the church of Constantine Lips; Kariye Camii (the church of St Saviour in Chora); the church of the Pantocrator; Fethiye Camii (the church of the Pammakaristos); the Genoese town of Galata; the Princes Isles; and the Bosphorus. In the last section of the gallery there is a section of the chain used by the Byzantines to close the entrance to the Golden Horn in times of siege.

The second floor of the new wing is devoted to **Anatolia and Troy Through the Ages**. This hall is arranged chronologically, beginning at the northern end, where there are displays explaining the topography of Troy and the history of the successive excvations under Heinrich Schliemann, Wilhelm Dörpfeld, Carl W. Blegen, and Manfred Korfmann The display cases on the right side of the hall show objects from the different levels of Troy, while those on the left display antiquities from the successive prehistoric periods at sites elsewhere in Anatolia.

At the south end of the hall there is a gallery devoted to **Phrygia** in the archaic period, with photographs of the extraordinary rock-carved Phrygian sanctuaries and sculptures of the fertility goddess Cybele-Kubaba. A display case has antiquities from Phrygian sites in western Anatolia, most notably the huge bronze cauldrons that are the most distinctive works of this culture.

The third floor of the new wing is devoted to the **Cultures of Anatolia's Neighbours**. This floor has antiquities from Syria, Palestine and Cyprus. The most striking exhibit on this floor is a reconnstructed hypogeum, or subterranean tomb, at Palmyra in Syria. This is modelled on the hypogeum in the Valley of the Tombs built in AD 108 by the Yarhai family; the portrait busts are originals from a number of tombs in Palmyra.

On our way back to the ground floor we pass through a room on the second floor of the old museum. The glass cases here contain terracotta votive figurines of the classical and Hellenistic periods, similar to the famous Tanagra statuettes in the Louvre and other musums. In the centre of the room there is a colossal bronze statue of the Emperor Hadrian from Nicomedeia, dating from the mid second century AD. From the windows here we have an excellent view of Çinili Köşk, the next stop on our itinerary.

Çinili Köşk was built by Mehmet the Conqueror in 1472 as an outer pavilion of Topkapî Sarayî, serving as a pied-à-terre for the Sultan on occasions when he wanted to escape the crowded confines of the Harem. From 1874 until 1891 it served as a storehouse for antiquities, which were subsequently moved to the Archaeological Museum. During the 1950s the kiosk was thoroughly restored to its original condition, and now it serves as a museum of Turkish tiles.

The kiosk is a unique masterpiece of Ottoman architecture, very Persian in its design and decoration. It is laid out in two almost identical storeys (the lower one completely visible only from the rear), cruciform in plan with chambers in the corners of the cross. It has a deeply recessed entrance alcove on the main floor entirely revetted in tiles of various kinds, most of them tile mosaic in turquoise and dark blue. On the back all these form simple geometric designs, but in the deep soffit of the arch there is an inscription in a geometricised form of Cufic calligraphy. On the three faces of the vault at the height of the lintel of the door there is a long double Persian inscription in the beautiful *cuerda seca* technique. The main inscription is in white letters on a dark blue ground. Above and entwined with this is a subordinate inscription in yellow, with the tendrils of a vine meandering in and out between the letters, the whole encased in a fame of deep mauve with flowers of dark blue, turquoise and white.

The interior consists of a central salon in the shape of an inverted Latin cross with a dome over the crossing. The cross is extended by a vestibule at the entrance end, an apse-like room at the far end, and two eyvans or open alcoves (now glassed in) at the ends of the shorter arms, with additional chambers at the corners of the cross. All of these rooms were once tiled and many of them still are, with triangular and hexagonal panels of turquoise and deepest blue, sometimes with superimposed gold designs.

The oldest of the exhibits is a small selection of Selcuk tiles – mostly wall tiles of enamel and majolica ware – of the twelfth to fourteenth century. Next in date are tiles of the transitional period

Haghia Eirene and the Museums

from Selcuk to Ottoman, i.e., from the fourteenth and fifteenth centuries. The principal exhibit of this period is the superb *mihrab* from the mosque of Ibrahim Bey at Karaman, in central Anatolia. The finest of the Ottoman tiles are from Iznik and date from the mid sixteenth century to the early seventeenth. An outstanding example from this period is a lunette from the *medrese* of Haseki Hürrem Camii in Istanbul. There are also ceramics from the eighteenth and ninetenth centuries, some of them pretty but Europeanised and lacking the brilliance and superb craftsmanship of the earlier works. The best of the later ceramics are charming plates made in the nineteenth century in Çanakkale, on the Asian shore of the Dardanelles.

We now go on to the **Museum of the Ancient Orient**, housed in the former Institute of Fine Arts, erected in 1883. The building was converted into a museum in 1917, and after restoration it reopened in its present form in 1974. The entryway is guarded by two colossal basalt lions of the neo-Hittite period, dated c.800 BC.

The museum, currently under restoration, contains an extremely important collection of antiquities gathered from Anatolia and the former Middle Eastern dominions of the Ottoman Empire, including works of the ancient Egyptians, Sumerians, Akkadians, Babylonians, Hatti, Hittites, neo-Hittites, Urartians, Assyrians, and Aramaeans, as well as from Arabia and Nabatea.

The most historic exhibits are the **Code of Hammurabi**, dated 1750 BC, the world's oldest recorded set of laws; and the Treaty of Kadesh, dated 1269 BC, the earliest known peace agreement, recording the end of a war between Ramses II of Egypt and the Hittite emperor Hattusilas. Another notable exhibit is a series of tile panels with reliefs of lions and mythological beasts; these are from Babylon, dating from the reign of Nabuchhadnezzar II (605–562 BC), and formed part of the processional way that led from the Ishtar Gate to the sanctuary where the New Year's festival was held. Other striking exhibits include objects from Arabia and Nabatea in the pre-Islamic period; Egyptian antiquities from the time of the First Dynasty (c.3200 BC) to the beginning of the Ptolemaic Dynasty (310 BC); works from Mesopotamia and the Urartian culture that flourished in easternmost Anatolia at the beginning of the first millennium BC; Assyrian objects from the palaces of Tiglath-Pileser III (745–727 BC), Sennacherib (705–688 BC) and Ashurbanipal (669–629 BC); monumental sculptures of the Hatti and Hittite cultures in central Anatolia, as well as earlier objects of this regon going back to c.5500 BC, the beginning of the Chalcolithic era;

79

inscriptions, reliefs and statues of the Assyrian, Aramean and neo-Hittite cultures, the most striking of the latter works being the colossal Ivriz Kaya relief, a copy of the original showing a diminutive king offering gifts of grain and fruit to a gigantic god, dating from the eighth century BC.

A visit to the Museum of the Ancient Orient completes the picture of the rich archaeological and artistic heritage of Turkey, heir to all of the treasures of the ancient world acquired by the Ottomans when they conquered Byzantium and the Middle East.

There is an outdoor cafe in the garden opposite the Archaeological Museum, a very pleasant spot to rest and have a drink before moving on. Among the antiquities arrayed in the garden is a huge block of marble with the heads of two Gorgons carved on either side, the one at the back missing the upper half of its face. The block was found near the Column of Constantine on the Second Hill, and was probably part of a Gorgon frieze on a Roman building in the Forum of Constantine. Two other Gorgon heads now in the Basilica Cistern, which we will see on the next itinerary, were undoubtedly part of the same structure, whose frieze probably originated in a classical temple in Asia Minor. Thus nothing of importance is ever really lost in Istanbul, but recycled in successive layers as one empire succeeds another in this ancient imperial city.

6

Around the First Hill

OUR NEXT ITINERARY will take us around the First Hill, beginning in Ayasofya Meydanî, the great square between Haghia Sophia and Sultan Ahmet I Camii, the Blue Mosque.

Ayasofya Meydanî occupies the site of the ancient Forum Augustaeum, the public forecourt of the Great Palace of Byzantium. The Augustaeum was first identified by the French scholar Petrus Gyllius (Pierre Gilles), who was in Istanbul in the years 1545–50. On its northern side the Augustaeum gave access to Haghia Sophia and the Patriarchal Palace, which was attached to the southwest side of the Great Church. The eastern side of the square bordered the Chalke, or Brazen House, the main entrance to the Great Palace, and also the Senate, one of the institutions that Constantine the Great brought from Rome to his new capital. Southwest of the Augustaeum was the Hippodrome, the famous stadium of ancient Byzantium, and on the southern side of the square were the Baths of Zeuxippus, the largest bathing establishment in the city. West of the Augustaeum there was another great public square, the Stoa Basilica, which was the site of the University of Constantinople, the central law courts of the Empire, and a large outdoor book-market. Thus the Augustaeum was the focal point of the ancient city's public life.

The only monument standing today on the site of the ancient Augustaeum is the **Hamam of Roxelana**, the handsome multi-domed structure on the northeast side of the park between Haghia Sophia and the Blue Mosque. The *hamam* was part of the *külliye* of Aya Sofya Camii, and was intended for the use of the clergy and staff of the mosque as well as those who came there for the Friday prayer service. It was commissioned by Süleyman the Magnificent in the name of his wife Roxelana, and it was designed and built by Sinan, who completed it in 1556. It is a double *hamam*, with separate baths for men and women, one at each end of the building, the men's entrance facing Haghia Sophia. Each end of the building consists of a great entrance hall, the *camekan*, covered by a large dome; from there one passes through the *soğukluk*, a corridor with three small domes; this leads to the *hararet*, or steam room, a domed chamber

81

surrounded by a series of little cubicles for bathing. This is one of the most handsome Ottoman baths in the city; it was restored in the 1980s and is now used for the display and sale of Turkish rugs and *kilims*, or flat-weave carpets.

The **Blue Mosque** is a foundation of **Ahmet I**, who in 1609 commissioned Davut Ağa to begin construction of the *külliye*, which was completed in 1617, the year before the Sultan's death. The mosque is one of the most splendid sights in the city, with its graceful cascade of domes and semidomes, its six slender minarets accentuating the corners of the building and the courtyard, and its generally imposing but harmonious proportions.

The mosque is preceded by a **courtyard** as vast as the mosque itself, with monumental entryways at each of the three sides. The courtyard is bordered by a peristyle of 26 columns forming a portico covered by 30 small domes, with a handsome octagonal *şadîrvan* at its centre. This is the only mosque in the city with **six minarets**. Four of the minarets stand at the corners of the mosque and the other two at the far corners of the courtyard. The minarets at the corners of the mosque each have three *şerefes*, while the other pair have only two each. The central dome of the mosque is flanked by semidomes on all four sides, with those to north and south surrounded by three smaller semidomes and those to east and west by two semidomes each, besides which there are also small domes over the corners of the building. The four piers supporting the main dome continue above the building as tall octagonal turrets with little cupolas, while smaller round turrets flank each of the corner domes. The north and south facades of the building each have two storeys of porticoed galleries, which are continued at a lower height by the arcades along the side walls of the mosque courtyard.

The central area of the mosque interior is very nearly a square, 51 metres long by 53 metres wide, covered by a dome 23.5 metres in diameter with its crown 43 metres above the floor, its cornice resting on four pointed arches and four smooth pendentives. The main support for the great dome comes from four colossal piers, five metres in diameter, which are divided in the middle by a band and ribbed above and below with convex flutes. The mosque is filled with light from its 260 windows; they were once filled with Turkish stained glass of the seventeenth century, but these have all vanished and have been replaced by inferior modern imitations. The painted arabesques in the dome and upper zone of the building are also modern works of inferior quality; their colour is an overly-bright

Sultan Ahmet I Camii, the Blue Mosque

The Hippodrome, with the Serpent Column and the Egyptian Obelisk

blue, from which the mosque derives its name. What is original and very beautiful in the decoration of the interior is the revetment of tiles on the lower part of the walls, particularly in the galleries. These are Iznik tiles of the best period; the magnificent floral designs display the traditional lily, carnation, tulip and rose motifs, as well as cypresses and other trees; these are all in exquisite colours, subtle blues and greens predominating. The *mihrab* and *mimber,* of white Proconnesian marble, are also original, and are fine examples of the carved stonework of the early seventeenth century. The bronzework of the great courtyard doors is of equal excellence, as is the woodwork of the doors and window-shutters of the mosque interior, encrusted with ivory, mother-of-pearl and sea-tortoise shell. Under the sultan's loge, in the upper gallery to the left of the *mihrab,* the wooden ceiling is painted with floral and geometric arabesques, one of the few surviving examples of this exquisite early Ottoman style.

A ramp outside the northeast corner of the mosque leads to the *hünkâr kasrî,* which is connected by an internal passageway with the royal loge within the mosque. The *hünkâr kasrî* now houses the **Kilim Museum**. This is a remarkable collection ranging in date from the fifteen century to the nineteenth, including a number of *kilims* that belonged to the sultans and were used in the royal tent on campaign. Beneath the east end of the mosque there are huge vaulted structures that once served as storerooms and stables. These chambers have been restored and now house the **Rug Museum**, a collection comparable in interest to that of the Kilim Museum, including rare and beautiful examples.

The mosque and its courtard were entirely surrounded by an outer precinct wall, of which only the northern section remains. This wall separated the mosque from the other institutions in the *külliye,* which included a *medrese, türbe,* hospital, caravansarai, primary school and *imaret.* All of these have survived except for the hospital and the caravansarai. The *imaret* is now incorporated into the structures at the south end of the Hippodrome and is no longer visible from the street. The primary school, recently restored, is elevated above the north precinct wall of the mosque. The *medrese* is just outside the precinct wall toward the northwest. Near it is the large square *türbe,* which has recently been restored and is now open to the public. Ahmet I is buried here along with his wife Kösem and three of his sons, Osman II, Murat IV, and Prince Beyazit, the Bajazet of Racine's tragedy.

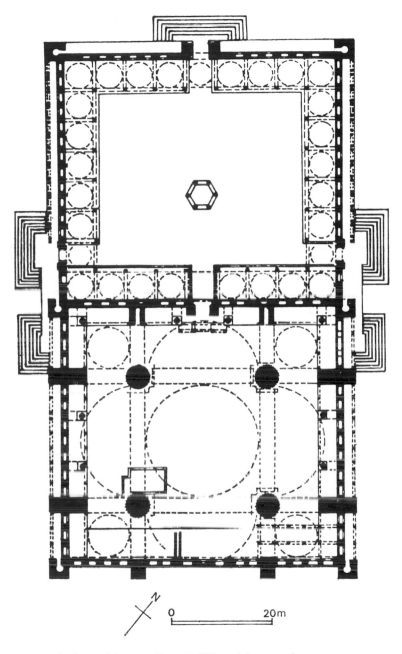

0   20m

Sultan Ahmet Camii (Blue Mosque)

The park in front of the Blue Mosque is laid out on the site of the ancient **Hippodrome**, with the street around its periphery following the course of the original racetrack. The Hippodrome was built by Septimius Severus c. AD 200 and probably reconstructed on a larger scale by Constantine the Great when he shifted his capital to Byzantium. Many of the great events in the history of Byzantium took place in the Hippodrome, beginning with the inaugural rites of the city of New Rome on 11 May 330. During the Byzantine era the triumphs of victorious generals and emperors were celebrated here and here too several emperors were executed, along with patriarchs of Constantinople, religious heretics, and rebels. During the early centuries of the Byzantine Empire the Hippodrome was the centre of the turbulent public life of Constantinople. It was here that the Nika Revolt against Justinian began on 13 January 532, and it was here that the rebellion was crushed five days later when Justinian's general Belisarius trapped the insurgents in the Hippodrome and slaughtered 30,000 of them in the arena.

The Hippodrome was some 480 metres long and 120 metres wide, with tiers of seats down the long sides of the track and around the curved southern end, the *sphendone*, which was supported on a great vaulted substructure that can still be seen from the southern slope of the First Hill. Around the top of the outer wall there was an arcade of columns with an epistyle in the classical manner. According to one estimate, there were seats for some 60,000 spectators, although as many as 100,000 may have been crammed into the stadium when there was standing room only. The spectators entered through great vaulted passageways at the straight northern end of the stadium; these were called *vomitaria*, because they literally 'vomited' forth the crowd at the end of a day's races. The Emperor and his party watched the races from a royal enclosure called the **Kathisma**; this was probably located midway along the eastern side of the arena, connected directly to the Great Palace. Down the long central axis of the stadium there was a raised terrace called the *spina*, adorned with a line of statues, obelisks, and columns, of which three monuments still remain *in situ*. The sanded race-track ran around the *spina*, with the turning-points at the northern and southern ends. Usually a race involved four two-wheeled chariots, each pulled by a team of four horses, with the charioteers garbed in the colours of their supporting factions – the Whites, Reds, Blues, and Greens – which divided up along social, economic and political lines. A normal race required seven laps around the track, for a total distance of about a mile and a half. The most successful charioteers became national heroes. The most famous was Porphyrios, of whom the Emperor Anastasius I (491–518) erected two bronze statues in the Hippodrome, their pedestals now preserved in the Archaeological Museum.

During the intervals between the races the crowd was entertained by exhibitions of wild animals, clowns, dwarfs, acrobats and musicians. Justinian's wife, the Empress Theodora, was the daughter of a bear-keeper in the Hippodrome, and she began her career there as a dancer; later she became a renowned courtesan, a career she had given up a few years before she met her husband-to-be. Sigurd, King of Norway, visited the Hippodrome in 1111, when he saw a spectacular display of fireworks and a fantastic spectacle in which performers appeared levitated in the air. Later in the twelfth century Benjamin of Tudela reported that in the intermission between the races he saw circus acts with lions, tigers, bears and leopards, as well as astonishing feats of juggling.

The Hippodrome, like so many other monuments in Constantinople, was pillaged and destroyed in the Latin Occupation of 1204–61. At the time of the Turkish conquest it was in ruins, though when Petrus Gyllius first examined the site, in 1545, he found that part of the Hippodrome was still standing, most notably the substructure of the *sphendone* and part of the epistyle that extended around the outer wall, though before he left the city five years later that colonnade had been destroyed. What remained of the superstructure of the Hippodrome was completely destroyed in the years 1609–16, when it was used as a quarry for the building of Sultan Ahmet's mosque. The site of the arena then came to be known as the Atmeydanî, the Square of Horses, a name stemming from the fact that it was used by the palace pages as a field for playing *cirit*. Plans for converting the square into a park were first drawn up in 1890 by the French architect Bouvard, and nine years later work was completed on the domed ornamental fountain that now stands near the northeastern end of the Hippodrome, a gift from Kaiser Wilhelm II to Abdül Hamit II. Excavations carried out in the 1960s at the northwestern corner of the Atmeydanî unearthed remains of the Hippodrome, including a few seats of the stadium and some other structures that may include baths. Other seats were uncovered in the late 1980s within the garden in front of Sultan Ahmet I Camii. Aside from these ruins, all that remains to be seen of the ancient Hippodrome are the substructure of the *sphendone* and the three monuments that have survived on the *spina* of the racetrack, all of them near its southern end.

The most prominent of the ancient monuments on the *spina* is the **Egyptian Obelisk**. This was originally due to the Pharaoh Thutmose III (1549–1503 BC), who erected it in the Great Temple at Karnak, at Deir el Bahri opposite Thebes in upper Egypt, to commemorate one of his campaigns in Syria and the crossing of the Euphrates River. The obelisk was originally 30 metres tall, but its present height is only 19.8 metres. It may have been shipped to Constantinople on the orders of the Emperor Julian (361–63), but it was not erected on its present site until c.390, when Theodosius I entrusted the work to Proclus, the Prefect of Constantinople.

The obelisk is mounted on four brazen blocks that rest on a marble base decorated with sculptures in low relief. These represent Theodosius and his family in the Kathisma, as they look down on various events taking place in the arena below. On the south side of the base the Emperor is shown watching the races depicted in the lower block; on the east he is presenting a laurel wreath to the victorious charioteer; on the north he is assisting in the erection of the Obelisk, the method of which is represented on the lower block; and on the west he is receiving homage from vanquished enemies. Inscriptions in Greek and Latin on the base praise Theodosius and his Prefect Proclus for erecting the Obelisk; the Latin inscription tells us that thirty days were required to do the job, while the one in Greek says that it took thirty-two days. The total height of the monument including the base is about 26 metres; the bottom of it represents approximately the original level of the race-course, some 4.5 metres below the present surface of the Atmeydanî.

Beyond the Obelisk is the **Serpent Column**, in the form of three intertwined serpents. This originally formed the base of a trophy that stood in the temple of Apollo at Delphi, presented as a token of thanksgiving by the thirty-one Greek cities that contributed contingents in the victory over the Persians at Plataea in 479 BC. The column was brought from Delphi to Constantinople by Constantine the Great and it may have stood elsewhere in the city before the Emperor erected it on the *spina* of the Hippodrome. The three serpent heads were broken off and lost at various times after the conquest, but the upper part of one of them was found in 1847 and is now in the Archaeological Museum.

The third of the three ancient monuments on the *spina* is a roughly-built pillar of stone 32 metres high that stands near the southern end of the Atmeydanî. Gyllius called it the **Colossus**, but most modern writers refer to it, incorrectly, as the **Column of**

Constantine Porphyryogenitus. Both names stem from the Greek inscription on its base, where the monument is compared to the Colossus of Rhodes, and where it is recorded that the pillar was restored and sheathed in bronze by Constantine VII Porphyrogenitus. But the inscription also states that the pillar was decayed by time; thus it must date from an earlier period, perhaps that of Constantine the Great. Gyllius was the first to decipher the inscription, and in his description of the monument he also records a spectacular misadventure that he witnessed there,

> One day, being the festival of the circumcision of the Prince of Boldania [Moldavia], I saw an ingenious fellow of a mountebank climb to the top of it and come down safe. The same attempt was immediately made by another, who made shift to reach the top, but the height so completely dazzled him, that despairing of getting down without injury, he threw himself with all his might from the Colossus to avoid the danger of being dashed to pieces on the foundation. So falling down right upon his feet, he struck the earth and died upon the spot.

The western side of the Atmeydanî is dominated by the **Ibrahim Pasha Sarayî**, part of which is obscured by a nineteenth-century building that stands in front of its northern wing. The palace was restored in the 1970s, and it now houses the **Museum of Turkish and Islamic Art**, the most important collection of its kind in the world.

The palace seems to have been built early in the reign of Süleyman the Magnificent, who gave it to the Grand Vizier Ibrahim Pasha as a wedding present in 1523, when he married the princess Hadice, the sultan's sister. The palace was the most splendid residence in the Ottoman Empire, far exceeding in its size and grandeur any of the imperial pavilions in Topkapî Sarayî. Ibrahim had been Süleyman's intimate companion since the beginning of his reign. But Roxelana poisoned Süleyman's mind against Ibrahim, and in 1536 the Grand Vizier was executed by the Sultan. Immediately afterwards all of Ibrahim's wealth and possessions were confiscated by the government, including his palace on the Hippodrome. The palace subsequently was used for a variety of purposes. At first it seems to have served as a dormitory and school for apprentice pages in Topkapî Sarayî, with its main hall on the Hippodrome housing the High Court of Justice; later it seems to have been a barracks for unmarried Janissaries, part of it serving as a prison. By the beginning of the twentieth century the palace was in ruins and its northeast wing demolished, but the rebuilding has superbly restored the remainder, making it an ideal home for the Museum of Turkish and Islamic Art.

Passing through the entrance lobby, we enter the central court-yard, which has a terrace overlooking the Hippodrome. Part of the north wing of the palace on the lower level has been restored as an old-fashioned Istanbul coffee-house, a delightful place to have a drink after seeing the exhibits in the museum. A stone lion of the Selcuk period stands beside an archway on the right; a staircase leads from there up to the second floor of the north wing, where the museum exhibits begin.

The cells in the north and west wings on the upper level, nineteen chambers in all, are used to display objects from the various periods of Turkish and Islamic art, including works from the Ummayid, Abbasid, Mamluk, Selcuk, Beylik and Ottoman periods, ranging in date from the seventh century to the nineteenth. The exhibits include *kilims*, manuscripts, calligraphy, miniatures, woodwork, metalwork, stonework, sculpture, ceramics, glassware, and folk-arts, altogether an extraordinary collection, superbly displayed. After passing through the north and west wings we enter the south wing, where we pass through a pair of ante-rooms into the great hall overlooking the Hippodrome, where some of the most precious treasures of the museum are exhibited. This originally served as Ibrahim Pasha's Hall of the Divan, where he presided over meetings of the Council. The balcony at the far end of the room was used as a review pavilion, and miniatures in Topkapî Sarayî show the Sultan seated there as he watches a Procession of the Guilds in the Hippodrome below.

The lower level beneath the great hall houses the museum's **Ethnographical Collection**. This consists principally of objects belonging to the Yürük, the nomadic Turkish tribespeople of Anatolia, whose wandering way of life has not changed in its essentials since the first Türkmen warriors swept across Asia Minor after the Selcuk victory over the Byzantines at Manzikert in 1071. The most fascinating exhibits here are the black goat-hair tents of the Yürük, furnished with objects that these nomads still use in their daily life.

After leaving Ibrahim Pasha Sarayî we continue along the west side of the Atmeydanî to the end of the square, where a narrow street named Şehit Mehmet Paşa Yokuşu winds downhill towards the Marmara. At the second turning on the left we come to the main gateway of **Sokollu Mehmet Pasha Camii**, one of the most beau-tiful of Sinan's grand vizierial mosques.

The mosque and its attached medrese were built by Sinan in 1571–72 for Sokollu Mehmet Pasha, one of the most outstanding Grand Vezirs in the history of the Ottoman Empire. Sokollu Mehmet, the son of a Bosnian priest, was taken into the Janissary Corps as a youth and educated at the Palace School at Topkapî Sarayî. His outstanding ability brought him early preferment and he rose rapidly in the Ottoman hierarchy, becoming Grand Vizier under Süleyman the Magnificent in 1565. He continued to hold that post under Süleyman's son and successor, Selim II, and married the Sultan's daughter, Princess Esmahan, in whose honour he founded this mosque, though it is popularly known as Sokollu Mehmet Pasha Camii. After Selim's death in 1574 Sokollu Mehmet Pasha continued to serve as Grand Vizier under Murat III until 1579, when he was murdered by a mad soldier in the Divan.

The entrance to the mosque courtyard is unique, the outer gateway being beneath the large domed chamber that served as the *dershane* of the *medrese*; a flight of stairs ascends from there to the avlu, which is centered on a domed *şadirvan* with widely over-hanging eaves. The domed cells of the *medrese*, sixteen in all, are arrayed around three sides of the courtyard, the portico being completed on the fourth side by the domed bays of the porch, where the entryway to the mosque faces the *dershane* opposite. In the lunettes of the mosque windows under the porch there are striking and elegant inscriptions in blue and white faience.

The internal plan of the mosque is a hexagon inscribed in an almost square rectangle, with the central area covered by a dome, counter-balanced at the corners by four small semidomes. There are no side aisles, but around three sides there is a low gallery supported on slender marble columns with typical Ottoman lozenge capitals. The polychrome of the arches, whose voussoirs are of alternate red and green marble, is characteristic of the period. The **tile decoration** of the mosque has been done with singularly charming effect. Only selected areas of the walls have been sheathed in tiles: the penden-tives below the dome, a frieze of floral design, and the exquisite central section of the east wall. The latter panel frames the *mihrab* in tiles decorated in vine and floral motifs in turquoise on a background of pale green, interspersed with panels of fine calligraphy with white letters on a deep blue field. The finely-carved marble *mimber* is surmounted by a tall conical cap, sheathed in the same turquoise tiles that frame the *mihrab*. Above the *mihrab* the framed arch in the east wall is pierced by elegant stained-glass windows. Above the entrance portal there is a small specimen of the original painted decoration. It consists of very elaborate arabesque designs in rich and varied colours. Also above the door, surmounted by a design in gold, there is a fragment of black basaltic stone from the Kaaba in Mecca, with other pieces set into the *mihrab* and *mimber.*

Leaving the mosque by its side gateway to the south, we turn left and make our way down to the Marmara through one of the most picturesque old quarters in the city. Looking back uphill, we see the huge retaining wall of the **sphendone**, whose vaulted substructure forms a great arc across the Marmara slope of the First Hill below the southern end of the Hippodrome. Eventually we come to Küçük Ayasofya Caddesi, a street that runs along the Marmara shore of the First Hill just inside the railway line. Here we turn right and come to **Küçük Ayasofya Camii**, the Mosque of Little Haghia Sophia, so called because of its supposed resemblance to the Great Church. This is one of the most beautiful and historic of the former Byzantine churches of the city, originally dedicated to **SS. Sergius and Bacchus**.

The church was begun by Justinian in 527, the first year of his reign, and was dedicated to the patron saints of Christians in the Roman army, centurions who had been martyred for their faith. Justinian's devotion to these saints stemmed from his belief that they had saved his life a decade before he succeeded his uncle Justin I (518–27) to the throne. This occurred during the reign of Anastasius, who had accused Justinian of plotting to usurp the throne and sentenced him to death. But SS. Sergius and Bacchus appeared to the Emperor in a dream and told him that the charges were untrue, whereupon he released Justinian. As soon as Justinian succeeded to the throne he expressed his gratitude to the saints by dedicating to them this church, the first of many that he was to build in Constantinople and elsewhere in his Empire. SS. Sergius and Bacchus remained a church for nearly a thousand years; then in the first decade of the sixteenth century it was converted into a mosque by Hüseyin Ağa, Chief Black Eunuch in the reign of Beyazit II. Hüseyin Ağa is buried in a *türbe* just to the north of the apse.

The edifice is in plan an irregular octagon crookedly inscribed in a very irregular rectangle. These irregularities may be due to the fact that it had to be squeezed between two already existing buildings, the church of SS. Peter and Paul and the palace of Hormisdas, both of which have disappeared without a trace. The method of transition from the octagon to the dome is astonishing: the dome is divided into sixteen compartments, eight flat sections alternating with eight concave ones above the angles of the octagon. The octagon has eight polygonal piers with pairs of columns in between, alternately of verd-antique and red Synnada marble, both above and below, arrayed straight on the axes but curved out into the exedrae at each corner. The space between this brightly-coloured, moving curtain of columns and the exterior walls of the rectangle becomes an ambulatory below and a spacious gallery above, the latter reached by a staircase at the south end of the narthex. The **capitals** and the classic **entablature** are exquisite specimens of the elaborately carved and deeply undercut style of the sixth century. On the ground floor the capitals are of the 'melon' type, in the gallery 'pseudo-Ionic', and a few of them still bear the monogram of Justinian and Theodora, who was co-founder of the church, though most of these have been effaced. In the gallery the epistyle is arcaded in a way that became habitual in later Byzantine architecture, already in Haghia Sophia, for example. But on the ground floor the entablature is still basically classical, trabeated instead of arched, with the traditional architrave, frieze and cornice, but very different from anything classical, like lace in its appearance. The frieze consists of a long and beautifully carved inscription in twelve Greek hexameters honouring Justinian and Theodora along with St Sergius, though for some reason St Bacchus is not mentioned. The walls, like those of Haghia Sophia, were revetted with veined and variegated marbles, while the vaults and domes glittered with mosaics. Procopius, in his *Edifices*, writes that 'By the sheen of its marbles it was more resplendent than the sun, and everywhere it was filled profusely with gold.'

We leave by the gate in the south wall of the church courtyard, from where we follow a winding path that takes us under the railway line and then out to the highway along the Marmara shore. There we turn left and begin walking along a well-preserved stretch of the **Byzantine sea-walls.**

The original sea walls along the Marmara were constructed by Constantine the Great, ending where his land walls came down to the shore at Samatya, below the Seventh Hill. When the Theodosian walls were built in the following century, the Marmara sea-walls were extended to meet them. Four centuries later the Marmara walls were almost completely rebuilt by the Emperor Theophilus (829–42), who sought to strengthen the city's defences against the Arabs. Several prominent inscriptions bearing the name of Theophilus are still visible on the huge towers along the Marmara walls. The Marmara defences consisted of a single line of walls 12 to 15 metres high studded with 188 towers at regular intervals. These walls extended from Saray Burnu to the Marble Tower, which anchored the Theodosian walls to the fortifications along the Marmara, a distance of eight kilometres, and were pierced by 13 gates. At Saray Burnu the Marmara walls joined up with the fortifications along the Golden Horn, thus completely walling in the city, a total distance of about 25 kilometres. Although a large part of the fortifications along the Marmara has been destroyed in the past century that which remains is still impressive, particularly the walls and towers below the First Hill.

Almost immediately in front of SS. Sergius and Bacchus there is a small postern gate once used by the monastery that was attached to the church, an institution that vanished after the Turkish conquest. The posts of the gateway are carved with a long inscription in Greek, containing a conflation from Habakkuk and Psalms. It seems to be generally agreed that these inscribed doorposts originally formed the base of the celebrated equestrian statue of Justinian that stood in the Augustaeum. This statue was still standing when Gyllius first came to the city, but during his stay he saw it being demolished and carted away, as he writes:

> I recently saw the equestrian statue of Justinian erected on the pillar that stood here [in the Augustaeum] and which had been preserved a long time in the imperial precinct, carried into the melting houses where they cast their ordnance. Among the fragments were the leg of Justinian, which exceeded my height, and his nose, which was over nine inches long. I dared not measure the horses legs as they lay on the ground but privately measured one of the hoofs and found it to be nine inches in height.

A short distance beyond this gate we find the ruins of another and grander Byzantine portal, known in Turkish as **Çatladî Kapî**, or the **Cracked Gate**. The marble sides and archway of the gate are finely carved with acanthus-leaf decorations as well as with a large monogram of Justinian. This postern is probably the one known as the Imperial Marine Gate, since it appears to have been one of the entrances from the port of Bucoleon, the private harbour of the Great Palace. It was also called the Porta Leonis, from the statues of the two lions that stood on the facade of Bucoleon, one of the seaside buildings of the Great Palace. These lions remained in place until the late nineteenth century, and they are now preserved in the Archaeological Museum. Bucoleon, the Palace of the Bull and the Lion, took its name from another statue group, now lost, which showed a lion attacking a bull. The main entryway from the port to the palace was by a monumental staircase in the huge tower just beyond the Çatladî Kapî. As we pass this tower we see all that now remains of **Bucoleon**, the eastern loggia of the palace, with its three marble-framed windows and a vaulted room behind them, along with a smaller arched window in which a column capital bears Justinian's monogram. Below the windows some projecting corbels indicate that a balcony extended along the façade, suspended over a marble quay below. Notice the curious-looking row of large marble slabs built into the lower part of the walls; these are the bottoms of Doric capitals of the fifth century BC, doubtless taken from some ancient temple that stood nearby.

These ruins are all that now remain above ground of the **Great Palace of Byzantium**, whose pavilions and courts and gardens covered the Marmara slopes of the First Hill. The palace was first built by Constantine the Great when he founded his new capital. Much of the Palace was destroyed during the Nika Revolt in 532 but it was immediately afterwards rebuilt and considerably enlarged by Justinian. Later emperors, particularly Basil I, the Macedonian, restored and extended the palace and adorned it with works of art. The Great Palace was divided into several different establishments: the Sacred Palace and the Palace of Daphne, which were near the present site of the Blue Mosque; the Chalke, or Brazen House, which adjoined the east side of the Augustaeum; the Palaces of Magnaura and Mangana, which stood on the Marmara slope of the First Hill east of what is now Topkapî Sarayî; and the Palace of Bucoleon, within which was the famous Porphyry Pavilion. This latter chamber was the lying-in room for the empresses of Byzantium, whose children were thus known as Porphyrogenitus, or 'born in the purple'. The Great Palace served as the imperial residence up until the sack of Constantinople by the Venetians and Crusaders in 1204. After the restoration of the Byzantine Empire in 1261 the palace was found to be in a state of advanced decay and was never afterwards restored. Instead, the emperors of the Palaeologus dynasty abandoned it and took up residence in the Palace of Blachernae, in the northwest corner of the city above the Golden Horn. At the time of the Turkish conquest the Great Palace by the Marmara was completely in ruins. Shortly after he entered the city, Mehmet the Conqueror walked through the ruined halls of the palace and was so saddened as to recite a melancholy distich by the Persian poet Saadi: 'The spider is the curtain holder in the Palace of the Caesars/ The owl hoots its night call on the Towers of Aphrasiab.'

The next defence-tower in the walls beyond Bucoleon served as the Pharos, or Lighthouse, in Byzantine times. The modern lighthouse is some five hundred metres beyond this. About 300 metres beyond the lighthouse we come to **Ahîr Kapî**, the **Stable Gate**, the only surviving gateway of the Byzantine sea-walls along the Marmara. Its Turkish name comes from the fact that it led to the Sultan's mews nearby. It may have had the same name in Byzantine times, for Michael III is known to have built some stables in the same area. It was a double gate, and much of both the inner and outer gateways has survived. Outside the gate, to the left, there is a simple but excellent restaurant named Karişma Sen, which in Turkish means 'Mind Your Own Business'.

After passing through the gate we immediately turn left on Ahîr Kapî Sokağî and then take the first right, Keresteci Hakkî Sokağî, which we follow as far as **Akbîyîk Meydanî**, the **Square of the White Moustache**. This is the centre of one of the oldest and most picturesque quarters in the city, the venerable Akbîyîk, and its labyrinthian streets have the most unusual and even bizarre names: the Street of the Bushy Beard, the Street of the Sweating Whiskers, the Street of the Shame-Faced, the Street of Ibrahim of Black Hell, and the Avenue of the White Moustache, from which the square and the surrounding neighbourhood are named.

There are two Ottoman fountains in the Square of the White Moustache, the most notable being the one on the left, the **Akbîyîk Meydanî Çeşmesi**. There are more than four hundred of these Ottoman *çeşmes* in the old city, ranging in size from monumental street fountains such as that of Ahmet III to simple wall fountains. These *çeşmes* were once the only source of water for the poorer people of Istanbul. Almost all of them have dedicatory inscriptions in old Turkish script; these are in the form of chronograms, in which the numerical value of the Arabic letters gives the date of foundation. The Akbîyîk Çeşmesi is an attractive example of a Turkish baroque fountain, with its rich decoration of flowers and cypress trees and its elaborately written chronogram, which reads as follows: 'When the mother of Ali Pasha, Vizier in the reign of Sultan Mahmut I, quenched the thirst of the people with the pure and clear water of her charity, Riza of Beşiktaş, a Nakşibendi dervish, uttered the following epigram: "Come and drink the water of eternal life from this fountain".' The numerical value of the words in the last phase gives the year of foundation as AH 1147, or AD 1734.

We leave the square on Akbîyîk Sokağî, which passes under the railway line and then veers to the right. At the first intersection we turn right on to Mimar Mehmet Ağa Caddesi, and then left at the next corner on to Torun Sokağî, the Street of the Grandchild. This brings us to the main entrance of the **Mosaic Museum**, which can also be entered from the street above. The entryway here is flanked by the fragmentary remains of ancient marble columns and capitals and other architectural members, all of them parts of the Great Palace of Byzantium, unearthed in excavations during the years 1933–38.

The museum houses mosaic pavements of the Great Palace, which up until recent years were still *in situ*, but are now exhibited in restored panels at their original sites. The pavements were part of the **Mosaic Peristyle**, a colonnaded walkway that may have led from the imperial apartments to the Kathisma, the royal enclosure on the Hippodrome. The mosaics depict mostly pastoral views and scenes of hunting and animal combat, along with a few scenes in the Hippodrome, including one in which two tipsy spectators pretend to be a horse and charioteer. The mosaics have been dated to the first half of the sixth century, probably part of Justinian's rebuilding of the Great Palace.

We leave the Mosaic Museum by its upper doorway. There we turn right on Kabasakal Sokağî the Street of the Bushy Beard, which passes directly behind and below the Blue Mosque. This was originally an *arasta*, or Turkish bazaar street, but it was destroyed in an earthquake in the nineteenth century. The present street is a reconstruction dating from the 1970s, its arcaded shops devoted entirely to the tourist trade. At the northern end of the street there is a way in to the Rug Museum of Sultan Ahmet I Camii. There we veer left and walk uphill, following Kabasakal Sokağî as it turns right to pass between the Hamam of Roxelana and the buildings just to its east. The first of these is the **Cedid Mehmet Efendi Medresesi**, a seventeenth-century structure that has been restored by the TTOK. The medrese now houses the **Istanbul Fine Arts Market**, with the cells around the courtyard used by artisans practicing old Ottoman crafts such as bookbinding, paper marbling, embroidery, miniature painting, engraving, and doll-making, with their products on sale to the public. The TTOK has also restored **Yeşil Ev**, the **Green House**, the handsome old Ottoman *konak*, or town house, next to the *medrese*; this has been converted into a deluxe hotel and restaurant, with tables set outside in the very attractive courtyard in good weather. This is a perfect place to stop for lunch after a stroll around the First Hill.

7

From the First Hill to the Third

O UR NEXT ITINERARY will take us from the First Hill to the Third, following the most ancient thoroughfare in the city.

The main avenue of Byzantine Constantinople was the **Mese**, or **Middle Way**, which led from the Augustaeum out to the land walls of the city. The first stretch of the Mese followed the same course as the present avenue that connects the summits of the First and Third Hills. Between the summits of the First and Second Hills this is known as **Divan Yolu**, the **Road of the Divan**, and its extension to the top of the Third Hill is **Yeniçeriler Caddesi**, the **Avenue of the Janissaries**. Both names derive from Ottoman times, for on days when the Divan was meeting in Topkapî Sarayî the Janissaries paraded along this road when passing between the palace and their barracks in the Et Meydanî, on the Third Hill.

At the beginning of Divan Yolu on the right we see an Ottoman *suterazi*, or water-control tower, one of the very few that have survived in the city. The ancient marble stele at its base was excavated in 1967–68 and was identified as the **Milion**, a triumphal archway of the late Roman period through which one passed in going from the Augustaeum to the Mese. The Milion was modelled on the Miliarium Aureum, or Golden Milestone, the monument that Augustus erected in Rome as the reference marker from which all road distances in his Empire were measured. The Milion performed the same role in Constantinople, serving as the zero point for all milestones on the Via Egnatia, the Roman road between Byzantium and the Adriatic. According to Gyllius, the Milion was surmounted by statues of Constantine the Great and his mother Helena, holding between them a large cross.

The street that heads off half-right from the Milion is Yerebatan Caddesi. A short way down the left side of this street is the entrance to **Yerebatansaray**, the **Underground Palace**, better known to foreigners as the **Basilica Cistern**. This is indeed an underground palace, by far the largest and grandest of the ancient Byzantine cisterns in the city.

The cistern takes its English name from the fact that it was built directly under the **Stoa Basilica**, or **Imperial Portico**, the great square west of the Augustaeum. This stoa, which may have been built by Constantine the Great, was destroyed by fire c.475. It was rebuilt by Justinian after the Nika Revolt in 532, and at the same time he reconstructed the cistern beneath it, using considerable material from more ancient structures. The Basilica Cistern was apparently the principal source of water on the First Hill throughout the Byzantine era and on into Ottoman times; nevertheless all knowledge of it was lost after the conquest until it was rediscovered by Gyllius. He came upon it only after a long search, as he writes:

> The Imperial Portico is not to be seen, though the Cistern remains. Through the inhabitants' carelessness and contempt for everything that is curious it was never discovered except by me, who was a stranger among them, after a long and diligent search for it. The whole area was built over, which made it less suspected that there was a cistern there. The people had not the least suspicion of it, although they daily drew their water out of the wells that were sunk into it. By chance I went into a little skiff. I discovered it after the master of the house lit some torches and rowed me here and there across through the pillars, which lay very deep in water. He was very intent upon catching his fish, with which the Cistern abounds, and speared some of them by the light of his torches. There is also a small light that descends from the mouth of the well and reflects on the water, where the fish usually come for air.

Up until the 1970s one could see only a small part of this vast cistern from the landing at the bottom of the stairs. But then, after being closed for years in a restoration project, Yerebatansaray was reopened to the public in 1987, with most of the water pumped out and walkways built so that one can explore its interior. The cistern originally had 336 columns in 12 rows of 28 each, with an intercolumniation of four metres, but 90 of them in the southeast corner were walled off at the end of the nineteenth century and are not visible today. Most of the columns are capped by Byzantine Corinthian capitals; these have imposts above them that support little domes of brick supported in a herring-bone pattern. The far left-hand corner of the cistern seems to have been part of a nymphaion, or ornamental fountain, and was possibly accessible from the Stoa Basilica when it was first built. Two of the columns there stand on pedestals carved with classical egg-and-dart design, and these rest on extraordinary bases in the form of **Gorgon heads**, one of them on its side and the other upside down. (**Medusa** was one of three Gorgons, daughters of Phorcys and Ceto; she was the only one who was mortal, while her sisters Stheno and Euryale were immortal.) These are identical to the two Gorgon heads we saw in the garden of the Archaeological Museum, and it would seem that they too came from the Forum of Constantine. The two Gorgons here were probably put in place when Justinian rebuilt the Stoa Basilica and the cistern beneath it. It is believed that all four heads were part of a Gorgon frieze on some classical temple in Asia Minor, brought to Constantinople to adorn some public building in the Forum of Constantine.

We now begin strolling down the left side of Divan Yolu, passing the northern end of the Hippodrome. About a hundred metres along we come to a small but elegant mosque, **Firuz Ağa Camii**. This was built in 1491 for Firuz Ağa, Chief Treasurer in the reign of Beyazit II. Firuz Ağa Camii is of interest principally because it is one of the few examples in Istanbul of a 'pre-classical mosque', that is, one built before 1500. This is the architectural style that flourished in Bursa when it was the capital of the Ottoman Empire. Firuz Ağa Camii is quite simple, consisting merely of a square room covered by a windowless dome resting on the walls, the so-called single-unit type of mosque. It is preceded by a little porch of three bays, with the minaret on the left-hand side. The tomb of the founder, in the form of a marble sarcophagus, is on the terrace beside the mosque.

Beyond the mosque there is an archaeological site first excavated in the 1960s. The fragmentary ruins exposed here seem to be those of two small **palaces** belonging to noblemen of the late Roman period named **Antiochus and Lausus**. The palace of Antiochus was the grandest of the two, a hexagonal building with five deep semicircular apses, between each pair of which there were circular rooms. In the early ninth century, this palace was converted into a **martyrium** for the body of St Euphemia, when it was taken from Chalcedon to Constantinople. The martyrium is decorated with frescoes dating from the late thirteenth century, which are preserved under a shed beside the Law Courts. Unfortunately, the site of the martyrium is not open to the public.

We now turn left on the street at the end of the park. A short way along we come on our right to the entrance to **Binbirdirek**, the **Cistern of a Thousand-and-One Columns**. Binbirdirek is now being restored as a covered market and will soon be open to the public.

Binbirdirek is the second largest of the city's ancient cisterns, but it is only a third the size of Yerebatansaray. The cistern was originally about 19 metres high from the floor to the tops of the little brick domes in herring-bone designs, but in the course of time mud has accumulated to a depth of some 4.5 metres. The columns are in two tiers bound together by curious stone ties, their total height originally 12.4 metres. There are 224 columns in 16 rows of 14 each, but twelve have been walled in, apparently from very early times. The impost capitals are plain but generally inscribed with monograms of the stone masons. Several ancient sources say that the cistern was built by Philoxenus, a Roman senator who came to the city with Constantine the Great, although there is evidence that some of the structure dates from the fifth or sixth century.

Returning to Divan Yolu, we turn left on Klodfarer Caddesi, named after the French novelist Claude Farrere. At the end of the street and on the right we come to the Eminönü Belediye Başbakanlîǧî, the town hall of this part of Istanbul. A door to the right of the main entrance has a sign indicating the entrance to the **'Theodosius Cistern'**, to which visitors are escorted by the watchman on duty.

Visitors are restricted to the platform just inside the entrance, from where one can look down upon the cistern, which is only partly illuminated by the present inadequate lighting system. The cistern measures some 25 by 42.5 metres, its brick roof supported by 32 columns of white marble, some of which are surmounted by Corinthian capitals and others by Doric capitals. The cistern is believed to have been built in the mid-fifth century by the Empress Pulcheria, sister of Theodosius II and wife of the Emperor Marcian (450–57). After restoration, the cistern was opened to the public in 1994.

We now return to Divan Yolu. Directly across the avenue we see the large enclosure of the *türbe* **of Mahmut II**, a domed structure in the Empire style. The *türbe* was completed in 1840, the year after Mahmut's death; buried with him are his son Abdül Aziz and his grandson Abdül Hamit II, along with a large number of princes and imperial consorts.

Directly opposite the türbe, on the south side of the avenue, we pass an Ottoman **library** that is still in use as a research centre. This is one of the institutions of the **Köprülü** *külliye*, whose other extant structures we will see farther along on this itinerary. These buildings were erected in 1659–60 by two members of the illustrious Köprülü family, Mehmet Pasha and his son Fazîl Ahmet Pasha, both of whom served as Grand Vizier, as did three others of their family in the following half-century. The library of the Köprülü *külliye* is a handsome little building with a columned porch and a domed reading-room, constructed in a mixture of brick and stone. The library contains an important collection of books and manuscripts, many of which were the property of its founders, who were known in their time as Mehmet the Cruel and Ahmet the Statist.

One block further along the same side of the avenue we pass two other structures of the Köprülü *külliye*, first the open ***türbe* of Mehmet Pasha** and then the mosque of the foundation. The mosque is a few steps beyond the *türbe*, projecting out onto the sidewalk of the avenue; this was once the lecture hall of the *medrese*, most of which has been demolished.

Directly across the avenue from the Köprülü mosque is the **Çemberlitaş Hamamî**, one of the finest extant examples of a classical Turkish bath. This was founded some time before her death in 1583 by the Valide Sultan Nur Banu, wife of Selim II and mother of Murat III. The bath was originally double, but part of the women's section was destroyed when the avenue was widened. What remains of the women's bath is now a café. The men's section is still in operation; its entrance is on the side street to the right off the avenue. In general, the men's bath follows the usual plan: a great domed *camekan* leads to a small three-domed *soğukluk*, which opens into the *hararet*. This latter has a rather charming arrangement, seen also at Cağaloğlu and elsewhere, in which a circlet of columns forms an arcade that supports the dome. The corners have little washing-cells, each with its own dome and an attractive door, the marble pavements laid out in geometric designs.

At the next turning on the right we see one of the most historic monuments in the city, the **Column of Constantine**, known also as the Burnt Column. The Turks call it Çemberlitaş, the Hooped Column, a name that is also applied to the surrounding neighbourhood. The column stands on the summit of the Second Hill, where it has been a landmark since the day that Constantinople was founded. The column was erected by Constantine the Great to commemorate the establishment of his capital in New Rome, dedicated on 11 May 330, the day that Byzantium became Constantinople. It stood at the centre of the Forum of Constantine, a colonnaded area of oval form that has been compared to Bernini's superb portico at St Peter's in Rome. The column, whose total height is now some 35 metres, consists of a rough masonry base about ten metres high surmounted by a shaft of six porphyry drums, the joints between them hooped with iron bands. Originally the monument had a square pedestal with five steps; this supported a porphyry plinth and column base on which were stacked seven porphryry drums. The original iron hoops were added in 416 when the lower part of the monument was damaged. At the summit there was a large capital, presumably Corinthian, upon which stood a statue of Constantine in the guise of Apollo. The statue remained in place until 1106, when it was toppled in a hurricane and destroyed. Half a century later Manuel I Comnenus (1143–80) replaced the capital with the present masonry courses, erecting on top of the monument a huge cross, which was presumably destroyed at the time of the conquest. In 1779 the column was damaged in a great fire that destroyed much of the surrounding quarter, leaving the black scars that one can still see on the porphyry drums. Soon afterwards Abdül Hamit I repaired the monument, which was stabilized by encasing its lower drum in the present masonry case. The column was restored in the 1970s, when the iron hoops were replaced by steel bands.

The side street that leads off to the right from Yeniçeriler Caddesi at the column is known as Vezirhanî Caddesi. The street takes its name from the **Vezir Hanî**, whose entrance is a short way down on the right from the column. The *han* was part of the Köprülü *külliye*, erected in 1659–60 as a hostel for travelling merchants, its facilities including stables for their animals as well as warehouses and shops for the storage and sale of their goods. The Vezir Hanî served as the slave market of Istanbul before the abolition of slavery in the Ottoman Empire in 1855.

Across the way from the Vezir Hanî we see **Nuruosmaniye Camii**, the Mosque of the Sacred Light (Nur) of Osman. This külliye, which also includes a *medrese*, library, royal loge, *türbe* and *sebil*, was begun in 1748 by Mahmut I and completed in 1755 by his brother and successor, Osman III, for whom it is named. Nurosmaniye Camii was the first monumental Ottoman edifice to exemplify the new baroque architectural style from Europe, designed by a Greek architect named Simeon. Like most of the baroque mosques, it consists essentially of a square room covered by a large dome resting on four arches in the walls; the form of these arches is strongly emphasized, especially on the exterior; also the arches are round, rather than pointed as in classical Ottoman architecture. In plan, the building has an oddly cruciform appearance because of the two side chambers at the east end, and it has a semicircular apse for the *mihrab*. On the west it is preceded by a porch with nine bays, and this is enclosd by an extremely curious courtyard which can only be described as a figure with seven sides and nine domed bays inscribed within a semicircle! The whole structure is erected on a low terrace to which irregularly placed flights of steps give access.

Continuing down Vezirhanî Caddesi, we come to **Mahmut Pasha Camii**, the oldest grand vizierial mosque in the city, built in 1462. Mahmut Pasha was of noble Byzantine origin, but he became a Muslim and soon rose to high rank in the Ottoman service, appointed as Grand Vizier soon after the conquest. But despite his great ability he eventually fell from favour and was beheaded by Mehmet the Conqueror in 1474.

The mosque consists of a long rectangular room divided in the middle by an arch, thus forming two square chambers each covered by a dome of equal size. On each side of the main hall there is a narrow, barrel-vaulted passage that communicates both with the hall and with three small rooms on each side. These side rooms were used as a *tabhane*, or hostel, for itinerant dervishes, a feature of larger Ottoman mosques of the pre-classical period. To the west a narthex with five bays runs the width of the building and is preceded by a porch with five bays. The porch is an unfortunate restoration, in which the original columns have been replaced by, or encased in, ungainly octagonal octagonal piers.

In the garden behind the mosque we find Mahmut Pasha's magnificent *türbe*, dated by an inscription to 1474. It is a tall octagonal building with a blind dome and two tiers of windows. The upper part of the fabric on the outside is entirely encased in a kind of mosaic of tile work, with blue and turquoise the predominating colours. The tiles make a series of wheel-like patterns of great charm; they are presumably of the first Iznik period (1453–1555), and there is nothing else exactly like them in Istanbul.

The *külliye* of Mahmut Pasha also includes a *hamam* and a *han*, both of which we will see later on this itinerary.

Returning to Yeniçeriler Caddesi, at the corner beyond the Column of Constantine we come to **Atik (Old) Ali Pasha Camii**. The mosque was built in 1496 by Hadîm (the Eunuch) Atik Ali Pasha, who served as Grand Vizier under Beyazit II. Its plan is somewhat unusual, in that it consists of a rectangular room divided into two unequal parts by an arch. The western and larger section is covered by a dome, the eastern by a semidome under which is the *mihrab*, as if in a sort of great apse. The western section is also flanked to north and south by two rooms with smaller domes. The semidomes and the four smaller domes have stalactite pendentives, a common feature of Ottoman mosques of early date. The *külliye* also included a *medrese*, an *imaret* and a dervish *tekke*, but the latter two institutions were demolished when the avenue was widened in the 1950s. The *medrese* is just across the avenue from the mosque.

On the next block beyond Atik Ali Pasha Camii we come to the *külliye* **of Koca (Old) Sinan Pasha**, enclosed by a marble wall with iron grilles. This attractive complex consists of a *medrese*, a *sebil* and the *türbe* of the founder, who was Grand Vizier under both Murat III and Mehmet III. The architect was Davut Ağa, who completed the *külliye* in 1593, two years before Sinan Pasha's death. The most outstanding building in this very attractive complex is the *türbe*, a sixteen-sided structure built of polychrome stonework, white and rose-coloured, and with a rich cornice of stalactites and handsome window mouldings. The *medrese*, which we enter by a gate in the alley alongside, has a charming courtyard with a portico of ogive arches. The *sebil*, too, is an elegant structure with bronze grilles separated by little columns and surmounted by an overhanging roof.

Across the alleyway from the *sebil* a marble wall with grilles encloses another attractive little complex of buildings, the *külliye* **of Çorlulu Ali Pasha**. This Ali Pasha was a son-in-law of Mustafa II and Grand Vizier under Ahmet III, on whose orders he was beheaded in 1711 on Mytilene. Ali Pasha's head was afterwards brought back to Istanbul and buried in the graveyard of his *külliye*, which had been completed in 1708. This *külliye*, consisting of a small mosque and a *medrese*, belongs to the transitional period between the classical and baroque styles in Ottoman architecture. Nevertheless, the buildings are still essentially classical, the only obviously baroque features being the capitals of the columns in the porch.

Directly across the avenue we see the *külliye* **of Kara Mustafa Pasha of Merzifon**, consisting of an octagonal mosque, a *medrese* and a *sebil*. The *külliye* was begun in 1663 by Kara Mustafa Pasha, who was Grand Vizier under Mehmet IV. The *külliye* was still unfinished in 1663, when Kara Mustafa Pasha was beheaded at Belgrade after the unsuccessful Turkish siege of Vienna, a turning-point in European history, for thenceforth the Ottomans were no longer a threat to the West. His remains were returned for burial in the graveyard of his *külliye*, which was finally completed by his son in 1690. The mosque is of the transitional type between classical and baroque. It is of interest chiefly as one of the few octagonal buildings to be used as a mosque. The *medrese* now houses a research institute commemorating the celebrated poet Yahya Kemal (1884–1958).

Just beyond Mustafa Pasha's *külliye* we turn left on to Gedik Paşa Caddesi, which at the second turning on the left brings us to a *hamam* of the same name. This is the oldest Turkish **bath** in the city, built in 1475. Its founder was **Gedik Ahmet Pasha**, one of Mehmet the Conqueror's Grand Viziers, commander of the fleet at the capture of Azof and the conqueror of the Greek island of Lefkada and the Italian port of Otranto. This *hamam* has an unusually monumental *soğukluk* consisting of a large domed area flanked by alcoves and cubicles, with the one on the right having a very elaborate stalactited vault.

Returning to Yeniçeriler Caddesi, we cross the avenue and continue straight ahead on Çarşîkapî Sokağî, the Street of the Market Gate. This takes its name from the **Kapalî Çarşî**, or **Covered Bazaar**, one of the most renowned marketplaces in the world, which we now enter through a gateway at the end of the street

The Kapalî Çarşî was built by Mehmet the Conqueror soon after the conquest, occupying much the same area that it does today. Although it has been wrecked by earthquakes and ravaged by fires, most recently in 1954, its basic structure and layout are unchanged from Mehmet the Conqueror's time. It is a small city in itself; according to a survey made in 1976, there are more than 3,000 shops of various kinds, along with innumerable storehouses and work-shops, many of them housed in old Ottoman hans, as well as several lunch-counters, a teahouse, and an excellent restaurant, the Havuzlu Lokantasî. At first the Kapalî Çarşî seems a bewildering labyrinth, but after wandering through it for a while you discover that it is really a well-planned complex, with most of its streets and squares laid out in a rectangular grid pattern. Shops selling the same kinds of goods tend to be congregated on the same street, with the streets themselves named after the merchants or artisans who are or were established there, such as **Kuyumcular Sokağî**, the **Street of the Jewellers**, where the most costly jewellers and dealers in gold and silver ornaments have their own arcade. Some of these names, such as the **Street of the Turban-Makers** and the **Street of the Sword-Cutlers**, remind one that much of the fabled oriental atmosphere of the Covered Bazaar has vanished since the passing of Ottoman times.

The core of the Bazaar is the **Old Bedesten**, a stronghold consisting of fifteen domed enclosures in five rows of three each

The Beyazidiye

supported internally by eight massive piers. This is one of the original structures built by Mehmet the Conqueror; then, as now, it was used to house the most precious wares, for it can be securely locked and guarded at night. Some of the most interesting and valuable objects in the Bazaar are sold here, including old trays and ewers of brass and copper, old coins, Ottoman weapons, and antiques of various kinds. The Bedesten has gates on all of its four sides, and each of these is named after one of the guilds that has or had its shops on the street outside. Dealers in gold objects still have their shops outside the Gate of the Goldsmiths. Above the outer portal of this gateway there is a relief with the figure of a single-headed eagle, the imperial emblem of the Comneni dynasty who ruled over Byzantium in the eleventh and twelfth centuries. (The Palaeologues, who ruled during the last two centuries of the Empire, had a double-headed eagle as their symbol.) This has led to the suggestion that the Bedesten was originally of Byzantine contruction, but authorities generally agreee that the building was erected by Mehmet the Conqueror, with the relief being re-used from a Byzantine structure, as was often the case in Istanbul.

There is a second bedesten near the southeastern corner of the Covered Bazaar. This is the **Sandal Bedesten**, which Mehmet the Conqueror built later in his reign, after the greatly increased trade and commerce of the Ottoman Empire filled the Old Bedesten to its capacity. The internal support for the lofty roof is provided by twelve massive piers, in three rows of four each, supporting twenty brick domes.

In and around the Covered Bazaar there are a number of old *hans*, commercial buildings where Ottoman merchants stored their goods before sale. Many of these *hans* are still serving the same purpose today, along with housing all types of commercial and industrial enterprises. Inside the Kapalî Çarþî itself the finest of these is the **Zincirli Han**, which is near the northeast corner of the Bazaar, a picturesque old caravansarai now used by a number of rug merchants and antique dealers.

The main market street leading down from the Kapalî Çarþî to the Golden Horn is **Mahmut Paþa Yokuþu** which has at its upper end a gate in the northeast corner of the Bazaar. About a hundred metres down this street on the left we see the very impressive hamam of the **Mahmut Pasha** *külliye*, which has recently being restored and now serves as a market hall. The hamam was completed in 1476, two years after Mahmut Pasha's death, making it the second oldest

Turkish bath in the city after that of Gedik Ahmet Pasha. Like most of the great Ottoman *hamams*, it was originally double, but the women's section was torn down to make way for the adjacent *han*. We enter through a large central hall, 17 metres on each side, with a high dome on stalactited pendentives. The *soğukluk* is a truly monumental room covered by a dome with spiral ribs in the form of a scallop shell; on each side are two square cubicles with elaborate vaulting. The *hararet* is octagonal with five shallow oblong niches, and in the cross-axis there are two domed eyvans, each of which leads to two more domed bathing cubicles in the corners.

A hundred metres farther down Mahmut Paşa Yokuşu we come to the **Kürkçü Hanî**, the **Han of the Fur Dealers**, who have been doing business here for more than four centuries. This is also part of the Mahmut Pasha *külliye* and is the oldest *han* in the city. Unfortunately, part of it has been destroyed. Originally it consisted of two large courtyards. The first, nearly square, is 45 by 50 metres, and has about 45 rooms on each of its two floors; in the centre there was a small mosque, now replaced by an ugly modern building. The second courtyard to the north was smaller and very irregularly shaped, with about 30 rooms on each floor; unfortunately it has now been for the most part destroyed.

Continuing down Mahmut Paşa Yokuşu, we turn left at the next corner on to Çakmakcîlar Yokuşu. Just beyond the first turning on the left we come to the entrance to the **Büyük Yeni Han**, which means literally the **Big New Han**. This was built in 1764 by Mustafa III and is the finest extant example of a baroque *han*. Its central courtyard is more than one hundred metres in length, divided in the middle by what appears to be a later construction. The courtyard is quite narrow for its great length; nevertheless it is very impressive and picturesque, with its three stories of great round-arched arcades.

A little farther up Çakmakcîlar Yokuşu and on the opposite side, we come to the entrance to the **Valide Hanî**. This is the largest and most interesting *han* in the city, built by the Valide Sultan Kösem, wife of Ahmet I and mother of sultans Murat IV and Ibrahim, not long before her death in 1651. We enter through a great gateway into the first courtyard, small and iregularly shaped because of the alignment of the *han* relative to the street outside. From there we pass into the main court, a vast area some 55 metres on a side surrounded by a two-tiered arcade, the innumerable chambers of which are devoted to every conceivable form of industry and commerce. A vaulted tunnel leads from the far left corner of the main courtard into the inner court, which because of the lay of the land is set at a lower level than the rest of the han. At the back of this courtyard we see the impressive remains of a Byzantine tower built into the structure of the *han*. This had traditionally been called the **Tower of Eirene** and is tentatively dated to the medieval Byzantine era, but the evidence for this is very uncertain.

We now retrace our steps through the Valide Hanî, after which we cross Çakmakcîlar Yokuşu and continue straight ahead on the narrow alley opposite the *han* gateway. This eventually takes us back to the upper end of Mahmut Pasa Yokuşu, where we continue straight ahead until we come to the western entryway to the outer courtyard of Nuruosmaniye Camii. Turning right here, we follow Kalpakçîlar Sokağî, the main street of the Kapalî Çarşî, which takes us all the way along the upper end of the Bazaar to the gateway at its southwestern corner. There we leave the Bazaar and turn right on Çadîrcîlar Caddesi, then after a few steps we turn left through an ancient stone portal known as Hakkaklar Kapîsî, the Gate of the Engravers.

After walking up a flight of steps we then come to the **Sahaflar Çarşîsî**, the **Market of the Secondhand Booksellers**. This is one of the most picturesque spots in the city, a vine-shaded courtyard lined with bookshops displaying both new and secondhand books, always crowded with browsing bookworms. The Sahaflar is one of the most ancient markets in the city, occupying the site of the Chartoprateia, the book and paper market of Byzantium. After the conquest it became the market for the turban-makers and metal-engravers, whose name is perpetuated in that of the entryway to the market. At the beginning of the eighteenth century the booksellers set up shop here too, moving from their old quarters inside the Covered Bazaar, where a street is still named for them. Later in that century, with the legalization of printing in the Ottoman Empire, the booksellers greatly increased their trade and came to dominate the market, which from that time on came to be named for them. During the nineteenth and twentieth centuries, the Sahaflar was one of the principal markets in the Ottoman Empire for the sale and distribution of books. During the past half-century, however, the establishment of modern bookshops elsewhere in the city has diminished its importance somewhat, though the Sahaflar still holds pride of place as the oldest book-market in Turkey. The guild of booksellers in this market is one of the oldest in Istanbul, and it is mentioned in Evliya Çelebi's Procession of the Guilds. In the garden at the centre of the square there is a modern bust of Ibrahim Müteferrika, a Hungarian who joined the Ottoman service, and who in 1732 began to print the first works in Turkish ever published in the Ottoman Empire.

After passing through the Sahaflar Çarşîsî we enter the outer courtyard of the Beyazidiye, the imperial mosque complex that dominates Beyazit Meydanî, the vast but formless square on the summit of the Third Hill. We will visit the Beyazidiye at the beginning of the next itinerary, and we might end the present stroll by having an informal lunch at the outdoor café in the outer courtyard of the mosque. This café had its beginnings in a coffee-house frequented by the Janissaries, who had their main barracks nearby before they were annihilated by Mahmut II in 1826. The coffee-house survived up into the 1960s, shaded by a giant *çînar*, or plane-tree, a favourite gathering-place for students and faculty from the nearby Istanbul University and for those working and shopping in the Covered Bazaar. The square has long been the most popular outdoor market of the city, and in recent years people from eastern Europe have been coming here to sell their wares, joining the throngs of local peddlers and hawkers. This has been a market square since Sultan Beyazit II first built his mosque and its associated pious foundations here five centuries ago, and it is much the same as it was when Evliya Çelebi described the Beyazidiye in his *Seyahatname*:

> Round the inner and outer courts of this mosque there are shops of all kinds of trades, with a public kitchen, a refrectory and hostel for travellers, and a school for instruction in the Koran. The court has six gates and is adorned with lofty trees, under the shade of which thousands of people gain a livelihood by selling all kinds of things.

8

Around the Third Hill

OUR NEXT STROLL will take us around the Third Hill to see
the imperial mosque complexes and other monuments in the
centre of the old city, beginning with the Beyazidiye.

The **Beyazidiye** was founded by Beyazit II, Mehmet the
Conqueror's son and successor. It was the second imperial mosque
complex to be erected in Istanbul after the conquest, the first being
Mehmet the Conqueror's *külliye*. But the original mosque of
Mehmet the Conqueror was destroyed by an earthquake in 1766, and
the present mosque in the Conqueror's *külliye* is a replacement
dating from 1771. Thus Beyazit II Camii is the oldest extant imperial
mosque in Istanbul. The Beyazidiye was built in the years 1501–56
by the architect Yakub-şah bin Sultan şah, whose only other known
building is a caravansarai at Bursa. The mosque of the Beyazidiye
marks the beginning of the classical period of Ottoman architecture,
which continued for more than two centuries, Besides the great
mosque itself, the *külliye* consists of a *medrese, imaret, hamam,*
primary school and several *türbes.*

Beyazit II Camii is preceded by the most beautiful of all the city's
mosque courtyards, with magnificent entrance portals on three sides.
A peristyle of 20 ancient columns – porphyry, verd-antique, and
Syenitic marble – forms an arcade with red-and-white or black-and-
white voussoirs, with the portico covered by 24 small domes. The
pavement is of polychrome marble, and in the centre there is a beautifully decorated *şadîrvan*. Capitals, cornices and niches are elabo-
rated with stalactite mouldings. The harmony of proportions, the rich
but restrained decoration, the brilliance of the variegated marbles,
together give the courtyard a quite unique charm.

An exceptionally fine portal leads into the mosque, which in plan
is a greatly simplified and much smaller version of Haghia Sophia.
As in the Great Church, the central dome, which is 17 metres in
diameter, and the domes to east and west form a nave, flanked by
side aisles to north and south. There are no galleries over the aisles,
which open wide into the nave, separated from it only by a pair of
ancient granite columns and the four huge piers that support the

114

dome. An unusual feature of the interior is that the Sultan's loge is to the right of the *mimber* rather than to the left, as in all other imperial mosques in the city; it is supported on columns of very rich and rare marbles. At the west side of the interior a broad corridor, divided into domed or vaulted bays, extends considerably beyond the main body of the mosque and creates the effect of a narthex. At the end of the south arm of the corridor there is a small library, added in the eighteenth century by the şeyh-ül Islam Veliyüttin Efendi. The two fine minarets rise from the ends of the corridor, their shafts picked out with geometric designs in terracotta; they stand far beyond the main part of the building in an arrangement which is unique and gives a very grand effect.

Behind the mosque is the **graveyard garden**, where Beyazit II lies buried in a simple, well-proportioned *türbe* of limestone picked out in verd-antique. Nearby is the even simpler *türbe* of his daughter Selçuk Hatun. Beyond these, a third *türbe* in a very ornate *Empire* style is that of Koca Mustafa Reşit Pasha, Grand Vezir under Abdül Mecit and leader of the Tanzimat, or Reform movement, who died in 1858. Below the eastern side of the *türbe* garden is an arcade of shops originally erected by Sinan in 1580; this had been demolished, but in the 1960s it was reconstructed according to the original plan. Just behind these shops is a double *sibyan mektebi*, or primary school, with two domes and a porch. This is part of the *külliye* of the Beyazidiye, and is the oldest Ottoman primary school in the city, since the one attached to the mosque of Mehmet the Conqueror has vanished; it now houses a research institute.

The *imaret* of the Beyazidiye is in the outer courtyard of the mosque opposite the northern minaret. This impressive building served as both a public kitchen and caravansarai; it was restored in 1882 by Abdül Hamit II and now serves as the State Library.

On the north side of Beyazit Square is the main entrance to **Istanbul University**, established on its present site in the early years of the Turkish Republic. The huge tower in the courtyard of the university, some 50 metres high, is one of the most prominent landmarks in the city. It was erected by Mahmut II in 1828 as a fire-watch station, a function that it performed up into the 1960s, when the public were still allowed to ascend it for the most panoramic of all views in the city, but unfortunately it has since been closed.

The *medrese* of the Beyazidiye is at the far west end of the square. It is of the standard form; the cells where the students studied are ranged around four sides of a porticoed courtyard, while the *dershane* is opposite the entrance portal. The building has been restored and now houses the Municipality Library and the Calligraphy Museum. The museum contains examples of all types and periods of Ottoman calligraphy; one cell of the *medrese* has been set up as a calligrapher's studio, with wax figures representing the artisan instructing his students in this quintessentially Islamic art.

The *hamam* of the Beyazidiye is beyond the *medrese* on the main avenue, which here takes the name Ordu Caddesi. This impressive building has been closed for years and is now beginning to deteriorate, which is a pity, since this must have been one of the most splendid Turkish baths in the city. Built into the base of the baths on the side along Ordu Caddesi are some fragmentary reliefs of the late Roman period, including one, placed in upside down, showing a line of marching centurions.

The reliefs built into Beyazit's *hamam* were taken from a Roman commemorative column that stood in the **Forum of Theodosius**, whose ruins are arrayed along both sides of Ordu Caddesi at the western end of Beyazit Meydanî. This forum was built on the summit of the Third Hill by Theodosius I c.390. The column was erected as part of a monument to Theodosius by his son and successor Arcadius in 396. The monument included a gigantic triumphal gateway in the Roman fashion, along with a commemorative column with reliefs showing the victories of Theodosius, like that of Trajan in Rome. The forum seems to have been in ruins at the time of the conquest, and what was left of the gateway and commemorative column were used in the construction of Beyazit's *hamam*. Gyllius identified the forum, but it was subsequently built over and completely vanished from sight, until its remnants were rediscovered when the avenue was widened in the late 1950s. Huge fragments of the gateway are arrayed on either side of the avenue, the most notable being the enormous Corinthian capitals and the columns curiously decorated with the peacock-eye or lopped branch design. A column of this type can be seen in the Basilica Cistern, and another outside the Archaeological Museum, both undoubtedly having been removed from the Forum of Theodosius.

Across the avenue from Beyazit's *hamam* there are two Ottoman *hans* of some interest. The one on the left is Şimkeshane, the **Han of the Silver-Thread Spinners**. This was originally built by Mehmet the Conqueror to house the Imperial Mint, but when that was moved to Topkapî Sarayî the Spinners of Silver Thread were installed here. The *han* was damaged by fire and then rebuilt in 1707 by Rabia

Gülnüş Ümmetüllah, wife of Mehmet IV and mother of Mustafa II and Ahmet III. The **han** on the right was built c.1740 by Seyyit **Hasan Pasha**, Grand Vizier under Mahmut I. Both *hans* lost their front half when Ordu Caddesi was widened, but they were restored in the 1980s.

We now begin walking down the south side of Ordu Caddesi, and on the third block beyond the Hasan Pasha Hani we come to the *külliye* **of Ragîp Pasha**, Grand Vizier during the years 1757–63. This little complex was built in 1762, probably by the architect Mehmet Tahir Ağa.

A flight of steps leads down from the avenue under a *mektep*, an Ottoman primary school that is now being used as a children's library. Across the courtyard is the main library, which has been restored and is once again serving its original purpose. From the courtyard a flight of steps leads into a domed lobby, and from there we pass into the reading room. This is square in plan, the central space covered by a dome supported on four columns; between these, beautiful bronze grilles form a kind of cage that contains the books and manuscripts. Round the sides of this vaulted and domed room are chairs and tables for readers. The walls are revetted in blue and white tiles, either of European manufacture or strongly under European influence, but charming nevertheless. The complex also includes a small graveyard, separated from the courtyard by a fine bronze grille; there we see the tombstone of Ragîp Pasha, surmounted by a representation of the large turban he wore as Grand Vizier.

Continuing along Ordu Caddesi, we now take the second turning on the left. We turn right at the next corner, and then at the end of this street we ascend a flight of steps onto a marble paved terrace.

Just beyond the far left corner of the terrace we see a former Byzantine church known in Turkish as **Bodrum Cami**, or the Subterranean Mosque, because of the crypt that lies beneath it. The church and the monastery to which it was attached were founded by the Emperor Romanus I Lecapenus (919–44). The monastery was known as the **Myrelaion**, the 'place of the myrrh oil', an ancient name of unknown origin that was also applied to the church. When his wife Theodora died in 922 he buried her in a funerary chapel that he built beneath the church. The church was converted into a mosque late in the fifteenth century by Mesih Pasha, a descendant of the imperial Byzantine dynasty of the Palaeologues who became a Muslim and rose to the rank of commanding general of the Ottoman army. The mosque was gutted by fire several times, and up until the 1970s it was reduced to a burned-out shell; but then it was restored after an archaeological study by Professor C. Lee Striker of Pennyslvania State University. The building now serves as a mosque once again.

Professor Striker's archhaeological study revealed that the two superimposed churches were built during the period 919–23, and that both of them were of the same design, namely the four-column church so common in Byzantium from the ninth and tenth centuries onward. Here, as in many other cases, the columns were replaced by piers in Ottoman times. In this type the four columns stand at the corners of a square supporting the circular cornice of a high drum that carries the central dome, with vaults radiating in four directions to form a Greek cross; on three sides there are aisles and galleries, with a narthex on the west and on the east a wide central apse flanked by two smaller side apses. On the exterior are some pretty and unusual buttresses that look like engaged columns. The crypt was excavated during the restoration and a few graves and some traces of frescoes were discovered.

Romanus also built a palace next to the church, erecting it on a late Roman substructure known as the **Rotunda**, which was also excavated by Professor Striker. The Rotunda was now been restored and opened as a subterranean market hall, entered via a stairway at the rear of the terrace and also from the side street below. The Rotunda is circular in plan, some thirty metres in diameter, its roof originally supported by 75 columns. The restoration was very successful, and the Rotunda makes a most attractive shopping mall, its Roman colonnade and walls exposed to view.

We now retrace our steps to Ordu Caddesi, which we cross and come to **Laleli Cami**, the **Tulip Mosque**. This is perhaps the best of all the baroque mosques in the city, founded by Mustafa III and built in 1759–63 by Mehmet Tahir Ağa. The mosque is built on a high terrace over a congeries of vaulted shops and passages, in the centre of which there is a great hall supported by eight enormous piers, with a fountain as its focus. It has been suggested that this subterranean arcade is a *tour de force* of Mehmet Tahir, designed to show that he could support his mosque virtually on thin air!

The moque itself is constructed of brick and stone, but the superstructure is of stone only, and the two parts do not appear to fit together very well. Along the sides there are amusing but pointless galleries, with the arcades formed of round arches, with a similar arcade covering the ramp leading to the imperial loge.

The plan of the interior is an octagon inscribed in a rectangle. All but the west pair of supporting columns are engaged in the walls, with the colonnade on that side supporting the western gallery. All the walls are heavily revetted in variegated marbles – yellow, red, blue and other colours – which give a gay if somewhat gaudy effect. In the west wall of the gallery there are medallions of opus sectile which incorporate not only rare marbles but also semi-precious stones such as onyx, jasper and lapis lazuli. A rectangular apse contains the *mihrab*, which is made of sumptuous marbles. The *mimber* is made from the same materials, while the *Koran kürsü* is a rich work of carved wood heavily inlaid with mother-of-pearl. The *külliye* also included a *medrese*, an *imaret*, a *han*, a *hamam*, a stable for the Sultan's horses, and a *türbe* in which Mustafa III is buried along with his son Selim III, who was deposed by the Janissaries in 1807 and murdered by them the following year. The *medrese* and *hamam* have vanished but the other structures are in good repair. The *han* is north of the mosque, approached by an alleyway leading off from Fethi Bey Caddesi, the street on the east side of the complex. It is known locally as **Büyük Taş Han**, the **Big Stone Han**. An outstanding restoration has converted the *han* into an attractive shopping mall with a restaurant and cafés.

We now walk along Fethi Bey Caddesi and then continue on Fevziye Caddesi as far as Şehzadebaşî Caddesi, where we cross the avenue and turn left. The latter avenue takes its name from **Şehzade Camii**, the **Mosque of the Prince**, which we now see looming ahead and to the right. This imperial mosque complex was erected by Süleyman the Magnificent in memory of his eldest son, Prince Mehmet, who died of smallpox at the age of twenty one in 1543. Sinan was commissioned to build the *külliye*, which he completed in 1548, his first imperial mosque complex on a monumental scale.

The mosque is preceded by a handsome *avlu* surrounded on all four sides by a portico, with the usual *şadîrvan* in the centre. The two minarets, which rise from the western corners of the mosque, are considered to be the most beautiful in the city; notice the elaborate geometrical sculptures in low relief, the intricate traceries of the *şerefes*, and the occasional terracotta inlay. These, together with the cluster of domes and semidomes, many of them with fretted cornices and bold ribbing, crown the building in an arrangement of repetition and contrast that are nowhere surpassed. Here, too, Sinan first adopted the brilliant expedient of placing colonnaded galleries along the entire length of the north and south façades in order to conceal the buttresses, an arrangement, as we will see, that he used with even greater effect at the Süleymaniye.

The interior is vast and empty; almost alone among the imperial mosques, it has not a single column, nor are there any galleries. Sinan, wishing from the beginning to centralize his plan, adopted the expedient of extending the area not by two semidomes, as in Haghia Sophia, but by four. Although this is the most obvious and logical way of both increasing the space and centralising the plan, the identical symmetry along both axes has a repetitive effect that tends toward dullness. Furthermore, the four great piers that support the dome are stranded and isolated in the midst of the vast space, and their inevitably large size is therefore unduly emphasized. The general effect of the interior is of an austere simplicity that is not without its charm.

There are half-a-dozen **tombs** in the walled garden behind the mosque, the largest and grandest being that of Prince Mehmet himself, a work of Sinan erected in 1543–44. This has the finest interior decoration of any *türbe* in the city; but unfortunately it and the other tombs in the garden are not open to the public. Two other remarkable tombs in this garden are those of the Grand Vizier Rüstem Pasha, son-in-law of Süleyman the Magnificent, and the Grand Vizier Ibrahim Pasha, son-in-law of Murat III, the former built in 1561 by Sinan and the latter in 1603 by Dalgîç Ahmet Ağa, both of them adorned with superb Iznik tiles. There are three other *türbes* in the *külliye*, those of Hatice Sultan, a daughter of Murat III; Fatma Sultan, granddaughter of Prince Mehmet; and Destari Mustafa Pasha. The latter is the most interesting of the three; dated by an inscription to 1611, it has the unusual form of a rectangle, with the walls between the windows revetted with Iznik tiles.

The other institutions of the şehzade *külliye* stand along the north side of the mosque precincts. The *medrese* is at the northwest corner of the outer courtyard, with the Valens Aqueduct directly behind it. The *imaret* and the *mektep* are on the east side of Dede Efendi Caddesi, the side street that leads off from Şehzadebaşî Caddesi just beyond the *türbe* garden.

At the corner of Dede Efendi Caddesi and Şehzadebaşî Caddesi, just opposite the *türbe* garden, there is a *medrese* with an exceptionally handsome *sebil* at the corner. This charming *külliye* was built in 1720 by **Nevşehirli Damat Ibrahim Pasha**, son-in-law of Ahmet III, whom he served as Grand Vizier from 1718–30, during the golden years of the Tulip Period. That delightful epoch ended on 20

September 1730, when Ahmet III was deposed and Ibrahim Pasha was killed by the Janissaries.

We now walk back eastwards along Şehzadebaşî Caddesi to the first intersection, where off to the left we see a handsome edifice named **Kalenderhane Camii**. This is a Byzantine church that in Mehmet the Conqueror's time was converted into a mosque by the Kalender order of dervishes, hence the Turkish name. During the 1970s the building underwent a thorough investigation directed by Professor C. Lee Striker, sponsored by the Dumbarton Oaks Society and Istanbul Technical University. During the course of the study the building was identified as the **church of the Theotokos Kyriotissa** (Our Lady, Mother of God) and dated to the twelfth century. Professor Striker's study also revealed that the church had been erected on the site of earlier structures and had been rebuilt in both the Byzantine and Ottoman periods. After the restoration the building was once again opened as a mosque.

The church is cruciform in plan, with deep barrel vaults over the arms of the cross and a dome with sixteen ribs over the centre. It originally had side aisles communicating with the nave, and galleries over the exonarthex and narthex.

The interior still preserves most of its elaborate and beautiful marble revetment.

During the restoration a series of **wall paintings** were discovered in a small chapel to the right of the apse. These proved to be a fresco cycle of the life of St Francis. This was done during the Latin occupation of the city, c.1250, and is thus the oldest cycle of the life of St Francis in existence, painted only a quarter of a century after the saint's death. It is also the only work of art that has survived *in situ* from the Latin occupation of Constantinople. The cycle consists of a standing figure of the saint and ten scenes from his life, anticipating in many ways the frescoes of Giotto at Assisi. Another important discovery was a mosaic of the Presentation of the Christ Child in the Temple, dating probably to the seventh century and thus the only pre-iconoclastic Christian figural mosaic ever found in the city. A late Byzantine mosaic of the Theotokos Kyriotissa came to light over the main door leading to the inner narthex, and another much earlier fresco of the Kyriotissa was found in the side chapel, thus settling the much disputed dedication of the church. These works of art were taken to the Archaeological Museum, where, as we have seen, they are displayed in the gallery devoted to 'Istanbul Through the Ages'.

Excavations under and to the north of the church have revealed a whole series of earlier structures on the site. The earliest is a Roman bath of the late fourth or early fifth century, including a trilobed room, a circular chamber, and evidence of a hypocaust. This was succeeded by a Byzantine basilica of the mid-sixth century, built up against the Valens Aqueduct and utilizing the arches thereof as its north aisle. Finally, in the pre-iconoclastic period another church was built on the site, part of the sanctuary and apse subsequently being incorporated in the present building. Sections of the opus sectile pavements of these earlier buildings were found under the floor of the existing apse.

An arched passageway beside Kalenderhane Camii lead us under the Valens Aqueduct, after which we turn immediately left onto Cemal Yener Tosyalî Caddesi. After crossing Dede Efendi Caddesi we come on our right to the *medrese* of **Ekmekçizade Ahmet Pasha**, built no later than 1618. The founder was the son of an Edirne baker who rose to the rank of Vizier and Defterdar, First Lord of the Treasury. The building has been abandoned and is not open to the public.

We continue in the same direction as far as the first turning on the right, Katip Çelebi Caddesi. Just beyond the turning, on the left side of Cemal Yener Tosyalî Caddesi, we see an Ottoman **primary school** built in 1775 by **Recai Mehmet Efendi**, First Lord of the Treasury and Keeper of the Seal under Abdül Hamit I. The upper floor is built of alternate courses of brick and stone, while the entire ground floor is sheathed in an elaborately decorated marble casing. In the centre is the projecting curve of a *sebil* with three fine bronze grilles between the columns; on the left is the ornate entrance portal, and balancing this on the right is a *çeşme*. Desite the poor condition of the fabric, this remains one of the most elaborate and charming of the small Ottoman *mekteps*.

We now turn right on Katip Çelebi Caddesi. As we do so we come immediately on our left to the famous **Vefa Bozahanesi**, where we might stop for a refreshing glass of *boza*, a millet drink that was once particularly favoured by the Janissaries. A silver cup once used here by Atatürk is preserved in a glass case on the wall.

Just beyond the Vefa Bozahanesi is a little mosque originally known as Kovacîlar Mescidi and now called **Mimar Mehmet Ağa Camii**. This was built in 1514 by a certain Revani Succaq Efendi, who was Sürre Emini, or official escort of the annual embassy of the sultan to Mecca. It is a small square building with a dome, and is of no particular interest, though it has a pretty minaret. The mosque has recently been somewhat over-restored.

At the next corner the street divides, and we veer to the right on Vefa Caddesi. A short way along on the left we come to **Vefa Camii**, the mosque from which the street and the surrounding neighbourhood take their name. This is a brand new mosque erected on the site of the original Vefa Camii, founded in the late fifteenth century. All that is left from the original mosque is the *türbe* of the founder, Şeyh Muslihiddin Vefa, who died in 1491. His *türbe* is a place of pilgrimage, for he has been one of the most popular Turkish folk-saints in Istanbul for more than five centuries.

Just beyond Vefa Camii and on the same side of the street we come to the **Atîf Efendi Kütüphanesi**, the most charming and original of the Ottoman public libraries in the city.

The library, founded in 1741–42, is constructed of stone and brick in the baroque style. The building consists of two parts, one of them an apartment block for the staff and the other the library itself. The former faces the street and its upper storey projects *en cremaillere*, that is, in five zigzags supported on corbels. Three small doors lead to the lodgings, while a large gate in the middle opens into a court-yard, on the other side of which stands the library. This consists of an entrance lobby, a room for book storage, and a large reading room of astonishing shape. This oblong area, cross-vaulted like the other rooms, is bordered at one end by a series of five deep bays arranged like a fan. A triple arcade supported on two columns divides the two parts of the room; on the exterior this fan-like arrangement presents seven faces. Displayed near the entrance to the reading-room is the entire *vakfiye*, or deed of foundation, inscribed on a marble plaque.

The street just opposite the library entrance is called Tirendaz Sokagi, the Street of the Archer. At the far end of this street, on the left, we come to a handsome Byzantine church with a fluted minaret. This is known in Turkish as **Kilise Cami**, literally Church Mosque. It is no longer used as a mosque and is kept locked, but one of the local children will invariably fetch the key and let you in, the usual procedure for gaining entry to abandoned monuments in Istanbul.

This was identified by Gyllius as the **church of St Theodore**, but nothing is known of its history other than the fact that it was converted into a mosque soon after the conquest. Constructed of stone, brick and marble, its elaborate design and decoration identify it at once as belonging to the last great flowering of Byzantine architecture in the fourteenth century. In the south dome of the exonathex there were some fine mosaics which have now disappeared except for one or two faded fragments. Both the exonarthex and the narthex contain some handsome columns, capitals and door frames, which appear to be reused materials from a much earlier church, probably of the sixth century. The present church is of the four-column type.

After leaving the church we turn left and then left again at the next corner. Walking straight ahead through the next intersection, we continue along Şifahanî Sokağî. This takes us to the south side of the **Süleymaniye**, the great mosque complex of Süleyman the Magnificent, which we will visit on our next itinerary.

9

The Süleymaniye

THE **SÜLEYMANIYE** IS the second largest but by far the most impressive mosque complex in the city, exceeded in size but not in splendour by the *külliye* of Mehmet the Conqueror. It is a fitting monument to its founder, Süleyman the Magnificent, and a master-work of the greatest of Ottoman architects, the incomparable Sinan.

Sinan began building the Süleymaniye complex in 1550 and completed the mosque in 1557, but it took two more years before all the buildings of the other *külliye* were finished. The mosque stands in the centre of a vast outer courtyard enclosed by a precinct wall, with the other buildings of the *külliye* arrayed around it on the surrounding streets with as much symmetry as the nature of the site would permit. Nearly all of these pious foundations have been well restored, and some of them are again serving the people of Istanbul as they did in the days of Süleyman. We will later look at all of of those that are open to the public, but first let us visit the great mosque itself.

We approach the entrance to the mosque precincts along **Tiryaki Çarşîsî**, the **Market of the Addicts**, the street that borders the south side of the complex. It seems that in Ottoman times the teahouses along the left side of this street, set into the *medreses* there, used to serve opium to their customers in addition to tea, coffee and tobacco, and hence the name.

Halfway along Tiryaki Çarşîsî we enter the outer courtyard of the mosque. We then pass through another gateway in the southeast corner of the *avlu*, the inner courtyard.

The *avlu* is a porticoed **courtyard** of exceptional grandeur, with columns of the richest porphyry, marble and granite. The western portal of the court is flanked by a great pylon containing two stories of chambers; these, according to Evliya Çelebi, were the *muva-kithane*, the house and workshop of the mosque astronomer. The four minarets rise from the corners of the courtyard, with each of the taller ones beside the mosque having three *şerefes* each and the smaller ones two each. The four **minarets** are traditionally said to symbolize the fact that Süleyman was the fourth sultan to rule in

Istanbul, while the ten *şerefes* denote that he was the tenth sultan of the imperial house of Osman.

The great dome is flanked by semidomes to east and west, and on the north and south sides by arches whose tympanum walls are filled with windows. Internally the dome rests principally on four huge piers supported laterally by huge buttresses, which Sinan sought to make unobtrusive by a very ingenious plan. On the north and south he incorporated the buttresses into the walls of the building, allowing them to project about equally within and without. He then proceeded to mask this projection by building galleries with arcades of columns between the buttresses. On the outside the gallery is double, with twice the number of columns in its upper storey as in its lower, while on the inside there is a single gallery only. In both cases – particularly on the outside – the device is extremely successful, and is indeed one of the features that gives the exterior its interesting and beautiful distinction.

The interior of the mosque is 61 metres long and 70 metres wide, its central area surmounted by the great dome, 26.2 metres in diameter and with its crown 49.5 metres above the floor. The central area is extended along the main axis by the semidomes and exedrae at the corners, while on either side there are five domed areas flanked by the galleries. The only separation between the central area and the side aisles are the four piers and the two pairs of porphyry monoliths that support the tympanum walls in triple arcades. Two other pairs of porphyry monoliths to north and south of those between the piers support the middle domed spaces on either side, with the gallery arcades extending between them and the side buttresses.

The general effect of the interior is of a severely simple grandeur. The east wall only is enlivened by some touches of colour; here the lovely **stained-glass windows** are by the glazier known as Sarhoş (the Drunkard) Ibrahim; the tiles, used with great restraint, are the earliest examples of the new techniques of the Iznik kilns introduced in the mid-sixteenth century: leaf and flower motifs in turquoise, deep blue and red on a pure white ground. The mihrab and *mimber* in Proconessian marble are of great simplicity and distinction, as are also the woodwork, inlaid with ivory and mother-of-pearl, of the doors, window-shutters, and the *Koran kürsü*. Throughout the building the inscriptions are by the most famous of Ottoman calligraphers, Ahmet Karahisarî.

The **tombs** of **Süleyman** and his wife **Roxelana** are in the graveyard garden behind the mosque. Süleyman's *türbe*, as is fitting, is the

The Süleymaniye

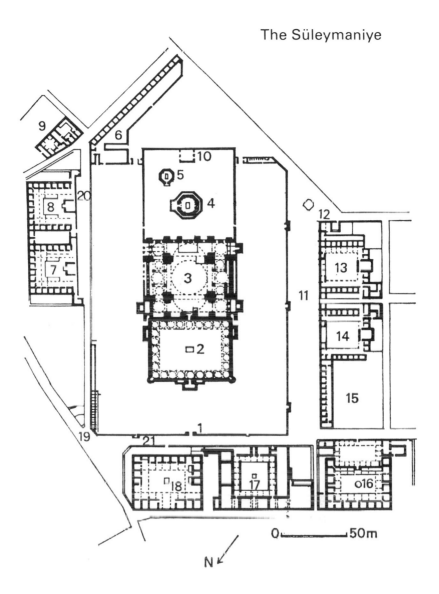

0 ————————— 50m

N

1 Entrance
2 Inner Courtyard
3 Mosque
4 Tomb of Süleyman
5 Tomb of Roxelana
6 Dar-ul-Hadis
7 Salis Medrese
8 Rabi Medrese

9 Hamam
10 Dar-ül Kura
11 Tiryaki Carsísí
12 Mektep
13 Evvel Medrese
14 Sani Medrese
15 Tip Medrese
16 Dar-üs Sifa

17 Imaret
18 Caravansarai
19 Tomb of Sinan
20 Avenue of Sinan the Architect
21 Sifahane Sokagi

largest and grandest of Sinan's mausoleums, although it is not quite as beautiful as that of his son Prince Mehmet. The *türbe* was completed in 1566, the year of Süleyman's death while on campaign in Hungary. The *türbe* is octagonal in form, surrounded by a pretty porch on columns. Like Sinan's tombs at Haghia Sophia and Şehzade Camii, **Süleyman's *türbe*** has a double dome, with the interior dome supported by columns, its inner surface still retaining its gorgeous painting in wine-red, black and gold. The walls of the interior are covered with Iznik tiles, twice as many in this small room as in all the vastness of the mosque itself. Süleyman is buried beneath the large cenotaph in the centre of the room. Next to his cenotaph is that of his daughter Mihrimah and beside them are the caskets of two later sultans, Süleyman II and Ahmet II. Despite its beauty, the *türbe* is dark and seems crowded with all the shawl-hung caskets. But there is no mistaking the majesty of Süleyman's own cenotaph, for at its head is the huge white turban that he wore as Sultan. Süleyman's reign was the longest and most illustrious in the history of the Ottoman Empire, as Evliya Çelebi writes in his encomium to the sultan whom the Turks call Kanuni, or the Law-Giver: 'During the forty-six years of his reign he subdued the world and made eighteen monarchs his tributaries. He established order and justice in his dominions, marched victoriously through the seven quarters of the globe, embellished all the countries which were vanquished with his arms, and was successful in all undertakings.'

The ***türbe* of Roxelana** stands just to the east of Süleyman's tomb. Her tomb is smaller than that of Süleyman, but its tile decoration is even finer. The cylindrical base of the dome, slightly recessed from the octagonal cornice of the building itself, is decorated with a long inscription forming a kind of sculptured frieze. The *türbe* is dated 1558, the year of Roxelana's death. She is known in Turkish as Haseki Hürrem, the Joyous Favourite. She is better known to the West as Roxelana, literally the Russian, because of her supposed origin. Süleyman fell in love with Roxelana during the early years of his reign and soon made her his legal wife, putting aside all of the other women in his harem. The Italian Bassano, a page in the Saray at the time, wrote thus of Süleyman's devotion to Roxelana: 'He bears her such love and keeps such faith in her that all his subjects marvel and say that she has bewitched him, and they call her Cadi, or the Witch.' The power of Roxelana over Süleyman grew so great that in 1553 she persuaded him to kill his eldest son, Mustafa, on the pretext that the Prince was plotting to usurp the throne. In this way

Roxelana's own son, Selim II, the Sot, succeeded to the throne after the death of Süleyman. Historians consider this to be the turning-point in the history of the Ottoman Empire, for with the alcoholic reign of Selim II began the long and almost uninterrupted decline of the Empire.

The other elements of the Süleymaniye *külliye* are arrayed around the mosque terrace and along the streets bordering the outer precinct wall. These include five **medreses** of Islamic law, one of them serving as a preparatory school for the others; a *tip medrese*, or medical college; a hospital, which included an insane asylum; an *imaret*; a caravansarai; a *dar-ül hadis*, or school of tradition; a *dar-ül kura*, or school for the various methods of reading and reciting the Koran; a *hamam*; and a street of shops.

The *dar-ül kura* is set into the middle of the eastern wall of the *türbe* garden. This school consists of a large domed area of very lovely proportions built over a small Byzantine cistern with four columns.

The far eastern end of the terrace, behind the *türbe* garden, is a large area that is triangular in shape because of the lay-out of the street below. In Süleyman's time this was known as the Iron Wrestling Ground, because of the weekly wrestling matches that were held there. This has always been an honoured sport in Islam, and the Prophet himself enjoyed wrestling with his companions. The left arm of this triangle, approaching it from the *türbe* garden, is taken up with the *dar-ül hadis*, a *medrese* of most unusual form. It consists of 22 cells arrayed in a long straight line rather than around a courtyard; opposite them is a plain wall with grilled openings enclosing a long narrow garden. At the near end of the line of cells a staircase leads up to a sort of open loggia, which appears to have served as the *dershane* in summer months.

From the outer edge of the terrace we can look down upon the street that borders the northern precinct wall. This was once an attractive *arasta*, a market street, with shops built into the retaining wall of the terrace and also opposite. These shops are still functioning, though they are now rather battered; but there is a plan to restore the *arasta* in its original form.

Just across the street we see two of the five *medreses* of the Süley-maniye *külliye*. There was a college for each of the four orthodox schools of Islamic law; they are called Evvel (First), Sani (Second), Salis (Third), and Rabi (Fourth), along with a school for preparatory students, the Mülazimler. The four colleges were laid out in two pairs, with one each on the north and south side of the outer precinct wall. The pair on the north side are **Salis** and **Rabi**, which are laid out in an ingenious manner on five different levels because of the steep slope of the ground. The north side of the courtyard is raised on high superstructures, beneath which is the Mülazimler *medrese*. These unique structures were restored in the 1970s but they are not open to the public.

At the eastern end of the market street, just below the *dar-ül hadis*, is the **hamam** of the Süleymaniye. This was restored in the early 1980s, but it too remains closed to the public.

We now retrace our steps to the eastern end of Tiryaki Çarşîsî to look at the elements of the *külliye* on that side of the complex. The polygonal structure that we see there in the middle of the street is an Ottoman water-distribution centre, or *taxim*, which is part of the *külliye*.

The first institution at the eastern end of the esplanade is the **mektep**, which served as the primary school for the children of the Süleymaniye staff. This little building, whose entrance is around the corner, has been restored and is now in use as a children's library.

The next two institutions are the **Evvel and Sani** *medreses*, whose entrance is at the far end of the narrow alley that separates them. The buildings are mirror images of one another; and although the layout is typical enough – cells around a porticoed courtyard – there are interesting variations. Thus there is no portico on the north side, but instead the three *hücres*, or cells, are open, forming a kind of loggia, while the portico on the south side is cut by the *dershane*. The two *medreses* now house the celebrated Süleymaniye iibrary, one of the most important in the city. All of the porticoes have been glassed in to accomodate the library; this has been attractively done, and the effect has been enhanced by a charming garden in each of the courtyards.

Just beyond the Sani *medrese* we come to what was originally the **tip medrese**, or **medical college**, once the foremost in the Empire. Unfortunately, all that remains of it now are the row of cells along the Tiryaki Çarşîsî, the other three sides having long since disappeared. A modern concrete structure has been built in its place, and this now serves, appropriately enough, as a maternity clinic.

Across the street from this to the west is the vast *dar-ü ifa*, or **hospital**, now a military printing-house and closed to the public. Evliya Çelebi writes of the excellence of this hospital: 'The hospital of the Süleymaniye is an establishment so excellent that the sick are

The Süleymaniye, the imperial mosque of Suleyman the Magnificent,
with the Golden Horn behind

Fatih Camii, the Mosque of the Conqueror

generally cured within three days of their admission, since it is provided with the most admirable physicians and surgeons.' Like most of the larger Ottoman hospitals, that of the Süleymaniye had a special section for the care of the insane. Foreign travellers to Istanbul were much impressed by these mental institutions and praised their number and size, charity and organization. Their mode of treatment is described by Evliya: 'They have excellent food twice a day; even pheasants, partridges and other delicate birds are supplied. There are musicians and singers who are employed to amuse the sick and insane and thus to cure their madness.'

Turning right from Tiryaki Çarşîsî on to the street that borders the west end of the precinct wall, we come next to the *imaret* of the *külliye*. It is enormous, as well it might be, for it had to supply food not only for the poor of the district but also for the several thousand people directly dependent on the Süleymaniye: the clergy of the mosque, the faculties and students of the several *medreses*, the staff and patients of the hospital, the travellers staying at the caravansarai, and the personnel of the other institutions of the *külliye*. The *imaret* now houses the Darüzziyafe Lokantasî, a good restaurant specializing in Ottoman cuisine. Its central courtyard is very charming, with its ancient plane trees and young palms and a lovely marble fountain in the centre.

The next building beyond the *imaret* is the **caravansarai**, now closed to the public. The caravansarai was also huge, including a kitchen, bakery, olive press, sleeping quarters for travellers, stables for their horses and camels, and storage rooms for their belongings. According to ancient Ottoman tradition, all accredited travellers were given free food and shelter at this and other caravansarais in the Empire. This hospitality is described by Evliya Çelebi: 'The caravansarai is a most splendid establishment where all travellers receive twice a day a bowl of rice, a dish of barley-soup and bread, every night a candle, and for each horse provender; but the gift to travellers is only for three days.'

Continuing beyond the caravansarai, we come to the west end of the market street of the *külliye*. There, opposite the northwest corner of the precinct wall, we see a domed *sebil* at the apex of a little triangular graveyard garden. Just within the angle of the apex is **Sinan's** own *türbe*, which he built during his latter years; it stands in what was the garden of the house where he lived from the time he began working on the Süleymaniye. It is an open *türbe*: an arcade with six ogive arches supports a marble roof with a tiny dome over Sinan's marble sarcophagus, surmounted by a stone tombstone in the form of the turban he wore as Chief Architect. On the south wall of the *türbe* garden there is a long inscription by Sinan's friend, the poet Mustafa Sa'i, which commemorates the architect's accomplishments. Mustafa Sa'i also wrote of Sinan in his *Tezkere-ül Ebniye*, which contains the definitive list of Sinan's buildings. Sinan was born of Christian parents in the Anatolian province of Karamania c.1497. When he was about fourteen he was inducted in the *devşirme*, the annual levy of Christian youths who were taken into the Sultan's service. As was customary, he became a Muslim and was sent to one of the palace schools in Istanbul. He was then assigned to the Janissaries and served in four of Süleyman's campaigns. Around 1538 he was appointed Chief of the Imperial Architects, and in the following year he completed his first large mosque complex in Istanbul, Haseki Hürrem Camii. During the following half century, serving as Chief Architect under Süleyman and his two immediate successors, Selim II and Murat III, Sinan was to adorn Istanbul and the other cities and towns of the Ottoman Empire with an incredible number of mosques and other buildings. The Turkish architectural historian Aptullah Koran credits Sinan with a total of 477 structures, of which 327 can be identified in Istanbul and its environs, the others scattered over the former European and Asian dominions of the Ottoman Empire. He continued working up until a few days before his death in 1588, when he was past ninety, having served as Chief of the Imperial Architects for fifty years. It is fitting that Sinan should be buried here, next to the majestic monument that he erected to crown the reign of Süleyman the Magnificent.

10

To the Summit of the Fourth Hill

OUR NEXT ITINERARY will take us from the Eminönü end of the Galata Bridge to the summit of the Fourth Hill. The first stretch of our walk will take us from the the bridge up the shore of the Golden Horn past the parking lot, where we come to the Zindan Hanî, a late Ottoman commercial building that has recently been restored.

The *han* takes its name from the quarter in which it stands, **Zindan Kapî**, the **Prison Gate**. This was one of the oldest and most picturesque quarters in Istanbul, but almost all of its buildings were destroyed in a misguided urban renewal programme in the 1980s. The prison from which the neighbourhood took its name was the ancient **tower** that still stands behind the *han*, the first stop on our itinerary.

This is one of the few surviving defense towers of the ancient **Byzantine sea-walls** along the Golden Horn. The walls have completely disappeared along the shore below the **Atatürk Bridge**, the second of the two spans across the Horn, and only this tower in Zindan Kapî remains. The tower was well restored in the 1980s, and its lower floor is open to the public. It dates from the medieval Byzantine period, probably from the ninth century, when the sea-walls were strengthened to repel the Arabs who several times besieged the city.

The tower was for centuries used as a prison, known as the **Bagno**, where many of the inmates were galley slaves.

Legend has it that one of those imprisoned here was Cafer Baba, an emissary from Harun al-Rashid to the Empress Eirene (797–802), who locked him up in the Bagno. He died and was buried there, according to the legend, which goes on to say that his remains were discovered by the Turks after the conquest, whereupon his grave became a place of pilgrimage for Muslims. The supposed tomb of Cafer Baba has been restored and is once again open as a shrine. Evliya Çelebi tells the story of Cafer Baba in his *Seyahatname*:

> Cafer Baba was buried in a place within the prison of the infidels, where to this day his name is insulted by all of the unbelieving

malefactors, debtors, murderers, etc. imprisoned there. But when (God be praised!) Istanbul was taken, the grave of Cafer Baba in the tower of the Bagno became a place of pilgrimage which is visited by those who have been released from prison and who call down blessings in opposition to the curses of the unbelievers.

A short distance beyond the tower we see the shattered remains of an arched gateway. This is all that is left of one of the portals in the ancient Byzantine sea-walls, perhaps the one that gave its name to the district of the Prison Gate. The original Byzantine name of this gate is uncertain, but in early Ottoman times the local Greeks referred to it as the Porta Caravion, the Gate of the Caravels, because of the large number of ships that were moored at the pier nearby, the ancient Scala de Drongario. This landing, known as **Yemiş Iskelesi**, or **Fruit Pier**, was the principal dock for the huge fruit and vegetable market that was located here from early Byzantine times up until the 1970s. The pier is still used by the old boats that ferry passengers across the Golden Horn at this point, a service that Petrus Gyllius says goes back to the days of the ancient Greek city of Byzantium.

A short way beyond the ruined gateway we come to an abandoned and dilapidated mosque known as **Ahi Çelebi Camii**. The mosque was founded at an uncertain date by Ahi Çelebi Ibni Kemal, Chief Physician of the hospital at the mosque of Mehmet the Conqueror, who died in 1523 while returning from a pilgrimage to Mecca. The building is of little architectural interest, aside from the fact that it was apparently restored at one point by Sinan. Its principal interest to us its association with Evliya Çelebi, who writes of it in his *Seyahatname*. One night in the month of Ramazan in 1632, on Evliya's twenty-first birthday, he fell asleep in his father's house in the nearby quarter of Unkapanî and dreamt that he was in the mosque of Ahi Çelebi. While praying there, in his dream, he was astonished to find the mosque fill up with what he described as 'a refulgent crowd of saints and martyrs', followed by the Prophet Mohammed, who led his companions in reciting the first chapter of the Koran. Evliya was brought before the Prophet, who blessed him and said that he would become a great traveller. When the prayers were concluded, Evliya went round and kissed the hands of the Prophet and his 'sainted companions', all of whom gave him their blessings, as he writes, describing the heavenly aromas they gave off.

Their hands were perfumed with musk, ambergris, spikenard, sweet-basil, violets and carnations; but that of the Prophet himself smelt of nothing but saffron and roses, felt when touched as if it

135

had no bones, and was as soft as cotton. The hands of the other prophets had the odor of quinces, that of Abu Bekr had the fragrance of lemons, Omar's smelt like ambergris, Osman's like violets, Ali's like jasmine, Hasan's like carnations, and Hüseyin's like white roses.

Evliya goes on to tell how the Prophet and his companions then left the mosque, giving him 'various greetings and blessings', after which he awoke and found himself back in his father's house, from which he left to consult an interpreter of dreams.

When I awoke I was in great doubt whether what I had seen was a dream or reality, and I enjoyed some time the beatific contemplations which filled my soul. Having afterwards performed my ablutions and offered up the morning prayer, I crossed from Constantinople to the suburb of Kasîm Pasha and consulted the interpreter of dreams, Ibrahim Efendi, about my vision. From him I received the comfortable news that I would become a great traveller, and after making my way through the world, with the intercession of the Prophet, would close my career by being admitted into Paradise. I then retired to my humble abode, applied myself to the study of history, and began a study of my birthplace, Istanbul, that envy of kings, the celestial haven and stronghold of Macedonia.

This was the dream that inspired the *Seyahatname*, or *Narrative of Travels*, an incredibly detailed and at times fabulous description of the Ottoman Empire in the mid seventeenth century, evoking for us the times in which Evliya lived, particularly in his beloved Istanbul.

We now cross the highway and begin walking up the shore of the Golden Horn, passing through what is perhaps the oldest and most colourful market quarter of the city. As we walk along the left side of the highway we pass in turn three little mosques that are among the very oldest in the city, all of them built just after the conquest, though they have since been rebuilt.

We come to the first of these of these ancient mosques about 200 metres up the highway. This one is called a mescit, a name used for smaller mosques. It is known as **Kantarcîlar Mescidi**, the **Mescit of the Scale-Merchants**, named after the guild whose members still make and sell old-fashioned scales and balances in this neighbourhod, just as they did in Evliya's time, when he describes them in the Procession of the Guilds. This mosque was founded during Mehmet the Conqueror's reign by one Sarî Demirci Mehmet Muhittin, whose first two names reveal him to be an iron-worker, probably one who made scales. It has since been reconstructed several times, and is of little interest except for its great age.

About 250 metres farther along we come to **Kazancîlar Camii**, the **Mosque of the Cauldron-Merchants**, here again named after a guild that is still active in this neighbourhood. It is also known as Üç Mihrablî Camii, the Mosque with Three Mihrabs. Founded by a certain Hoca Hayreddin Efendi in 1475, it was enlarged first by Mehmet the Conqueror himself, and then by Hayreddin's daughter-in-law, who added her own house to the mosque. Apparently an extra *mihrab* was added in each of these reconstructions, so that it came to have three *mihrabs*, hence its name.

The third mosque is about 150 metres farther along, a short distance before the Atatürk Bridge. This is called **Sağrîcîlar Camii**, the **Mosque of the Leather-Merchants**, which guild once has its shops in this neighbourhood, though no longer. The mosque is of the simplest type, a square room covered by a dome, the walls of stone. The building is of little interest architecturally, but its historical background is rather fascinating, particularly since it is probably the oldest mosque in the city. It was founded in 1455 by Yavuz Ersinan, an ancestor of Evliya who was Mehmet the Conqueror's standard-bearer during the siege of Constantinople. Yavuz Ersinan built a house beside the mosque, as well as a small graveyard in which he was buried. Evliya was born in this house in 1611, and it was there, twenty-one years later, that he had the dream that inspired him to become a traveller and to write the *Seyahatname*. Buried along with the founder in the little graveyard is his comrade-in-arms, Horoz Dede, or Grandfather Rooster. Horoz Dede received this name during the siege of Constantinople, when he made his rounds each morning and woke the troops of Mehmet the Conqueror's army with his loud rooster call. Horoz Dede was killed during the final assault and was buried here, with Mehmet the Conqueror himself among the mourners.

We now come to **Atatürk Bulvarî**, the broad highway that leads from the Atatürk Bridge up the valley between the Third and Fourth Hills. We walk up the left side of the avenue for about 300 metres, which brings us to a rather handsome baroque mosque known as **Şebsafa Kadîn Camii**.

The mosque was built in 1787 by Fatma Şebsafa Kadîn, one of the women in the harem of Abdül Hamit I. It is of brick and stone; the porch has an upper storey with a cradle-vault, and inside there is a sort of narthex, also of two storeys, covered with three small domes.

These upper storeys form a deep and attractive gallery overlooking the central area of the mosque, which is covered by a high dome resting on the walls. To the north of the mosque is a long *mektep* with a pretty cradle-vaulted roof.

We now cross Atatürk Bulvarî, whose western side is lined with enormous Roman substructures that lie beneath the houses on the ridge of the Fourth Hill above. The substructures appear to be of the late Roman period, perhaps the fifth century. One of them has recently been excavated to reveal a large subterranean cistern, which is not open to the public.

We now turn off the avenue on to Zeyrek Mehmet Pasa Sokaği, which leads up to the heights of the Fourth Hill. A short distance up the hill we find a small Ottoman primary school known as **Zenbelli Ali Baba Mektebi**, surrounded by a walled garden. The building has been restored and is now used as a children's library; it is a very pleasing example of the minor architecture of the early sixteenth century. It was built by the Şeyh-ül Islam Ali Ben Ahmet Efendi, also known as Zenbelli Ali Baba, who died in 1525. The founder is buried beneath a marble sarcophagus that stands in the *mektep* garden.

Taking the side street to the right past the entrance to the *mektep*, we soon come to the former Byzantine church complex known as **Zeyrek Camii**, whose entrance is on a picturesque square surrounded by decaying wooden houses dating back to late Ottoman times. This is the **Pantocrator**, one of the most renowned religious establishments in Byzantium, converted into a mosque after the conquest.

The Pantocrator is a composite building that originally consisted of a monastery with two churches and a chapel between them, all built between about 1120 and 1136. The monastery and the south church were built by the Empress Eirene, wife of John II Comnenus, some time before her death in 1124. Her church was dedicated to St Saviour Pantocrator, Christ the Almighty, a name that was also applied to the entire complex. After Eirene's death her husband John decided to erect another church a short distance to the north of hers, dedicated to the Virgin Eleousa, the Merciful or Charitable. When this building was completed the Emperor decided to join the two churches with a mortuary chapel, dedicated to the Archangel Michael. After the completion of the chapel Eirene was reinterred there, and when John died in 1143 he was buried beside her. John's son and successor Manuel I was buried there as well when he died in

1180. The last dynasty to rule Byzantium, the Palaeologoi, also used the mortuary chapel, with Manuel II buried there in 1425 and John VIII in 1449.

The monastery of the Pantocrator was one of the most renowned in Byzantium. It was a very extensive foundation, including a hospice for old men, an insane asylum, and a famous hospital. All of these have since disappeared, doubtless the source of the widespread ruins and substructures in the neighbourhood of the church.

During the period of Latin rule in Constantinople, 1204–61, the Pantocrator was taken over by the Roman Catholic clergy of the Venetians. Immediately after the recapture of the city by the Byzantines, on 25 July 1261, their Genoese allies crossed over from Galata and stormed the Pantocrator, where some of the Venetians were still holding out, and in the fighting the monastery was burned down. The monastery was soon afterwards rebuilt, and during the last two centuries of the Byzantine period it regained its status as one of the most important religious centres in the city. The most famous resident of the monastery in its latter years was George Scholarius, better known as Gennadius. Gennadius accompanied John VIII Palaeologus to the Council of Ferrara–Florence in 1438, when the Emperor agreed to a union between the Greek and Latin churches in a vain effort to obtain help from the West in fighting the Turks. Gennadius bitterly opposed the union, and when he returned to Constantinople he denounced the Emperor for having given in to Rome, and the great majority of the populace joined him in a boycott of the Greek Orthodox church. Shortly after the Turkish conquest Mehmet the Conqueror appointed Gennadius as Patriarch of Constantinople, which under Ottoman rule made him head of all members of the Greek Orthodox Church in the empire. Subsequently the Pantocrator was converted into a mosque by a cleric known as Zeyrek Molla Mehmet Efendi, from whom it takes its Turkish name of Zeyrek Camii.

In plan, the **south church** erected by the Empress Eirene is of the four-column type, with a central dome, a triple apse, and a narthex with a gallery overlooking the nave. (The columns have as usual been removed in Ottoman times and replaced by piers.) This church preserves a good deal of its original decoration, including the marble pavement, the handsome door frames of the narthex, and the almost complete marble revetment of the apse. A study of the church by the Byzantine Institute unearthed part of the magnificent opus sectile floor of the church, arranged in great squares and circles of coloured marbles with figures in the borders. Notice also the curious Turkish *mimber* made from fragments of Byzantine sculpture, including the canopy of a ciborium. The investigations of the Byzantine Institute in addition discovered fragments of stained glass from the east window.

The **north church** is somewhat smaller but of essentially the same type and plan as the south church, where here again the columns have been replaced by piers. Unfortunately, it has retained none of its original decoration. The **mortuary chapel** between the north and south churches is a structure without aisles and with but one apse, covered by two domes. It is highly irregular in form because it has to fit between the two churches, which are not of exactly the same size. Parts of the walls of the churches were demolishd so that all three sections opened widely into one another. John also added an outer narthex which must once have extended in front of all three churches, but which now ends awkwardly in front of the mortuary chapel.

A program of restoration and study of the Pantocrator has now been begun by Professor Robert Ousterhout of the University of Illinois and Professors Metin and Zeynep Ahunbey of Istanbul Technical University. The roof and domes have now been restored, while a start has been made on restoration of the interior and an archaeological study of its structure.

Behind the Pantocrator an old Ottoman structure has been restored as a restaurant-café called the **Zeyrekhane**, a good place to have lunch before continuing on this itinerary.

An old wooden house that stood in the square outside the church has now been demolished and replaced by a new structure, which serves as the local cultural centre. Visitors are welcome to visit the centre, which has beneath it a spring that supplies a copious supply of water through an old Ottoman fountain.

We now take the street that leads off from the far left corner of the square, following it to the first intersection. Turning left there, we come almost immmediately on our left to a small tower-like building known locally as **Şeyh Süleyman Mescidi**. This is a Byzantine structure that may once have been part of the Pantocrator complex, perhaps a funerary chapel or a library. The lower part of the exterior is square and its upper part octagonal; within it is altogether octagonal, with shallow niches in the cross axes, with a crypt beneath. This strange building, which now serves as a Koran school, has never been seriously studied.

Returning to the last intersection and crossing it, we continue in the same direction along Hacî Hasan Sokağî. We turn left at the next corner and come on our left to the courtyard entrance of a small mosque, **Hacî Hasan Mescidi**, with a quaint and pretty minaret. The minaret has a stone base at the top of which there is a curious rope-like moulding. The shaft is of brick and stone arranged to form a criss-cross or chequerboard design, unique in Istanbul. The *şerefe* has an elaborate stalactite corbel and a fine balustrade, though it seems a bit too big in scale for the minaret. The mosque itself is rectangular, built of squared stone and with a wooden roof; in its present condition it is without interest. The founder was the Kazasker (Judge) Hacî Hasanzade Mehmet Efendi, who died in 1505, so the mosque must belong to about this date.

Continuing past the mosque, we turn right at the next corner, whereupon we see a beautiful Byzantine church at the end of the street. This is the **church of St Saviour Pantepoptes**, known in Turkish as **Eski Imaret Camii**.

The church was founded around 1085–90 by the Empress Anna Dalassena, mother of Alexius I Comnenus. Anna ruled as co-empeor with her son for nearly twenty years, and during that time she exerted a powerful influence on the Byzantine state. The Empress retired in 1100 to the convent of the Pantepoptes and spent her last years there in seclusion as a nun. When she died in 1005 she was buried in the convent. The church was converted into a mosque soon after the conquest, and for a time it served as an *imaret* for the mosque of Mehmet the Conqueror, from which it takes its name of Eski (Old) Imaret Camii.

The Pantepoptes is closely hemmed in on three sides by houses, which obscure much of its form. Nevertheless, what we can see of the exterior is very charming and characteristic of an eleventh-century Byzantine church, with its twelve-sided dome and its decorative brickwork in the form of blind niches and bands of Greek-key and swastika motifs and rose-like medallions.

On entering, we can see that it is a quite perfect example of a church of the four-column type, with three apses and an outer and inner narthex, many of the doors of which retain their magnificent frames of red marble. Over the inner narthex is a gallery which opens into the nave by a charming triple arcade on two rose-coloured marble columns. The church itself has retained most of its original characteristics, though the four columns have as usual been replaced by piers, and the windows of the central apse have been altered. The side apses, however, preserve their windows and their beautiful marble cornice. The dome too has retained its original form, resting on a cornice with a meander pattern of palmettes and flowers, with twelve windows between which twelve ribs taper up towards the crown.

We now retrace our steps to Şeyh Süleyman Mescidi, turning left there and then right at the next corner. This brings us to Itfaiye Caddesi, where a short way along on the left we come to an old Turkish bath of considerable interest.

This is **Çinili Hamam**, the **Tiled Bath**, an early work of Sinan; it was built in about 1545 for Hayrettin Pasha, Süleyman's great pirate-admiral, better known in the West as Barbarossa. It is a double bath, the men's and women's sections lying side by side and the two entrances, rather unusually, being in the same façade, with almost identical plans. In the centre of the great *camekan* is an elaborate and beautiful marble fountain with goldfish swimming in it. The narrow *soğukluk*, with two little semidomes at each end, leads to the cruciform *hararet*, where the open arms of the cross are covered with tiny domes, the rooms in the corners each having a large cupola. Here and there on the walls are small panels of faience, and the floor is of opus sectile. In the *camekan* fragments of a more elaborate wall revetment of tiles of a later period may be seen. Early in the Turkish Republic this fine *hamam* was abandoned and in ruins, but in the late 1960s it was restored and is once again in use.

Beyond the *hamam*, Itfaiye Caddesi widens and becomes quite picturesque, with a double row of plane tres shading the open stalls of a colourful street-market, most of whose shopkeepers are Kurds from eastern Anatolia. We follow this avenue for a few blocks and then turn left just before the aqueduct, taking the street which runs parallel to the great Roman arches.

Just before we come to the intersection with Atatürk Bulvarî, we come on our right to the entrance of a small classical *külliye* built up against the aqueduct. This formerly housed the Municipality Museum, but it now serves as the **Caricature Museum**, with changing exhibitions of works by Turkish artists.

The *külliye* was founded in 1599 by **Gazanfer Ağa**, who, as we have learned, succeeded his brother Cafer Ağa as Chief White Eunuch of Topkapî Sarayî in 1557. It includes a small *medrese*, the *türbe* of the founder, and a charming *sebil* with handsome grilled windows. The complex was restored in 1945, at which time the cells of the *medrese* had doors cut between them to serve as exhibition areas for the Municipality Museum.

To the Summit of the Fourth Hill

After leaving the museum we walk a few steps to Atatürk Bulvarî, where we now pass under the aqueduct, one of the most prominent landmarks of the old city as seen from the Golden Horn.

The **aqueduct** is thought to have been built c.375 by the Emperor **Valens** (364–78), although it has been suggested that originally it may have been constructed by the Emperor Hadrian c.125. The water that it conducted, tapped from various streams and lakes outside the city, appears to have entered through subterranean pipes near the Edirne Gate and to have passed underground along the ridges of the Sixth, Fifth and Fourth Hills to a point near the present site of the mosque of Mehmet the Conqueror. From there the water was carried by the aqueduct across the deep valley that divides the Fourth and Third Hills. On the Third Hill, near the present site of Beyazit Square, the water was received in a huge cistern, the *nymphaeum maximum*, from which it was distributed to various parts of the city. The length of the aqueduct was originally about a kilometre, of which about 900 metres remain, and its maximum height, where it crosses Atatürk Bulvari, is about 20 metres. The aqueduct was damaged at various times but was kept in good repair by both the Byzantine emperors and the Ottoman sultans. The aqueduct fell into disuse in the late Ottoman period and began to deteriorate, but in the early 1990s its surviving structure was restored. The long line of the double arches marching across the valley betwen the Third and Fourth Hills has a grand and Roman look, and is almost as essential a characteristic of the city's skyline as the great procession of imperial mosques that crowns the ridge along the Golden Horn.

After passing through the aqueduct we reach the summit of the Fourth Hill, the goal of this itinerary.

11

Around the Fourth Hill

OUR PRESENT ITINERARY will take us around the Fourth Hill. After seeing the monuments there, on our next itinerary we will go on in turn to the Fifth and Sixth Hills, walking along the ridge that parallels the Golden Horn to the south.

Having passed through the Valens aqueduct on the last itinerary, we now walk to the northern side of the park just beyond it to Itfaiye Caddesi. There we come to the **Itfaiye Müzesi**, or **Fire Brigade Museum**, which is in an old firehouse. The most interesting exhibits in the museum are figures representing the *tulumbacî*, the men of the fire brigades in ninetenth-century Istanbul, who raced barefoot through the streets of the city in response to the cry of 'Yangin var!' ('There's a fire!'), carrying their little fire-engine and their fire-fighting gear.

We now come to the intersection of Atatürk Bulvarî and Şehzade-basî Caddesi. This major intersection is still known by its old Ottoman name of **Saraçhane**, or Saddlery, since those who made and sold saddles once had their shops here. This is approximately the site of the ancient **Forum Amastrianum**, where public executions were held in Byzantine times. The main thoroughfare of Byzantine Constantinople, the **Mese**, divided into two branches at this point, one of which followed the present course of Şehzadebasî Caddesi, while the other went along the same route as Atatürk Bulvarî to the **Forum Bovis**, the present Aksaray, the intersection beyond the underpass.

Here we take the underpass that leads to the northeast corner of the intersection, from where we walk to the pretty little mosque that stands just to the west of the Şehzade Camii complex.

This is known as **Burmalî Minare Camii**, the Mosque with the Spiral Minaret. The mosque was built c.1550 by the Kadî (Judge) of Egypt, Emin Nurettin Osman Efendi. Although of the very simplest kind – a square room with a flat wooden ceiling – the mosque has several peculiarities that give it a cachet of its own. Most noticeable is the brick minaret with spiral ribs, from which the mosque gets its name; this is unique in Istanbul and is a late survival of an earlier

Anatolian tradition. Another distinctive feature of the mosque is its pitched porch, which is supported by four columns with Byzantine Corinthian capitals. Finally, the entrance portal is not in the middle but on the right-hand side. This is usual in mosques whose porches are supported by three columns only – so as to prevent the door being blocked by the central column, but here there is no apparent reason for it. The interior has no special features.

We now cross over to the southeast corner of the intersection. The huge building that dominates this side of the avenue opposite Şchzade Camii is the **Belediye**, or **Municipality**, the headquarters of the civil government of Istanbul.

Behind the Belediye is the little *medrese* of the Şeyh-ül Islam **Ankaravî Mehmet Efendi**, founded in 1707. It is a small and attractively irregular building, chiefly of red brick, with a long, narrow courtyard, at the far end of which a flight of steps leds to the lecture hall. The *medrese* was restored in the 1960s and now houses part of the Economics Faculty of Istanbul University.

We now cross to the southwest corner of the Suraçhane intersection, where in the park on the left side of the avenue we see a standing marble column and some other ancient architectural members. These and the extensive remains to the rear of the park were unearthed when the Saraçhane underpass to Aksaray was constructed in the 1960s. An archaeological excavation was conducted by Dumbarton Oaks under the direction of Martin Harrison, who identified the church and reconstructed its architectural plan.

The **church** was dedicated to **St Polyeuktos**, it was built in the years 524–27 by the Princess Anicia Juliana, a granddaughter of Valentinian III (425–55), Emperor of the West. St Polyeuktos was an enormous edifice, some 52 by 58 metres (compare the Süleymaniye, which is about 52 metres square), preceded by an atrium. The church was essentially basilical in form, divided into a nave and side aisles by an arrangement of piers and columns. The excavations uncovered fragments of columns, capitals, an elaborately carved entablature, and parts of a long and beautifully carved inscription by which the church was identified. The church was destroyed and looted by the Latins during their sack of the city in 1204, and it was never rebuilt. The so-called Pilastri Acritani on the south side of San Marco were taken from St Polyeuktos, as evidenced by fragments that were found on the site.

We now head westward along the south side of the avenue, which here takes the name Macar Kardesler Caddesi. On the next block we come to the handsome *külliye* of **Amcazade Hüseyin Pasha**, another foundation of the illustrious Köprülü family. Hüseyin Pasha was a cousin (in Turkish, *amcazade*) of Fazîl Ahmet Pasha, and was the fourth member of the family to become Grand Vezier, serving from 1697–1703 under Mustafa II.

An inscription over the entryway to the *külliye* records its foundation date as 1698. The principal element of the *külliye* is the *medrese*, whose separate octagonal *dershane* served also as a *mescit*; besides these the complex includes a library, a large primary school over a row of shops, two little graveyards with open *türbes*, a *şadîrvan*, a *sebil*, and a *çeşme*, all arranged with almost romantic disorder.

We now continue down the avenue and then turn left on Kîz Taşî Sokağî, the Street of the Maiden's Column. The name stems from the Roman commemorative **column** that stands in the centre of the little square at the end of the street, a monument known in Turkish as **Kîz Taşî**. The base of the monument is formed by a pedestal of Corinthian marble on three steps. Above this stands a granite column ten metres high, surmounted by a battered Corinthian capital and a plinth with eagles at the corners; this once supported a seated statue of the **Emperor Marcian**. Fragments of sculpture remain on the base, including the figure in high relief of a Nike, or Winged Victory, which is what led the Turks to call this the Maiden's Column. There is also on the base an elegiac couplet in Latin recording that the column was erected by the Prefect Tatianus in honour of the Emperor Marcian.

We now return to the main avenue, whose name soon changes to Fevzi Paşa Caddesi. This soon brings us on the left to a *medrese* founded in 1700 by the Şeyh-ül Islam **Feyzullah Efendi**, a distinguished scholar and one of the most enlightened men of his day. His *medrese* now serves as the **Millet Kütüphanesi**, or **People's Library**. The cells of the *medrese* surround two sides of the courtyard, in which a *şadîrvan* stands in the midst of a pretty garden. The street side of the courtyard is wholly occupied by a most elaborate and original *dershane* building: a flight of steps leads up to a porch covered by nine domes of very different patterns, the arches of which are supported on four columns. To the right of the porch are the large domed lecture-rooms, now used as library reading-rooms.

We now continue down the avenue to the next intersection, passing on our right behind four of the massive *medreses* of the enormous mosque complex of Mehmet the Conqueror, known to the Turks as Fatih Camii. At the intersection just beyond the *medreses* we turn right, crossing the avenue and continuing straight ahead on Islambol Caddesi, which borders the west side of the **Fatih Camii complex**. We then turn right again to enter the vast outer courtyard of the complex, with the mosque and its *avlu* and *türbe* garden in the middle, flanked to north and south by the *medreses* and other buildings of the *külliye*.

The huge mosque complex founded by Mehmet the Conqueror was the most extensive and elaborate *külliye* ever built in the Ottoman Empire. An inscription records that the complex was built during the years 1463–70 and that the architect was Atik Sinan, who is believed to have been a Greek. Besides the great mosque itself, the *külliye* consisted of eight *medreses* and their annexes, along with a hospice, *imaret*, hospital, caravansarai, primary school, *hamam*, and two *türbes*. The complex was laid out over a vast, almost square area, about 325 metres on a side, with almost rigid symmetry. It occupies approximately the site of the famous Church of the Holy Apostles and its attendant buildings. This church and its imperial mausoleum, already in ruins at the time of the conquest, were used as sources of building materials for the construction of Fatih Camii.

The original mosque built by Mehmet the Conqueror was completely destroyed by an earthquake on 22 May 1766. Mustafa III immediately undertook its reconstruction, and the present mosque, designed on a completely different plan in the baroque style, was completed in 1771. What remains of Mehmet the Conqueror's original mosque complex is, most probably, the *avlu*, the main entrance portal of the mosque, the *mihrab*, the minarets up to the first *şerefe*, the south wall of the graveyard and the adjoining gate in the east precinct wall. All of the other buildings in the *külliye* were badly damaged in the earthquake but restored by Mustafa III, presumably in their original form. The surviving buildings include the eight great *medreses*, which stand on the north and south sides of the mosque precincts; these have been restored, along with the *tabhane*, or hospice, and they now serve as student dormitories. Only two fragments remain of the *imaret*, and the caravansarai has disappeared entirely.

Part of the west wall of the precinct has been demolished, together with the small library and *mektep* that once stood just outside it. We enter the precincts through **Boyacî Kapîsî**, the **Gate of the Painter**. We then approach the *avlu*, the **courtyard** of the mosque itself; this, with its monumental portal, is original. In the lunettes of the six western windows are some of most remarkable inscriptions in the city: the first *Surah* of the Koran written in white marble letters on a ground of verd-antique. The effect is extremely lovely. The dignified but simple portal has rather curious engaged columns at the corners. The convex flutes or ribs of their shafts become interlaced at top and bottom to form an intertwined serpentine pattern, while the columns end in a sort of hourglass-shaped capital and vase.

In the centre of the picturesque courtyard stands the *adîrvan*, with a gay witch's cap conical roof resting on eight marble columns and surrounded by tall cypress trees. In essentials it is original, even to the cypresses, which are constantly mentioned by travellers, though doubtless replanted from time to time. The antique marble columns of the portico have stalactite capitals of fine, bold workmanship. At either end of the mosque porch are two more exquisite lunette inscriptions, this time in faience, showing a vivid yellow combined with blue, green and white in the *cuerda seca* technique typical of this early period. The west façade of the mosque itself belongs for the most part to the reconstruction after the earthquake of 1766, except for the entrance portal. On the exterior this portal has the same engaged columns as the gate to the courtyard, and is surmounted by a stalactite canopy enclosed in a series of projecting frames which give depth and emphasis. The historical inscriptions are written in bold calligraphy on the sides and over the door. But the interior side of the portal is even more remarkable; its canopy is a finely carved scallop shell supported on a double cornice of stalactites. However, it is sadly masked by a later baroque balcony built in front of it.

The present **mosque** is a copy of the type in which the central dome is flanked by four semidomes on the axes, a plan invented by Sinan for Şehzade Camii and used again for Ahmet I Camii and Yeni Cami. Here the exterior lines are still reasonably classical and pleasing, but the interior is at once weak and heavy. The lower part of the walls is sheathed in common white tiles of such inferior quality that they have become covered with damp. The *mihrab*, which is from the original building, resembles in style the entrance portal, though the gilt-framed panels in the lower part are probably a baroque addition. Certainly baroque but equally handsome is the *mimber*, an elaborate structure of polychrome marble.

The **tombs** of **Mehmet the Conqueror** and his wife **Gülbahar**, mother of Beyazit II, stand in the graveyard garden behind the mosque. Both of these structures were completely rebuilt after the earthquake, though on their original foundations. Mehmet the Conqueror's *türbe* is very baroque and its interior extremely sumptuous in the *Empire* style. His tomb has been a popular religious shrine for more than five centuries, and there are always people praying inside the *türbe*.

The *türbe* of Gülbahar is simple and classical and must resemble the original quite closely. An old and persistent legend, quite definitly apocryphal, has it that Gülbahar was a daughter of the King of France, sent by him as a bride for the Emperor Constantine XI Dragases but captured by the Turks when they were besieging the city in 1453. The legend goes on to say that Gülbahar, although she was the wife of Mehmet the Conqueror and the mother of Beyazit II, never embraced Islam and died a Christian. Evliya Çelebi recounts a version of this legend and has this to say of Gülbahar's *türbe*: 'I myself have often observed at morning prayer. that the readers appointed to chant lessons from the Koran all turned their backs upon the coffin of this lady, of whom it was so doubtful whether she departed in the faith of Islam. I have often seen Franks [Europeans] come by stealth and give a few aspers to the tomb-keeper to open her *türbe* for them, as its gate is always kept locked.' The story is also repeated by the Italian traveller Cornelio Magni, who was led by the tomb-keeper to believe that Gülbahar was a Christian princess who never became a Muslim. 'The türbe,' he says, 'remains always shut, even the windows. I asked the reason for this and was told: "The sepulcher of her whose soul lives among the shades deserves not a ray of light!" ' After much entreaty and the intervention of an Emir who passed by, the tombkeeper let him in. 'I entered,' he says, 'with veneration and awe . . . and silently recited a *De profundis* for the soul of this unfortunate maiden.'

The little library in the south corner of the graveyard was built by Mahmut I and dates from 1742.

The eight great **medreses** flank the mosque precincts to north and south; they are severely symmetrical and almost identical in plan. Each contains 19 cells for students and a *dershane*. The entrance to the *dershane* is from the side, and beside each entrance is a tiny garden planted with trees, an effect as rare as it is pretty. Beside each *medrese* there was originally an annexe about half as large; these have disappeared but their plan can be reconstructed, rooms opening on porticoes round three sides of a terrace. All in all there must have been about 256 *hücres*, or student rooms. Thus the establishment must have provided for over a thousand students, a university on a big scale. These fine buildings have been restored and are once again used as residences by students.

The southeast gate of the precinct, called **Çorba Kapîsî**, or the **Soup Gate**, from the proximity of the *imaret*, is part of the original structure. Notice the elaborate and most unusual designs in porphyry and verd antique set into the stonework of the canopy as well as the '*panache*' at the top in verd antique. Through this gate we approach what is perhaps the finest building of the *külliye*, the restored *tabhane*, or hospice for travelling dervishes. It has a very beautiful courtyard and is in general an astonishing, indeed unique, building. The twenty domes of the courtyard are supported on sixteen exceptionally beautiful antique columns of verd antique and Syenitic marble, doubtless from the Church of the Holy Apostles. At the east end a large square room (which has unfortunately lost its dome) originally served as a zaviye, or room for the dervish ceremonies. On each side of this are two spacious domed rooms opening onto two open eyvans. These are very interesting: each has two domes supported on a rectangular pillar that one would swear at first sight to be baroque. Closer examination, however, shows the same engaged ribbed columns ending in intertwined designs and an hourglass capital and base that we found on the entrance portals of the mosque itself.

The great vacant lot to the south was the site of the caravansarai, to the east, and the imaret, to the west. Two fragments of the latter remain in the southwest corner. Another building of the *külliye* which has disappeared is the *dar-üş-şifa*, or hospital. This was placed symmetrically with the *tabhane* on the north side of the graveyard.

Outside Mehmet the Conqueror's *tabhane* is the *türbe* complex built in 1817–18 for **Nakşidil Valide Sultan**, wife of Abdül Hamit I and mother of Mahmut II. The legend goes that this lady was Aimée Dubuc de Rivéry, cousin of the Empress Josephine, captured by Algerian pirates and presented to the Sultan by the Bey of Algiers. A romantic tale has been made of this story by Leslie Blanch in *The Wilder Shores of Love*; unfortunately, there seems to be little or no foundation for the legend.

The *külliye* consists of Nakşidil's enormous *türbe*, a *sebil*, and a *mektep*. Her *türbe* is a pretty building in the baroque *Empire* style, forming a pleasant contrast with the austerity of the classical structures of Mehmet the Conqueror's *külliye*. At the corner stands the enormous *türbe*, which has fourteen sides; of its two rows of windows the upper one are oval, a unique and pretty feature. The fourteen faces are divided from one another by overly slender columns which bear, on top of their capitals at the first cornice level, tall flame-like acanthus leaves carved almost in the round, giving a fine bravura effect. The wall stretching along the street opposite the *tabhane* contains a gate and a grand *sebil* in the same flamboyant style as the *türbe*. The gate leads into an attractive courtyard from which one enters the *türbe*, whose interior decoration is rather elegant and restrained. Diagonally opposite at the far end of the court is another *türbe*, round and severely plain. In this *türbe* are interred Gülüştü Valide Sultan, mother of Mehmet VI Vahidettin, the last Sultan of the Ottoman Empire, together with other members of the family of Sultan Abdül Mecit.

We leave the Mehmet the Conqueror Camii complex at its eastern end and turn right on Aslanhane Sokağı, the Street of the Lion House, whose name indicates that Mehmet the Conqueror must have had a menagerie here. This brings us back to Fevzi Paşa Caddesi, which we cross and continue straight ahead on the side street that passes the west side of the *medrese* of Feyzullah Efendi.

Proceeding downhill, we take the second turning on the right, and then one block along on our left we come upon an ancient mosque known as **Iskender Pasha Camii**. The mosque is dated 1505, but the identity of the founder is not certain, but it is thought that he was one of the viziers of Beyazit II who was governor of Bosnia. It is a simple dignified building with a blind dome on pendentives resting on the walls; the three small domes of the porch are supported on ancient columns with rather worn Byzantine capitals. The *şerefe* of the minaret has an elaborately stalactited corbel; the curious decoration on top of the minaret probably belongs to an eighteenth-century restoration.

At the next corner we turn left on Halıcılar Caddesi, which we follow downhill until it comes to the wide Adnan Menderes Caddesi, formerly known as Vatan Caddesi. Here on the left we come to a large Byzantine church now serving as a mosque known as **Fenari Isa Camii**.

The church, which was part of the **Monastery of Constantine Lips**, was studied and restored by archaeologists of the Byzantine Institute. Their findings have clarified the architectural history of this complicated building, parts of which were constructed at various dates. It actually consists of two churches, along with a double narthex and a side chapel; its original structure was altered in

Ottoman times, when it was converted into a mosque. The first church on the site, the one to the north, was built along with a monastery in 907 by Constantine Lips, a high official in the reigns of Leo VI and Constantine VII Porphyrogenitus. This church and monastery were dedicated to the Theotokos Panachrantos, the Immaculate Mother of God. The establishment apparently fell into disuse during the Latin Occupation of 1204–61, for soon after the recapture of the city by the Byzantines the monastery was refounded by the Empress Theodora, wife of Michael VIII Palaeologus. At the same time Theodora added another church to the south dedicated to St John the Baptist. She also build an outer narthex for both churches as well as a funerary chapel to the south of the church of St John.

Several members of the Palaeologus dynasty were interred in the funerary chapel, beginning with the Empress Theodora herself in 1304. Other members of the family buried here include Theodora's sons, the Emperor Andronicus II and Prince Constantine; the Princess Irene of Brunswick, first wife of Andronicus III (1328–41); and the Princess Anna, first wife of John VIII. Neither Irene nor Anna lived to become Empress of Byzantium, for they died before their husbands came to the throne. A contemporary chronicle tells of how Anna was buried in the church in the dead of night, at a time when the city was stricken by the Black Death.

The church was converted into a mosque in 1496, and at that time the monastery was given over to a community of dervishes. The first head of this dervish *tekke* was called Isa, the Muslim name for Jesus, and thenceforth the establishment came to be called Fenari Isa Camii, the Mosque of the Lamp of Jesus.

The original **north church** built by Constantine Lips was of the four-column type (the columns were replaced by arches in Ottoman times), but quite unusually it had five apses, the extra ones to north and south projecting beyond the rest of the building. The northern apse has been demolished while the southern one is incorporated into the south church. Another unusual, perhaps unique, feature of the north church is that there are four little chapels on the roof, grouped around the dome.

The **south church** erected by the Empress Theodora was of the ambulatory type; that is, its nave was divided from the aisles by a triple arcade to north, west and south, with each arcade supported by two columns. (All this was removed in Ottoman times, but the bases of some of the columns still remain, and you can see the narrow arches of the arcade above, embedded in the Turkish masonry.) Of its three apses the northern one was the southern supernumerary apse of the older church. Thus there were in all seven apses, six of which still remain and make the eastern facade of the building exceedingly attractive. On the interior walls a certain amount of good sculptured decoration survives in cornices and window frames, particularly in the north church.

We now cross Menderes Caddesi and turn right to walk westward along the avenue. A short way long we come on our left to a classical *medrese*. This was built by Sinan in 1562–63 for Süleyman the Magnificent, who dedicated to the memory of his father, **Selim I**. The twenty cells of the *medrese* occupy three sides of the courtyard, on the fourth side stands the large and handsome lecture-hall, which was at some point turned into a mosque. The original entrance, through a small domed porch, is behind the *dershane* and at an odd angle to it; the wall that encloses this whole side is irregular in a way that is hard to explain. Nevertheless, the building is very attractive, and once inside you do not notice its curious asymmetry.

Just west of this *medrese* across a side street there is a small *külliye* consisting of a *mektep* and a *türbe* in a walled garden. The entrance to the garden is through a gate in the north wall; on the left is the octagonal *türbe*, that of **Şah Huban Kadîn**, a daughter of Selim I, who died in 1572. While there is nothing remarkable about the *türbe*, the **mektep** is a grand one. It is double, that is, it consists of two spacious square rooms, each covered by a dome and containing an elegant *ocak*, or fireplace. The wooden roof and column of the porch are part of a modern restoration. Both the *mektep* and the *türbe* are works of Sinan, and they are dated to the year of Şah Huban's death. The *mektep* now serves as an out-patient clinic for mental illnesses.

Recrossing Menderes Caddesi, we continue straight ahead on Akdeniz Caddesi and walk uphill as far as the fourth turning on the left, Hüsrev Paşa Sokağı. One block down this street, on the far corner to the left, we come to a handsome and elaborate *türbe*. This is the **tomb of Hüsrev Pasha**, built by Sinan and dated by an inscription to 1545–46.

Hüsrev Pasha was a grandson of Beyazit II and had been one of the leading generals in Süleyman's great victory at Mohacs in 1526, when the fate of Hungary was decided in less than two hours. After that victory Hüsrev Pasha governed Bosnia for a decade with great pomp and luxury, but also with severe justice. Later he became governor of Syria, and in 1536–37 he commissioned Sinan to build a mosque for him in Aleppo; this is the earliest dated building by the great architect and is still in existence. While governor of Rumelia in 1544 Hüsrev fell into disgrace through his complicity in a plot against the Grand Vizier Süleyman Pasha. Despairing because of his fall from power, he took his own life soon afterwards by literally starving himself to death, one of the very rare incidents of suicide among the Ottomans.

The *türbe* of Hüsrev Pasha is octagonal in form. The eight faces are separated from one another by slender columns that run up to the first cornice, which is elaborately carved with stalactites; the dome is set back a short distance and has a cornice of its own, also carved.

We now turn north on the side street that leads uphill past the *türbe*, and in the middle of the second block we come on our right to **Bali Pasha Camii**. An inscription over the portal records that the mosque was founded in 1504 by Huma Hatun, daughter of Beyazit II, who had died in 1495. The mosque appears in the *Tezkere*, the listing of Sinan's works. But the early date of the founding suggests that Sinan must have built Bali Pasha Camii some time later, though whether on its old plan or a new one it is impossible to say.

The plan of Bali Pasha Camii is simple and to a certain extent resembles Iskender Pasha Camii, visited earlier on this itinerary. The chief difference between the two mosques is that in Bali Pasha Camii the dome arches to north, west and south are very deep, almost barrel vaults; thus room is left, on north and south, for shallow bays with galleries above.

We now turn left at the next corner, and then, after three blocks, we turn right on Akşemsettin Caddesi. We cross the street at the first turning on the left, which brings us to **Mesih Pasha Camii**.

An inscription dates the mosque to 1485, but the name of the architect is not given; it is popularly attributed to Sinan, though without any evidence. The founder was the eunuch Mesih Mehmet Pasha, infamous for his cruelty as Governor of Egypt, who became Grand Vizier for a short time at the age of ninety in the reign of Murat III.

The courtyard of the mosque is attractive but rather sombre. It consists of the usual domed porticoes under which, rather unusually, are the ablution fountains; this is because the usual place of the *şadîrvan* in the centre of the courtyard has been taken up by the picturesque open *türbe* of the founder.

The mosque is preceded by a double porch, but the wooden roof of the outer porch has disappeared, leaving nothing for the arcades to support; the inner porch had the usual five bays. In plan the building is an octagon inscribed in a square with semidomes as squinches in the diagonals; to north and south are galleries. But the odd feature is that whereas in most mosques of this form aisles are under the galleries, here they are turned into porches. That is, where one would expect an arcade of columns, one finds a wall with windows opening onto an exterior gallery which, in turn, opens to the outside by enormous arches, now glazed in. The *mihrab* and *mimber* are very fine works in marble, as are the galleries above the windows. Tiles of the best period complete the decoration of this interesting building.

One block farther along Akşemsettin Caddesi brings us to Fevzi Paşa Caddesi, where we continue straight ahead on Yavuz Selim Caddesi. This avenue takes us through the lively quarter known as **Çarşamba**, or **Wednesday**, named for the street-market that throngs the neighbourhood on that day. Here we have completed our stroll around the Fourth Hill, as we head toward the summit of the Fifth Hill.

12

The Fifth and Sixth Hills

OUR NEXT ITINERARY will take us around the **Fifth and Sixth Hills**, which rise from the western end of the ridge that parallels the Golden Horn. We begin where we left off on the last itinerary, walking along Yavuz Selim Caddesi toward the summit of the Fifth Hill. (Yavuz, or the Grim, is a nickname given to Selim I, who was known for his merciless ferocity, which led him, among other things, to behead his Grand Viziers at the rate of one a year.)

Ahead and somewhat to the left we see the imperial mosque of Selim I. **Selim I Camii** stands at the northern end of an enormous open cistern that takes up the entire block along which we approach the mosque. This is the **Cistern of Aspar**, named for the Gothic general in the service of the Empire who built it in 459, twelve years before he was put to death by Leo I (457–74). It is the second largest of the three great Roman reservoirs that survive in the city. The reservoir is square in plan, 152 metres on a side, and was originally ten metres deep. During the latter Byzantine period the reservoir was allowed to go dry and within it there developed a small village, which was still in existence up until the 1970s, when it was demolished to make way for a playground and sports complex.

We now pause at the side street to the right leading off from the southeast corner of the reservoir. Here we find a late Roman basement that is now being used as a workshop. The brick ceiling of the basement is supported by a colonnade of marble columns consisting of four rows of seven monoliths each, topped with Corinthian capitals and imposts. The date and identity of this structure are uncertain, although there is some reason to believe that it was built in the mid-fifth century by the Empress Pulcheria. The structure has recently been well restored.

Selim I Camii stands on a high terrace overlooking the Golden Horn. This is one of the most beautiful buildings in Istanbul, and its dramatic position atop the Fifth Hill makes it a most conspicuous landmark on the ridge above the Golden Horn. It is the second oldest imperial mosque in the city, exceeded in age only by the Beyazidiye. The mosque was finished in 1522 under Süleyman the Magnificent, who dedicated it to his father, but it may have been begun two or three years earlier by Selim himself, as the Arabic inscription over the entrance portal would seem to imply. The identity of the architect is unknown.

The **mosque**, with its great shallow dome and cluster of little domes on either side, is impressive and worthy of the site. The courtyard is one of the most charming and vivid in the city, with its columns of various marbles and granites, the polychrome voussoirs of the arches, the very beautiful tiles of the earliest Iznik period in the lunettes above the windows – turquoise, deep blue, and yellow – and the pretty *şadîrvan* surrounded by tapering cypress trees. The plan of the mosque is quite simple: a square room, 24.5 metres on a side, covered by a shallow dome 32.5 metres in height under the dome, with the cornice resting on the outer walls through smooth pendentives. The room itself is vast and empty, but saved from dullness by its perfect proportions and by the exquisite colours of the Iznik tiles in the lunettes of the windows. The mosque furniture though sparse is fine, particularly the *mihrab*, *mimber* and sultan's loge. The border of the ceiling under the loge is a quite exceptionally beautiful and rich example of the painted and gilded woodwork of the great age; notice the deep, rich colours and the varieties of floral and leaf motifs in the four or five separate borders, like an Oriental rug, only here picked out in gold. North and south of the great central room there are annexes consisting of a domed cruciform passage giving access to four small rooms. These, as in other early mosques elsewhere in the city, served as dervish hospices.

The grand *türbe* **of Selim I** is directly behind the mosque in the graveyard garden. It is octagonal in form and covered with a dome that is deeply ribbed on the exterior. In the porch on either side of the door there are two beautiful panels of tilework, presumably from Iznik but unique in colour and design. Facing Selim's *türbe* is another called the Tomb of the Princes, probably a work of Sinan, which shelters the remains of four children of Süleyman the Magnificent who died in their early childhood. Beyond this there is another large octgonal *türbe*, that of Abdül Mecit, who died in 1861. The *külliye* of Selim I also included an *imaret*, a *medrese* and a *mektep*, of which only the latter has survived, the little domed building in the outer courtyard.

After leaving the *külliye* of Selim I we walk along Sultan Selim Caddesi, which takes us past the western side of the Cistern of Aspar. We then turn right on Manyasizade Caddesi, which at the far corner of the first street on the right brings us to **Ismail Efendi Camii**.

This is a quaint and interesting example of a building in the transitional style between classical and baroque, built in 1724 by the Şeyh-ül Islam Ismail Efendi. The vaulted substructure contains shops, with the mosque standing on a terrace above them. This design was adopted so that it would resemble the Kaaba at Mecca, according to Hafîz Hüseyin Ayvansarayî, author of the *Hadika*, a comprehensive description of the mosques of Istanbul written in 1780. Above the main entrance to the courtyard is a very characteristic *mektep* of one room. To the right a long double staircase leads up to the mosque; the porch has been tastelessly reconstructed, but the general effect is pleasing except for the glassed-in portico. On the interior there is a very pretty, and perhaps unique, triple arcade in two storeys of superposed columns repeated on the south, west and north sides and supporting galleries, giving the dome an unusually high appearance.

At the back of the garden there is a small *dar-ül hadis*, or school of tradition. It has been greatly altered and walled in, so that it has little resemblance to the original structure. Nevertheless, it is once again being used for something like its original purpose, for it now houses a Koran school. All-in-all this little *külliye* is quite charming, with its warm polychrome of brick and stone masonry; it was, on the whole, fairly well restored from near ruin in 1952.

Returning to the main avenue, at the next corner we turn right on to Murat Molla Caddesi. This street is named for the founder of the handsome library that we see about a hundred metres along on the right, standing in an extensive walled garden. The **library** was founded in 1775 by Kadasker Damatzade **Murat Molla**, who served as Chief Judge and Minister of War under Abdül Hamit I.

The library is a large square building of brick and stone built on Byzantine substructures, fragments of which can be seen in the garden. The central area of the main reading room is covered by a dome supported by four columns with re-used Byzantine capitals; the corners of the room also have domes with barrel vaults over them. It is a typical and very attractive example of an eighteenth-century Ottoman library, to be compared with those of Ragîp Pasha and Atîf Efendi; like these, it is constantly in use.

Returning to Manyasizade Caddesi, we continue for about 150 metres and then turn left on to Mehmet Aga Camii Sokağî, named for the small mosque in its walled garden to the right. This pretty

Selim I Camii

Fethiye Camii, the Church of the Virgin Pammakaristos

mosque is of interest because it is one of the relatively few that can be confidently attributed to the architect Davut Ağa, who built it in 1585. The founder, **Mehmet Ağa**, was Chief Black Eunuch in the reign of Murat III.

In plan the mosque is of the simplest type: a square room covered by a dome and with a projecting apse for the *mihrab* and an entrance porch with five bays. But unlike most mosques of this simple type, the dome does not rest directly on the walls, but on arches supported on pillars and columns engaged in the walls; instead of pendentives there are four semidomes in the diagonals. Thus the effect is that of an inscribed octagon, as in several of Sinan's mosques, but in this case without side aisles. The effect is unusual but not unattractive. The interior is adorned with faience inscriptions and other tile panels of the best Iznik period; but the painted decoration is tasteless. In the garden to the left is the *türbe* of the founder, a rather large square building of little interest.

The *külliye* also included a *hamam*, presumably built by Davut Ağa, which is around the corner and to the left. This is a double bath, both the men's and women's sections having the same plan. In the men's bath there is a large *camekan* whose dome is supported on squinches in the form of conches, and a cruciform *hararet* with cubicles in the corners of the cross. However, the lower arm of the cross has been cut off and turned into a small *soğukluk*, which leads through the right-hand cubicle into the *hararet*. In the cubicles there are small private wash-rooms separated by low marble partitions, a unique disposition.

Returning to Manyasizade Caddesi, we turn left at the next corner to find a tiny mosque known as **Hirami Ahmet Pasha Camii**. This has been identified as the Byzantine **church of St John in Trullo**. The building is a characteristic example of the four-column church with a narthex and three semicircular apses, evidently of the eleventh or twelfth century. Traces of its fresco decoration could still be seen up until 1961, when it was spoiled in a clumsy restoration.

We return to the main avenue, which here changes its name to Fethiye Caddesi, after which we turn right at the next corner on to Fethiye Kapîsî Sokağî. This brings us to **Fethiye Camii**, the former Byzantine **church of the Theotokos Pammakaristos**, the Joyous Mother of God, which stands on a terrace overlooking the Golden Horn.

Fethiye Camii was superbly restored in the early 1960s by the Byzantine Institute of America, whose studies have now clarified the architectural history of this complicated church. It consists of a simple bay with a narthex; a small chapel, or parecclesion, on the south; and a curious perambulatory forming a side aisle on the north; with an outer narthex on the west; and two bays of an aisle on the south in front of the parecclesion. Each of these three sections was radically altered when the building was converted into a mosque. The main church was built in the twelfth century by a nobleman named John Comnenus and his wife Anna Doukina. In form this church was of the ambulatory type, with a triple arcade in the north, west and south dividing the central domed area from the ambulatory; at the east end there were the usual three apses, and at the west a single narthex.

Towards the end of the thirteenth century the church was reconstructed by a general named Michael Dukas Glabas Tarchaniotes, who served as Protostrator, or Master of the Horse, under Andronicus II Palaeologus (1282–1328). Around 1310 a parecclesion was added on the south side of the church by Michael's widow, Maria Doukina Comnena Palaeologina Blachena, serving as a funerary chapel for her departed husband. The chapel was of the four-column type and was preceded by a four-storeyed narthex covered by a tiny dome. In the second half of the fourteenth century the north, west and south sides were converted into a perambulatory, which ran into and partly obliterated the south chapel.

After the Turkish conquest the church served as the Greek Orthodox Patriarchate from 1456–1586. Then in 1591 Murat III converted it to Islam, calling it Fethiye Camii, the Mosque of the conquest, to celebrate his recent victory over Persia and the Ottoman annexation of Georgia and Azerbaijan. This conversion radically altered the interior of the building. After restoration by the Byzantine Institute, the main prayer room was divided off from the side chapel and reconsecrated as a mosque, while the parecclesion was converted into a museum to exhibit the surviving mosaics.

The exterior presents one of the best examples in the city of the fine stone and brick work of the Palaeologian period. Because of the two storeyed narthex, the chapel has a cubic form divided in three storeys of blind arcades, with a succession of wide and narrow arches, slender niches, annd concave roundels.

The **side chapel** has been most beautifully restored by the Byzantine Institute, its missing columns replaced, and its surviving mosaics uncovered and cleaned. The mosaic in the crown of the dome is Christ Pantocrator, the All-Powerful, surrounded by twelve Prophets of the Old Testament. In the conch of the apse is Christ

Hyperagathos, the All-Loving; on the left wall of the bema is the Virgin; on the right wall is St John the Baptist; and in the domical vault above them are the four Archangels. The Baptism of Christ is depicted on the east section of the domical vault in the side aisle. Elsewhere, in the conches and in the soffits of the arches and on their supporting pilasters, there are representations of seventeen saints. The mosaics in Fethiye Camii are dated to the early fourteenth century, and are a brilliant example of the renaissance of culture that took place in Byzantium under the Palaeologus dynasty.

Between the marble facing on the lower part of the south wall and the mosaics on the upper part there is a long inscription in gold letters on a blue ground. This is a threnody written by the poet Philes to commemorate the love that Maria Blachena, the founder of the church, bore for her departed husband, the Protostrator Michael Tarchaniotes, whom she addresses as 'fairest also of the dead'.

We now return to the main avenue, which 200 metres farther along changes its name to Draman Caddesi. The street here takes its name from the small mosque on the left, perched on a high terrace reached by a double staircase. This is **Draman Camii**, a minor work by Sinan. Inscriptions record that the mosque was founded in 1541 by Yunus Bey, the famous interpreter (in Turkish, *draman*, or *dragoman*) of Süleyman the Magnificent. Unfortunately, it was very badly restored in the 1970s and has now lost any interest it may have had. Originally it was the centre of a small complex consisting of a *medrese* and a *mektep*, both presumably by Sinan, The *medrese* has perished but the *mektep* remains, though in ruins, a fine domed building to the northeast of the mosque.

Some 200 metres farther along the left side of Draman Caddesi we come to **Kefevi Mescidi**, formerly known as Kefeli Camii. This is a Byzantine edifice, of uncertain identity, converted into a mosque in 1630.

The building is in good condition and still in use as a mosque. It is a long narrow structure with two rows of windows and a wooden roof; the entrance is now in the middle of the west wall. The building may have belonged to the Monastery of the Prodromos (St John the Baptist) in Petra, which is known to have been in this area. The building here was probably a refectory, not a church, since it has only one apse and is oriented north instead of east. It had been dated variously from the ninth century to the twelfth.

We continue along Draman Caddesi to its intersection with Salma Tomruk Caddesi, where we turn left and continue to Fevzi Pasha

Caddesi. We turn left again there, having reached the Sixth Hill and now heading back toward the Fifth Hill.

Below us on the left is a huge open cistern now used as a football stadium. This is one of the three late Roman reservoirs in the city; its attribution was long in doubt but it has been identified with great probability as the **reservoir** constructed c.421 by **Aetios**, Prefect of Constantinople in the reign of Theodosius II. Huge as it is, it is yet the smallest of the three Roman reservoirs that still survive in the city, meauring 224 by 85 metres, its original depth being about 15 metres. Like the others it was already dry in Byzantine times.

About a hundred metres beyond the end of the cistern we come to an attractive *medrese* that has been restored and converted into a children's clinic. This is known as **Zincirli Kuyu Medresesi**, founded by Semiz (Fat) Ali Pasha, Grand Vizier in the reign of Süleyman the Magnificent. Ali Pasha was so fat that he had difficulty finding a horse strong enough to carry him; if a dead nag was found in an Istanbul street wags would say that the Grand Vizier had tried to ride it. He was known for his wit and conviviality as well as for his honesty, a pleasant contrast to his predecessor Rüstem Pasha, the Louse of Fortune. Since Ali Pasha died in office in 1564, the *medrese* must have been built before that time. It is a work of Sinan, but presents no special features except the two symmetrical entrances on either side of the *dershane*.

A short way farther along we come to a little mosque called **Zincirli Kuyu Camii**. This was built c.1500 by that Atik Ali Pasha whose larger and better known mosque we saw on the Second Hill. Zincirli Kuyu Camii is a small rectangular building of brick and stone construction, covered by six equal domes in two rows of three supported by two massive rectangular pillars; its original porch of three bays has disappeared and has been poorly reconstructed.

The building is interesting as being a tiny example of the Selcuk Ulu Cami, or Great Mosque, a type that was fairly common before the Ottomans established their capital in Istanbul. The type consists of a square or rectangular space covered by a multiplicity of domes supported by pillars or columns. It can be very large and impressive, as in the Ulu Cami of Bursa with its twenty domes. On the small scale of Zincirli Kuyu Camii it is rather heavy and oppressive.

Opposite the mosque on the side street to its left is a small late baroque *türbe*, dated by an inscription to 1825. This is the tomb of the famous calligrapher **Hattat Rakîm Efendi**, who designed the beautiful inscriptions on the *türbe* and *sebil* of Nakşidil at the mosque of Mehmet the Conqueror.

We turn right from the side street on to Hasan Fehmi Paşa Caddesi, which soon becomes Fatih Nişancî Caddesi. At the first intersection we come to a small square called Üç Baş Meydanî, literally the Square of the Three Heads. The square takes its name from **Üç Baş Mescidi**, the tiny mosque on the left, an early and minor work of the great Sinan.

Evliya Çelebi writes that Üç Baş Mescidi received this odd name 'because it was built by a barber who shaved three heads for a single copper coin, and, notwithstnding, grew so rich that he was able to build this mosque, which is small but particularly sanctified.' A more prosaic explanation is given by the *Hadika*; there it is recorded that the founder of this mosque, Nurettin Hamza ben Atallah, came from a village in Anatolia called Üç Baş. An inscription over the gate gives the foundation as 1530–31. This is the earliest building that can be ascribed to Sinan, though all that remains of the original mosque are the minaret and the inscribed portal.

Opposit the mosque there is a ruined *medrese* founded in 1575 by a certain Halil Efendi. In the centre of the square there is an ancient *çeşme*, with a beautifully written inscription recording that it was founded in 1681 by one Mustafa Ağa.

About 250 metres farther along on Fatih Nişancî Caddesi we come on our right to a beautiful classical mosque, **Nişancî Mehmet Pasha Camii**. The mosque is popularly ascribed to Sinan, but it does not appear in the best texts of the *Tezkere*, the list of his works; therefore it is probably not by him. The mosque was built between 1584 and 1588 for Mehmet Pasha, who was Nişancî, or Keeper of the Seal, in the reign of Murat III.

Even from a distance the elegance of line and the masterly arrangement of the upper structure of the mosque can be seen: the great dome surrounded by the eight little weight-turrets, the eight semidomes of two sizes, and the minaret unusually close to the dome base; an excellently proportioned distribution of curves and verticals. We enter through a very charming courtyard where the arches are of the ogive type; under the porch of five bays an inscription with the *tuğra* of Mustafa III records a restoration in 1766, presumably after the very severe earthquake of that year.

The plan of the mosque is an interesting variation of the octagon inscribed in the square. Eight partly engaged columns support the dome arches; in the axes there are four semidomes, while in the diagonals four smaller semidomes serve as squinches instead of pendentives. The eastern semidome covers a projecting apse for the *mihrab*, while those to north and south also cover projections from the square. The western corners of the cross so formed are filled with small independent chambers; above on three sides there are galleries. The whole arrangement is masterly, and there are interesting details.

In the corners of the east wall there are two charming little platforms, which can be reached by staircases built into the thickness of the wall from the recesses. In the voussoirs and balustrades of these platforms, in the window frames, and elsewhere throughout the mosque, an interesting conglomerate marble of pale violet and grey is used. For the columns that support both platforms and galleries there is another conglomerate marble of tawny brown flecked with yellow, grey, black and green. The arches of the galleries, like those of the courtyard, are of the ogive type. As a whole, the mosque is a masterpiece; it is as if the unknown architect, in the extreme old age of Sinan, had decided to play variations on themes invented by Sinan himself, and to show that he could do them as well as the Master. In the little graveyard behind the mosque is the small and unpretentious *türbe* of Nişancî Mehmet Pasha.

About 150 metres farther along on our right we come to **Kumrulu Mescidi**, the Little Mosque of the Turtle Dove. The mosque takes its name from a fragment of Byzantine sculpture used in the adjoining *çeşme*, in which a relief represents two turtle-doves drinking from the Fountain of Life.

Kumrulu Mescidi is of interest principally because its founder and builder was Atik Sinan, the architect of the original Mosque of the Conqueror. According to Demetrius Cantemir, the architect of the mosque of the Conqueror was a Greek named Christodoulos. Evliya Çelebi writes that Sultan Mehmet ordered both of the architect's hands cut off, on the grounds that the dome of his mosque was not as large as that of Haghia Sophia. Atik Sinan's tombstone is to be seen in the mosque garden, with an inscription recording that he was executed by Mehmet the Conqueror in 1471; thus Kumrulu Mescidi is dated prior to that year.

A few steps farther along brings us back to Yavuz Selim Caddesi, where we complete our stroll around the Fifth and Sixth Hills.

13

Kariye Cami

OUR NEXT ITINERARY will take us to **Kariye Camii**, the former **Church of St Saviour in Chora**, which is on the Sixth Hill just inside the land walls. We approach it via Fevzi Paşa Caddesi, turning right at the signposted street just beyond the Cistern of Aetios.

St Saviour in Chora is, after Haghia Sophia, the most interesting Byzantine church in the city. This is not due to the building itself, pretty as it is, but because of the superb mosaics and frescoes that it contains, a magnificent heritage of Byzantine art that has no equal in the world.

The phrase 'in Chora' means 'in the country', because the original church and monastery on this site were outside the walls of Constantine. The name also has a symbolic sense: Christ as the 'Country' or 'Land of the Living', and the Blessed Virgin as the 'Dwelling-place of the Uncontainable', as they are referred to in inscriptions in the church.

No trace remains of the original ancient church, nor is anything certain known of its history. The present building in its first form dates from the late eleventh century. This church was built in the years 1077–81 by Maria Doukina, mother-in-law of Alexius I Comnenus; it was probably of the four-column type so popular at that time. An elaborate remodelling of the church was carried out early in the twelfth century by Maria Doukina's grandson Isaac Comnenus, third son of Alexius I. Then a third period of building two centuries later created the present church and its works of art; this was carried out in the years 1315–21 by Theodore Metochites, who served as both Prime Minister and First Lord of the Treasury under Andronicus II Palaeologus. Thus the art works here are contemporary with those at Fethiye Camii, another creation of the Palaeologian renaissance.

The Chora continued to function as a church for more than half a century after the Turkish conquest, but then in 1510 it was converted into a mosque by Atik Ali Pasha, Grand Vizier under Beyazit II. The mosaics and frescoes were never wholly obliterated, though in the

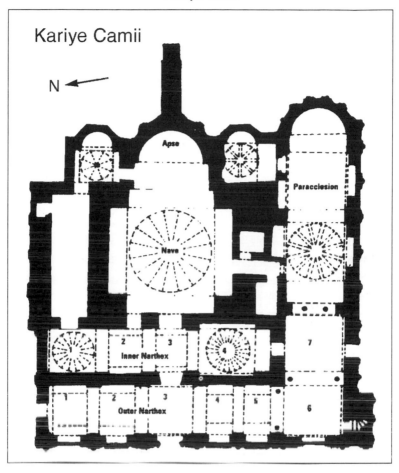

course of time most of them were obscured by plaster, paint and grime, and many were shaken down by earthquake. The church and its extraordinary works of art were unknown to the scholarly world until 1860, when the Greek architect Pelopidas Kouppas brought it to the attention of Byzantinists in the West. A programme of restoration was organized in 1948 by Thomas Whittemore and Paul A. Underwood, sponsored by the Byzantine Institute of America and the Dumbarton Oaks Center for Byzantine Studies. The project was directed by Ernest Hawkins and took a decade to complete; the results were published in a magisterial four-volume work, *Kariye Djami*, written by Paul A. Underwood (Princeton University Press, 1966), a masterpiece on which the present description of the church is based.

Kariye Camii: Outer and Inner Narthexes

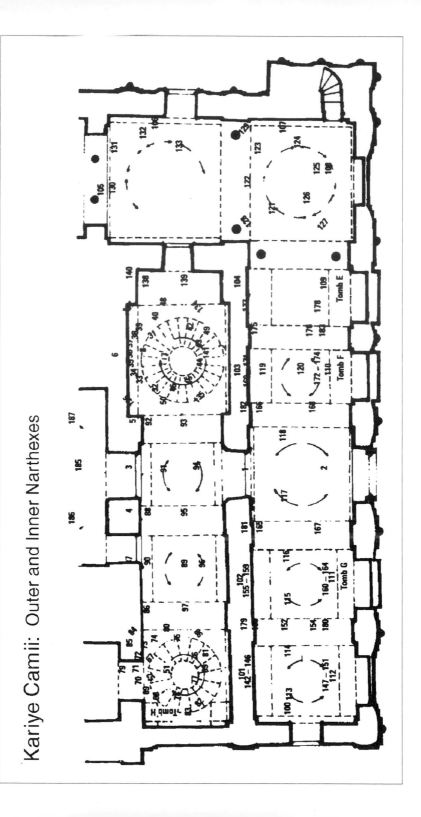

The church is preceded by an exonarthex and a narthex, with a parecclesion to the right and a two-storeyed passageway on the left. The central area of the church is covered by a dome carried on a high drum; this is supported by four huge pilasters that stand at the corners of the nave, with great arches springing between them and with pendentives making the transition to the circular cornice. The present dome is Turkish, but the drum is from the reconstruction of 1315–21. There are two smaller domes carried on lower drums above the first and fourth (numbering from left to right) bays of the narthex, as well as one above the westernmost bay of the pareclession with still smaller domes above the prothesis and diaconicon, the apsidal chambers that flank the main apse to north and south, respectively.

The mosaics and frescoes in the Chora are by far the most important and extensive series of Byzantine paintings in the world. They are contemporaneous with the paintings of Giotto in Italy, and though quite unlike Giotto's work in detail they seem to breathe the same spirit of life and reality, so typical of the dawn of the Renaissance, a far cry from the formal and stylized painting of the earlier Byzantine tradition.

The mosaics in the church follow a definite iconographic order. They fall into seven quite distinct groups: six large Dedicatory or Devotional panels, in the inner and outer narthexes; the Ancestry of Christ, in the two domes of the inner narthex; the Cycle of the Life of the Blessed Virgin, in the first three bays of the inner narthex; the Cycle of the Infancy of Christ, in the lunettes of the outer narthex; the Cycle of Christ's Ministry, in the vaults of the outer narthex and the fourth bay of the inner narthex; Portraits of Saints; and the Mosaics in the Nave.

The genealogy in the domes serves as a prelude to the narrative cycles of the lives of the Blessed Virgin and Christ, which comprise the major elements in the programme. These themes are closely linked together and form one continuous narrative, for the cycle in the outer narthex takes up the account at the precise point in Mary's life, as it is narrated in the apocryphal Protoevangelium of James, where the Gospel accounts begin, superseding it as the authority. However, while the mosaics depicting the Infancy of Christ are based upon the Gospels and quote their texts in inscriptions, at many points they illustrate events derived from the Protoevangelium. In the account that follows the mosaics will be described in the order in which they occur in the seven groups, with each subject identified by a parenthetical number keyed to the plans.

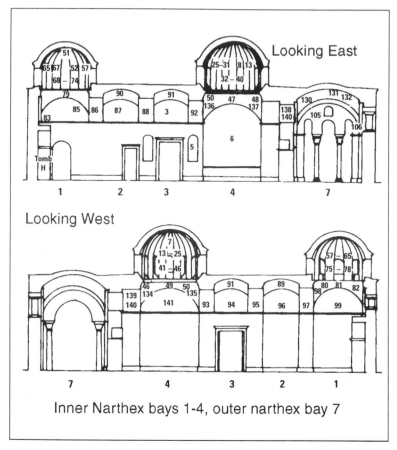

Looking East

Looking West

Inner Narthex bays 1-4, outer narthex bay 7

I. Dedicatory and Devotional Panels

(1) Christ Pantocrator (in lunette over door to inner narthex). (2) The
Virgin Blachernitissa and Angels (opposite the above, over door to
the building). Here the Virgin is of the type venerated at the sacred
spring of Blachernae, which we will see on a later itinerary. (3) The
Enthroned Christ with the Donor (inner narthex in lunette over door
to nave). Metochites offers a model of his church to the enthroned
Christ. The donor is dressed in his official robes, wearing an extraordinary turban-like hat called a *skiadon*, literally a sunshade. (4) St
Peter and (5) St Paul (to left and right of door leading into nave). (6)
The Deesis (right of door in east wall of south bay). Below are
figures of two donors. At the Virgin's right is Isaac Comnenus, third

170

son of Alexius I, who was probably responsible for the rebuilding of the church in the twelfth century; the other figure, partly lost; what remains of the inscription reads: '. . . of Andronicus Palaeologus, the Lady of the Mongols, Melanie the nun'. This was either Maria, half-sister of Andronicus II, who married a Mongol Khan and founded the still-extant church of St Mary of the Mongols; or else another Maria, an illegitimate daughter of Andronicus II, who also married a Mongol Khan. To add to the confusion, both of these women took the name of Melane when they became nuns, making it impossible to say which of them is represented in the mosaic.

II. The Genealogy of Christ

In the crown of the south dome there is a medallion of (7) Christ Pantocrator and in the flutes two rows of his ancestors, from Adam to Jacob in the upper zone (18–31), and in the lower twelve sons of Jacob and some others (32–46). In the crown of the north dome there is a medallion of the (51) Blessed Virgin with the Christ Child below; in the upper zone sixteen kings of the House of David (52–67), in the lower eleven figures (68–78) representing 'other ancestors in the genealogy.'

III. The Cycle of the Life of the Blessed Virgin

These mosaics are located in the first three bays of the inner narthex. The Cycle of the Life of the Virgin is based mainly on the Apocryphal Gospel of St James, better known as the Protoevangelium, which dates back to at least the second century. This gives an account of her birth and life from the rejection of the offerings of Joachim, her father, to the birth of Jesus. It was very popular in the Middle Ages, and is the source of many cycles of pictures in the East and the West. The most notable is Giotto's fresco cycle in the Arena Chapel at Padua, done at a slightly earlier date than the mosaics at Kariye Camii and representing many of the same scenes. Here in Kariye Camii there were twenty scenes, of which nineteen are either completely or partially preserved.

The scenes are: (82) Joachim's Offerings Rejected (first bay, northwest pendentive of dome): Zacharias, the High Priest, raises his hands in a gesture of refusal. The rest of the scene in the northwest pendentive is lost; it must have shown Joachim and his wife bearing offerings, which were rejected because they had no children.

(83) Fragmentary Scene (in lunette of north wall): probably Joachim and Anne returning home; only a maid looking out of a doorway is preserved. (84) Joachim in the Wilderness (in southeast pendentive): ashamed at the rejection of his offerings, Joachim goes into the wilderness to pray for offspring. (85) The Annunciation of St Anne (in lunette of east wall, left half of scene lost). The right half shows the angel of the Lord announcing to Anne that her prayer for a child has been heard. (86) The Meeting of Joachim and Anne (in east soffit of arch between first and second bays): Anne informs Joachim on his return from the wilderness of the annunciation of the angel. (87) The Birth of the Blessed Virgin (in east lunette of second bay) (88) The First Seven Steps of the Virgin (in east soffit of arch between second and third bays): the Virgin took her first seven steps when she was six months old. (89) The Virgin Blessed by the Priests (west side of domical vault in first bay). (90) The Virgin Caressed by her Parents (east side of domical vault in first bay: note the two magnificent peacocks, representing incorruptibility, in the two pendentives. (91) The Presentation of the Virgin in the Temple (in domical vault of second bay): at the age of three the Virgin was presented as an attendant in the Temple, where she remained until she was about twelve. (92) The Virgin receiving Bread from an Angel (in east soffit of arch between third and fourth bays): while the Virgin remained in the Temple she was miraculously fed by an angel. (93) The Instruction of the Virgin in the Temple (in west soffit of arch between third and fourth bays): the central figures of the scene have unfortunately been destroyed. (94) The Virgin receiving the Skein of Purple Wool (in lunette above door from outer narthex): the priests decided to have the attendant maidens weave a veil for the Temple; the royal colours, purple and scarlet, fell to Mary's lot. (95) Zacharias, praying before the Rods of the Suitors (in west soffit of arch between second and third bays): when the time came or the Virgin to be married, Zacharias the High Priest called all the widowers together and placed their rods on the altar, praying for a sign showing to whom she should be given. (96) The Virgin entrusted to Joseph (in west lunette of second bay): when the rods were returned to the widowers, Joseph's rod began to sprout green leaves and the Virgin was awarded to him. (97) Joseph taking the Virgin to his House (in west soffit of arch between first and second bays): here they are just leaving the temple; the youth is one of Joseph's sons by his former wife. (98) The Annunciation to the Virgin by the Well (in southwest pendentive of dome in first bay). (99) Joseph

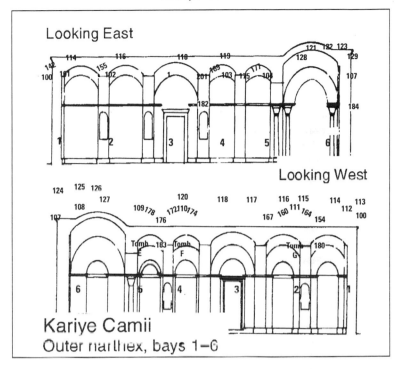

Looking East

Looking West

Kariye Camii
Outer narthex, bays 1–6

taking leave of the Virgin and Joseph reproaching the Virgin (two scenes in west lunette of first bay): Joseph had to go away for six months on business; when he returned he found the Virgin pregnant and was angry (until reassured by a dream, as in the first scene of the next cycle).

IV. The Cycle of the Infancy of Christ

Each of the thirteen extant or partly extant scenes occupies a lunette of the outer narthex, proceeding clockwise round all seven bays. In the soffits of the arches are saints, while in the domical vaults are the scenes of Christ's Ministry, which will be described later. The Infancy Cycle is largely based on the canonical Gospels, and most of the scenes are inscribed with quotations which sufficiently identify them.

(100) Joseph Dreaming; The Virgin with Two Companions; The Journey to Bethlehem (three scenes in north lunette of first bay). (101) The Enrollment for Taxation (in east lunette of first bay). (102)

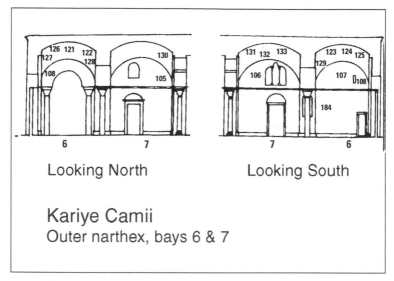

Looking North   Looking South

Kariye Camii
Outer narthex, bays 6 & 7

The Nativity (in east lunette of second bay). (103) The Journey of the Magi; the Magi before Herod (two scenes in east lunette of fourth bay). (104) Herod enquiring of the Priests and Scribes (in east lunette of fifth bay).

We now turn the corner into the seventh bay. The lunette above the door to the inner narthex, now blank, probably contained the Adoration of the Magi. The lunette above the columns and arches that lead to the pareclession retains traces of (105) The Return of the Magi to the East. (106) The Flight into Egypt (in south lunette of seventh bay): main scene destroyed, only title remaining. To the right of the window is the Fall of Idols from the Walls of an Egyptian Town as the Holy Family passes by (from an apocryphal source).

The mosaics in the west lunette of the sixth bay depict the Massacre of the Innocents; (107) (to the left) Herod orders the Massacre; (108) The Soldiers go forth to slay the Children: central part and inscription destroyed. (109) Mothers mourning their Children (in west lunette of fifth bay). (110) The Flight of Elizabeth (in west lunette of fourth bay): the scene depicts Elizabeth, with her baby son, John the Baptist, seeking refuge from the massacre in the mountains that open to receive her. (111) Joseph Dreaming, The Return from Egypt (two scenes in west lunette of second bay). (112) Christ taken to Jerusalem for the Passover (in west lunette of first bay).

Kariye Cami

V. The Cycle of Christ's Ministry

This cycle occupies the domical vaults of all seven bays of the exon-arthex as well as parts of the south bay of the inner narthex. Unfortu-nately, all but one of the vaults in the exonarthex are very badly damaged, many scenes being lost or reduced to mere fragments. The series begins in the vault of the first bay.

(113) Christ among the Doctors (in vault of first bay, north side), fragments only). (114, 115) John the Baptist bearing witness of Christ (two scenes, in vault of first bay, south side, and vault of second bay, north side). (116) The Temptation of Christ (in vault of second bay, south side). (117) The Miracle at Cana (in vault of third bay, north side, badly ruined). (118) The Multiplication of the Loaves (in vault of third bay, south side, badly ruined). (119) Christ Healing a Leper (in vault of fourth bay, east side, fragments only). (120) Christ walking on the Water (in vault of fourth bay, west side, fragments only).

The fifth vault is completely empty. The vault of the sixth bay contains fragments of the following nine scenes, the identification of some of which are uncertain, at best. (121) Christ healing the Para-lytic at the Pool of Bethesda. (122) An unidentified scene showing the fragmentary figures of two disciples. (123) Christ healing the Dropsical Man. (124) Christ healing the Paralytic at Capernaum. (125) An unidentified scene, showing the fragmentary figures of nine disciples. (126) Fragment showing the lower part of a bare-footed figure, thought to be either the Healing of the Gadarene Demoniac or the Healing of the Blind and Dumb Demoniac at Capernaum. (127) Christ and the Samaritan Woman (in the north-west pendentive). (128) The Paralytic carrying off his Bed (in the northeast pendentive). (129) Christ Healing the Blind Born (in the southeast pendentive). In the seventh vault there are fragments of four scenes, three of which (130, 131 and 133) are so meagre that they cannot be identified; the fourth (132) has been identified as a representation of Christ calling Zacchaeus from the Sycamore Tree.

We now re-enter the inner narthex, where the last eight scenes of Christ's Ministry, almost all well-preserved, are to be found in the pendentives, vaults and lunettes under the southern dome that contains the Ancestors of Christ. (134) Christ healing the Blind and Dumb Man (in southwest pendentive). (135) Christ healing the two Blind Men (in northwest pendentive). (136) Christ healing Peter's Mother-in-Law (in northeast pendentive). (137) Christ healing the Women with the Isue of Blood (in southeast pendentive). (138)

175

Christ healing the Man with the Withered Hand (in soffit of south arch, east side). (139) Christ healing the Leper (in soffit of south arch, west side). (140) Christ healing . . . (inscription and half of mosaic lost) (in south lunette). (141) Christ healing various Diseases (in western lunette).

VI. Portraits of Saints

The soffits of the arches of the outer narthex are decorated with the portraits of martyr-saints; there were originally fifty, of which thirty-seven still exist (142–178). Those that are identified are in all cases saints of the Eastern Church, most of them little known to the West. In addition to these there are also a dozen portraits of saints on the pilasters that receive the transverse arches in the exonarthex, of which only the battered fragments of six unidentified figures have survived.

The six panels in the first, second and third bays would seem to have been devoted to portraits of those who, by divine intervention, were precursors of the Incarnation. Facing one another across the exonarthex between the first and second bays are (179) (to the east) St Anne, with the infant Mary in her arms, and (180) (to the west) her husband Joachim. Between the second and third bay is (181) (to the east) the Virgin Mary and the Christ Child; facing this (to the west) there was in all probability a figure of Joseph, but this has been entirely destroyed. On the east pilaster between the third and fourth bays there is a small fragment of (182) St John the Baptist across from this there would have been a portrait of either John's father Zacharias or his mother Elizabeth, but this too has disappeared. The panels on the other six pilasters undoubtedly also bore portraits of saints; of these only two fragments remain: (183) an unidentified military saint (on the west pilaster between the fourth and fifth bays); and (184) St Euthymius, the Palestinian hermit (on the south pilaster between the sixth and seventh bays).

VII. The Panels in the Nave

(185) The Dormition (in Greek, Koimesis) of the Virgin (over the central door from the narthex). Here the Virgin is shown laid out on her bier. Behind stands Christ holding her soul, represented as a babe in swaddling clothes. Over Christ's head hovers a six-winged seraph. Around stand apostles, evangelists and early bishops. The idea is

176

taken from an apocryphal work, *Concerning the Koimesis of the Holy Mother of God*, ascribed to St John the Divine.

(186) Christ (in panel at left of bema). Christ holds the Gospels open to Matt. 11: 28: 'Come unto me, all ye that labour and are heavy laden, and I will give you rest.'

(187) The Virgin Hodegitria (in panel to right of bema). The type is that of the Hodegitria, the Guide or Teacher, the original of which is supposed to have been painted by St Luke from life. An icon, believed to have been the original by St Luke, was revered as the protectress of Constantinople, and was carried in procession along the walls of the city whenever Byzantium was besieged.

THE PARECCLESION: THE FRESCOES

The superb fresco decoration of the **parecclesion** was the last part of Theodore Metochites' work of decoration to be carried out, probably in 1320–21. The great but unknown master painter of these frescoes was probably the same as the one who did the mosaics in the rest of the church. The decoration of the chapel was designed to illustrate its purpose as a place of burial. Above the level of the cornice the paintings represent the Resurrection and the Life, the Last Judgement: Heaven and Hell, and the Mother of God as the Bridge between Earth and Heaven. Below the cornice there is a procession of saints and martyrs, interrupted by four tombs.

I. Scenes of Resurrection

(201) The Anastasis (Resurrection) (in the semidome of the apse). This scene, called Anastasis in Greek, is known in English as the Harrowing of Hell. The central figure is Christ, who has just broken down the gates of Hell, which lie beneath his feet, while Satan lies bound before him. With his right hand he pulls Adam out of his tomb and with his left hand Eve. Behind Adam stands John the Baptist, David, Solomon and other righteous kings; standing with Eve in her tomb is Able, and behind him another group of the righteous. This is surely one of the greatest paintings in the world, the apogee of Byzantine art in its last renaissance.

(202) Christ raising the Widow's Son (north side of bema arch).
(203) Christ raising the Daughter of Jairus (south side of bema arch). In the crown of the arch the Archangel Michael is in a medallion.

177

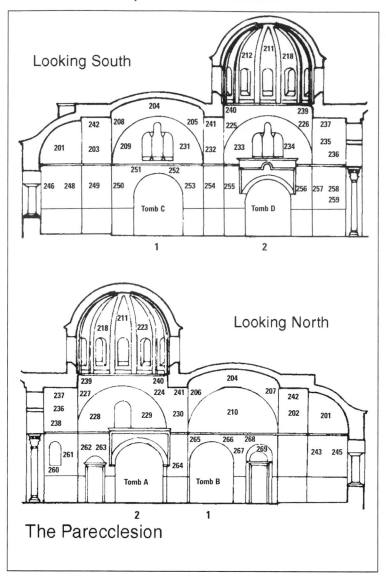

II. The Last Judgement: Heaven and Hell

(204) The Second Coming of Christ (in vault of east bay). This vast scene occupies the whole vault; the title is inscribed in the centre. It represents the doctrine of Last Things; death, judgement, immortality in heaven or damnation in hell. In the crown is the Scroll of

178

Heaven (Apocalypse 6:14). In the eastern half Christ sits in Judgement. To the souls of the saved he says: 'Come, ye blessed of my Father, inherit the kingdom prepared for you from the foundation of the World.' (Matt. 25:34). To the condemned souls on his left he says: 'Depart from me, ye cursed, into everlasting fire, prepared for the devil and his angels.' (Matt. 25:41). Below to the left a River of Fire broadening into a lake in which are the damned. Below Christ is the Etimasia or empty throne prepared for the Second Coming: Adam and Eve lie prostrate before it. Below this is the Weighing and Condemnation of Souls. The western half of the vault is occupied by the Choirs of the Elect in clouds. (205) The Land and Sea giving up their Dead (in southwest pendentive). (206) An Angel conducts the Soul of Lazarus to Heaven (northwest pendentive). (207) Lazarus the Beggar in Abraham's Bosom (northeast pendentive). (208) The Rich Man in Hell (southeast pendentive). (209) The Torments of the Damned (in lunette of south wall, east half). This scene consists of four rectangular panels identified as: (upper left) The Gnashing of Teeth; (upper right) The Outer Darkness; (lower left) The Worm that Sleepeth Not; (lower right) The Unquenchable Fire. (210) The Entry of the Elect into Paradise (in lunette of north wall). The Elect are led by St Peter toward the Gate of Paradise, guarded by a Cherub; the Good Thief welcomes them and points to the enthroned Mother of God.

III. The Mother of God and Her Prefigurations

This cycle, in the western dome and bay, represents the Blessed Virgin and a series of five episodes from the Old Testament which came to be symbolical interpretations or 'types' of the Virgin and the Incarnation. The Virgin and Child (211) in the crown supported by the heavenly court of angels (212–223) in the spaces between the ribs. (224–227) Four Hymnographers (in the pendentives of the dome): (northeast) St John Damascene; (southeast) St Cosmas the Poet; (southwest) St Joseph the Poet; (northwest) St Theophanes. These poets were chosen because of their hymns, verses of which are inscribed on their scrolls; they refer to the prefigurations of the Virgin depicted below. (228) Jacob's Ladder; Jacob wrestling with the Angel (in west half of north lunette). This symbolizes the ladder or bridge to heaven as a prefiguration of the Virgin. (229) Moses and the Burning Bush; (230) Moses hides his Face (in east half of north lunette and on soffit of arch). The burning bush that is not consumed is a prefiguration of the Virgin.

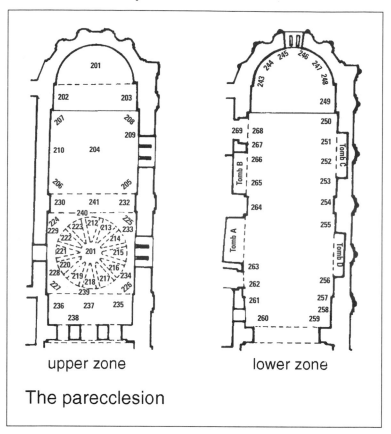

upper zone   lower zone

The parecclesion

Four scenes on the south wall depict the Dedication of Solomon's Temple: (231) The Bearing of the Ark of the Covenant; (232) The Bearing of the Sacred Vessels; (233) Solomon and All Israel; (234) The Installation of the Ark in the Holy of Holies. The Ark of the Covenant is here symbolized as a prefiguration of the Virgin.

(235) Isaiah Prophesying: The Angels Smiting the Assyrians before Jerusalem (in south soffit of west arch). Here the inviolable city is a prefiguration of the Virgin. (236) Aaron and his Sons before the Altar (in north soffit of west arch). Here the altar is a prefiguration of the Virgin. (237, 238) The Souls of the Righteous in the Hands of God (in crown of west arch). This scene is almost entirely lost, but one can make out part of the Hand of God holding out the souls of the Righteous, represented as infants in swaddling clothes.

MEDALLION PORTRAITS IN THE ARCHES

The only portraits on the walls still to be described are those in the four medallions in the crowns of the transverse arches. (239) Melchidezek the Righteous (at the centre of the vertical face of the west arch, in the narrow space between the dome cornice, head missing in its entirety). (240) Jesus Christ (facing (239) in the corresponding position on the arch at the east side of the dome; the head is damaged but the essential features remain). These two portraits were placed in confrontation to illustrate that Melchizedek the righteous, King of Salem and priest of the most high God, who offered bread and wine to Abraham and blessed him (Gen. 14:18–19) was the foreshadowing of Christ. A second medallion portrait of Christ (241) is found on the same arch as (240), on the horizontal surface in the centre of the soffit. The fourth medallion portrait (242) is a bust of the Archangel Michael at the centre of the bema arch; this is larger than the other three medallions and is in a much better state of preservation. The large scale and prominent position of the portrait have led some scholars to suggest that Theodore Metochites may have dedicated this funerary chapel to the Archangel Michael.

PORTRAITS ON THE WALLS

A long procession of saints and martyrs marches about the lower walls of the parecclesion below the cornice. In the apse stands the full-length figures of six Fathers of the Church; they are, from left to right: (243) a ruined figure of a bishop; (244) St Athanasius; (245) St John Chrysostom; (246) St Basil; (247) St Gregory the Theologian; (248) St Cyril of Alexandria. In the rectangular panel on the pier to the south side of the bema arch there is a life-sized portrait bust of the (249) Virgin and Christ-Child. The portrait of the Virgin is of the type called Eleousa, the Merciful, or Compassionate. There was originally a portrait of Christ on the opposite panel on the north side of the bema arch, but this has entirely disappeared.

Outside the bema, the frieze in the lower zone of the parecclesion consists mainly of portraits of martyrs and warrior-saints, the most prominent of them full-length military figures dressed in full armour. There are twenty of them (250–269), most of them belonging to the Eastern Church and almost unknown in the West.

THE TOMBS

There were four tombs in the parecclesion, each in a deep niche which originally held a sarcophagus with mosaics or frescoes above; some fragments of this decoration are still visible. Tomb A, the first in the north wall, is almost certainly that of Theodore Metochites himself, though it has lost its identifying inscription. It has an elaborately carved and decorated archivolt above. Tomb B is entirely bare. Tomb C has well-preserved paintings of a man and woman in princely dress but has lost its inscription. Tomb D is that of Michael Tornikes, general and friend of Metochites, identified by a long inscription over the archivolt. The inscription is even more elaborately carved than that of Metochites himself; fragments of mosaic and painting still adorn the tomb.

There are also three tombs in the outer narthex, and one in the inner narthex. Tomb E, in the fifth bay of the outer narthex, is that of the princess Eirene Raoulina Palaeologina, a connection by marriage of Metochites; it preserves a good deal of its fresco decoration. Tomb F, in the fourth bay of the outer narthex, is that of a member of the imperial Palaeologus family, but cannot be more definitely identified, though it preserves some vivid paintings of imperial costumes. Tomb G, in the second bay of the outer narthex, is the latest in the church; it probably dates from not long before the Turkish conquest, with fresco decoration strongly influenced by the Italian Renaisance. Unfortunately the inscription has vanished and the identity of the deceased is unknown. Tomb H, in the north wall of the inner narthex, is that of the Despot Demetrius Doukas Angelus Palaeologus, youngest son of Andronicus II. Demetrius died c.1340. Only a small part of the mosaic decoration has survived, and the only intact figure is that of the Virgin. Beneath her a fragmentary inscription reads: 'Thou art the Fount of Life, Mother of God the Word, and I Demetrius am thy slave in love.'

Before leaving Kariye Camii we might reflect on the man to whom we owe this church and its incomparble works of art. Theodore Metochites was a true renaissance man, one of the great figures of his time; a diplomat and high government official, theologian, philosopher, historian, astronomer, poet and patron of the arts, the leader of the artistic and intellectual revival during the Palaeologian era. But after Andronicus III usurped the throne in 1328, Metochites and other leaders of the old regime fell from power, stripped of their possessions and banished into exile. Only when his life was drawing to a close was Metochites allowed to return to the city and retire in the monastery of St Saviour in Chora. He died there on 13 May 1331 and was buried in the parecclesion of his beloved church. During his last days Metochites was comforted by his friend and protege, the scholar Nicephorus Gregoras, who was also confined to the monastery. When Gregoras later wrote the history of his times, he penned this affectionate tribute to Metochites, describing his friend at the height of his career under Andronicus II: 'From morning to evening he was most wholly and eagerly devoted to public affairs as if scholarship was absolutely indifferent to him; but later in the evening, having left the palace, he became absorbed in science to such a degree as if he were a scholar with absolutely no connection with any other affairs.' Among all his accomplishments, Metochites was proudest of the church that he had built and adorned, and towards the end of his life he wrote of his hope that it would secure for him 'a glorious memory among posterity to the end of the world'. It has indeed.

The TTOK has restored some of the old Ottoman houses around Kariye Camii. One of the houses is now the Kariye Hotel, which has an excellent restaurant known as the Asithane, an ideal place to have lunch after visiting Kariye Camii.

14

The Seventh Hill

THE FIRST SIX hills of the city march in an almost straight line along the Stamboul shore of the Golden Horn. **The Seventh Hill** stands by itself toward the Marmara shore, its slopes including most of the southwestern part of Stamboul. It is separated from the Fourth, Fifth and Six Hills by the deep valley of the Lycus River, now canalized, that flows into the centre of the Constantinopolitan peninsula, where it bends sharply south to flow into the Sea of Marmara.

Our present itinerary will take us around the Marmara slopes of the Seventh Hill, starting in the centre of the old city and going out as far as the land walls. This will take us through some of the most pleasant and picturesque parts of the city, particularly through the old quarter known as Samatya, on the Marmara shore of the Seventh Hill.

We will start our tour at the crossroads in **Aksaray**, in the centre of the old city. Like Beyazit Square and Saraçhane, Aksaray occupies approximately the site of an ancient Roman forum, in this case the **Forum Bovis**. At the Forum Bovis the Mese, the main thoroughfare of Byzantine Constantinople, once again divided into two branches, one leading off to the northwest along the route of the modern Turgut Ozal Caddesi (fomerly Millet Caddesi), the other heading southwest along approximately the course of Cerrah Paşa Caddesi.

Aksaray was once a pleasant crossroads and market square, but today it has been brutalized by a fly-over highway intersection. The principal monument in Aksaray has been totally isolated by this traffic circle and its overpasses, which cut it off from the people who once used it. This is **Valide Sultan Camii**, the imperial mosque just to the north of the overpass. It was built in 1871 for Pertevniyal Valide Sultan, mother of Sultan Abdül Aziz. It used to be ascribed to the Italian architect Montani, but it seems actually to be by Hagop and Sarkis Balyan, from the family of Armenian architects who built all of the late Ottoman palaces and imperial mosques we will see along the Bosphorus. The mosque, which was much admired in late Ottoman times, but not generally today, combines elements from Moorish and Turkish, Gothic, Renaissance and Empire architectural styles.

At the west of the overpass and to the left down the first cross street, we come to a handsome Ottoman primary school. This *mektep* was founded in 1723–24 by **Ebu Bekir Pasha**; it has been restored and is now in use as a children's library, like several others of its type.

Beyond the western end of the overpass the two principal highways in mid-Istanbul meet in an acute angle; the southern one, Turgut Ozal Caddesi, runs along the north side of the Seventh Hill to Top Kapí, the Cannon Gate; the northern one, Adnan Menderes Caddesi, follows the course of the Lycus River, which is canalized beneath it.

Crossing to the angle between these two avenues, we come to **Murat Pasha Camii**, one of the oldest mosques in the city. This attractive building is one of the two mosques of the 'Bursa type' that still exists in the city, the other being Mahmut Pasha Camii, which we saw on an earlier tour. Murat Pasha was a member of the imperial Palaeologus family; like Mahmut Pasha, he converted to Islam after the conquest, rising to the rank of Vizier before being killed in battle as a relatively young man. The beautiful calligraphic inscription over the portal of the mosque gives its date of foundation as 1469, seven years later than Mahmut Pasha Camii.

Murat Pasha Camii is smaller and less elaborate than Mahmut Pasha Camii but resembles it in general plan: a long rectangular room divided by an arch into two squares each covered by a dome, with two smaller side-chambers to north and south forming a *tabhane*, a hospice for travelling dervishes. The prayer room is covered by two large domes; the eastern one rests on pendentives with bold and deeply cut stalactites, while the western one has a curious arrangement of triangles. The porch has five domed bays with six very handsome ancient columns, two of Syenitic marble, four of verd antique. The capitals are of three different kinds, two types of stalactites and the lozenge capital. The construction of the building is in courses of brick and stone. The *külliye* originally included a *medrese* and a large double *hamam*, but these were demolished when the two avenues were widened.

We now cross Turgut Ozal Caddesi and continue south for a short distance until we come to Cerrah Paşa Caddesi, where we turn right and begin walking up the slope of the Seventh Hill.

A short way along on our left we come to an imposing mosque in its walled garden. This is **Cerrah Pasha Camii**, after which the avenue and the surrounding neighbourhood are named. The founder,

Cerrah Mehmet Pasha, had been a barber and therefore a surgeon (*cerrah*), having obtained this official title by performing the circumcision of the future Sultan Mehmet III. He was appointed Grand Vizier in 1598 by Mehmet III, who warned him that he would be drawn and quartered if he did not do his duty. But he was dismissed after six months, without being drawn and quartered, because of the failure of an expedition that he led into Hungary.

An Arabic inscription over the main portal of the mosque gives the date of foundation as 1593; the architect was Davut Ağa, who succeeded Sinan as Chief Architect of the empire. Cerrah Pasha Camii is generally considered to be one of the most successful of the grand vizierial mosques. Its plan presents an interesting modification of the hexagon-in-rectangle type. The four domes which flank the central dome at the corners, instead of being oriented along the diagonals of the rectangle, are parallel with the cross axis. The plan has the advantage that, for any hexagon, the width of the building can be increased without limit. The *mihrab* is in a rectangular apse which projects from the east wall. The galleries, which run around three sides of the building, are supported by pretty ogive arches with polychrome voussoirs of white stone and red conglomerate marble; in some of the spandrels there are very charming rosettes. The interior is thus elegant in detail and gives a sense of spaciousness and light. The exterior too, is impressive by its proportions. The porch originally had seven bays; its eight handsome antique columns are still standing, four of Proconnesian marble, two of Theban granite, and two of Syenitic marble. The *türbe* of the founder, a simple octagonal building, is in front of the mosque beside the entrance gate.

Immediately across the street there is an interesting *medrese* that is not part of the Cerrah Pasha *külliye*. This was built in the second half of the sixteenth century by **Gevher Sultan**, daughter of Selim II and wife of the great admiral Piyale Pasha. The *medrese*, which has been restored, has the standard form of a rectangular porticoed courtyard with student cells around the periphery.

We now continue along Cerrah Paşa Caddesi for another 100 metres and take the second turning on the right, Haseki Kadîn Sokagî. A short way up the street we come on our right to a massive stone structure wedged between two houses. This is all that remains of a commemorative column erected in 402 by the **Emperor Arcadius**. It stood in the centre of the **Forum of Arcadius** and was decorated with spiral bands of sculpture in low relief representing the emperor's triumphs, like Trajan's column in Rome. At the top of the column, which was more than fifty metres high, there was a colossal statue of Arcadius, erected in 421 by his son and successor, Theodosius II. The statue was toppled from the column and destroyed during an earthquake in 704. The column itself remained standing until 1715, when it was demolished because it appeared to be in danger of collapsing on the adjacent houses. Now all that remains are the mutilated base and some fragments of sculpture from the column that are on display in the Archaeological Museum.

We now continue along Haseki Kadîn Sokağî to the end of the street. There we find the *külliye* of **Bayram Pasha**, which is divided by the street itself; on the right are the *medrese* and *mektep*, and on the left the *mescit, tekke, türbe* and *sebil*. An inscription on the *sebil* gives the date of construction of the *külliye* as 1634. At that time Bayram Pasha was Istanbul's Kaykamam, or Governor; two years later he became Grand Vizier under Murat IV and soon afterwards died on the Sultan's expedition against Baghdad.

At the corner to the left is the handsome *sebil*, with five grilled openings; behind it is the palatial *türbe* of the founder, looking rather like a small mosque. At the far end of the enclosed garden is the *mescit*, which is flanked by the cells of the dervish *tekke*. The *mescit* is a large rectangular building which served also as the room where the dervishes performed their mystical ceremonies, accompanied by music and dancing. The whole complex is finely built of ashlar in the high classical manner, and the very irregularity of its design makes it singularly attractive.

Turning left at the corner and passing the complex of Bayram Pasha, we come immediately to the *külliye* of **Haseki Hürrem**, which is contiguous with it to the west. This is the third largest mosque complex in Stamboul, surpassed only by those of Mehmet the Conqueror and Süleyman the Magnificent.

The *külliye* was built by Süleyman for his wife Haseki Hürrem, the famous Roxelana. The mosque and its dependencies were designed by Sinan and completed by him in 1539, his first *külliye* in Istanbul. According to tradition, Süleyman kept the project secret from Roxelana while the mosque complex was being built, and brought here there only on her birthday, when he dedicated the *külliye* in her honour.

The mosque itself is disappointing, especially as it is a work of Sinan. Originally it consisted of a small square room covered by a dome on stalactited pendentives, preceded by a rather pretentious porch of five bays that overlapped the building at both ends. It may have had a certain elegance of form and detail in its original design. But then in 1612 a second and identical room was added on the north; and at the same time the original north wall was removed and replaced with a great arch supported on two columns. Also, the *mihrab* was moved to the centre of the extended east wall, so that it is squeezed behind one of the two columns. The effect of these changes is distinctly unpleasing.

The other buildings of the mosque complex are magnificent, comprising a *medrese*, primary school, public kitchen, and hospital, all of which have been restored. The *medrese* is immediately across the street from the mosque. It is of the usual type: a porticoed courtyard surrounded by the students' cubicles and the *dershane*; but apart from its truly imperial size, it is singularly well-proportioned and excellent in detail. Its twenty columns are of granite, Proconnesian marble, and verd-antique; their lozenge capitals are decorated with small rosettes and medallions of various elegant designs and here and there a sort of serpentine garland motif, a quite unique design. Also unique are the two pairs of lotus flower capitals, their leaves spreading out at the top to support a sort of abacus; though soft and featureless, they make a not unattractive variation from the almost equally characterless lozenge. Two carved hemispherical bosses in the spandrils of the arcade call attention to the *dershane*, a monumental square room with a dome. The great charm of this courtyard must have been still greater when the faience panels with inscriptions were still in place; many years ago when the building was abandoned and dilapidated they were removed to the Çinili Köşk, where they are now exhibited. Next to the *medrese* is the large and very oddly-shaped *mektep* in two storeys with wide projecting eaves.

The ***imaret*** is beyond the *mektep*, entered through a monumental portal which leads to an alleyway. At the end of this, one enters the long rectangular courtyard of the *imaret*, shaded with trees. Vast kitchens with large domes and enormous chimneys (better seen from outside at the back) line three sides of the courtyard.

The **hospital** is behind the *medrese*, entered from the street behind the *külliye* to the north. It is a building of most unusual form: the court is octagonal but without a columned portico. The two large corner-rooms at the back, whose great domes have stalactited pendentives coming far down the walls, originally opened to the courtyard through huge arches, now glassed in; with these open rooms or eyvans all the other wards and chambers of the hospital

188

communicated. Opposite the eyvans on one side is the entrance portal, approached through an irregular vestibule, like that so often found in Persian mosques. On the other side are the lavatories, also irregular in shape; while the eighth side of the courtyard forms the façade on the street with grilled windows. This building too has been well restored, and it is once again in use as a hospital.

Returning to the street outside Haseki Hürrem Camii, we continue in the same direction for about 400 metres. Then to our left, set back from the road and partly concealed by trees and houses, we see the fine old mosque that has given its name to this quarter. This is **Davut Pasha Camii**, dated by an inscription over the door to 1485. Davut Pasha, the founder, was Grand Vizier under Beyazit II.

In plan the mosque belongs to the simple type of the square chamber covered by a large blind dome; but the *mihrab* is in a five-sided apse projecting from the east wall, and to north and south are small rooms, two on each side, once used as *tabhanes* for travelling dervishes. What gives the building its distinction and harmony, however, is the beautiful shallow dome, quite obviously less than half a hemisphere. The pendentives of the dome are an unusually magnificent example of the stalactite form, here boldly incised and brought far down the corners of the walls.

Behind the mosque, a graveyard surrounds the founder's *türbe*, octagonal in form and with an odd dome in eight triangular segments. Across the narrow street to the north stands the *medrese* of the *külliye*, almost completely surrounded and concealed by houses. The courtyard must have been extremely handsome – indeed it still is – with its re-used Byzantine columns and capitals, but it is in an advanced state of ruin. The *külliye* once also had an *imaret* and a *mektep*, but these have completely disappeared.

Some 200 metres beyond Davut Pasha Camii and on the same side of the street, we come to a grand and interesting **complex**, that of **Hekimoğlu Ali Pasha**, Grand Vizier for fifteen years under Mahmut I. A long inscription in Turkish verse over the door gives the date of construction as 1734 35; the architect was Ömer Ağa.

One can consider this *külliye* either the last of the great classical complexes or the first of the new baroque style, for it has characteristics of both. At the corner of the precinct wall beside the north entrance is a very beautiful *sebil* of marble with five bronze grilles; above runs an elaborate frieze with a long inscription and fine carvings of vines, flowers and rosettes in the new rococo style that had recently been introduced from France. The façade of the *türbe* along the street is faced in marble, corbeled out at the top, and has a *çeşme* at the far end. It is a long rectangular building with two domes dividing it into two equal square areas. Farther along the precinct wall stands the monumental gateway with a domed chamber above; this was the library of the foundation.

The mosque itself, raised on a substructure containing a cistern, is purely classical in form. Indeed its plan is almost an exact replica of that at Cerrah Pasha, which we saw earlier on this tour. The tiles are Turkish, from the recently established kilns at Tekfursaray, in Istanbul. The traditional stalactite and lozenge capitals have been abandoned in favour of a very weak and characterless form like an impost capital, which seems quite out of scale and out of place.

Outside the precinct, across the street to the northeast, stands the *tekke* of the foundation, but little is left of it save a very ruinous *zaviye*, or room for the dervish ceremonies.

Returning to the main street and continuing for a short way we turn right on Köprülüzade Sokağî, which we follow uphill for five blocks. This brings us to one of the two peaks of the Seventh Hill, where we see immediately on our right an enormous open reservoir, now used as a recreational area. This is the largest of the three Roman **reservoirs** in the city, that of **St Mocius**, so called from a church that stood nearby. The cistern was built in the reign of Anastasius I, c.500; like the other two reservoirs, it fell into disuse in later Byzantine times. It is rectangular in form, 170 by 147 metres, its present depth ranging betwen 10 and 15 metres. Its walls are of good late Roman construction, composed of brick, alternating both inside and outside with beds of dressed stone.

We now retrace our steps to the intersection just east of Hekimoğlu Ali Pasha Camii. From there we head south on Ese Kapîsî Sokağî, which we follow to its intersection with Koca Mustafa Paşa Caddesi (the continuation of Cerrah Paşa Caddesi). Then we take the street opposite and slightly to our left, Tekkesi Sokağî. On the opposite side of the street, within the grounds of a government building, we see the ruins of an interesting building that is partly Byzantine and partly Ottoman.

This complex consists of two walls of a Byzantine church and the wreck of a medrese by Sinan. Of the church only the south and east walls remain. It was of the simplest kind: an oblong room without aisles ending at the east in a large projecting apse and two tiny side apses. The church is probably to be dated to the beginning of the fourteenth century, but nothing is known of its history nor even the name of the saint to whom it was dedicated. About 1560 the church was converted into a mosque by the eunuch Ibrahim Pasha, who added to it a *medrese* built by Sinan, now in ruins. The building is known locally as **Isa Kapî Mescidi**. The name Isa Kapî means the Gate of Christ, and the theory is that it preserves the memory of one of the gates in the city walls of Constantine the Great, which are thought to have passed nearby. This is possible, but the arguments of the authorities are contradictory and inconclusive.

We continue along Tekkesi Sokağî to the first turning on the right, Gümrükçü Sokağî, which we follow for one block and then turn left on Sancaktar Tekkesi Sokağî. After a few turnings this takes us to an octagonal Byzantine building called **Sancaktar Mescidi**.

This has been identified, on very slender evidence, as one of the buildings of the Monastery of Gastria. The legend is that this monastery was founded in the fourth century by St Helena, mother of Constantine the Great, and that it derived its name of Gastria, which means 'vases', from the vases of flowers she brought back from Calvary where she had miraculously discovered the True Cross! This story has been refuted by the French scholar Janin, who shows that there is no trace of the existence of the monastery before the ninth century. The present little building has the form of an octagon on the exterior with a projecting apse at the east end; within it has the form of a domed cross. It is thought that it was once a funerary chapel, and it has been dated variously from the eleventh to the fourteenth century. The building was for long a ruin, but it has now been restored and is once again serving as a mosque.

Leaving Sancaktar Mescidi, we walk straight ahead for a few paces to the next intersection and then turn right on Marmara Caddesi. This brings us back to Koca Mustafa Paşa Caddesi, where we turn left and stroll through the pleasant district of Samatya.

We now take the second right onto Ramazan Efendi Caddesi, where a short way along on the right we come to a charming little mosque with a pretty garden in front.

The official name of the mosque is Hoca Hüsrev Camii, for the court official who founded it, but it is more usually called **Ramazan Efendi Camii**, after the first *şeyh* of the dervish *tekke* that was part of the foundation. The building is by Sinan, and a long inscription over the door by his friend Mustafa Sa'i gives the date as 1586; thus, this is undoubtedly the last mosque built by the great architect, who would then have been in his late nineties.

It is a building of the simplest type: a small rectangular room with

191

a wooden roof and porch. It is thought that it was originally covered by a wooden dome, and that it had a porch with three domed bays supported by four marble columns; the present wooden porch and flat wooden ceiling are botched restorations after an earthquake. The minaret is an elegant structure both in proportion and in detail, while the small *şadîrvan* in the courtyard is exquisitely carved. But the great fame of the mosque comes from the magnificent panels of faience with which it is adorned. These are from the Iznik kilns at the height of their artistic production and are thus some of the finest tiles in existence; the borders of 'tomato red' or 'Armenian bole' are especially celebrated.

We now return to Koca Mustafa Paşa Caddesi and continue in the same direction as before. A short distance along, the avenue forks to the right and we soon come to a pleasant square shaded with trees and lined with teahouses. On the left side of the square is the entrance to the mosque complex of Koca Mustafa Pasha, after whom the avenue and the surrounding neighbourhood are named.

The central building of this picturesque complex is **Koca Mustafa Pasha Camii**, which was originally a Byzantine **church** dedicated to **St Andrew in Krisei**. The identification and history of this church are, however, very obscure and much disputed. The general opinion of Byzantinists may be summarized as follows: This may have been one of the churches in this region dedicated to a St Andrew; if so, it is probably that dedicated to St Andrew of Crete c.1284 by the Princess Theodora Raoulaina. (Byzantine documents refer to it as St Andrew in Krisei, after the neighbourhood – Krisei – in which it was located.) Also, the present building was almost certainly of the ambulatory type; it may have been built on the foundations of an earlier church dedicated to St Andrew the Apostle; and it certainly re-used sixth century materials, especially capitals. In any event, the church was converted into a mosque by Koca Mustafa Pasha, Grand Vizier in the reign of Selim I.

When the church was converted into a mosque, the interior arrangements were re-oriented by ninety degrees because of the direction in which the mosque was laid out. Thus the *mihrab* and *mimber* are under the semidome against the south wall; the entrance is in the north wall, in front of which a wooden porch has been added. We enter through a door at the west end of the north aisle into the narthex, walking to its central bay before we stop to look in detail at the interior. This bay has a small dome supported by columns with beautiful sixth-century columns of the pseudo-Ionic type. From here we pass through the central portal into a sort of inner narthex or aisle, separated from the church only by two verd antique columns; this aisle is regretably obstructed by a large wooden gallery. From this point the whole church is visible; it now has a trefoil shape but was originally ambulatory; that is, there would have been a triple arcade supported by two columns to north and south, like the one that still exists on the west. To the east the conch of the apse is preceded by a deep barrel vault; to north and south open out the two later Ottoman semidomes. Even in its greatly altered form it is an extremely attractive building.

The dependencies of Koca Mustafa Pasha Camii include a *medrese*, a *tekke*, a *mektep*, and two *türbes*; what survives of these are of much later date than the conversion of the church into a mosque. The mosque is one of the most popular Islamic religious shrines in the city, for in one of the two *türbes* in the courtyard is buried the famous Muslim folk-saint Sümbül (Hyacinth) Efendi. Sümbül Efendi was the first *şeyh* of the dervish *tekke* which was established here in the early sixteenth century, and to this day the common people of the city flock to his tomb to pray to him for help. The second *türbe* is the tomb of Sümbül's daughter Rahine, who is generally prayed to by young women looking for a good husband. The ancient and blasted tree hovering above her *türbe* is also said to possess miraculous powers.

We now retrace our steps for a short way back along Koca Mustafa Paşa Caddesi past the fork in the road, after which we take the first right onto Müdafayî Milliye Caddesi. This street, which is part of a huge outdoor market on Saturdays, takes us down the slope of the Seventh Hill towards the Marmara shore. About 250 metres along we turn left on Marmara Caddesi, and after a few paces we come on our right to the large Armenian church of **Surp Kevork** (St George), known in Turkish as **Sulu Manastîr**, the Monastery with Water.

Surp Kevork is built on the site of the ancient Byzantine **church of the Virgin Peribleptos** ('Seeing All Around'), whose remains have recently been excavated in the foundations of the present church. The Peribleptos was founded c.1030 by Romanus III Argyrus, and it was one of the very few churches that was not converted into a mosque after the Turkish conquest. The tradition heretofore generally accepted was that the church remained in the hands of the Greeks until 1643, when it was given to the Armenians by Sultan Ibrahim under the influence of his favourite concubine, the

Armenian giantess known as Şeker Para. This story, however, appears to be fictitious, for we read in the recently published work of the Armenian traveller Simeon of Zamosc in Poland, who visited the city in 1608, that it was already at that date in the hands of the Armenians and was the cathedral church of the Armenian Patriarch. The Patriarchate remained here until 1641, when it was moved to its present location in Kumkapî, on the Marmara shore below the Third Hill. The present church of Surp Kevork is due to a complete rebuilding in the nineteenth century. The building in the church courtyard is the entrance to an *ayazma*, or holy well, from which Surp Kevork takes its Turkish name of Sulu Manastîr.

Once past the church we turn right on Canbaziye Sokağî, which leads steeply downhill towards the Marmara. As we walk along we see below and to the left the domes of a large double *hamam*. This is called **Ağa Hamamî** and is a work of Sinan. However it is no longer used as a bath and is now part of a commercial enterprise, its structure having suffered from long neglect.

At the lower end of the street we turn right on Abdurrahman Nafiz Gürman Sokağî, formerly known as Samatya Caddesi. This avenue skirts the foot of the Seventh Hill not far from the sea, following the branch of the ancient Mese that led to the Golden Gate.

After the first intersection we see across the street to the left the courtyard wall of the Greek church of **Haghios Georgios Kyparissas, St George of the Cypresses**. This church was founded in the ninth century and has remained in the hands of the Greeks ever since. The first mention of the church after the conquest is in 1583 by Tryphon Karabeinikov, who came to Istanbul as a representative of the Russian Czar to distribute funds to the Greek churches and monasteries of the city. (He visited the city again in 1589 for the same purpose.) The present structure is due to a complete rebuilding in 1834, when the reforms of Mahmut II made it possible for the Christians in the Ottoman Empire to replace their old houses of worship with new and larger churches.

A little farther along the avenue we see the campanile of a church on the heights above the right side of the avenue. This is the Greek **church of Haghios Menas**. The earliest mention of the church is again by Tryphon in 1583, while the present structure dates to a complete rebuilding in 1833.

Beneath the church, though in no way connected with it, are some very ancient structures of great interest. They are entered from the main avenue and are presently used as a workshop for producing doors and window frames. These substructures, discovered in 1935 by the German archaeologist Alfons Maria Schneider, have been identified as the crypt of the **Martyrium of SS. Karpos and Papylos,** two martyrs who perished in the Decian persecutions of 250–51. The crypt is a large domed chamber of circular form which reminds one of the beehive tombs at Mycenae, only constructed not of stone but of brick, in the excellent technique of the fourth or fifth century. A vaulted chamber, also of brick, extends completely around the chamber, which has a deep apse at the east. This unique structure appears to be one of the oldest places of Christian worship in the city, and one hopes that it will be thoroughly investigated and restored.

About 150 metres farther along, after crossing Hacî Kadîn Çeşme Sokaği, we see on our right the Armenian Catholic **church of Surp Nikoğos (St Nicholas)**, a modern structure of little interest.

The side street to the left directly opposite leads to two interesting old Greek Orthodox churches. The first of those that we come to is **Haghios Nikolaos (St Nicholas).** This is mentioned in Tryphon's list of 1583, the present church dating from a reconstruction in 1830. A short way beyond it toward the Marmara is the **church of Christos Analepsis (the Resurrection of Christ),** first referred to in 1573 by the German traveller Stefan Gerlach, with the present building due to a reconstruction in 1832. Some consider this to be the most beautiful of the post-conquest Greek churches in Istanbul, particularly because it retains its original wooden colonnade and iconostasis.

Returning to the main avenue, about half a kilometre father along we see on our left the Greek church of **Haghioi Konstantinos kai Eleni,** dedicated to Constantine the Great and his mother Helena. It is believed that this church was founded in the early fifteenth century. After the conquest it was used principally by Turkish-speaking Christians from Anatolia known as Karamanlî. The earliest reference to the church is by Petrus Gyllius in 1547; the present building is due to a reconstruction in 1833. On the outer wall of the church there is a relief showing Constantine and Helena holding between them the True Cross (Timios Stavros), patterned on the famous statue that surmounted the Milion at the beginning of the Mese.

We turn left at the second street beyond SS. Constantine and Helena and come to the walled garden of a very ancient and important Byzantine church. The church is known in Turkish as **Imrahor Camii,** whose walled precincts we enter through an old iron gate.

This is the **basilica of St John of Studius**, known also as the Studion, the oldest church in the city, surpassing even Haghia Sophia in its antiquity. (The church of the Virgin Chalcoprateia, which we saw on an earlier tour, is slightly older than the Studion, but only a small fragment of its structure remains, while here the greater part of the building survives.) The church is not officially open to the public, but the family who live on the grounds can usually be persuaded to admit visitors.

The church of Ayios Ioannis Prodromos, St John the Forerunner, was erected some time between 454 and 463, and its associated monastery was completed shortly afterwards. The founder was the Roman patrician Studius, who served as consul during the reign of Marcian. His name was perpetuated in that of his monastery, the Studion, which became the most renowned in Byzantine Constantinople.

The first monks in the Studion were from an order known as the Akoimati, the 'Sleepless Ones', so called because they prayed in shifts throughout the day and night. The Studion housed about a thousand monks in its prime, and throughout the Byzantine period it was a centre of the religious, intellectual and artistic life of the city. The golden age of the Studion began in 799, when the great abbot Theodore arrived to take direction of the monastery. During the next twenty-seven years Theodore made the Studion the most powerful and influential monastery in the empire. He was a leader in the struggle against the iconoclastic emperors. who on three occasions banished him from the city. Theodore returned from his third exile to serve as abbot once again for the last five years of his life, a period when the Studion established the reputation that has led modern historians to call it 'the Cluny of the East'. The monks of the Studion were renowned as poets and composers of hymns, as scholars and transcribers of ancient manuscripts, as illuminators of books and painters of icons. Theodore kept the monks busy at their various tasks, and when their assigned work was done they were expected to improve their minds by reading in the monastic library. 'Is it work time?' said Theodore, 'then to your labours; is it leisure time? then to your studies.'

The church of St John of Studius was one of the most renowned in Constantinople and figured prominently in the history of the city. Michael V attempted to find refuge in the church when he was over-thrown on 19 March 1042, but he was dragged from its altar by an angry mob who gouged out his eyes before he was sent off into exile,

Church of St John of Studion

never to return. Isaac I Comnenus (1057–59) retired to the Studion when he abdicated his throne late in 1059, and after his death early the following year he was buried in the monastery, the 'illustrious school of virtue' where he had studied in his youth. Michael VII Ducas (1071–78) also retired to the Studion after his abdication in 1078, though he later left the monastery when he was appointed Bisop of Ephesus. Michael VIII Palaeologus celebrated a Te Deum in the church of St John on 15 August 1261, the day that he entered the city to restore Constantinople as the capital of the Byzantine Empire.

The Studion continued to function for nearly half a century after the Turkish conquest, celebrating its millennium in 1463. Late in the fifteenth century the church of St John was converted into a monastery by Ilyas Bey, who served as Imrahor, or Chief Equerry, under Beyazit II. Thenceforth it was known as Imrahor Camii. It continued to serve as a mosque until it was destroyed in the earthquake of 1894, after which it was abandoned, the monastery having by then disappeared.

The church was originally preceded by an atrium, whose site is now occupied by the picturesque walled garden in front of the edifice. This served as the courtyard of Imrahor Camii and also as a Turkish graveyard, of which the principal remnant is the fenced-in tomb of a Muslim saint. At the centre of the courtyard is the *şadîrvan* of the mosque, which in Byzantine times would have been the site of a *phiale*, or fountain. The remains of the minaret of the mosque rise from the southwest corner of the building.

At the far end of the garden is the narthex, which is presently closed to the public. The narthex is divided into three bays, of which the wide central one has a very beautiful portal consisting of four columns *in antis*, with magnificent Corinthian columns supporting an elaborate entablature with richly sculptured architrave, frieze and cornice. Two of the marble door-frames still stand between the columns. From the narthex five doors lead into the church.

In form the church is a pure basilica, with a nave ending in an apse, semicircular within and three-sided on the exterior. Around its inner curve there was a synthronon, tiers of benches for the clergy, with the altar in front. The nave was flanked by side aisles separated from the sanctuary by two rows of seven columns. Six of the columns on the north side still stand; they are monoliths of verd-antique with capitals and entablature as in the narthex. Above the entablature of the aisle colonnades there was originally a second row

198

of shorter columns that supported the wooden roof, but these and the columns in the south aisle were destroyed by the earthquake in 1894. The interior was revetted with marble and the upper parts decorated with mosaics. The floor was also of mosaic in opus sectile design, and some portions of this may still be seen, although they are fast disappearing.

Before we leave the church, we might read what one of the monks of the Studion wrote about the monastery in the last days of Byzantium, apparently at a moment of transcendant happiness:

> No barbarian looks upon my face, no woman hears my voice. For a thousand years no useless man has entered the monastery of the Studion, none of the female sex has trodden its court. I dwell in a cell that is like a palace, a garden, an olive grove and a vineyard surround me. Before me there are graceful and luxuriant cypress trees. On one hand is the great city with its market places and on the other hand the mother of churches and the empire of the world.

This concludes our present tour of the Seventh Hill, though we will see other parts of it on our next itinerary, which will take us along the land walls of the city.

We now make our way out to the Marmara, starting along Narlî Kapî Çeşme Sokağî and following it as far as the railway tracks, where an underpass leads out to the shore highway. Here we pass the site of an ancient portal in the Byzantine sea-walls known as Narlî Kapî, the Pomegranate Gate. According to the *Book of Ceremonies*, on the feast-day of St John the Baptist the Emperor of Byzantium would come to pay a visit to the Studion, travelling in his royal barge from the Great Palace, and the abbot of the monastery would be waiting to receive him at this gate, whence they would walk together in procession to the church.

Outside Narlî Kapî we come to a nineteenth-century church built up against the Byzantine sea-walls. This is the Armenian Catholic **church of Surp Mîgîrdîç (St John the Baptist)**. It has been suggested that the original church on this site was Byzantine in foundation, and that it was a dependency of the Studion, but there is no evidence to support this.

We now start walking back along the Marmara shore to Kumkapî, the last stop on our itinerary. This is a very long walk and there are only a few specific places of interest en route, and so those who are tired might be inclined to take a taxi. Much of the Marmara shore is now parkland, so that those who choose to complete this itinerary on foot can at least escape some of the noise and fumes generated by the high-speed traffic on the highway. The present highway was laid out on filled-in land and was completed in 1959. Before that time the sea came right up to the Byzantine sea-walls along the Marmara shore. Considerable stretches of the sea-wall have survived, along with a number of defence towers, and we will see them paralleling the railway line as we pass along the shore.

About two kilometres past Narlî Kapî we come to the ancient **Harbour of Theodosius**, whose defence walls have now been partially rebuilt. This harbour was originally created during the reign of Constantine the Great by an official named Eleutherios, by whose name it was first known. Half a century later Theodosius I dredged the harbour and surrounded it with massive defence walls, of which those on the seaward side have now been rebuilt. The Harbour of Theodosius, as it was thenceforth known, had to be dredged periodically because the Lycus River here flows into the sea, and one can still see its brown effluents discolouring the blue waters of the Marmara.

The quarter inside the sea-walls here is called Vlanga, a name that goes back to Byzantine times. Up until fairly recent times much of Vlanga was given over to kitchen gardens, whose soil was formed by alluvial earth carried seaward by the Lycus River.

About 1.5 kilometres past the Harbour of Theodosius we come to **Kumkapî**, where we see the principal fishing-port of the city, a picturesque harbour now protected by a modern breakwater. The original port was called the **Kontoscalion**, known in Turkish as Kumkapî, the Sand Gate. This harbour was originally created by the Emperor Julian the Apostate in 362, and it was subsequently dredged and its fortifications strengthened and repaired by several later emperors. After the Greek reconquest of the city from the Latins in 1261, Michael VIII Palaeologus made the Kontoscalion the main base for the rebuilt Byzantine navy. After the conquest the Kontoscalion became the principal harbour for the city's fishing fleet. The original harbour was destroyed when the coastal highway was built in 1959, but since then a new port has been created on the seaward side of the road.

At Kumkapî we enter the city via an underpass that takes us beneath the railway line. This is the site of the Porta Kontoscalion, one of the principal gateways in the Byzantine sea-walls along the Marmara, though not a trace remains of the ancient portal.

At the first intersection we come to **Kumkapî Meydanî**. This is a very lively and picturesque market square surrounded by fish-restaurants, an ideal place to eat after our long tour of the Seventh Hill.

15

The Land Walls

THIS ITINERARY WILL take us along the periphery of the ancient **land walls** of the city, beginning on the Sea of Marmara and ending at the Golden Horn, with several detours to visit places inside and outside the city. For the most part, no specific directions will be given for this itinerary, because in some stretches it is more convenient to stroll inside the walls, in others outside, while sometimes you can walk along the walls themselves.

The Byzantine land-walls extend for a distance of four Roman miles across what were once the downs of Thrace, now a modern wasteland whose only greenery is in the numerous cemeteries outside the city.

The land walls, for the most part, were constructed during the reign of Theodosius II. The first phase of the Theodosian walls was completed in 413 under the direction of Anthemius, Prefect of the East. This consisted of a single wall studded with a total of nearly one hundred defence towers at regular intervals. But this was destroyed by an earthquake in 447, toppling 57 towers. This happened at a very critical time, for Attila the Hun was then advancing on Constantinople with his Golden Horde. Reconstruction of the wall began immediately under the direction of the new Prefect of the East, Constantine. The circus factions of the Hippodrome all worked together, and within two months the walls were completely rebuilt and were far stronger than before. Besides restoring and strengthening the original wall, Constantine added an outer wall and a moat. The walls were completed just in time to deter Attila, who turned aside from Constantinople and instead ravaged the western Roman Empire.

The **Theodosian walls** originally extended from the Sea of Marmara to the Golden Horn, though the last stretch leading down to the Horn was subsequently replaced in several stages of rebuilding by later emperors. The main element in the Theodosian defence system was the inner wall, which was about five metres thick at its base and rose to a height of twelve metres above the ground level inside the city. This wall had a total of 96 towers, each 18 to 20

202

metres high, at an average interval of 55 metres; these were mostly square but some were polygonal. Between the inner and outer walls there was a terrace called the *peribolos*, which varied from 15 to 20 metres in breadth, and whose level was about five metres higher than the ground inside the city. The outer wall, the *protichisma*, was about ten metres thick and 8.5 metres in height. This also had 96 towers, alternating in position with those in the inner wall; in general they were either square or crescent-shaped in turn. Beyond this was an outer terrace called the *parateichion*, bordered on the outside by the counterscarp of the moat, which was a battlement nearly two metres high. The moat itself was originally about ten metres deep and 20 metres wide, and could be flooded whenever the city was threatened, although there is some doubt as to whether this was ever done.

The Theodosian walls were anchored to the sea-walls along the Marmara by a bastion known as the **Marble Tower**, which remains a landmark in the southwestern corner of the old city. This is a handsome structure standing on a little promontory by the sea, now separated from the Theodosian walls by the shore highway. The tower, 13 metres on a side and 30 metres high, its lower half faced in marble, is unlike any other structure in the defence-system. It may have been designed as a sea-pavilion, a pied-à-terre for the Emperor when he came for an excursion on the Marmara. Beyond the tower we see the sunken remains of a mole that was part of the castle harbour.

A short way in from the shore highway, just beyond the first tower of the inner wall, we see the first of the ancient gateways that we will pass on this stroll. This is called the **Gate of Christ** because of the laurate monogram XP above it. There were ten gates and a few small posterns in the Theodosian walls. Five of the gates were public entryways and five were used only by the military, such as the Gate of Christ, also called the First Military Gate. The distinction was not so much in their structure as in their approach, for the public gates had bridges over the moat leading to roads in the countryside beyond, while the military gates gave access only to the outer fortifications.

The first stretch of walls between the Marmara highway and the railway line is in a remarkably good state of preservation, with hardly a stone out of place. The first small tower of the *protichisma* bears an inscription of John VIII Palaeologus; the fourth tower of the inner wall has one of Romanus I Lecapenus; and the seventh inner tower has one with the names of Leo III and his son Constantine V, all of them recording repairs on the defence-walls. There are 30 such inscriptions recording repairs on the walls and towers that remain standing between the Marmara and the Golden Horn, ranging over a period of more than a thousand years, evidence of the care that the Byzantine emperors took to maintain this great bulwark of Byzantium.

The railway line cuts through the walls between the sixth and seventh towers of the inner wall. Along this stretch it is best to follow the main road outside the walls, crossing the railway line on a bridge. This brings us past **Yedikule**, the **Castle of the Seven Towers**, which is built up against the Theodosian walls just beyond the railway line.

Yedikule is a curious structure, partly Byzantine and partly Turkish. The seven eponymous towers consist of four in the Theodosian walls itself, plus three additional towers built inside the walls by Mehmet the Conqueror. The three inner towers are connected together and joined to the Theodosian walls by four heavy curtain-walls, forming a five-sided enclosure. The northwest and southwest corners of the castle are formed by two polygonal defence-towers in the Theodosian walls, while the two other square towers between them are marble pylons flanking the famous Golden Gate, which predates the rest of the structure.

The much celebrated **Golden Gate**, or **Porta Aurea**, is actually a Roman triumphal arch erected c.388 by Theodosius I, the Great. At that time the present city walls had not been built and the triumphal archway, as was customary, stood by itself straddling the road that led out of Constantinople along the Marmara coast, about a mile outside of town. The arch was of the usual Roman form, with a triple arcade containing a large central archway flanked by two smaller ones. The gates themselves were covered with gold plate – hence the name – and the façade was decorated with sculptures, the most famous of which was a group of four elephants placed there to commemorate the triumphal entry of Theodosius the Great after his victory over Maximius in 388. When Theodosius II decided to replace Constantine's land walls a quarter of a century later, he incorporated the Golden Gate within his new line of fortifications. In later centuries the Golden Gate was the scene of triumphal entries of a number of emperors, the last occasion being on 15 August 1261, when Michael VIII Palaeologus entered Constantinople after the city had been retaken from the Latins, who had held it since 1204.

We now enter the city through **Yedikule Kapî**, a small Byzantine portal that has above its inner arch the relief of a single-headed

The Golden Gate

The land walls of Byzantine Constantinople

eagle, the emblem of the Comneni dynasty. After passing through the gateway we turn right at the first corner to come to the entryway of Yedikule castle.

Two of the towers of Yedikule served as prisons, most notably the one to the left of the entrance, where foreign ambassadors and prisoners-of-war were kept, while the other towers were used as storehouses for part of the imperial treasury. A stairway in the Tower of the Ambassadors, as it is called, leads up to the top of the bastion, where one can walk along the *chemin de ronde* as far as the Golden Gate. The pylon to the north of the Golden Gate was also used as a prison in Ottoman times, and it was one of the principal places of execution in the city. On exhibition are the instruments of torture and execution that were used there, as well as the infamous 'well of blood' down which the severed heads of those executed in the tower were dumped to be flushed into the sea. Osman II was executed here by the Janissaries after they deposed him on 22 May 1622, when he was only 17 years old. Evliya Çelebi gives this brief account of the murder of Young Osman, as he was called: 'They carried him in a cart to Yedikule, where he was barbarously treated and at last most cruelly put to death by Pevlivan [the Wrestler]. Whilst his body was exposed upon a mat, Kafir Ağa cut off his right ear and a Janissary one of his fingers for the sake of a ring upon it.'

We now return to Yedikule Kapî and resume our walk along the walls. From Yedikule Kapî to the next gate, Belgrad Kapî, is a distance of 620 metres. All of the eleven towers that guard the inner wall along this stretch are still standing, as are all but one of those in the outer wall. An inscription on the inner wall records repairs by Leo III and his son Constantine V c.730, and one on the tenth tower of the outer wall notes a restoration by John VIII in 1434.

Belgrad Kapî was known in Byzantium as the **Second Military Gate**. The gate came by its Turkish name because Süleyman the Magnificent settled in its vicinity many of the artisans he brought back with him after his capture of Belgrade in 1521.

The distance from Belgrad Kapî to the next gate, Silivri Kapî, is 680 metres. The fortifications in this stretch are also in good condition, with all 13 towers still standing in the inner wall and only one of the 13 missing in the outer wall. The third and fourth towers of the inner wall both bear inscriptions of Leo II and Constantine V, while the fifth, tenth and twelfth towers of the *protichisma* have inscriptions of John VIII.

Silivri Kapî was known in Byzantium as the **Porta tou Pigi**, owing to its proximity to the famous **shrine** of the **Panayia Zoodochus Pigi**, Our Lady of the Life-Giving Spring, which is some 500 metres outside the gate. The shrine is known in Turkish as **Balîklî**, because of the fish (in Turkish *balîk*), that swim in the pool round the sacred spring. This spring was first enclosed in a Christian shrine by Leo I in the third quarter of the fifth century, with later emperors repairing and enlarging it. The present church dates from a rebuilding in 1833. The graveyard at the shrine is the last resting-place of most of the Patriarchs of Constantinople over the past century and a half. The courtyard is paved with old tombstones inscribed in the curious Karamanlî script, that is, Turkish written in the Greek language, used by the Turkish-speaking Greeks of Anatolia.

Silivri Kapî is the first of the large public gates which we come to when walking from the Marmara. Like all of the larger gates it is double, with entryways through both the inner and outer walls. The most memorable day in the history of this gate was 25 July 1261. On that day a small body of Greek troops led by Alexius Strategopoulos overpowered the Latin guards at the gate and forced their way inside, thus opening the way to the recapture of Constantinople and the restoration of the Byzantine Empire in its ancient capital.

Excavations just inside the gate in 1988 unearthed a hypogeum, or subterranean burial chamber, dating from the fourth or fifth century AD. Several sarcophagi decorated with reliefs were found in the chamber and are now on exhibit in the Archaeological Museum.

Just inside the Silivri Gate to its south there is a fairly large and charming **mosque** by Sinan. This was built in 1551 for **Hadîm** (the Eunuch) **Ibrahim Pasha**, the second of the two grand viziers of that name under Süleyman the Magnificent.

The mosque has a fine porch with five domed bays, with the portal of the mosque surmounted by an elaborate stalactited baldachino. In form it is an octagon inscribed in a rectangle with galleries on each side. It has no columns, but in the angles of the octagon pretty pendentives in the form of shells support the dome. The marble *mimber* and sultan's loge are of admirable workmanship, as are the panels of the doors, inlaid with ivory. The founder is buried in a marble sarcophagus within an attractive open *türbe* in the garden of his mosque.

The next stretch of walls, from Silivri Kapî to Yeni Mevlevihane Kapî is some 900 metres in length. All of the original 15 towers are still standing along both the inner and outer walls between these two gates, but neither they nor the walls themselves are as well-preserved as those closer to the Marmara. Less than midway along, betwen the fifth and seventh towers, there is a curious indentation in the walls known as the Sigma from its resemblance to the uncial form of that Greek letter, like the Latin letter C. Just beside the Sigma is the Third Military Gate, now walled up. Over this little gate there once stood a statue of Theodosius II, builder of these walls, which remained there until the fourteenth century. The second tower of the inner wall has an inscription of Leo III and Constantine V; and on the tenth tower there is one with the names of Leo IV (775–80), Constantine VI (780–97) and the Empress Eirene. The towers in the inner wall on either side of the Sigma bear inscriptions of John VIII.

Yeni Mevlevihane Kapî took its name from a *tekke* of Mevlevi dervishes that once stood outside the gate. In Byzantium this portal was called the Gate of Rhegium, and sometimes also the Gate of the Reds, after the members of the circus faction of the Hippodrome who built it, as recorded in Greek and Latin inscriptions on the south corbel of the outer gateway. Inscriptions on the lintel of the outer gate bear the names of Justin II, Basil II, and Constantine VIII.

The line of walls between Yeni Mevlevihane Kapî and the next gate, Top Kapî, measures some 900 metres. All but one of the 15 towers in the inner wall are still standing, along with all 14 towers of the *protichisma*. The seventh tower bears the names of Leo III and Constantine V, along with this inscription: 'Oh Christ, God, preserve thy city undisturbed and free from war. Conquer the wrath of our enemies.' Between the ninth and tenth towers the inner wall is pierced by the Fourth Military Gate, now walled up.

Between the tenth and eleventh towers the walls have been pierced to allow the passage of Turgut Ozal Caddesi, one of two wide avenues that were cut through the centre of the old city during the 1960s.

Top Kapî, the **Cannon Gate**, was known in Byzantium as the Gate of St Romanus, because of its proximity to a church of that name, now vanished. Its Turkish name, the Cannon Gate, comes from the fact that outside it in 1453 Mehmet II placed his largest cannon, the famous Urban, named for the Hungarian military engineer who made it for the Sultan. Inside the gate are suspended some of the huge stone cannon balls fired by Urban during the siege. The gateway stands on one of the two summits of the Seventh Hill; the other, about a mile to the southeast, is surmounted by the Cistern of St Mocius, which we saw on the last itinerary.

About 250 metres inside the gate, walking along the left side of Topkapî Caddesi, we come to a large mosque complex that is one of the most masterful of Sinan's works. This is **Kara Ahmet Pasha Camii**, which Sinan built in 1554 for another of Süleyman's Grand Veziers.

We enter by a gate in the south wall into a spacious and charming courtyard shaded by plane trees. The court is formed by the cells of the *medrese*; to the left stands the large *dershane* with pretty shell-shaped pendentives under the dome; beside it a passage leads to the lavatories. The porch of the mosque has unusually wide and attractive arches supporting its five domes. Over the embrasures or niches of the porch are some rather exceptional tiles, predominately apple-green and vivid yellow, done in the old *cuerda seca* technique. A few more such panels, but with blue and white inscriptions, will be found inside the mosque itself on the east wall. The marble revetment around the entrance portal evidently belongs to a restoration carried out in 1896; though very *Empire* in style, it is restrained and does not clash too badly with the rest.

The plan of the mosque is a hexagon inscribed in a rectangle. The four semidomes lie along the diagonals of the building and each rests on two small conches; six great columns support the arches, and there are galleries on three sides. The proportions of the building are unusually fine, as are many of the details, for example, the polychrome voussoirs of the arches and the elegant *mihrab* and *mimber*. But what are rarer are the wooden ceilings under the western galleries, painted with elaborate arabesques in rich reds, dark blue, gold and black. This is perhaps the most extensive and best preserved example of this kind of painting in the city; it is singularly rich and beautiful. Unfortunately, the ceiling on the left has been spoiled by an attempt at restoration, but the one on the right retains its somber brilliance.

Outside the precinct wall, towards the west, is the *türbe* of the founder, a simple octagonal building. Beyond it stands the large *mektep*, double and of very interesting design, a long rectangular building with a wooden roof; after restoration it is once again being used as a primary school. The *külliye* also included a *medrese*, but this has vanished.

A short distance outside Top Kapî there is a small but interesting mosque that is well worth a detour. It is approached by taking Topkapî Davut Pasa Caddesi, the road that leads off from the gate; it stands about 500 metres along on the left. There we see **Takkeci**

Ibrahim Ağa Camii, recognizable immediately by its unique wooden porch and dome.

The mosque was founded in 1592 by a certain Ibrahim Ağa, who was a maker of the felt hats known as *takke*, the most distinctive of which were the tall conical headdresses worn by the dervishes. Takkeci Ibrahim Ağa Camii is the only ancient wooden mosque in the city to have retained its original porch and dome, spared by its remote location outside the city from the fires that destroyed all of the other structures of its type within Stamboul.

A stone wall with a grille and the remains of a fine *sebil* at the corner surround the mosque precincts. The deeply projecting tiled roof of the porch is supported by a double row of wooden pillars. Since the porch extends halfway around both sides of the mosque, the pillars give the effect of a little copse of trees, the more so since the paint has long since worn off. The roof itself has three dashing gables along the façade, a very pretty and quaint arrangement. On the right rises the fine minaret with a beautifully stalactited *şerefe*. Handsome but rather heavy inscriptions adorn the spaces over the door and windows.

Within, a wooden balcony runs around the west wall and half of the side walls; it has a cornice that preserves the original arabesque painting, such as that just seen at Kara Ahmet Pasha Camii. The ceiling is of wood painted dark green, and in the centre is a wooden dome on an octagonal cornice. Here you see how greatly the dome adds to the charm of the interior, and what a disaster it is when these ceilings are restored flat. Two rows of windows admit light; the tiny one over the *mihrab* preserves some ancient and brilliant stained glass. Beneath the upper row of windows the walls are revetted entirely with tiles of the greatest Iznik period, in large panels with vases of leaves and flowers. These are celebrated, and are as fine as those that we saw at Ramazan Efendi Camii on the last itinerary.

We now return to Top Kapî and resume our stroll along the walls toward Edirne Kapî, the next of the Byzantine public gates. The stretch of walls, between Top Kapî and Edirne Kapî is about 1,250 metres in length; it is interrupted between the sixth and eighth towers by Adnan Menderes Caddesi, whose construction caused the demolition of the seventh towers of both the inner and outer walls. Menderes Caddesi and the Istanbul Metro beneath it follow the course of the ancient **Lycus River**, which still flows in a pipeline under the highway, passing through the walls in the deep valley between the Sixth and Seventh Hills.

The Land Walls

The stretch of fortifications between Top Kapî and Edirne Kapî was known as the **Mesoteichion**, the 'middle of the walls', since it formed the central arc in the long line between the Marmara and the Golden Horn. The Mesoteichion was the most vulnerable section of the Theodosian walls, since here the fortifications descend into the valley of the Lycus. During the siege of 1453 the defenders on the Mesoteichion were at a serious disadvantage, being below the level of the Turkish guns on either side of the valley. Consquently the walls along this stretch are the most badly damaged of all the fortifications, and most of the defence towers that have survived, 16 out of 22 in the inner wall and 12 out of 22 in the *parateichion*, are mere piles of rubble or great shapeless hulks of masonry.

The northern stretch of the Mesoteichion, between the Lycus River and Edirne Kapî, was known in Byzantium as the **Murus Bacchatureus**. The only entryway through this stretch of walls was the **Pyli ton Pempton**, the **Fifth Military Gate**. The Emperor Constantine XI had his command post near this gate during the final hours of the siege. He was last seen there just before the walls were breached, fighting valiantly beide his cousins, Theophilus Palaeologus and Don Francisco of Toledo, and his faithful comrade John Dalmata. Tradition has it that the Emperor's body was recovered near the Gate of the Pempton later on the day that the city fell, and that it was secretly buried by the Greeks in one of the city's churches. The Gate of the Pempton is known in Turkish as Hücum Kapîsî, the Gate of the Assault, perpetuating the memory of that last fateful battle.

Edirne Kapî was known in Byzantium as the **Porta Adrianople**, for from here began the main road to Adrianople, the modern Edirne. It was also called the **Porta Polyiandriou**, the **Gate of the Cemetery**. The latter name stemmed from the fact that there was a vast necropolis outside the walls in this area, as indeed there still is today, with large Turkish, Bulgarian, Greek and Armenian cemeteries. It was through Edirne Kapî that Mehmet the Conqueror entered the city early in the afternoon of 29 May 1453, an historic occasion that is commemorated by a plaque beside the gate. Evliya Çelebi, whose ancestor Yavuz Ersinan was Mehmet the Conqueror's standard-bearer, gives this vivid description of the Conqueror's triumphal entry into the city:

> The Sultan, then having the pontifical turban on his head and sky-blue boots on his feet, mounted on a mule and bearing the sword of Mohammed in his hand, marched in at the head of seventy or

eighty thousand Muslim heroes, crying out 'Halt not Conquerors! God be praised! Ye are the Conquerors of Constantinople!'

Just inside the walls to the south of Edirne Kapî is the magnificent **mosque of Mihrimah Sultan**, which stands on the summit of the Sixth Hill at an altitude of 76 metres, the highest point in the old city. This *külliye* was built by Sinan in the years 1562–65 for the Princess Mihrimah, daughter of Süleyman and Roxelana. Besides the mosque, the *külliye* includes a *medrese*, a *mektep*, a double *hamam*, a long row of shops, and the *türbe* of the Grand Vezir Semiz Ali Pasha, Mihrimah's son-in-law. Unfortunately the mosque was severely damaged by the earthquakes in 1766 and 1894. Each time the mosque itself was restored, but the attendant buildings were for the most part neglected; in recent years some not altogether satisfactory reconstruction was carried out.

We enter from the main street through a gate giving access to a short flight of steps leading up to the terrace. On the right is the great courtyard, around three sides of which are the porticoes and cells of the *medrese*. The west side of the *medrese* has only had its portico restored, and it is difficult to be sure how many cells there were along this side and whether the *dershane* stood there as one might expect. The mosque is preceded by an imposing porch of seven domed bays supported by eight marble and granite columns. This porch was originally preceded by another, doubtless with a sloping wooden roof supported on twelve columns, traces of which may be seen on the ground.

The central area of the interior is a square, covered by a great dome 20 metres in diameter and 37 metres high under the crown, resting on smooth pendentives. The tympana of all four dome arches are filled with three rows of windows. To north and south high triple arcades, each supported on two great granite columns, open into side aisles with galleries above, which reach only to the springing of the arches, each of them divided into three domed bays. The plan thus gives a sense of enormous space and light.

The interior decoration is modern, insipid in colour and characterless in design. The *mimber*, however, is a fine original work of white marble with a beautiful medallion perforated like an iron grille. The voussoirs of the gallery arches are a fretted polychrome of verd antique and Proconnesian marble.

From the exterior the mosque is strong and dominant as befits its position at the highest point of the city. The square of the dome base with its multi-windowed tympana, identical on all sides, is given solidity and boldness by the four great weight-towers at the corners, prolongations of the piers that support the dome arches. Above this square rises the dome itself on a circular drum pierced by windows.

Just beyond Edirne Kapî the walls are breached by the broad Fevzi Paşa Caddesi. The Theodosian walls continue for 600 metres beyond Edirne Kapî, at which point they give way to a stretch of walls constructed in later times. The inner wall in this last stretch is well-preserved and has nine towers that are more or less intact, while six of those in the outer wall survive.

At the end of the last surviving stretch of the Theodosian walls stands one of the most remarkable buildings remaining from the days of Byzantium. It is known in Turkish as **Tekfursaray**, the **Palace of the Sovereign**, while in English it is called the **Palace of the Porphyrogenitus**. The palace is believed to date from the latter part of the thirteenth century, and may have been an annexe of the nearby Blachernae Palace, which was the principal imperial residence during the last two centuries of Byzantium.

Tekfursaray is a large three-storied building wedged in between the inner and outer fortifications at the very end of the Theodosian walls. On the ground floor an arcade with four wide arches opens into a courtyard, which is overlooked on the first floor by five large windows. The top floor, which projects over the walls, has windows on all sides, with seven of them overlooking the courtyard; on the opposite side there is a curious bow-like apse, and a window with the remains of a balcony to the east. The roof and all the floors have disappeared. The whole palace, but particularly the façade on the court, is elaborately decorated with geometrical designs in red brick and white marble, so typical of the latter period of Byzantine architecture.

After the conquest the palace was used for a variety of purposes. During the sixteenth and seventeenth century it was used as a menagerie, particularly for larger and tamer animals such as elephants and giraffes. The latter animal particularly amazed European travellers, for they had never seen one before. Fynes Moryson, who visited Istanbul in 1597, thus describes the giraffe that he saw in the sultan's menagerie at Tekfursaray:

> . . . a beaste newly brought out of Affricke (the Mother of Monsters), which beaste is altogether unknowne in our parts, he many times put his nose in my necke, when I thought myself furthest distant from him, which familiarity I liked not; and howsoever his Keepers assured me he would not hurt me, yet I avoided those his familiar kisses as much as I could.

Before the end of the seventeenth century the animals were used elsewhere and the palace served for a while as a brothel. Then in 1719 a pottery was set up in the palace, producing the famous Tekfursaray tiles, which although inferior to those of Iznik and beginning to show European influence, are nevertheless quite charming. The pottery was short-lived, however, and by the second half of the eighteenth century the palace was in full decline and finally lost its roof and floors. During the first half of the nineteenth century it served as a poorhouse for the indigent Jews of the nearby quarters of Ayvansaray and Balat. Around 1860 the American missionary Cyrus Hamlin seriously considered purchasing the palace as a site for a new school, but he abandoned the idea in favour of a site at Rumeli Hisarî on the Bosphorus, where in 1863 he founded Robert College, the present University of the Bosphorus. Later Tekfursaray served as a bottle works and storehouse, but in recent years it has been restored as an historical monument.

Just beyond Tekfursaray the Theodosian walls come to an abrupt end, and from there on the fortifications are continued by walls of somewhat later construction. It would appear that the original Theodosian walls followed a more or less straight line down to the Golden Horn, whereas the present walls are bent in an arc farther out into Thrace. These later fortifications are quite different in construction from the Theodosian walls. For the most part the line of fortifications from Tekfursaray to the Horn is a single wall, without a moat; to make up for this it is higher and more massive than the inner Theodosian wall and its towers are stronger, taller and closer together. It is extremely impressive when seen from outside the city, its great towers marching down in a mighty procession from the heights of the Sixth Hill to link up with the sea-walls along the Golden Horn.

The first stretch of fortifications beyond Tekfursaray is known as the **Wall of Manuel I Comnenus**. This wall, dating from the mid-twelfth century, is admirably constructed; it consists of high arches closed on the outer face, with nine towers, eight of them circular and one square, pierced by one public entryway, known in Turkish as **Eğri Kapî**, or the **Crooked Gate**. This name stems from the fact that the narrow lane that enters the city here must bend around a *türbe* that stands almost directly in front of the gate. This is the supposed tomb of Hazret Hafîz, a Companion of the Prophet Mohammed who, according to tradition, was killed on this spot during the first Arab attacks on Constantinople in the years 674–78. Eğri Kapî was known

214

in Byzantium as the **Porta Kaligeria**, the **Gate of the Shoemakers**; it took its name from the quarter inside the walls here, where military boots, called *kaliga*, were manufactured.

It was at the Porta Kaligeria that the Emperor Constantine XI Dragases was last seen alive by his friend, George Sphrantzes, who would later write a history of the fall of Byzantium. Late in the evening of 28 May 1453 the Emperor, accompanied by Sphrantzes, had stopped briefly at the Palace of Blachernae after returning from his last visit to Haghia Sophia. According to Sphrantzes, Constantine assembled the members of his household and said goodbye to each of them in turn, asking their forgiveness for any unkindness he might ever have shown them. 'Who could describe the tears and groans in the palace?' Sphrantzes wrote. 'Even a man of wood or stone could not help weeping.' The Emperor then left the palace and rode with Sphrantzes to the Porta Kaligeria. They dismounted there and Sphrantzes waited while Constantine ascended one of the towers nearby, whence he could hear the sounds of the Turkish army preparing for the final assault. After about an hour he returned and mounted his horse once again. Sphrantzes said goodbye to Constantine for the last time and then watched as the Emperor rode off to his post on the Murus Bacchatureus, where he met his death the following morning in defence of his doomed city.

The Wall of Manuel I ends at the third tower beyond Eğri Kapî. The rest of this stretch of wall, from the third tower to where it joins the retaining wall of the Blachernae terrace, appears to be of later construction. The workmanship here is much poorer than that of Manuel's section, as can clearly be seen where the two join, without being bonded together, just beyond the third tower from Eğri Kapî. This section contains four towers, all square and also much inferior to those built by Manuel. Manuel's wall has no dated imperial inscription; the northern and later one has three: the first dated 1188 (Isaac II Angelus), the second 1317 (Andronicus II Palaeologus), and the third 1441 (John VIII Palaeologus). There is also in this northern section a postern, now walled up, which is thought to be the ancient **Gyrolimne Gate**. This was an entryway to the Blachernae Palace, whose outer retaining wall and two towers continue the line of fortifications in this area.

We now come to the terrace that once supported the upper part of the **Blachernae Palace**, whose substructures are still virtually intact below, going all the way down to the level of the ground outside the walls.

We enter the precincts by a pasageway beside **Ivaz Efendi Camii**, a classical mosque that stands at the southern end of the Blachernae terrace. The identity of the architect is unknown, although there is an unsupported tradition that it is a work of Sinan. There is no historical inscription, and the date of construction is given variously as 1581 or 1585, the latter being the year when Ivaz Efendi died. The founder had been Chief Judge of Istanbul in the reign of Murat III.

The west facade of the mosque is most unusual. Instead of a central entrance-portal, there are double doors at each end of the façade, the rest of it being filled with windows, producing a very pretty effect. Another odd, indeed unique, feature is that the minaret is at the southeast corner of the building. Originally there was a porch, evidently with a sloping porch supported by columns, which ran around three sides of the building.

The mosque is almost square, its dome resting on four semidomes with stalactite cornices; the *mihrab* is in a projecting apse and is decorated with Iznik tiles of the best period. The centre of the west wall is occupied by a gallery in two storeys supported on slender marble columns. There are also wooden galleries to north and south, but these are probably not original, certainly not in their present form. The interior is very elegant, and the many windows in all its walls gives a great sense of light.

On the terrace in front of the mosque there is a modern concrete stairway that leads down into the substructures of the **Blachernae palace**. The first imperial residence on this site was built in the last decade of the fifth century by Anastasius I, which he used as a pied-à-terre when he visited the nearby shrine dedicated to the Virgin of Blachernae, which gave its name to the palace. The Blachernae Palace was rebuilt and enlarged several times, particularly under the dynasty of the Comneni in the eleventh and twelfth centuries. After the Latin Occupation of 1204–61 the Great Palace on the Marmara slope of the First Hill was abandoned and for the remainder of the Byzantine period the imperial family lived exclusively at Blachernae. They were still in residence there when the city fell to the Turks on 29 May 1453. Because it was built right up against the defence walls the palace suffered severe damage during the last siege, and virtually all that has survived are the substructures.

The substructures of the palace are quite impressive, but to explore them one must be equipped with an electric torch. The penetralia consist of two nearly parallel walls some 60 metres long, the space between which varies from eight to ten metres in width, divided by arched cross-walls into three storeys of compartments, 42 in all. Since the wooden floors have vanished these dungeons give an impression of immense height.

The ruined tower at the outer edge of the terrace is all that remains of the superstructure of the Blachernae Palace, the rest undoubtedly having been destroyed during the siege in 1453. It is traditionally called the **Tower of Isaac Angelus** and the substructure below it the **Prison of Anemas**. The tower is named for Isaac II Angelus (1185–95, 1203–04), who was supposedly confined there between his first and second reigns, along with his son Alexius IV. The prison takes its name from Michael Anemas, a rebel who was incarcerated there by Alexius I Comnenus. This prison-tower appears frequently in the history of the last centuries of Byzantium. Six Byzantine emperors were at one time or another imprisoned in the tower, where they were tortured and mutilated, three of them dying in the process, namely Andronicus I Comnenus (1183–85), Isaac II, and his son Alexius IV.

The fortifications from the north corner of the Blachernae terrace to the Golden Horn consist of two parallel walls joined at their ends to form a citadel. The inner **wall** was built by the **Emperor Heraclius** in 627, apparently replacing the original Theodosian walls in this very vulnerable area, where the barbarian Avars had nearly broken into the city in 626. The three hexagonal towers are perhaps the finest in the whole system of fortifications. Then in 813 **Leo V** (813–20) decided that this wall by itself was inadequate and thereupon added to it the present outer wall, protected by four small towers, a fortification that is less massive and much inferior to the one behind it. (The city was at that time being threatened by Krum of the Bulgars.) The citadel can be entered between the first and second towers of the Heraclian wall, a portal known as the **Gate of Blachernae**. Within the citadel there is a small Muslim graveyard and the türbes of two Companions of the Prophet, Ebu Seybet ül-Ensari and Hamd ül-Ensari, who were supposedly killed in the first Arab siege of the city, their graves miraculously discovered here after the conquest.

From the Blachernae Gate we follow Toklu Dede Sokağî, a winding lane that brings us to the site of the ancient Porta Kiliomene, the westernmost gate in the sea-walls along the Golden Horn. There we turn left and walk along the last stretch of the sea-walls to join the land walls, at the point where the Walls of Heraclius and Leo converge. Here we come to the end of our long walk along the ancient Byzantine land walls, whose northernmost stretch we now see towering above us on the slope of the Sixth Hill leading down to the Golden Horn.

16

Up the Golden Horn

OUR NEXT ITINERARY will take us up the Stamboul shore of the **Golden Horn**, beginning at the **Atatürk Bridge** and ending at **Ayvansaray**, where the great land walls of the city come down to the Horn.

We cross Atatürk Bulvarî and continue up the Golden Horn, whose shore above the Atatürk Bridge has now been converted into a park. The creation of this park involved the demolition of several old quarters along the shore of the Golden Horn, although the few buildings of historic interest there have been for the most part preserved. Among these are the massive stone and brick houses known as 'meta-Byzantine', i.e., erected after the conquest in the Byzantine style.

Here and there along the way we will see some stretches of the **Byzantine sea-walls**. The Byzantine sea-walls for the most part were built in the second quarter of the ninth century by the Emperor Theophilus, who erected them along the shores of both the Sea of Marmara and the Golden Horn, linking them at both ends with the land walls. The defence-works along the Golden Horn consisted largely of a single line of walls ten metres in height and five kilometres long, with 110 defence-towers placed at regular intervals. Only two of the gateways in the sea-wall have survived; nevertheless, the location of the others can easily be identified, since the streets of the quarters along the Golden Horn converge to the sites of these ancient portals.

The first part of our stroll up the Golden Horn takes us past the quarter known as **Cibali**. The huge building that towers above the shore road to our left is the former **Cibali Cigarette Works**, one of the first large factories in the Ottoman Empire, built in 1884. The factory is no longer operating, but it is open to the public as a museum, an interesting look into the tobacco industry and the world of working men and women in late Ottoman and early Republican times. (The building is now being converted to house a new university.)

After passing the factory we see on our left one of the two surviving gateways of the Byzantine sea-walls; this is **Cibalî Kapî**, known in Byzantium as the **Porta Putea**. A plaque records that the gate was breached by Mehmet the Conqueror's forces on 29 May 1453, when Constantinople fell to the Turks. This gate also marks the point that faced the left wing of the Venetian fleet when the Latins first attacked Constantinople in 1203, and again when they finally captured the city in 1204.

About 250 metres beyond Cibalî Kapî we see on our left the Greek Orthodox **church of Haghios Nikolaos**. The earliest mention of this church is by Stefan Gerlach in 1573; the present structure dates to a rebuilding in 1833. In the narthex there is a model of a galleon hanging from the ceiling, placed there as an ex-voto by a mariner in thanksgiving for having been saved from the perils of the sea by St Nicholas, patron saint of sailors. Built into the wall of the courtyard there is an ancient Greek tombstone with a relief showing the deceased bidding farewell to his loved ones. In the exonarthex there is an *ayazma*, a holy well dedicated to Haghios Charalambos. The inner courtyard is enclosed by a well-preserved stretch of the ancient Byzantine sea-walls.

Just beyond the church we come to **Aya Kapî**, the **Holy Gate**, a small portal in the Byzantine sea-walls. This was in Byzantine times called the Gate of St Theodosia, after the nearby church of the same name, known today as Gül Camii. After passing through the gateway we go straight ahead for 50 metres and then turn left, after which we walk for another 50 metres. This brings us to a short stairway leading to the side street on the right, where we see **Gül Camii**, the former **church of St Theodosia**.

The church was founded in the first half of the eleventh century; originally it seems to have been dedicated to St Euphemia, but when the relics of the very popular St Theodosia were enshrined here it came to be known by her name instead. Theodosia had been martyred by the iconoclasts, and she became the patron saint of the iconodules, those who sought to restore icons to the churches of Byzantium.

The Turkish name of the church comes from a story, possibly true, originating in the last hours of Byzantium. Theodosia's feast-day is 29 May, and on that day in 1453 the church was as usual decked with roses for the saint's festival, as the congregation prayed to her to intercede with God to save their city from destruction. When the Turkish soldiers burst into the church later that day they found the roses still in place, and so when it was subsequently converted to a house of Islamic worship it was called Gül Camii, the

Mosque of the Roses, or so the story goes. The Greeks of the city still call it the Church of the Undying Rose.

The church is tentatively dated to the eleventh or twelfth century, principally because of the recessed brick technique used in its construction. It is a cross-domed church with side aisles supporting galleries; the piers supporting the dome are disengaged from the walls, and the corners behind them form alcoves of two storeys. The upper parts of the building were considerably altered in Ottoman times, a reconstruction that gives its exterior the appearance of a medieval fortress. Among the more pleasing aspects of the exterior is the minaret, which is handsomely proportioned and clearly belongs to the classical period of Ottoman architecture when the church was converted into a mosque.

After leaving Gül Camii we return to Aya Kapî and continue in the same direction along the shore road. About 100 metres beyond Aya Kapî we come to **Yeni Aya Kapî**, the **New Holy Gate**. This was not one of the original gateways in the Byzantine sea-walls, but was constructed in 1582 by Sinan to give access to a public bath he had built just outside the sea-walls. This bath, the Havuzlu Hamam, is on the corner just to the east of the gate; unfortunately it has been abandoned and is falling into ruins.

A hundred metres or so beyond Yeni Aya Kapî we come to a point where a street named Sadrazam Ali Pasha Caddesi branches off at a slight angle from the main road along the Golden Horn. This was the site of an ancient gateway known to the Turks as Petri Kapîsî, which led into a fortified enclosure known as the **Castle of the Petrion**, dating back to Justinian's time. The Petrion figured prominently in the sieges of 1203–04 and 1453. On 13 July 1203 the Venetian galleys under Doge Dandolo pushed their prows up against the sea-wall of the Petrion and captured 25 defence towers along the Golden Horn. The French knight Villehardouin, in his chronicle, *The Conquest of Constantinople*, describes Dandolo in action at the height of the assault:

> The Doge of Venice, though an old man and totally blind, stood at the bow of his galley with the banner of St Mark unfurled before him. He cried out to his men to put him on shore or he would deal with them as they deserved. They obeyed him promptly, for the galley touched ground and the men in it leapt ashore, carrying the banner of St Mark to land before the Doge.

During the final Latin assault upon the city, on 12 April 1204, the Petrion was once again at the centre of the action. It was here that two brave knights jumped from the flying-bridge of the Venetian galleon *Pelerine* onto a defence tower, and from there led the charge that breached the sea-walls and brought about the capture of the city.

On 29 May 1453 the Petrion withstood a sustained attack by the Turkish fleet, and the defenders surrendered only when they heard that the city had fallen. Since the Castle of the Petrion had surrendered rather than being taken by assault, Mehmet the Conqueror decreed that the houses and churches within its walls be spared in the general sack of the city.

Leaving the main road and veering left on Sadrazam Ali Pasha Caddesi, we soon come to the entrance to the **Greek Orthodox Patriarchate** and the **church of Haghios Yorgios, St George**. The Patriarchate has been on this site since 1601, having previously moved around to several other churches after being forced out of the Pammakaristos when it was converted into a mosque in 1586. The first reference to the church of St George is by Stefan Gerlach in 1573, while the present structure is due to a rebuilding in 1836. Opposite the church are the administrative headquarters of the Greek Orthodox Patriarchate. During the Ottoman period the Patriarch of Constantinople, under the suzerainty of the Sultan, was the religious leader of all Orthodox Christians in the Empire. The present Patriarch, Bartholomeus, traces his succession back to the first bishop of Byzantium, St Stachys, anointed by the Apostle Andrew. Bartholomeus is the head of the Greek Orthodox Church and the spiritual leader of Orthodox Christians throughout the world, a position that he has used to advance the ecumenical movement.

The street corner just beyond the entrance to the Patriarchate was the site of the ancient **Porta Phanari**, the Gate of the Lighthouse, known to the Turks as **Fener Kapîsî**. The gate itself has long vanished but the name survives in that of the quarter, the famous Fener. Beginning in the early sixteenth century Greeks of this quarter – the Feneriotes – amassed considerable wealth as merchants and traders under the protection of the Sublime Porte, and some rose to high rank in the Empire. One of the posts traditionally held by the Feneriotes was that of Hospodar (Viceroy) of Moldavia and Wallachia, trans-Danubian principalities that were client states of the Ottoman Empire up until the nineteenth century.

We continue past Fener Kapîsî on Vodina Caddesi, after which we take the first left and then the first right. At the end of this street we come to a long flight of steps which leads uphill past a huge area on the hillside enclosed by a high wall. This enclosure was once the site of the palace of the Hospodars of Moldavia and Wallachia, known in Turkish as **Vlach Saray**, which has long vanished. Two churches remain within the enclosure. One of these, the church of the **Panaghia Paramithias (St Mary the Consoler)**, is more commonly known as Vlach Saray, since it served as the chapel of the Hospodars. Vlach Saray was destroyed by fire in 1976 and is now just a charred shell. The other church, which has its entrance on Vodina Caddesi, is known as **Haghios Yorgios Metochi**. The first mention of this church is by Tryphon in 1583, while the present structure dates from a rebuilding in 1730. A manuscript of a lost work of Archimedes was discovered here in 1906. This document, a tenth-century copy in palimpsest, was a perfect and complete text of Archimedes' *Method of Treating Mechanical Problems, Dedicated to Eratosthenes*.

Halfway up the stairway we pass a portal that once led to the palace of the Hospodars. Beside the gate is a plaque honouring Demetrius Cantemir, Prince of Moldavia, who in 1727 wrote a history of the Ottoman Empire, and who also wrote pioneering works on the ethnography and linguistics of Moldavia as well as the first treatise on Turkish folk-music.

At the top of the steps we turn left, whereupon we saw at the end of the street a rose-red Byzantine church with an unusually high drum. This is the church of the **Theotokos Panaghiotissa**, the All Holy Mother of God, more generally known as the **Mouchliotissa, Our Lady of the Mongols**. This is the only Byzantine church in the city that still belongs to the Greek Orthodox Patriarchate, and services continue to be held here, although the congregation is now few in numbers.

Recent studies show that the original church was built as early as the tenth century. The church was rebuilt c.1282 by the Princess Maria Palaeologina, an illegitimate daughter of Michael VIII Palaeologus, whom the Emperor had sent off to Persia in 1265 as a bride to Hulagu, the Great Khan of the Mongols. Hulagu died before Maria reached the Mongol capital, so she was married instead to his son and successor Abagu. Maria lived in the Mongol court for about fifteen years, and through her influence the Khan and many of his people became Christians. Then in 1281 Abagu was assassinated by his brother Ahmet and Maria was forced to return to Constantinople. Shortly afterwards her father offered her as a bride to another Khan of the Mongols, Charabanda, but this time Maria refused, for she had decided to retire to a nunnery. She thereupon rebuilt the present

223

church along with a convent, dedicating them to the Theotokos Panaghiotissa, and spent the rest of her days there as the nun Melane. Since she was famous in Byzantium as the former Queen of the Mongols, her church came to be called the Mouchliotissa, Our Lady of the Mongols. After the conquest Mehmet the Conqueror issued a *firman*, or decree, allowing the parishioners of the Mouchliotissa to continue using their church without hindrance, having done so at the request of his Greek architect Christodoulos (who may be Atik Sinan, the architect of the original mosque of Mehmet the Conqueror). Subsequent sultans confirmed this right, and their *firmans* are displayed on the wall of the church in addition to that of Mehmet the Conqueror.

The church was originally quatrefoil in plan internally and trefoil externally. That is, the small central dome on a high drum was surrounded by four semidomes along the axes, all but the western ones resting on the outer walls of the building, which thus formed exedrae; the whole was preceded by a narthex of three bays. But in the late Ottoman period the entire southern side of the church ws demolished and replaced by a squarish narthex which is in every direction out of line with the original building. The effect is most disconcerting. Nevertheless, the interior of the church is quite attractive, particularly when it is illuminated for a service, with the silver cladding on its ancient icons gleaming in the candle light.

We now walk back around the church to the huge structure that dominates the skyline in this quarter, a red-brick Victorian building completed in 1882. It houses a very old and illustrious institution, the Greek Lyceé of the Fener, known in Greek as **Megali Schole**, or the **Great School**. This probably had its origins in the first Greek school founded in Istanbul after the conquest, although some scholars believe it may go back to the renowned Patriarchal Academy of Byzantine times. Here were educated many of the Greek Voivodes (governors) and Hospodars of Moldavia and Wallachia, as well as the chief interpreters who often wielded such great influcnce at the Sublime Porte, men from the renowned families of the Byzantine and post-Byzantine aristocrcy: Palaeologus, Cantacuzenus, Cantemir, Mavrocordato, and Ypsilanti. The school continues in operation, its present enrolment numbering about fifty.

We now retrace our steps to Fener Kapîsi, where we continue walking up the shore road. Some 125 metres beyond Fener Kapîsî we come to a restored meta-Byzantine mansion that houses the **Kadîn Eserleri ve Bilgi Merkezi, the Women's Library and**

Research Centre, which is open to the public. The library is devoted to books by and about women, with works in both Turkish and other languages, its most important resource being a complete collection of women's periodicals from the late Ottoman and early Republican periods.

About 150 metres farther along, we come to the **church of St Stephen of the Bulgars,** surrounded by an enclosed garden and graveyard on the shore of the Golden Horn. This was erected in 1896, when the Bulgarian Church was asserting its independence from the Greek Orthodox Patriarchate of Constantinople. The church of St Stephen, the patron saint of Bulgaria, is a Gothic building entirely constructed of cast iron, even its furniture and wall-panelling. Nevertheless, the church is rather handsome, both its interior and exterior, and it is kept in good repair by the small community of Bulgars who still worship here. In the little graveyard there are buried several metropolitans of the autocephalic Bulgarian Church.

About 250 metres beyond St Stephen's we come to the Greek **church of St John the Baptist** on the shore of the Golden Horn. The church is believed to be Byzantine in foundation, referred to in historical sources as early as 1334. The first mention of it after the conquest is by Tryphon in 1583; the present building dates from 1830 and was most recently restored in the 1980s.

The battered old stone mansion that adjoins the church courtyard is the former **Metochion of the Monastery of St Catherine on Mount Sinai,** which had an archimandrite in residence here from 1686 up until the late 1960s. This is the most impresive of all the meta-Byzantine buildings along the Golden Horn, but it is in appalling condition and is rapidly falling into ruins.

About 150 metres beyond the church of St John we come to **Balat Kapîsî,** the site of another of the ancient gates in the sea-walls along the Golden Horn. The Turkish name of the gate and the old quarter inside it – Balat – is a corruption of the Greek Palation, or Palace, stemming from the nearby presence of the Blachernae Palace, whose ruins we have seen just inside the land walls.

Balat was for centuries the principal Jewish quarter of the city, though in recent years many of the Jews who lived here have moved to more modern quarters of the city or emigrated to Israel. There are still half-a-dozen synagogues functioning in Balat, one of them dating in foundation to Byzantine times, though the present structures seem to be of the late Ottoman era.

There are also a number of old Greek and Armenian churches in Balat and the adjacent quarter of Ayvansaray, some of them dating in foundation to the Byzantine period, although in most cases the present structures are also nineteenth century.

There are a few monuments of minor interest in the immediate vicinity of Balat Kapîsî. The first of these is to be found on the second street in from the shore road and somewhat to the left of the gate. (Although the gate no longer exists, there is no mistaking its site, for all the local streets converge on it.) After a few twists and turns through the torturous streets, we come to the Armenian **church of Surp Reşdagabet** (Holy Archangels). This was founded as a Greek Orthodox church in the thirteenth or fourteenth century; in 1692 it was taken over by the Armenians, who rebuilt it in the mid-nineteenth century. Beneath the crypt there is an *ayazma*, apparently an ancient one, as evidenced by the Graeco-Roman funerary stelae set into its walls.

We now make a short detour to the south along Kürkçü Çeşme Sokağî. At the end of the street we come to a T, and across the way we see the **Akrida Synagogue**. Akrida was founded the first half of the fifteenth century, the only synagogue in the city that can defintely be dated back to the Byzantine period. The synagogue has been restored and is now open, but to visit it one must obtain permission from the Hahambaşalîk, or Chief Rabbinate, near Tünel in Beyoğlu (see Chapter 18).

We now return to Balat Kapîsi, and a short way west of the gateway we come to a small **mosque** by Sinan. A long and elegantly-written inscription over the fine entrance portal records that the mosque was built in 1562–63 by **Ferruh Ağa**, who was **Kethüda**, or Steward, of the Grand Vizier Semiz Ali Pasha.

The mosque is of the simple rectangular type; it most probably once had a wooden ceiling with a little dome, but this has been replaced in a restoration by a flat concrete ceiling. The building is very long and narrow, with a shallow apse for the *mihrab*, which is adorned with tiles of the Tekfursaray period. A wooden balcony runs along the west wall, but this is clearly not like the original, for it obstructs the windows in an awkward way. A deep porch precedes the mosque; it must have been rather impressive, supported, it would appear, on eight columns, the plinths of which remain; but it has been very summarily restored and glazed in. All the same, it is attractive with its grand marble portal, two handsome niches with pretty conch tops, and at end a curious sort of 'anta' or projection of the mosque wall with windows above and below. This is the handsomest and most interesting of Sinan's many mosques of this simple type, and it deserves a more sympathetic restoration.

We now continue up the Golden Horn along the street that runs past the north side of the mosque. About 150 metres along we see on our left a little Greek church in its walled enclosure. This is the **church of the Panaghia Balinou**, which is mentioned in Tryphon's list of 1583, though the present structure is due to a rebuilding in 1833.

We continue along, passing from Balat into the quarter known as Ayvansaray. About 100 metres beyond the Panaghia Balinou, on the right past a bend in the road, we come upon another of the churches mentioned by Tryphon in his list of 1583. This is the **church of Haghios Demetrios Kanabou**. Athough the present structure dates only to 1730 at the latest, its origins go back to Byzantine times, for a church of that name is known to have existed on this site as early as 1334. Haghios Demetrios served as the Patriarchal church from 1597 until 1600, the period just before the Patriarchate was etablished on its present site. It has been suggested that the church was founded by the family of Nichola Kanabou, who was emperor for a few days in April 1204, just before the city was sacked by the Latins of the Fourth Crusade.

The very pretty garden of the church is built up against a section of the ancient Byzantine sea-walls. From the outer edge of the garden we look out over the Golden Horn, which is at this point spanned by the old Galata Bridge, moved here from its original site after its demolition in the early 1990s. The bridge was reconstructed in 1994, and now spans the Golden Horn between Ayvansaray and Hasköy

Beyond the church we bear right and continue up the Golden Horn on Mustafapaşa Bostanî Sokağî, the first street in from the shore highway. We take the first turning toward the highway, and on the right side of this short street we come to a former Byzantine church known as **Atik Mustafa Pasha Camii**. The church may have been dedicated to **SS. Peter and Mark**, although there is little evidence to support this identification.

It is a domed-cross church dated to the ninth century, converted to a mosque at the end of the fifteenth century by Atik Mustafa Pasha, Grand Vizier of Beyazit II. The wooden porch, the dome and its drum, and probably some of the roofs and many of the windows are Turkish restorations. For the rest, the church preserves its original plan, which is simple and for a Byzantine structure, regular. A dome, doubtless originally on a fairly high drum with windows, covers the centre of the cross; the arms are barrel-vaulted, as are the four small rooms beyond the dome piers that fill up the corners of the cross, entered through high narrow arches. The three apses, semicircular within, have three faces on the exterior. The south apse contains the tomb of Cabir Ibn Abdullah-ül Ensari, a Companion of the Prophet who supposedly died in the first Arab siege of Constantinople, and whose grave was discovered here after the conquest.

Returning to Mustafapaşa Bostanî Sokağî, we continue to the next corner. There on the left we enter the gateway of a large walled enclosure, whereupon we find ourselves in the pretty garden of an ancient Greek Orthodox shrine. This is the **Ayazma of Blachernae**, a sacred spring within a little church at the back of the garden.

The shrine dates back to at least 451, when a great church was built over the sacred spring by the Empress Pulcheria, sister of Theodosius II and wife of Marcian, who dedicated it to the Blachernitissa, Our Lady of Blachernae. A few years later the church served to house the celebrated robe and mantle of the Virgin. These garments, which had been stolen from a Jewess in Jerusalem by two Byzantine pilgrims, were considered to be the most sacred relics in Constantinople, 'the palladium of the city and the disperser of all warlike foes'. The Virgin of Blachernae was credited with saving the city when the barbarian Avars threatened to break through the walls here in 626. The anniversary of this deliverance has been celebrated annually in this shrine ever since, the liturgy accompanied by a beautiful hymn known as the Akathistos. The shrine was rebuilt a number of times, most notably by Justinian, though the present building dates only from the nineteenth century. The Ayazma of Blachernae is still a popular place of pilgrimage, as well as being one of the loveliest spots in Istanbul, a tranquil haven in the rough and noisy city around it.

After leaving the shrine we walk straight ahead on the street that leads out to the shore highway. At the end of the street we pass the site of the last sea-gate in the Byzantine sea-walls along the Golden Horn, the **Porta Kiliomene**, of which not a trace remains.

Our present itinerary ends here, where the great Byzantine land walls of the city come down to the Golden Horn. From here we can either take a taxi back into the city, or else continue up the Golden Horn to Eyüp, a mile or so outside the city walls, where the next itinerary will begin.

17

Eyüp and across the Golden Horn

OUR NEXT ITINERARY will take us to **Eyüp**, a suburban village whose centre is about 1500 metres outside the city walls on the upper reaches of the Golden Horn. Ferries for Eyüp leave from the *iskele* above the Eminönü side of the Galata Bridge, near Zindan Kapî, the Prison Tower. On the way up the Golden Horn the ferry stops at Kasîmpaşa, Fener and Balat, going under the Ayvansaray-Hasköy bridge before coming to the Eyüp *iskele*.

Eyüp is named for Eyüp (Job) Ensari, Companion of the Prophet, who was killed during the first Arab siege of Constantinople. Mehmet the Conqueror and his spiritual advisor, the Şeyhülislam Akşemsettin, miraculously discovered Eyüp's supposed grave there during the siege of Constantinople in 1453, a story told by Evliya Çelebi in his *Seyahatname*:

> Sultan Mehmet II, having laid siege to Constantinople was, with his seventy saintly attendants, seven whole days searching for the tomb of Eyüp. At last Akşemsettin exclaimed, 'Good news, my Prince, of Eyüp's tomb!' Thus saying he began to pray and then fall asleep. Some interpreted this sleep as a veil cast by shame over his ignorance of the tomb; but after some time he raised his head, his eyes became bloodshot, the sweat ran from his forehead, and he said to the Sultan, 'Eyüp's tomb is on the very spot where I spread the carpet for prayer!' Upon this, three of his attendants together with the Şeyh and the Sultan began to dig up the ground, when at a depth of three yards they found a square stone of verd antique on which was written in Cufic letters: 'This is the tomb of Eba Eyüp.' They lifted up the stone and found below it the body of Eyüp wrapped in a saffron-coloured shroud, with a brazen play-ball in his hand, fresh and well-preserved. They replaced the stone, formed a little mound of earth they had dug up, and laid the foundation of the mausoleum amidst the prayers of the whole army.

This pleasant story, though still current and recounted in one form or another in guidebooks, seems rather unlikely – apart from its supernatural elements – because it appears that the tomb had long been known and respected even by the Byzantines. Various Muslim historians note that it was made a condition of peace, after the first Arab siege of Constantinople, that the tomb of Eyüp should be preserved. An Arab traveller in the mid-twelfth century mentions the tomb as still existing in his day, while another Muslim visitor to the city, Zakariye al-Kazwini (c.1203–83) relates that 'this tomb is now venerated among them [the Byzantines] and they open it when they pray for rain in times of drought, and rain is granted to them.' It is possible that these Arab travellers were associating the legend of Eyüp's tomb with the shrine of SS. Cosmas and Damian, the sainted physicians, whose church on the upper reaches of the Golden Horn had been a healing centre since early Byzantine times. In any event, it appears that the tomb of Eyüp was already known at the time of the Turkish siege in 1453, and its location would have been pointed out to Mehmet the Conqueror.

Within five years after the conquest Mehmet the Conqueror built a great *külliye* on the site, including a mosque and a *türbe* to enshrine Eyüp's remains. Here on their accession to the throne the Ottoman sultans from Beyazit II onwards were girded with the sword of their ancestor Osman Gazi, a ceremony equivalent to coronation. Eyüp's shrine became a Muslim Lourdes, and pilgrims came there from all over the empire to be cured of their ailments, just as they did to the church of SS. Cosmas and Damian in the Byzantine era. During Ottoman times many prominent men and women of the Empire were buried in the environs of Eyüp's shrine in splendid *türbes*, a number of which were the centres of extensive *külliyes*. Consequently Eyüp is a veritable outdoor museum of Ottoman architecture, particularly of sepulchral monuments. Many other Ottomans of lower station chose to be buried on the hillside above the shrine, creating the second largest cemetery in Turkey, surpassed only by the burial-ground of Karaca Ahmet above Üsküdar.

The village square is always lively and colourful, with pedlars selling food and religious trinkets to the throngs of pilgrims who have come to visit Eyüp's *türbe*, along with the groups of young boys, each dressed in an ornate cape and sparkling fez, coming with their families to pay their respect to the saint after their circumcision rites.

The *külliye* originally included, besides the *türbe* and the mosque, a *medrese*, *han*, *hamam*, *imaret* and market, all completed by Mehmet the Conqueror in 1458. By the end of the eighteenth century the mosque had fallen into ruins, but Selim III rebuilt it from the foundations in the years 1798–1800, except for the two minarets, which were erected earlier by Ahmet III.

The **mosque** is approached through an exceptionally picturesque outer courtyard, shaded by huge and ancient plane trees, in whose hollows live lame storks and in whose branches beautiful gray herons build their nests in spring. We then enter the inner court, surrounded on three sides by an unusually tall and stately colonnade, all in the deep shade of venerable plane trees.

In plan the mosque is an octagon inscribed in a rectangle. Despite its late date the mosque is singularly attractive, with its pale honey-coloured stone, the decorations picked out in gold, the elegant chandelier hanging from the centre of the dome, and the magnificent turquoise carpet that covers the entire floor (a gift of the late Prime Minister Adnan Menderes, who presented it to the mosque in thanksgiving for his life having been spared in a plane crash). The side of the building opposite is a blank wall, most of it covered with panels of tiles without an overall pattern and of many different periods, some of them of great individual beauty. A door in the wall leads to the *türbe* **of Eyüp Ensari,** an octagonal building, three sides of which project into the vestibule. The latter is itself sheathed in tiles, many of them of the best Iznik period. The *türbe* is sumptuously decorated, though with work largely of the baroque era.

The only other building of the *külliye* that has survived is the *hamam*, and even there the original *camekan* has been destroyed, replaced by a rather make-shift one largely of wood. But the *soğukluk* and *hararet* of the *hamam* remain and are still in use; they have handsome marble floors and the elaborate and attractive dome structure typical of the early period. The Victoria and Albert Musum has a very fine panel of 24 Iznik tiles of c.1570 from this *hamam*, very probably from the demolished *camekan*

After visiting the shrine we leave the village and walk up into the great **cemetery of Eyüp** on the hill above the mosque. This is one of the most fascinating and picturesque spots in Istanbul, with many thousands of Turkish tombs and tombstones scattered about in romantic disorder in the dappled shade of a vast grove of spectral cypresses. The older tombstones are beautifully carved and crowned with representations of the headdress of the deceased, turbans for the men and shawls for the women, with the occasional tiara for a princess. Those of the women are decorated with floral designs, usually roses, with the number of flowers indicating how many children she bore. The tombstones of the men usually have epitaphs carved in old

Turkish script, occasionally with some witty or philosophical fare-well, some composed by the deceased before their death, others by friends after their departure, such as this collection by Cevat Şakir Kabaağaç, the great Turkish writer better known as the Fisherman of Halicarnasus:

Passerby, spare me your prayers, but please don't steal my tomb-stone!

I could have died as well without a doctor than with the quack that friends set upon me.

My name is Süleyman, not Süleyman the Magnificent but Süley-man the stoker. My greetings to you!

A pity to good-hearted Ismail Efendi, whose death caused great sadness among his friends. Having caught the illness of love at the age of seventy, he took the bit between his teeth and dashed full gallop to paradise.

Stopping his ears with his fingers, Judge Mehmet hied off from this beautiful world, leaving his wife's cackling and his mother-in-law's gabbling.

[On a tombstone with the relief of three trees: an almond, a cy-press and a peach, the fruit of the latter being a Turkish metaphor for a woman's breasts] I've planted these trees so that people may know my fate. I loved an almond-eyed, cypress-tall maiden, and bade farewell to this beautiful world without savouring her peaches.

I have swerved away from you a long time. But in soil, cloud, rain, plant, flower, butterfly or bird, I am always with you.

At the top of the hill we come to the **Teahouse of Pierre Loti**, which the French novelist used to frequent during his stay in Istanbul. Several scenes from his novel *Aziyade* are placed in this cemetery. The view from the teahouse is particularly romantic at sunset, when the Golden Horn regains its lost beauty in the oblique light of the falling sun, all the more colourful because of the pris-matic refraction in Istanbul's polluted atmosphere.

We now return to Eyüp Camii. After a last look around we leave the *külliye* by the north gate, where we find ourselves on a narrow street that leads down to the Golden Horn.

Most of the left side of this street is occupied by the enormous *külliye* built in 1794 by **Mihrişah Sultan**, mother of Selim III. This is one of the largest and most elaborate of all the baroque complexes, and includes the *türbe* of the foundress together with a *mektep*, an *imaret*, a splendid *sebil*, and *çeşmes*. The *türbe* is round, but the façade undulates so as to turn it into a polygon, the various faces being separated by slender columns of red or dark grey marble; in general it recalls the tomb of Nakşidil at the mosque of Mehmet the Conqueror, though it is not quite so flamboyant. The entrance is in a little courtyard crowded with picturesque tombstones shaded by trees, along one side of which runs the columned courtyard of the primary school. Farther along the street another monumental gateway leads into a vast courtyard with even more tombstones and surrounded on three sides by the porticoes of the huge *imaret*. This is the only *imaret* in Istanbul that is still functioning, with some 500 people served here daily with food to take away. When leaving we should notice the magnificent *sebil* at the end of the garden wall on the street side.

Continuing toward the Golden Horn, we pass on the right the *türbe* and on the left the **library** of **Hüsref Pasha**; both are dated 1839 and are in heavy Empire style. The domes of the library reading-rooms contain a good example of that horrendous Italianate comic opera painted decoration of garlands, draperies and columns, which is so distrssing when it occurs in classical buildings but is quite appropriate here.

We now take the street that heads southward parallel to the Golden Horn. As we do so we pass on our left the neo-classical *türbe* of **Mehmet V Reşat**, who died in 1918; he was the only one of the sultans to be buried in Eyüp and the last of the imperial Osmanlı dynasty to be laid to rest in his own country. His *turbe* is a rather heavy building; the interior is revetted in modern Kütahya tiles predominately of an overly vivid green.

We now come to a crossroads surrounded by several clasical tombs. The finest and most elaborate of these is the *türbe* of Ferhat Pasha, dated 1595, an octagonal structure with a richly decorated cornice and polychrome voussoirs and window-frames.

We now turn left into the street that leads back toward Eyüp Camii, where halfway along we pass between two classical *türbes* of great simplicity.

The one on the left is the *türbe* **of Sokollu Mehmet Pasha**, built by Sinan c.1572 as part of a small *külliye*. Elegant and well-proportioned, it is severely plain, but the interior contains some interesting stained glass, partly ancient and partly a modern imitation but very well done; alternate windows are predominately green and blue. A little colonnade attaches the *türbe* to the *dershane* of the very fine *medrese* of the complex. Notice the handsome identical doorways of the two buildings, differing only in that the rich polychrome work of the *türbe* is in verd antique, that of the *dershane* in red conglomerate marble. The *dershane* also has stained glass windows, but they are modern and not as good as those in the *türbe*. Its dome is supported on squinches of very bold stalactites. The opposite door leads into the *medrese* courtyard, which is long and narrow, its colonnade having ten domes on the long sides, only three on the ends. The building has been well restored and is used as a children's clinic; it is pretty and charming, with a well-kept garden. In the little graveyard of the *türbe* are buried the family and descendants of Sokollu Mehmet. Just beyond the graveyard is a building in the same style as the *dershane*; this is the *darülkura*, or school for the various methods of reading the Koran. This little complex is certainly one of Sinan's finest.

Sokollu Mehmet Pasha was perhaps the greatest of the long line of able grand viziers of the sixteenth century. He was the son of a Bosnian priest and was brought up in the castle of Sokol, 'the falcon's nest', in Bosnia. When he was in his mid-teens he was taken in the *devşirme* and brought up in the Palace School in the Saray. His outstanding ability brought him early preferment and he succesively held the posts of Lord High Treasurer, Grand Admiral, Beylerbey (Governor) of Rumelia, Vizier, and finally Grand Vizier. He held the position of Grand Vezir for fifteen years, serving under Süleyman, Selim II and Murat III. While serving as Grand Vizier under Selim II he married the Sultan's daughter Esmahan. He continued to hold office until his death in 1579, when he was murdered in the Divan by a mad soldier. His death was noted with regret by the Venetian ambassador Maffeo Venier, who in a report to the Doge noted that 'With Sokollu Mehmet, Turkish virtue sank into the grave'.

The *türbe* across the street from Sokollu Mehmet's is that of **Siyavuş Pasha**, austere like the other but adorned within by inscriptions and pendentives in excellent Iznik tiles. It is also by Sinan, though Siyavuş outlived the great architect by a dozen years and died in 1601. Siyavuş seems to have had Sinan build this *türbe* originally for some of his children, who died young, and then was finally buried here himself.

Still another *türbe* by Sinan is to be found halfway up a narrow and picturesque little alleyway beside the tomb of Siyavuş. This is the **tomb of Mehmet Pertev Pasha**, who died in 1572. The *türbe* is of a very unusual design, rectangular in plan and more like a house than a tomb. It is a ruin, but was originally divided into two nearly equal areas each covered by a dome of wood exquisitely painted; this survived until 1927, when it fell victim to neglect. Inside are still to be seen some charming marble sarcophagi of Pertev and his family.

Here we have come full circle to the north gate of the Eyüp Camii courtyard. We now cross the court and take the inner of the two roads parallel to the Golden Horn, which soon brings us to the second group of buildings that make Eyüp illustrious.

The first of these, **Kîzîl Mescit**, is perhaps hardly worth a visit, though it has been reasonably well restored. Founded in 1581 by Kiremitçi Süleyman Çelebi, it is of the simplest type, a rectangular room of stone and brick with a tiled roof and a brick minaret.

A little farther on, on the opposite side of the street, we come to **Silahi Mehmet Bey Mescidi**, dated c.1490. This little mosque is also of the simplest type, but with an unusual and fascinating minaret. The minaret is hexagonal in shape, built of stone and brick; instead of the usual balcony it has a sort of lantern with six windows and a tall conical cap. There are in the city three or four other minarets with this lantern arrangement, but this is much the most striking and pretty.

Opposite Silahi Mescidi is the grandest and most intersting **mosque** in Eyüp, that of **Zal Mahmut Pasha**, a mature but unique work of Sinan. Its date of construction is unknown; that usually given, 1551, is at least twenty years too early, and a date in the mid-1570s seems most probable. The founder was an unsavoury character, his rise to power beginning in 1553 when he was assigned by Süleyman to execute Prince Mustafa, the Sultan's eldest son, who was suspected of planning to usurp the throne. Mahmut (who got his forename Zal from that of a Persian hero famous for his Herculean strength), finally ovecame the prince's resistance and strangled him. Later he married the Princess Şah Sultan, daughter of Selim II, the Sot, as a reward, it is said, for having smoothed that prince's way to the throne by the elimination of his older brother. In 1580 Zal and his wife died in a single night, for reasons unrecorded.

A fine view of the south façade of Zal Mahmut Camii can be had from the garden of Silahi Mescidi, which is a little higher. With its four tiers of windows and its great height and squareness it looks more like a palace than a mosque. The north façade is even more towering, for the mosque is built on a slope and supported on vaulted substructures in which rooms for the lower *medrese* have been made.

The mosque is constructed of alternate courses of stone and brick. A handsome porch of five bays gives access to the interior. This is a vast rectangular room; the massive dome arches spring out on the east from supports in the wall itself, on the west from thick and rather stubby pillars some distance in from the west wall. Galleries supported on a rather heavy arcade, some of whose arches are of the ogive type, run around three sides of the prayer room. The walls, which rise in a rectangle to the full height of the dome drum, are pierced with many windows and in spite of the width of the galleries provide plenty of light. The general effect of the interior is perhaps a little heavy but nonetheless grand and impressive, and it is quite different than that of any other mosque. The leaves of the main entrance door are fine inlaid work in wood, while the *mimber* and *mihrab* are equally fine works in carved marble.

The complex includes two *medreses*, like the mosque itself built of stone and brick. One of the *medreses* is laid out around three sides of the main courtyard, the other on a lower level to the north, enclosing two sides of the *türbe* garden. They are both of them extremely picturesque and irregular in design. In the upper *medrese* most of the south side consists of a building without a portico which looks rather like an *imaret* and may in fact have served as one. The *dershane* is not in the centre of the west wall but has been shifted to near the north end, and the last arches of the porches on this side are smaller than the others. There is no obvious reason for any of these abnormalities, but they have a certain charm, enhanced by the ogive arches of the arcade. At the northeast corner a long flight of steps leads down to the garden of the *türbe*, which is partly enclosed by two sides of the lower *medrese*. The *türbe* is an octagonal building of the usual type, in which ate buried Zal and his wife Şah Sultan.

A door in the east wall of the *türbe* garden leads to another **külliye** of a very different type, one of the most delightful of the smaller baroque complexes. It consists of an elaborate *türbe* and *mektep* with a *sebil* on the street and a *çeşme* in the garden. This was built at the end of the eighteenth century by **Şah Sultan**, a sister of Selim III. The undulating façades of the *türbe* and the amusing turned-back staircase of the *mektep* are very charming.

We now return to the inner street, along which there are two more buildings that are at least worth a glance.

At the next intersection we see on our left the small **mosque** of **Cezarî Kasîm Pasha**, erected in 1515. It has a pretty porch with four handsome antique columns of red granite, with the balcony of the minaret supported on an unusual zigzag corbel. Inside there are some late tiles; near the *mimber* there is an interesting one dated 1726 and signed 'Mehmet, son of Osman of Iznik'. This is a very fine panel showing the Kaaba at Mecca with interesting details including several large tents in the background.

At the next intersection we see on our right the **mosque of the Defterdar (Lord High Treasurer) Mahmut Efendi**; this is a very early mosque but was wholly rebuilt in the eighteenth century and is of little interest in itself. In the garden is the founder's curious open *türbe* surmounted by a dome supported on arches with scalloped soffits.

We now walk to the shore road, which along this stretch is called Feshane Caddesi. The name comes from the huge building on the far side of the road, the **Feshane**, or **Fez Factory**. The original Feshane on this site was erected in 1833 to produce the hat known as the 'fez' for the New Army of Mahmut II. The building was redesigned in 1843 and in 1894 it was expanded. After the fez was banned in the clothing reform in 1925, the Feshane was converted to other uses; then in 1986 it was closed and a number of its buildings were demolished during the programme for cleaning up the Golden Horn and renovating its shores. The Feshane has recently been restored; it is now used as an exhibition hall, and there are plans to convert it into a museum and art gallery.

The last stage of our itinerary will take us across the Golden Horn on the Ayvansaray-Hasköy bridge. We will see a number of sites along that side of the Golden Horn before returning to town, including some that are seldom visited by tourists or indeed Turks, though they are as interesting as many places in Stamboul that are far better known. These places are quite widely separated, and the areas in which they are located are, for the most part, not easy to negotiate on foot, and so it is probably best to do this part of the itinerary by taxi, or a seris of taxis.

The first places that we will visit are in **Hasköy**, directly across from Ayvansaray on the rebuilt span that was formerly the Galata Bridge.

Hasköy had in times past a large numbers of Greeks and Jews, the latter including members of the Karaite sect who had been moved here from Eminönü in the early seventeenth century when the construction of Yeni Cami began. Very few of these minorities now remain in Hasköy. The Orthodox Jews worship at the Mualem Synagogue on Harap Çeşme Sokağî, while the Karaites use the Bnai

Mikra Synagogue on Mahlul Sokağî. The large Jewish cemetery on the hill above Hasköy has sections for both the Orthodox and Karaite communities.

The few Greeks who remain in Hasköy worship at the **church of Haghia Paraskevi**, which is at the inner end of Baçtar Sokağî, the street that leads in from the *iskele*, or ferry-landing. The original church on this site dates back to the Byzantine period; after the conquest it is first mentioned in 1547 by Petrus Gyllius. The church was rebuilt in 1692 by Constantine Brankovanos, Prince of Wallachia, and in 1833 it was restored and took on its present appearance. Within the picturesque courtyard there are a number of interesting old tombstones, as well as a relief representing the Emperor Constantius Chlorus (305–06) and his wife Helena, parents of Constantine the Great, who are shown holding between them the True Cross.

Some 250 metres above the bridge we come to the new **Rahmi M. Koç Industrial Museum**. This is housed in a superbly restored Ottoman Lengerhane, or forge for making ship's chains and anchors, a structure dating from the first quarter of the eighteenth century. The exhibits, all attractively displayed, are mostly engines, machines and scientific instruments, as well as model automobiles, steam locomotives, aeroplanes, boats and ships, including a replica of a ship's bridge whose instruments may be operated by visitors. At the entrance there are a number of ancient Greek tombstones that were found at various sites in the city. One of the buildings of the Lengerhane has been converted into an attractive restaurant, the Café du Levant.

We now take a taxi back along the shore road past Hasköy to **Aynalîkavak Kasrî**, the **Palace of the Mirroring Poplars**, where the highway bends in from the Golden Horn to pass around the gardens of this late Ottoman pleasure-dome.

The original imperial building on this site was a pavilion erected at the beginning of the seventeenth century by Ahmet I. The palace was rebuilt on a larger scale and sumptuously decorated by Ahmet III in the early eighteenth century as one of the sites or his famous Tulip Festivals. Early in the third quarter of that century Aynalîkavak was extensively repaired by Koca Yusuf Pasha, Grand Vezir under Abdül Hamit I. The palace gave its name to the Treaty of Aynalîkavak, which was signed here on 9 January 1784 by representatives of Russia and the Ottoman Empire. The palace took on its present form in the last decade of the eighteenth century under Selim

II, who wrote some of his musical compositions while staying here. The palace was restored in the Republican era, and on 26 July 1984 it was officially opened as a museum by President Kenan Evren.

The palace is surrounded by particularly beautiful gardens and shaded by a grove of venerable trees, including a magnificent larch. It is in two storeys on the side facing the Golden Horn and a single storey to the rear, an arrangement due to the natural slope of the site. Aynalîkavak is celebrated for its many windows, with those in the upper course delicately fringed in stained glass. The furniture and décor are from the period of Selim III, including many original works. The elaborate inscriptions are from poems by Şeyh Galip and Enderunlu Fazîl, and the *tuğra* is the imperial monogram of Selim III, all written by the calligrapher Yesarî.

The principal rooms are the Arz Odasî, or imperial audience chamber; the Divanhane, or council hall; the Mother-of-Pearl Room, named after the inlaid suite there; and the Composition Room, where Selim III wrote and performed his music. The palace also houses the **Turkish Musical Research Centre and Musical Instruments Museum**, where concerts are held from time to time. The museum has a fascinating collection of the instruments used in Turkish classical music, with enlargements of miniatures showing their use in Ottoman times. Tapes of this music are played in the museum, including some of the compositions of Selim III.

There is a simple little café in the garden, a delightful place to pause before going off on the last stage of our itinerary.

The last place that we will visit on this itinerary is **Piyale Pasha Camii**, which is some two kilometres inland from the *iskele* at Kasîmpaşa, the first ferry-station on the north shore of the Golden Horn above the Atatürk Bridge. The mosque is at the head of Bülbül Deresi, the Valley of the Nightingales, whose once arcadian stream has long been built over by the streets and houses of the Kasîmpaşa quarter.

Piyale Pasha Camii is one of the most interesting and enigmatic of the classical mosques. The mosque was completed in 1573 by an unknown follower of Sinan. Piyale Pasha, the founder, began life as a Christian, the son of a Croatian shoemaker; he was taken up in the *devşirme*, educated in the Palace School, and eventually rose to the rank of Grand Admiral. While in command of the Ottoman fleet he terrorized the eastern Mediterranean, raiding as far as the coast of southern Italy, and captured a number of Aegean isles, including Chios. He was a favourite of Selim II, and capped his career by marrying one of the Sultan's daughters, Hace Gevheri Muluk Sultan.

Piyale Pasha Camii is unique in the clasical period in more than one respect. In the first place, it is the only classical mosque to revert to the Ulu Cami or multi-domed type common in the Selcuk and early Ottoman periods. Its six ample and identical domes in two rows of three each are supported internally by two great columns of red marble. Thus far the plan follows the earlier type, but all else is different.

Round three sides of the building there is a deep porch whose vaults are supported by stout rectangular pillars. Above the side porches are galleries with sloping roofs supported on small columns, while in front of the main porch there was another porch with 22 columns. Unfortunately, the roofs of this and the upper galleries on the sides have vanished, but from old prints and photographs of the mosque one can see how fascinating this unique arrangement was. The founder's *türbe* behind the mosque also had a colonnaded porch, but this too has gone. In the centre of the west wall there was a small balcony supported on six columns; behind this rises the single minaret, which is thus in the very unusual position of being in the middle of the west façade. The entrance portals are to the right and left of the balcony.

The mosque is lighted by numerous windows; many of the upper ones are round, *oeils-de-boeuf*. Between the second and third tier of windows a wide frieze of faience has inscriptions from the Koran in white on a blue ground; these are from the hand of the famous calligrapher Karahisarî, who wrote the inscriptions in the Süleymaniye. The *mihrab* is also a very beautiful work, with Iznik tiles of the best period. (One of the tile panels from Piyale Pasha Camii, a beautiful lunette, is now above one of the entrances to the Asiatic wing of the Boston Museum of Fine Arts.) The whole interior is not only unusual but exceptionally charming.

After seeing Piyale Pasha Camii we take a taxi back to town, concluding our itinerary around the Golden Horn.

18

Galata and Beyoğlu

THE OLDEST PARTS of the city on the north bank of the Golden Horn are **Galata** and **Beyoğlu**, the latter being the area formerly known as Pera. In Greek 'Pera' means 'beyond', at first in the general sense of 'across the Golden Horn', then in the medieval Byzantine period referring to the town that developed across the Horn from Constantinople; and later still to the fashionable suburbs above the walled town of Galata.

The historic origins of Galata predate the founding of Constantinople, going back to the times of the ancient Greek city of Byzantium. When the city was still known as Byzantium there are references to a small settlement on the north shore of the Golden Horn. This was originally called **Sycae**, or the **Fig Trees**, and it was also known as Peran en Sycais, meaning Sycae 'on the opposite shore'. As early as the fifth century AD Galata, whose name is of uncertain origin, had developed into a town, which was included within the limits of Constantinople as the Regio Sycaena, the thirteenth of the Byzantine capital's fourteen regions, surrounded by a defence wall and including a harbour, theatre, forum, public bath, and several churches. In 528 Justinian restored its theatre and other structures, renaming the town after himself as Justinianae, a name that ceased to be used after his reign and was soon forgotten, as the town once again came to be called Galata. Half a century later Tiberius II (578–82) is believed to have built a fortress in Galata at the confluence of the Golden Horn and the Bosphorus. This was known as the Castle of Galata, and it was used to anchor one side of the great chain that was stretched across the entrance to the Golden Horn in times of attack, the other side being moored to a tower of the sea walls under the Byzantine acropolis.

The town of Galata took its present form under the Genoese. Genoa, along with Venice and other Italian city-states, had obtained concessions from the Byzantine emperors as early as the eleventh century on the south bank of the Golden Horn in Constantinople. When the Venetians and the knights of the Fourth Crusade conquered Constantinople in 1204, the Genoese were forced to move across the Golden Horn to Galata, where they took control of the town and its port. During the last year of the Latin Occupation the Genoese entered into an alliance with Michael VIII Palaeologus, whose capital was then in Nicaea. This alliance, which was sealed with the signing of the Treaty of Nymphaeum on 12 March 1261, gave the Genoese extensive trading and commercial concessions in the Byzantine Empire. After the Byzantines recaptured Constantinople four months later, the Emperor allowed the Genoese to exploit these concessions to the fullest in Galata, which soon became an independent city-state under the aegis of Genoa. The city government was headed by a governor called the Podesta, who was appointed for a one-year term by the Senate of Genoa and sent out to Galata, where he and his council ruled from the Podestat, or Town Hall. Although the Genoese were expressly forbidden to fortify Galata, they began to do so almost immediately and went on expanding their colony with new walled enclosures throughout the remainder of the Byzantine period.

The first fortified area, walled in as early as 1304, was a long and narrow rectangle along the Golden Horn between the present Galata and Atatürk bridges. Then, in order to defend themselves more adequately on the upper landward side, the Genoese fortified a wedge-shaped area on the hillside above the eastern half of their first walled enclosure; and at the apex of these walls they erected the present **Galata Tower**, originally known as the **Tower of Christ**, which they completed in 1348. The final system of fortifications consisted of six walled enceintes, with the outer wall bordered by a deep ditch. The walls remained largely intact up until 1845, but then they were demolished so that Galata could expand beyond its medieval bounds. Today virtually all that remains of the Genoese fortifications are the Galata Tower and the remains of two defence towers and one postern.

Galata remained neutral during the Turkish siege of Constantinople in 1453, though many of the Genoese fought as allies of the Greeks in defending the city, most notably the brave Giustiniani, the Emperor Constantine's right-hand man. On 1 June 1453, three days after the fall of Constantinople, Mehmet the Conqueror met with leaders of the Genoese community in Galata and signed a treaty with them. The treaty confirmed the rights that had been given to the Genoese by the Byzantine emperors, but the Sultan refused to recognize Galata as a separate state. Mehmet the Conqueror ordered the Genoese to demolish some of their defence-towers and walls as a demonstration of his sovereignty over Galata, also decreeing that one of the largest Catholic churches be converted into a mosque. The following year Galata officially became a part of the Ottoman Empire, with the Sultan appointing a Voivode to govern the town. Nevertheless, the Genoese in Galata retained some degree of self-rule, running their municipal affairs through a body known as the Magnificent Community of Pera, which met in the **Podestat**, then known as the **Palazzo del Communale**. This body continued to control the civic affairs of Galata up to the mid-seventeenth century, after which its powers were limited to administering the Roman Catholic churches within the community. By the end of the nineteenth century the Magnificent Community of Pera had lost all of its remaining powers; then it lingered on for a while as a fraternal and religious society before disappearing altogether in the last years of the Ottoman Empire.

Immediately after the conquest Mehmet the Conqueror built a huge Tershane, or Naval Arsenal, on the shore of the Golden Horn just above Galata, where it still functions today as a shipyard. This, together with the very busy harbour, made Galata the centre of the city's maritime industries, where the Italian, Greek, Armenian and Jewish merchants made their living principally by catering to the needs of the ships in the port and their motley crews. Evliya Çelebi describes the scene in Galata in his day:

> In Galata there are eighteen wards inhabited by Moslems, seventy by Greeks, three by Franks, one by Jews, and two by Armenians. . . . The different wards of the town are patrolled day and night by watchmen to prevent disorders among the population, who are of a rebellious disposition, on account of which they have from time to time been chastised by the sword. The inhabitants are either sailors, merchants, or handicraftsmen such as joiners or caulkers. They dress for the most part in the Algerine style, because a great number of them are Arabs and Moors. The Greeks keep the taverns; the Armenians are merchants and bankers; the Jews are negotiators in love matters and their youths are the worst of all the devotees of debauchery. . . . In Galata there are two hundred taverns and wine-shops where the infidels divert themselves with music and drinking. The taverns are celebrated for the wine from Ancona, Sargossa, Mudanya, and Tenedos. The word *günaha* [temptation] is most particularly to be applied to the taverns of Galata because there all kinds of playing and dancing boys, mimics and fools, flock together and delight themselves day and night. When I passed through here, I saw many hundreds barefooted and bare-headed lying drunk in the streets.

243

Within a century after the conquest the wealthier merchants began to move out of the crowded confines of Galata to the hills and vineyards above, the area that came to be called Pera and is now known as Beyoğlu. Here the foreign powers built palatial mansions surrounded by gardens, all of them standing along the road that would later be called the Grand Rue de Pera. The population of Pera was mostly non-Muslim up until the end of the Ottoman Empire, but since then it has become as Turkish as the rest of Istanbul, with only small numbers of Greeks, Armenians, Jews and Levantine Europeans remaining, including a very few Genoese who can still trace their ancestry back to the days of the Magnificent Community of Pera.

We will begin our exploration of Galata by walking along the lively and colourful quay between the Galata Bridge and the ferry terminal, passing a raucous line of fishermen who from their rowboats sell fried fish sandwiches to passersby.

Just across from the ferry terminal we find one of the entrances to **Kemankeş Camii**, which has another entryway one street in from the port. This is better known as **Yer Altî Cami**, the **Underground Mosque**, for its prayer-hall is below street level in the vaults of an ancient Byzantine dungeon. Some scholars have identified this as the keep of the historic Castle of Galata built by Tiberius II. All that remains of the castle, if this be it, are the vast dungeons that house Yer Altî Cami, a labyrinth of vaults supported by 54 squat pillars in six rows of nine each. Deep within this maze we find the contiguous tombs of two Muslim saints separated from the mosque by gilded bronze grilles, together making up a sacred shrine visited by a constant stream of pilgrims, mostly women. The saints are Abu Sufyan and Amiri Wahibi, two more Warriors for the Faith (Gazi) who were supposedly captured by the Byzantines in the first Arab siege of Constantinople, dying as prisoners in the dungeons of the Castle of Galata. Their graves were revealed to a Nakşibendi dervish in a dream in 1640. When Murat IV learned of this he had the two saints reburied in ornate *türbes* on the site; then in 1757 the dungeons were converted into a mosque by the Grand Vizier Köse Mustafa Pasha.

Leaving Yer Altî Cami by its upper door, we might wander about for a while in the labyrinth of narrow streets of Galata near the lower shore of the Bosphorus. This was the last part of Galata to be walled in by the Genoese, just seven years before the Turkish conquest. Walking northward to Kemeraltî Caddesi, we see on the far side of the avenue a tall medieval tower. This is the oldest part of the Roman Catholic **church of St Benoit**. The church was founded by the Benedictines in 1427 and later became the royal chapel of the French ambassadors, several of whom were buried here. After being occupied by the Jesuits for several centuries, it was given on the temporary dissolution of that order in 1773 to the Lazarists, to whom it still belongs. In 1804 the Lazarists established a school here which is still one of the best of the foreign lycees in the city. Only the tower remains from the original church of 1427, with the nave and south aisle dating from 1732 and the north aisle from 1871.

Somewhat farther along Kemeraltî Caddesi and on the opposite side stands the new building of the Armenian **church of Surp Kirkor Lusavoriç, St Gregory the Illuminator**. This was erected a few years after the original church nearby had been demolished, when Kemeraltî Caddesi was widened in 1956. The original church was built in 1436, a decade before this part of Galata was walled in by the Genoese, the line of fortifications stretching along the present course of Kemeraltî Caddesi, the Avenue Under the Arches. The present church of Surp Kirkor is a replica of the famous church of St Gregory built in the seventh century in the Armenian city of Echmiadzin.

In the labyrinth of streets between Kemeraltî Caddesi and the Bosphorus there are three very old and interesting Greek churches. These are **Ayios Ioannis (St John)**, **Ayios Nikolaos (St Nicholas)**, and the **Panayia (the Blessed Virgin)**; all three were founded in the fifteenth century, although the present buildings date only from the nineteenth century. The Panayia is the headquarters of the so-called **Turkish Orthodox Church**, a tiny group who broke off from the Greek Orthodox Church in 1923 under a priest named Papa Eftim. Eftim proclaimed himself Patriarch of the Turkish Orthodox Church, and laid claim to the churches of the Panayia, Ayios Ioannis and Ayios Nikolaos. This led to a long and bitter battle with the Greek Orthodox Patriarchate, which still simmers even after the deaths of Eftim and his son and successor, Eftim II, with the Turkish Orthodox Church now having dwindled to just a handful of mostly old people. The mass in the three churches is said in Turkish, the first language of Papa Eftim and his original congregation.

We now return to **Karaköy**, the area around the Galata Bridge, a chaotic intersection that can only be crossed safely via the pedestrian underpasses, emerging by the exit marked **Tünel**. Tünel is the old funicular railway, opened in 1876, which takes one from

Galata to the heights of Pera in less than two minutes; the entrance is just a short way down the right side of the main avenue that runs along near the Golden Horn between the Galata and Atatürk bridges.

Crossing the avenue, we turn in to Kardeşim Sokağî, the Street of My Friend. We then turn right at the first corner, which immediately brings us to the gateway of an old Ottoman *han*. This once-handsome structure was built by Sinan for the Grand Vizier **Rüstem Pasha** shortly before 1550. The date of construction is fixed by Gyllius, who says that the *han* was built on the foundations of the Roman Catholic church of St Michael; this was still standing when Gyllius arrived in the city in 1545, but before he left in 1550 it was pulled down to make way for Rüstem Pasha's new building. A Byzantine Corinthian capital from the church can be seen just to the left inside the entryway to the han, where it serves as a well-head. The *han* is in two storeys with a long narrow courtyard; from the centre of this a stairway leads to the upper floor in an arrangement as picturesque as it is unique. The lower arcade of the building has round arches, while those of the galley are of the ogive type. The *han* is badly battered from four and one-half centuries of constant commercial use, and it is in urgent need of restoration.

We now continue down the left side of the main avenue toward the Atatürk Bridge. About 100 metres along we come to the oldest Ottoman monument in Galata, a handsome and solidly constructed commercial building with nine equal domes in three rows of three each. This is the **Galata Bedesten**, a covered bazaar built by Mehmet the Conqueror soon after the conquest. The structure is almost square in plan, its domes supported by four massive rectangular piers, creating nine domed spaces in its interior, while outside on its sides and rear there are a series of vaulted shops. The Bedesten was well restored in the early 1970s and it is now once again being used for commercial purposes.

We continue walking along the avenue, which 800 metres farther on ends at the approach to the Atatürk Bridge. At the end of the avenue we come to the **Azap Kapî Çeşmesi**, one of the most famous street-fountains in the city. (The fountain takes its name from that of the local quarter – Azap Kapî, the Marine Gate – the main entryway to the great Tershane above the Atatürk Bridge.) This beautiful baroque fountain was built in 1732–33 by the Valide Sultan Saliha Hatun, mother of Mahmut I. It consists of a projecting *sebil* with three grilled windows flanked by a pair of splendid *çeşmes*, the façades of the fountains entirely covered with floral decorations in low relief. Unfortunately, the original fluted dome has been restored in concrete.

On the shore of the Golden Horn just below the Atatürk Bridge we see the handsome mosque known as **Azap Kapî Camii**. This is the second of two mosques that Sinan built in Istanbul for Sokollu Mehmet Pasha, erected in 1577–78, six years after the one that he built for the Grand Vizier on the First Hill. While it hardly equals the earlier mosque, Azap Kapî Camii is nevertheless a fine and interesting building.

Internally the plan of the mosque is an octagon inscribed in a nearly square rectangle. The dome is supported by eight small semidomes, those in the axes slightly larger than those in the diagonals, while the eastern dome covers a rectangular projecting apse for the *mihrab*, with narrow galleries surrounding three sides. The *mihrab* and *mimber* are very fine works in carved marble, The interior was once decorated with Iznik tiles, but these disappeared and have been replaced by modern Kütahya tiles.

We now cross the highway and start walking back toward the Galata Bridge. But rather than walking along the busy highway itself we will wander through the labyrinth of streets to its left. One of the first turnings on the left leads to Yanîk Kapî Sokağî, the Street of the Burnt Gate, which takes its name from an ancient **portal** near its beginning. This is the only surviving gateway of the medieval Genoese town of Galata, connecting two of the walled enceintes. Above the archway there is a bronze tablet upon which is emblazoned the cross of St George, symbol of Genoa the Superb, between a pair of escutcheons bearing the heraldic arms of the noble houses of Doria and De Meruda.

We now make our way back to the first street in from the main highway and continue walking towards the Galata Bridge. This soon brings us to what at first sight appears to be a large Italian church with a huge campanile. This is **Arap Camii**, the Mosque of the Arabs, whose courtyard and main entrance are approached via an arched passageway beneath the campanile.

There are a number of apocryphal legends concerning the origin and history of this building, but evidence indicates that it was constructed by the Dominicans in 1323–37 and dedicated to St Dominic. The church seems to have included a chapel of St Paul, by whose name it was also called. It was converted into a mosque at the time of the conquest, and some four decades later it was given over to the colony of Moorish refugees who had settled in Galata, hence its Turkish name of Arap Camii.

The building has been damaged by fires and restored several times, and in a rebuilding in 1913–19 it was considerably widened by moving the left-hand wall several metres to the north. Nevertheless it remains a rather typical Latin church, originally Gothic; a long hall ending in three rectangular apses, and with a campanile (now the minaret) at the end. The flat wooden roof and the rather pretty wooden galleries date only from the restoration of 1913–19. At that time the original floor was uncovered and large quantities of Genoese tombstones came to light, which are now preserved in the Archaeological Museum. A number of these tombstones are dated 1348, the year that the Black Death struck Constantinople, to spread from here to the rest of Europe.

About fifty metres beyond Arap Camii we turn left on Perşembe Pazarî Sokağî, the Street of the Thursday Market. This takes us uphill through the oldest part of Galata, the enceinte that the Genoese walled off in 1304. Along this street we pass a number of massive old edifices built in alternating courses of brick and stone, the upper storeys projecting outwards in zigzags held up by corbels. These were once thought to be Genoese houses of the late Byzantine era, but one of them has been dated by an inscription in Arabic to 1735–36, and present opinion is that they are all of this period.

At the upper end of Perşembe Pazarî Sokağî we cross Bankalar Caddesi, after which we ascend a flight of steps to the lower end of Galata Kulesi Sokağî. The large building to the right of the steps is the former **Podestat** of the Genoese city, built in 1316 to house the Podesta sent out each year from Genoa to administer Galata. The Podestat was heavily reconstructed in 1939 and has lost its original medieval appearance.

We now make a brief excursion down the short street to the left at the top of the steps. Most of the right side of this street is taken up by a huge old building in the European style, its walls blackened with grime. This is the **Han of Ste. Pierre**, built in 1771 by the Comte de Saint Priest as 'the lodging-place and bank of the French nation', as he writes in his bequest. A plaque high on the facade of the building bears the arms of the Comte de Saint Priest and of the Bourbons, Kings of France. Another plaque records that the French poet Andre Chenier was born here on 30 October 1762, in an earlier house that stood on this site.

We now start up Galata Kulesi Sokağî, which halfway along its

The Galata Tower

course bends to the right as it passes the Roman Catholic church of St Peter, better known as San Pietro. San Pietro was founded in the late fifteenth century by the Dominicans, who are still in possession of the church. During the Ottoman period it was taken under the protection of France, serving as the parochial church of the French community in Pera. Later it served as the parish church of the Maltese community, as evidenced by the number of tombstones with Maltese names built into the courtyard wall. The structure of the present church dates only from 1841 and is a work of the Fossati brothers, who restored Haghia Sophia for Abdül Mecit in 1847–49.

We now continue up Galata Kulesi Sokağî to the **Galata Tower**, the great landmark on the northern side of the Golden Horn. Its base is 35 metres above the level of the Golden Horn, and from there the tower rises another 67 metres to the finial of its conical cap. An elevator ascends to the penultimate floor from which we ascend a stairway to the top level, where there is a restaurant with an observation deck 53 metres above the ground below, commanding an unsurpassed view of the city. Looking directly down along the route we have just followed, we can see two towers of the medieval Genoese city just to the right of Galata Kulesi Sokağî, one of them just above the church of San Pietro.

The Galata Tower was the great bastion of the Genoese city from 1348–1453. After the conquest the tower was used to incarcerate prisoners-of-war taken by the Turks; then in later Ottoman times it became a fire-watch station, a function that it performed until the late 1960s, when it was closed for a few years before its reopening as a touristic site. A plaque beside the upper stop on the elevators records an astonishing feat performed in the mid-seventeenth century by Hezarfen Ahmet Çelebi, who flew from the top of the Galata Tower with a pair of man-made wings and crossed the Bosphorus to land in Üsküdar.

In the square beside the entrance we can still see part of the Genoese **barbican**, an outer wall that extended in a semicircle around the Galata Tower. Up into the early 1970s a section of the very deep ditch that surrounded the outer walls of Galata could still be seen here. The upper gateway through the walls was beside this barbican, approached by a draw-bridge across the ditch, and up until 1845 the watchmen there still demanded a fee from travellers entering Galata, as Murray's Handbook for that year warns tourists.

One of the city's oldest street-fountains is set into the wall of the barbican just above the entrance to the Galata Tower. The **fountain** was commissioned just after the conquest by Bereketzade Hacî Ali Ağa, the first Turkish governor of the citadel of Galata, and it originally stood outside a mosque that he founded a short distance down the hill. The fountain was reconstructed in 1732, and it was moved to its present location in 1950.

We now cross the square above the Galata Tower and turn left on Galip Dede Caddesi. This is the upper end of **Yüksek Kaldîrîm**, which up until half-a-century ago was still a street of steps, the main route for pedestrians walking between Galata and the heights of Pera. A short way along Galip Dede Caddesi we pass **Yazîcî Camii**, the **Mosque of the Writer**, built in 1582 by Meyitzade Mehmet Efendi. The first name of the founder, Meyitzade, is a very curious one, meaning the Son of the Dead. The origin of the name is explained by Evliya Çelebi in his description of Meyitzade's tomb.

> Meyitzade's tomb: Before going to the siege of Erla his father recommended the child, then in his mother's womb, to the care of God Almighty. Soon after his departure the woman died and was buried; she then gave birth in the tomb and nourished her child by a miracle. The father, on his return, having heard of his wife's death, desired to be shown the grave, where he found the child still living and suckled by his mother's breast. He praised God and took the child home, who became a great and learned man; he died in the time of Ahmet I and was again buried close to his mother. A cupola was erected over the grave, which is a place of general pilgrimage.

At the upper end of Galip Dede Caddesi we come on the right to the entrance of the **Galata Mevlevi Tekke**, which is beside a pretty *sebil* founded in the early nineteenth century by Halil Efendi. The *tekke* was founded in 1492 by Şeyh Muhammed Semai Sultan Divani, a direct decendant of Mevlani Rumi, the sainted divine and mystic poet who in the thirteenth century founded the dervish brotherhood known as the Mevlevi, famous in the West as the 'Whirling Dervishes'. On entering the grounds we pass on our left the *türbe* of Galip Dede, a renowned mystic poet of the seventeenth century. This takes us into the main courtyard of the *tekke*, passing on our left its picturesque graveyard. At the end of the courtyard we come to the *semahane*, the building where the Mevlevi performed their famous dance. This is a beautiful octagonal chamber surrounded by several auxiliary rooms on two storeys. The *semahane* was superbly restored in the 1970s and now houses the **Museum of Divan Literature**, a form named for the mystical poetry written by Galip Dede and other

251

inspired mystics of Ottoman times. The exhibits include manuscripts of their works as well as memorabilia of the Mevlevi who lived in this *tekke* until 1925, when all of the dervish orders were banned in Turkey. Performances of the Mevlevi dance are given here occasionally, usually during the Istanbul Festival in summer.

The *tekke* was one of the sights that foreign travellers were shown in late Ottoman times, as John Cam Hobhouse writes in the journal that he kept during his travels in Greece and Turkey in 1809–10 with Byron: '. . . the people of Constantinople run in crowds to amuse themselves (for no other motive can be assigned to them) at the exhibition of the turning. . . . Dervishes, to which all strangers are carried, as to the theatre or other places of entertainment in the cities of Christendom.'

At the back of the *tekke* graveyard we find the **tombstone** of the famous **Count Bonneval**, known in Turkish as **Kumbaracî Ahmet Pasha**. Bonneval was a French officer who enrolled in the Ottoman army in the reign of Mahmut I, who appointed him Kumbaracîbaşî, or Commandant of the Corps of Artillery, after which he became a Muslim and changed his name to Ahmet. He spent the rest of his career in the Ottoman service, building a mansion on the Grand Rue de Pera just beyond the Mevlevi tekke, where he was buried after his death in 1747. A contemporary of Bonneval wrote of him that he was 'a man of great talent for war, intelligent, eloquent with turn and grace, very proud, a lavish spender, extremely debauched and a great plunderer.'

At the upper end of Galip Dede Caddesi we come to **Istiklal Caddesi**, the former **Grand Rue de Pera**, whose southern end is just to the left at the upper terminus of Tünel. The old tramway of the Grand Rue de Pera has resumed service between Tünel and Taksim, the square at the upper end of Istiklal, stopping enroute only at Galatasaray Square. Aside from the tramway, Istiklal Caddesi has been converted into a pedestrian mall, so that strolling along the avenue is now as pleasant as it must have been when this was the Grand Rue de Pera.

The great European embassies began to build their palatial embassies along the Grand Rue de Pera in the sixteenth century. Each of these legations became the centre of separate 'nations', with their own residences, churches, post offices and other institutions, operating almost independently of Turkish control. This continued to be true up until the founding of the Turkish Republic in 1923, when the embassies of the foreign powers were shifted to the new capital in Ankara. The old embassy buildings now serve as consulates. Nevertheless, they are still referred to as embassies, such is their grandeur.

Turning right on to Istiklal from Galip Dede Caddesi, we pass on our right the old **Swedish Embassy**, a very handsome mansion that probably dates back to the end of the seventeenth century in foundation.

At the next corner we turn right on Kumbaracî Yokuşu, which takes its name from the fact that Kumbaracî Ahmet Pasha had his mansion at the upper end of the street. Some 200 metres down the street we see up on the right the **Crimean Memorial Church**, the only monumental Protestant house of worship ever erected in the city. This impressive edifice was built during the years 1858–69 as a memorial to the British soldiers who died in the Crimean War. Its leading sponsor was Lord Stratford de Redcliffe (Stratford Canning), who laid the cornerstone of the church on 19 October 1858. The church was designed by C. E. Street, the architect of the London Law Courts; it is the earliest example in the city of the neo-Gothic style that became popular in the West during the Victorian period. The church was closed for a number of years, but it has now been restored and has reopened for services.

We now return to Istiklal and continue walking in the same direction. On the next block we pass on our right the old Russian Embassy, built in 1837 by the Fossati brothers, their earliest building in the city. A short way beyond that we come to the Roman Catholic **church of St Mary Draperis**, operated by the Franciscan fathers. The Franciscans built their first church of St Mary in Constantinople early in 1453 on the present site of Sirkeci Station, but after the conquest they were forced to abandon this building. They then held services at several temporary houses in Galata before settling into a building on the site of the present Customs House; this was given to them by a benefactress named Clara Bartola Draperis, whose last name was thereafter appended to that of the church. St Mary Draperis was moved to its present site in 1660, though the church we see today dates only from 1769.

At the next corner we turn right on **Postacîlar Sokağî**, the **Street of the Postmen**. This steep and narrow lane leads downhill past the contiguous grounds, on the left, of the old **Dutch** and **French Embassies**, whose main entrances are on Istiklal Caddesi. A short way down the left side of the street we come to the entrance of the **Dutch Chapel**, which since 1857 has housed the Union Church of

253

Istanbul, an English-speaking congregation from many lands. The chapel probably dates in foundation to the erection of the Dutch Embassy on the Grand Rue de Pera in 1612.

A short way farther down Postacîlar Sokağî we pass the entrance to the old **Spanish Embassy**, of which there remains only its **chapel**, dedicated to **Our Lady of the Seven Sorrows**. This was founded at the time of the establishment of the Spanish Embassy in 1670, but the present chapel dates only to 1870.

At the bottom of Postacîlar Sokağî there is a small square flanked by two large buildings in the European style. The building to the left is the former **French Tribunal of Justice**, a nineteenth-century structure in which the legal affairs of the European 'nations' were administered in late Ottoman times. The handsome old mansion on the right is the **Palazzo di Venezia**, which in the late Ottoman period served as the Italian Embassy. From the late sixteenth century until 1797 this was the residence of the Venetian *bailo*, the ambassador to the Sublime Porte from the Serene Republic of Venice. We learn from his *Memoirs* that **Giacomo Casanova** was a guest here in the summer of 1744; in his three months in the city this great lover made not a single conquest and was himself seduced by one Ismail Efendi, whom he met at Count Bonneval's house.

Returning to Istiklal, we now pass on our right the main entrances to the Dutch Embassy and then the French Embassy. The mansion that houses the Dutch Embassy was built by the Fossati brothers in 1855, replacing the original embassy building of 1612 that was destroyed in the great fire of 1831. The present **French Embassy**, the **Maison de France**, also dates from after the 1831 fire, as does the embassy chapel, which is dedicated to St Louis of France. France was the first European nation to establish formal diplomatic relations with the Ottoman Empire, beginning with a mission sent by Francois I in 1535 to Süleyman the Magnificent. The original Maison de France was erected in 1581, the first of the European embassy buildings on the Grand Rue de Pera.

After passing the second turning on the right we come to the Roman Catholic **church of St Anthony of Padua,** run by the Franciscans. This parish traces its origins back to the original church of St Francis that the Franciscans built at the upper end of the Grand Rue de Pera in 1725. The present church was completed in 1913, and is a fine example of Italian neo-Gothic architecture.

We now come to **Galatasaray Square**, the mid-point of Istiklal Caddesi. This square and the surrounding quarter take their name from the **Galatasaray Lycée**, whose ornate gateway is at the far corner of the intersection on the right. Although the present buildings of the Lycee date only from 1908, Galatasaray traces its origins back to the end of the fifteenth century, when Beyazit II founded a school here for the palace pages, ancillary to the one at Topkapî Sarayî. The school was reorganized by Abdül Aziz in 1868, becoming a modern lycee on the French model, with instruction in both French and Turkish. Since then it has produced many of the leading statesmen and intellectuals in Turkey, an important factor in the modernization of the country.

The street that heads off to the left from Galatasaray Square leads to the entrance of the **British Embassy**. England was second only to France in establishing ties with the Ottoman Empire, beginning with the agreement between Murat III and Elizabeth I that led to the founding of the Levant Company by English merchants in 1580. The company was founded by William Harborne, the first English ambassador to the Sublime Porte. The first British embassy building on this site was erected by Lord Elgin c.1800, but this was destroyed in the 1831 fire. The present building was originally designed by Sir Charles Barry, architect of the Houses of Parliament, but it was completed in 1845 by W. J. Smith along somewhat different lines.

We now turn left at the first corner beyond Galatasaray on to Şahne Sokağî, the Street of the Theatre. This street and those that lead off from it on its way downhill are the site of the **Galatasaray Balîk Pazar**, or **Fish Market**, where fish, fruit, vegetables and meat are sold in the shops and barrows along the way, the most picturesque and colourful area in Beyoğlu. A short way down Şahne Sokağî we come to one of the entrances to the famous **Çiçek Pasajî** – the **Passage of Flowers** – whose other entryway is on Istiklal. This L-shaped alleyway passes though a once-elegant apartment block known as the **Cité de Pera**, erected in 1871. Among the shops in the alleyway there were a number of florists, the last of which moved out to Şahne Sokağî more than two decades ago. Nevertheless the alleyway is still called the Passage of Flowers, though for more than half a century it has been lined with *meyhanes*, or beer halls. The *meyhanes* of the Çiçek Pasajî have become more respectable and less boisterous than they were in times past, but those who love the old Passage of Flowers miss the presence of the wandering minstrels, street singers, beggars, acrobats, contortionists, sword-swallowers and other raffish members of Beyoğlu's night-town, who are no longer allowed to congregate here.

255

At the first turning to the right off Şahne Sokaǧî we come to Nevizade Sokaǧî, which in recent years has replaced the Çiçek Pasajî as the centre of Beyoǧlu's night life, with both sides of the street lined with *meyhanes*, which have tables outside in good weather.

The upper end of Istiklal Caddesi, between Galatasaray and Taksim, is lined with shops, restaurants cafés, bars and cinemas, for here we are in the heart of downtown Istanbul. A number of the older buildings along the avenue date to the late Ottoman and early Republican eras, most notably Tokatlîyan Hanî, Cercle d'Orient, the Atlas Cinema, and Cité Rumelie. Halfway along this stretch of the avenue we pass on our left **Aǧa Camii**, the only mosque on Istiklal Caddesi. The first mosque on this site was founded in 1594–95 by Hüseyin Aǧa of the Galatasaray School; this was rebuilt in 1839 and restored in 1936.

At the upper end of Istiklal we pass on our left the old **French Consulate**. This was constructed by the French government in 1719 and originally served as a hospital for those suffering from the plague. Beyond that is the octagonal building from which the square and the surrounding neighbourhood take their name. This is the *taksim*, or water-distribution centre, built in 1732 by Mahmut I; here the waters from the Belgrade Forest north of Istanbul are channeled off to the various quarters of the modern city north of the Golden Horn. Off to the right is the Greek Orthodox church of Ayia Triada, the Holy Trinity, a huge edifice in the neo-Byzantine style with a high drum and two towering campaniles in front. This was completed in 1882 and is the biggest of Istanbul's modern churches, its imposing dimensions reflecting the large Greek population that Pera had a century ago.

The statue group near the western end of **Taksim Square** is the **Monument of Independence**, completed in 1928 by the Italian sculptor Pietro Canonica; this represents Atatürk and other leaders of the Nationalist movement whose efforts lead to the creation of the Turkish Republic in 1923. The glass-walled edifice at the eastern end of the square is the **Atatürk Cultural Centre**, home of the Istanbul Opera and the city's principal site for productions of music, theatre and dance, particularly during the Istanbul Festival.

Taksim Square is the hub of the modern city, with Siraselviler Caddesi leading off to the south, Taki Zafer Caddesi (and its continuation, Inönü Caddesi) to the west, and Cumhuriyet Caddesi to the north. The first two of these avenues lead down to the Bosphorus, while Cumhuriyet Caddesi leads to the more modern quarters of the town: Elmadaǧ, Harbiye, Maçka, Sişli and Nişantaşî.

Harbiye has two muscums of interest, as well as the **Spor ve Sergi Sarayî** and the **Cemal Reşit Rey Concert Hall**, the latter being two other sites where performances of the Istanbul Festival are held. The largest of the two museums in Harbiye is just beyond the Hilton Hotel. This is the Askeri Müzesi, or Military Museum, which has an outstanding collection of objects from all periods of Turkey's military history; there the famous Mektar Band gives regular performances of Ottoman army marches.

Harbiye's other **museum** is at 25 Halaskargazi Caddesi, the house where **Atatürk** lived in 1918–19, just before he went off to Anatolia to lead the Turkish Nationalist movement in the War of Independence. The house preserves a collection of memorabilia associated with Atatürk's residence here, in the last days of old Pera, giving us a glimpse of the man behind the pages of the history books.

19

Üsküdar and the Princes Isles

OUR NEXT ITINERARY will take us across the Bosphorus to Üsküdar and then out to the **Princes Isles**, Istanbul's suburban archipelago in the Sea of Marmara.

Üsküdar, the largest and most historic of Istanbul's Anatolian suburbs, is situated on the Asian shore of the lower Bosphorus, directly opposite the Constantinopolitan peninsula. Üsküdar was known in antiquity as Chrysopolis, the City of Gold, founded by Athens in 409 BC. Throughout the Byzantine period Chrysopolis was a suburb of Constantinople, and thus had much the same history as the capital. But its site was not nearly so well suited for defence, and it was on several occasions occupied or destroyed by invading armies, while Constantinople remained protected by its great walls until the Crusader sack of 1204 and the final Turkish siege of 1453. Chrysopolis, known in the late medieval era as Scutari, was taken by the Turks in the mid-fourteenth century and was never recovered by the Byzantines. During the Ottoman period some of the great men and women of the realm endowed Üsküdar with splendid mosque complexes and other pious foundations, all of which still adorn the town.

Ferries leave for Üsküdar from both Eminönü and Kabataş on the European shore of the lower Bosphorus. Either way one lands at the *iskele* beside the great square of Üsküdar, much of which occupies the site of the ancient harbour of Chrysopolis. The official name of this area is Hakimiyeti Milliye Meydanî, the Square of Popular Sovereignty, though almost everyone calls it simply **Iskele Meydanî**. In Ottoman times this was the mustering-place for the Sürre-i-Hümayun, the Sacred Caravan that departed for Mecca and Medina each year with its long train of pilgrims and its sacred white camel bearing gifts from the Sultan to the Şerif of Mecca.

The northern end of the square by the ferry-landing is dominated by **Iskele Camii**, an imposing but graceful mosque complex standing on a high terrace close to the shore. This *külliye*, which includes the mosque, a *medrese* and a *mektep*, was built by Sinan in 1557–58 for Mihrimah Sultan, daughter of Süleyman and Roxelana.

This was the first of two *külliyes* that Sinan erected for the Princess, the later one being the imperial mosque we have seen on the summit of the Sixth Hill.

The exterior of the mosque is very imposing because of its dominant position and its great double porch, a curious projection of which covers a charming fountain. The interior is perhaps less satisfactory, for the central dome is supported by three instead of the usual two or four semidomes, which gives it a rather truncated appearance. The *medrese* is to the north of the mosque, a pretty building of the rectangular type, now used as a clinic. The primary school is behind the mosque, built on sharply rising ground so that it has very picturesque supporting arches; it is now a children's library. At the foot of the steps below the mosque terrace is the very handsome baroque **fountain of Ahmet III**, dated 1726.

Passing the fountain and entering the main street of Üsküdar, we soon come to a supermarket housed in the remains of a *hamam*. The sign calls it **Sinan Hamam Çarşîsî**, thus ascribing the bath to Sinan; there is no evidence for this but it is certainly of his time.

A little farther along on the same side of the street is **Nişancî Kara Davut Pasha Camii**, which dates from the late fifteenth century. The prayer hall is a broad shallow room divided into three sections by arches, each section having a dome, an arrangement unique in Istanbul.

Across the street and opening into Iskele Meydanî is the large mosque complex known as **Yeni Valide Camii**; this was built for Ahmet III in 1708–10 and dedicated to his mother, the Valide Sultan Rabia Gülnüş Ümmetüllah. At the corner is the Valide's charming open *türbe*, which looks like a large aviary, and next to it a grand *sebil*. The mosque itself is one of the last to be built in the classical Ottoman style; its plan is a variation of the octagon-in-a-square theme. The *mektep* of the *külliye* is over the main gate, and outside this portal is the large *imaret*, at one corner of which is a baroque *çeşme*, a later addition.

On the shore of the Bosphorus south of Iskele Meydanî we come to **Şemsi Pasha Camii**, which Evliya Çelebi aptly describes as 'a little pearl of a mosque on the lip of the sea'. Sinan built this mosque in 1580 for Şemsi Ahmet Pasha, a famous Vizier who traced his descent back to the royal line of the Selcuks who ruled in Anatolia before the rise of the Ottomans.

The mosque is of the simplest type: a square room covered by a dome with conches as squinches. Şemsi Pasha's *türbe* opens into the mosque itself, from which it is divided merely by a green grille, a most unusual and pretty feature. The well-proportioned *medrese* forms two sides of the courtyard, while the third side consists of a wall with grilled windows opening directly onto the quay and the Bosphorus.

On the hill behind Şemsi Pasha Camii we see **Rum Mehmet Pasha Camii**, the oldest mosque in Üsküdar, erected in 1471. We approach it by crossing the highway to Şemsi Pasha Caddesi, which we follow uphill to the mosque.

The mosque exterior is very Byzantine in appearance. The high cylindrical drum of the dome, the exterior cornice following the curve of the round-arched windows, the square dome base broken by the projection of the great dome arches, and several other features suggest a strong Byzantine influence, perhaps connected with the fact that Mehmet Pasha was a Greek (in Turkish, Rum) who became one of Mehmet the Conqueror's Viziers. Internally the mosque has a central dome with smooth pendentives and one semidome to the east, with side chambers that are completely cut off from the central prayer-hall. Behind the mosque is Mehmet Pasha's gaunt *türbe*.

Leaving the mosque precinct by the back gate and following the winding street outside, keeping to the right, we eventually come to an imposing baroque mosque known as Ayazma Camii. Built in 1760–61 by Mustafa III and dedicated to his mother Mihrişah, it is one of the more successful baroque mosques, particularly its exterior.

A handsome entrance portal opens onto a courtyard from which a pretty flight of semicircular steps leads up to the mosque porch; on the left is a large cistern and beyond that an elaborate two-storied colonnade gives access to the imperial loge. The upper structure is also diversified with little domes and turrets, and many windows give light to the interior. The interior, as generally in baroque mosques, is less successful, though the grey marble gallery along the entrance wall, supported by columns, is effective.

Leaving by the south gate of the mosque and following the first street to the east, we come to a wider street, Doğancîlar Caddesi, the Avenue of the Falconers, where we see two pretty *çeşmes* of the baroque era at the intersection. Turning right here, we find at the end of this street a severely plain *türbe* built by Sinan for **Hacî Mehmet Pasha**, who died in 1559. It stands on an octagonal terrace bristling with tombstones and overshadowed by a dying terebinth tree.

The wide street just ahead leads downhill past a little park. The third turning on the right after the park, followed immediately by one on the left, leads to an elaborate and delightful *külliye*, the Ahmediye mosque, library and *medrese*.

The *külliye* was built in 1722 by Eminzade Hacî Ahmet Pasha, comptroller of the Arsenal under Ahmet III; it is perhaps the last ambitious building complex in the classical style, though verging towards the baroque. Roughly square in layout, it has the porticoes and cells of the *medrese* along two sides; the library, one entrance portal and the mosque occupy a third side; while the fourth has the main gate complex with the *dershane* above and a graveyard alongside. The plan is very irregular because of the alignment of the streets and the rising ground. The dome of the little mosque is supported by scallop-shell squinches and has a finely carved marble *mimber* and Koran *kursu*. But the library and the *dershane* over the two gates are the most attractive features of the complex and show great ingenuity of design. The whole *külliye* ranks with those of Amcazade Hüseyin Pasha and Bayram Pasha as among the most charming and inventive in the city.

We leave the Ahmediye by the main gate at the southeast corner of the courtyard, where a stairway under the *dershane* leads to the street below. A short and narrow street opposite the outer gate soon leads to a wider avenue, Toptaşî Caddesi, the Avenue of the Cannonball, where we turn right. (The eponymous cannonball, a stone sphere about a foot in diameter, has now been placed on a pedestal at the intersection.) We follow this avenue for about 600 metres as it winds uphill, until finally we see on our left the imperial *külliye* of **Atik Valide Camii.**

This great mosque complex was built by Sinan in 1583 for the Valide Sultan Nur Banu, wife of Selim II and mother of Murat III. This is the most splendid and extensive of all of Sinan's constructions in Istanbul with the sole exception of the Süleymaniye. Besides the mosque itself, the *külliye* consists of a *medrese*, hospital, *imaret*, *darülkura*, caravansarai, and *hamam*; all these buildings are still in existence and most are in good condition. (At the moment of writing the entire complex is under restoration, and it may be difficult or impossible to enter some of the buildings.)

We enter the precincts by an alley beside a graveyard and find ourselves in one of the most beautiful of all the mosque courtyards in the city, a grandly proportioned cloister with domed porticoes supported on marble columns; in the centre the *şadîrvan* is shaded by ancient plane trees and cypresses. The mosque is entered through an elaborate double porch, the outer one with a penthouse roof, the inner domed and with handsome tiled inscriptions over the windows.

The prayer-hall of the mosque is a rectangular room with a central dome supported by a hexagonal arrangement of pillars and columns; to north and south are side aisles each with domed bays. There are galleries round three sides of the room; the wooden ceilings under them preserve the rich painting typical of the period: floral and arabesque designs in black, red and gold. The *mihrab* is in a square projecting apse entirely revetted in magnificent tiles of the best Iznik period; note also the window-frames of deep red conglomerate marble with shutters richly inlaid with mother-of-pearl. The *mihrab* and *mimber* are fine works in carved marble.

The *medrese* of the complex stands at a lower level than the mosque and is entered by a staircase in the west wall of the court-yard. The courtyard of the *medrese* is almost as pretty as that of the mosque itself; it is oddly irregular, having five domed bays to the south but only three to the north. The *dershane* is in the centre of the west side in the axis of the mosque though at an obtuse angle to it, and it projects over the street below, which passes under it through an archway. At the next corner beyond the *medrese* stands the huge hospital, also irregular in plan but quite as attractive as the other buildings. The other buildings of the complex are currently inaccessible.

The street to the east of Atik Valide Camii leads after a walk of about a kilometre to **Çinili Cami**, the **Tiled Mosque**, which is surrounded by a pretty garden filled with flowers and trees. This small complex was built in 1640 for the Valide Sultan Kösem, wife of Ahmet I and mother of sultans Murat IV and Ibrahim. The mosque is small and simple, just a square prayer-room covered by a dome. It takes its name from the Iznik tiles that cover both its façade and interior; these are chiefly pale blue and turquoise on a white ground, and though after the best period they are still fine. The *mimber* of white marble has its carving very prettily picked out in gold, red and green, and its conical roof is tiled. The porch of the mosque is a baroque addition, as is the minaret, of which the *şerefe* has a corbel of very pretty folded back acanthus leaves, apparently unique in Ottoman architecture. Within the precinct is a very fine *şadîrvan* with a huge witch's cap for a roof, and a tiny *medrese* triangular in form sloping headlong downhill. Just outside the precinct is the handsome *mektep* of the *külliye*, and the *hamam* is a short way along the main street beyond the mosque.

We now walk back downhill to Iskele Meydanî, where we can consider an excursion in the vicinity of Üsküdar. As Evliya Çelebi writes, 'Üsküdar is surrounded on all sides with delightful walks.'

A very popular excursion is to **Büyük Çamlîca**, the **Great Mountain of Pines**, whose summit is 267 metres above sea-level, the highest point in the immediate vicinity of the Bosphorus. There is an extremely pleasant café and teahouse on the summit, with belvederes that command stunning views of the lower Bosphorus and the imperial city between the Golden Horn and the Sea of Marmara. Procopius, Justinian's court chronicler, describes the view from this hill in his *Edifices*, writing of how 'the city is surrounded by a garland of waters'.

Ferries leave from Eminönü and Kabataş for the Princes Isles (in Turkish, Adalar), the sybaritic archipelago off the Asian coast of the Marmara. En route the ferry from Eminönü stops at Kadîköy, on the Asian shore south of Üsküdar.

As the ferry crosses the strait we pass Üsküdar and then, some 700 metres beyond Şemsi Pasha Camii, we see a little fortified islet off the Asian shore. This is **Kîz Kulesi**, the **Maiden's Tower**, better known in English as **Leander's Tower**. The English name comes from the mistaken notion that Leander died here in his swim across the strait to see his lover, the priestess Hero, a tragedy that legend actually places near Abydos on the Dardanelles. The Turkish name comes from another legend that is associated with virtually every sea-girt tower or castle along the Anatolian coast. According to this legend, a king hid away his daughter in the tower when a prophetess foretold that she would die from the bite of a snake, but his enemy hid a serpent in a bowl of fruit and smuggled it out to the islet, where it killed the princess. According to the Byzantine chronicler Nicetas Choniates, Manuel I Comnenus was the first to fortify the islet, in the mid-twelfth century, using it to anchor one end of the great chain that was stretched across the Bosphorus in times of siege. Since then the islet has been used successively as the site of a lighthouse, semaphore station, quarantine post, customs control point, home for retired naval officers, and inspection station by the Turkish Navy. The present quaint structure dates from the late eighteenth century; it is currently being restored.

The most prominent monument along the Marmara shore south of Üsküdar is the enormous four-towered structure in Haydarpaşa, the district just north of Kadîköy. These are the **Selimiye Barracks**, a huge rectangle around an open square, with the very characteristic towers at the corners, famous as the scene of Florence Nightingale's ministrations during the Crimean War. They were originally erected in wood by Selim III to house the troops of his New Army. Later they were partly rebuilt in stone by Mahmut II, and later still the rest was done in stone by Abdül Mecit. They are still used by the military and are not open to the general public, except by special permission from the officer in charge. One of the rooms in the northeast tower has been converted into a museum commemorating Florence Nightingale.

The next prominent building to the south of the Selimiye Barracks is the **Haydarpaşa Lycée**, a huge structure with twin towers flanking its entrance. This was built in 1894 to house the Military Medical Academy, which remained here until 1933, after which the building became a secondary school for boys.

Farther to the south we see the **Haydarpaşa Railway Station**, a huge building on the water's edge with a façade flanked by twin towers. This was built in 1906–08 by the German architects Otto Rittner and Helmuth Cuno. The tiled ferry-station in front of it was built in 1915–17 by the Turkish architect Vedat Tek.

The **Crimean War Cemetery** is almost hidden away to the east of the train station, laid out in the angle formed by the two highways that intersect there. The cemetery was founded originally as a burial-place for the British soldiers who died in the Selimiye Barracks when it was being used as a hospital during the Crimean War, and among the tombstones there are a number marking the graves of Florence Nightingale's nurses. Also buried here are British and Commonwealth servicemen who were killed at Gallipoli and others who fell in the Middle East during World War I, along with civilians who died in Istanbul.

A short distance south of the Haydarpaşa Railway Station the ferry stops at **Kadîköy**. This is the site of ancient **Chalcedon**, founded, according to tradition, seventeen years before Byzas the Megarian established the city of Byzantium. Absolutely nothing remains of ancient Chalcedon, other than the antiquities we have seen in the Archaeological Museum. There are no Byzantine remains either, and the only Ottoman monument is the mosque on the shore road directly opposite the ferry station. This is Iskele Camii, founded in 1761 by Mustafa III; after being destroyed by fire it was rebuilt in 1858 by Abdül Mecit, and it was most recently restored in 1975.

After the ferry leaves Kadîköy it heads toward the **Princes Isles**, which we can now see out in the Marmara, on a still day appearing to float on the mirroring water between the pale blues of sea and sky.

The group consist of nine islands, four of them of substantial size and with villages that are populated year-round, the others tiny and uninhabited except for two that have summer villas. The four large islands, in order of their distance from Istanbul, with their Greek names in parentheses, are Kînalî (Proti), Burgaz (Antigone), Heybeli (Chalki), and Büyükada (Prinkipo), the largest and most populous of the isles, which in Byzantine times gave its name to the whole group.

Each of the four large islands, and some of the smaller ones as well, have one or two old Greek Orthodox monasteries; most of these institutions were founded in the Byzantine era, but their present structures date from the late Ottoman period. All of these monasteries were in Byzantine times used as places of exile for deposed Emperors, Empresses and Patriarchs of Constantinople, whose tales of misery give the islands a lugubrious history. During the Ottoman era the islands were inhabited mostly by Greeks, along with substantial numbers of Armenians and Jews and a few aristocratic Turkish families. There are still sizeable Greek, Armenian and Jewish communities on the islands, but today the majority of those living there are Turkish. Despite the multitudes of day-trippers who come out to the isles on weekends, particularly in the summer months, the archipelago is still largely unspoiled, particularly because automotive transport is banned except for a few municipal vehicles. Otherwise the only transport is provided by *faytons*, or horse-drawn carriages, an exceedingly pleasant way to travel around these lovely isles.

The ferry stops first at **Kînalî**, whose form is now disfigured by the numerous television antenna masts that have been erected on the peak of its highest hill. Its Turkish name of Kînalî, or Dyed with Henna, stems from the reddish colour of its cliffs along the shore. The Greeks called it **Proti**, or First, since it is the first of the isles that one comes to in sailing out to the archipelago from the city. The island was in times past inhabited principally by Armenians, who still make up a significant percentage of its population.

Southwest of Kînalî are the two small isles of **Sivri** and **Yassî**, the first of them to the north and the second to the south. The Greek name of Sivri is **Oxya** and that of Yassî is **Plate**. The Turkish and Greek names are descriptive and mean the same thing in each case: Sivri-Oxya meaning Pointed and Yassî-Plate meaning Flat. Sivri is nothing more than a tall craggy reef, while Yassî is just a flat rock, both of them virtually uninabited. In times past Sivri was used as a dumping-place for the street-dogs of Istanbul, who were periodically rounded up and left there to starve to death. Yassî was formerly the residence of Sir Henry Bulwer, British Ambassador to the Sublime Porte; he lived there in what Murray's Handbook of 1892 quaintly describes as 'a dilapidated Anglo-Saxon castle', where he is popularly supposed to have indulged in nameless orgies.

The ferry stops next at **Burgaz**, the Greek **Antigone**. In times past the island was inhabited principally by Greeks, but today their community is much reduced in number. The most prominent landmark in the village that clusters around the *iskele* is the Greek Orthodox **church of St John the Baptist**. This was founded in Byzantine times, but the present church is a modern structure. One place of interest in the village is the former **home of Sait Faik** (1907–54), the famous Turkish writer, whose house is now open as a museum.

A narrow strait, less than a kilometre wide, separates Burgaz from **Heybeli**, Greek Chalki, the next island served by the ferry. On the way across the ferry passes the tiny islet of **Kaşîk**, or **Spoon**, a name vaguely suggested by its topography. Known to the Greeks as **Pita**, it is the smallest of the isles in the archipelago. It was virtually uninhabited up until recent times, but now a number of summer villas have been built there.

Heybeli is the second largest of the isles, after Büyükada, which it rivals in beauty. The Turkish name of Heybeli comes from '*heybes*', or 'saddle-bag', stemming from the shape of the island, which had two symmetric hills separated by a rounded valley.

The village is a pretty cluster of tiered houses on the eastern side of the island. The buildings and grounds of a Turkish naval base are to the left of the landing. Beyond the base a road leads to the Greek Orthodox **church of Haghios Nikolaos**, which is a short way along the shore in a most picturesque setting beside the sea.

The most prominent landmark in Heybeli is the **Greek Orthodox Seminary**, whose huge building can be seen on Ümit Tepesi, the hilltop to the right above the village. The seminary, founded in 1841, is currently closed as a school, but its library is still open. According to tradition, the seminary is built on the site of the monastery of the Holy Trinity, founded in 857 by the Patriarch Photius, one of the most renowned figures in the intellectual history of Byzantium.

There was another Byzantine monastery on the western slope of

Değirmen Tepesi, the second of the island's two hills. The site is on land belonging to the Turkish Naval base, and cannot be visited without permission of the officer in charge.

This monastery, dedicated to the Panaghis Theotokou, the Virgin Mother of God, was founded in the second quarter of the fifteenth century by John VIII Palaeologus. All that remains of the monastery are its graveyard and chapel. The **chapel** is known as the **Panaghia Kamariotissa, Our Lady of the Arches**; this was founded by John's third wife, Maria Comnena, the last Empress of Byzantium, who died in 1439.

There are a number of interesting tombs in the graveyard. Among them are those of seven Patriarchs of Constantinople, four of whom were executed in the seventeenth and eighteenth century. The most famous of these is Cyril Lucaris, six times Patriarch of Constantinople and once of Alexandria, during which time he was in conflict with the Popes in Rome, with whom he exchanged excommunications. Cyril was executed by Murat IV on 25 June 1638, ending the remarkable career of the man whom Pope Urban had called 'the son of darkness and the athlete of hell'.

Also buried here is Edward Barton, second ambassador from Queen Elizabeth I to the Sublime Porte. Barton's tomb bears his coat-of-arms and a long and somewhat garbled insciption in Latin, which was probably intended to read as follows: 'To Edward Barton/ the Illustrious and Serene Ambasador of/ the Queen of the English/ Who on his return from the War in Hungary/ Whither he had accompanied the Invincible Emperor of the Turks [Mehmet III] /Died in the 35th year of his age/ And of our Salvation 1597/ The 15th day of September.'

We now come at last to **Büyükada**, the **Great Island**, known to the Greeks as **Prinkipo**. This has always been the most popular of the isles, both as a place to live and among day-trippers who come out on weekends in good weather. The village, renowned for its beautiful mansions, some of them dating back to the late Ottoman era, has a number of good hotels and restaurants as well as a very posh country club. Çelik Gülersoy, director of the Turkish Touring and Automobile Club, has recently restored a late Ottoman mansion on Çankaya Caddesi and converted it into the **Büyükada Cultural Centre**, which has an excellent café and restaurant.

Büyükada consists of two large hills separated in the middle by a broad valley, so that the road that goes around the island makes a figure eight. The best way to tour the island is to take a *fayton*; these leave from the square uphill and to the left of the *iskele*. The Büyük (Grand) Tour goes completely around Büyükada, while the Küçük (Little) goes only halfway, cutting back across the waist of the island.

At the central valley a path leads up to **Yüce Tepe**, the southern hill. Donkeys are available for hire at the foot of the hill, where there is a café-restaurant.

Yüce Tepe is surmounted by the famous **monastery of Haghios Georghios Koudona, St George of the Bells**. Legend has it that a shepherd was grazing his flocks on the hillside, when he heard the sound of bells coming from under the ground. When he dug down he found an icon of St George buried in the earth, after which he and the other islanders built a monastery on the site. The present monastery has six separate chapels on three levels, the older ones being the lowest, which tradition dates back to the Byzantine era. The building to the west of the main church on the upper level is a hostel, used by those who visit the monastery on the feast days of the several saints who have chapels dedicated to them here. The monastery celebrates its principal feast-day on 23 April, St George's Day, when thousands of pilgrims, including Turks as well as Greeks and other Orthodox Christians, hike up to the monastery for the dawn service, with many women making the round trip in their bare feet. Afterwards many of the merrier pilgrims sit down to a feast at the ramshackle outdoor restaurant on the summit, drinking the home-made wine that for centuries has been barreled by the monks at the monastery. The scene is surpassingly beautiful, with all of the isles visible against the background of the green hills along the Asian coast, the Marmara a shimmering mirror of turquoise reflecting the occasional passing cloud, and hardly a sign of the modern world in sight.

From the summit of Yüce Tepe we can see the two tiny islets beyond Büyükada; to the east is **Sedef Adasî, Mother-of-Pearl Island**; and to the west is **Tavşan Adasî, Rabbit Island**. In Byzantine times Sedef was known as **Terbinthos** and Tavşan was called **Neandros**. Tiny as they are, both islets were the site of religious establishments in the Byzantine era, with a monastery on Terebinthos and a convent on Neandros. Both of these were founded in the mid-ninth century by the famous Patriarch Ignatius, son of Michael I, who was buried in the monastery on Terebinthos in 877. Sedef today has a community of summer villas, while Tavşan is virtually uninhabited.

20

The Bosphorus

W E HAVE SAVED the best for last, for our final itinerary in
Istanbul will take us up and down the **Bosphorus**, the incom-
parably beautiful strait that separates the European and Asian halves
of the city.

Ferries leave from Eminönü for the villages along both shores of
the Bosphorus (in Turkish, Boğaziçi, which means literally 'in the
throat'). Some of these villages date back to antiquity as fishing
ports, but now many of them have been amalgamated into the vast
urban sprawl of Istanbul, which, spreading along the coastal highways, is increasingly marring the beauty of the Bosphorus and its
shores. Nevertheless, they still have a village-like quality about
them, particularly on the upper Bosphorus, where many of the locals
still earn their living as fishermen.

As Gyllius eloquently points out, the Bosphorus is 'the first
creator of Byzantium, greater and more important than Byzas, the
founder of the City'. And he later sums up the predominant importance of this 'Strait that surpasses all straits' with the epigram: 'The
Bosphorus with one key opens and closes two worlds, two seas.' The
two worlds to which Gyllius refers are Europe and Asia, and the two
seas are the Marmara and the Black Sea, which he calls by their
ancient Greek names, the Propontis and the Pontus Euxinus, the
'Hospitable Sea', known more simply as the Euxine.

Any description of the Bosphorus involves the names Rumeli and
Anadolu, for these are used in referring to the opposing continental
shores of the strait, the first to the European side and the second to
the Asian. The first of these toponyms derives from that of the old
Ottoman province of Rumelia, which included most of southeastern
Europe. This name comes from the Turkish 'Rum', or Rome, referring to the eastern Roman dominions that later came to be called the
Byzantine Empire. Anadolu is the Turkish for Anatolia, the Asian
part of Turkey; it is also the Greek word for 'east', more literally the
'land of sunrise'. The name Asia may originally have had the same
meaning as this in both the Indo-European and Semitic families of
languages, while Europe may have meant 'sunset' or the 'land of

darkness'. These two continents were first named by the early Greek geographers in referring to the Bosphorus and the Dardanelles, the ancient Hellespont, where the two great land masses are divided from one another by straits that Hellenic mariners probably began exploring at the end of the Bronze Age, in the thirteenth century BC. The distinction between the names of the two continents would have been dramatically evident to ancient mariners making their way up the Bosphorus from the Propontis to the Euxine, with the sun rising above one shore of the strait and then setting below the other, the deep waters of the channel clearly dividing the 'land of sunrise' from the 'land of darkness'.

There are several Greek myths about the Bosphorus, all of them probably dating from the end of the Bronze Age and the first voyages of discovery through the straits. One of these tells the story of Zeus and his mistress Io, daughter of the river-god Inachus, whom he changed into a heifer to conceal her from his jealous wife Hera. But Hera saw through the disguise and drove Io away, pursuing her with a relentless gadfly that forced her to swim across the northern-most of the two straits separating Europe from Asia. Thenceforth this strait bore the name Bosphorus, the Ford of the Cow, commemo-rating the flight of Io, the 'Inachean daughter, beloved of Zeus'.

The legend of Jason and his search for the Golden Fleece perhaps perpetuates the memory of the first Greek voyages of discovery through the straits. Homer placed Jason's voyage a generation before the Trojan War, which both ancient and modern scholars have dated to c.1220 BC. When Jason decided to set out in search of the Golden Fleece he commisioned a ship called *Argo*, and heroes from all over the Greek world volunteered to fill the fifty seats on its rowing benches, including Orpheus and Heracles. These were the Argo-nauts, the crew of the vessel that Spenser in *The Faery Queene* called 'the wondred *Argo*, which . . . first through the Euxine Sea bore all the flower of Greece.' The only full account of the voyage of *Argo* that has survived is the *Argonautica* of Apollonius of Rhodes, written in the mid-third century BC. Gyllius used the *Argonautica* to identify a number of places along the Bosphorus with the voyage of Jason and the Argonauts, and we will see several of these on our own exploration of the strait.

The Bosphorus is about 32 kilometres in length, measured along a line down the centre of its sinuous channel. But the distance along its shores is significantly longer than this, for the shoreline is indented by a succession of promontories, coves and bays, some of the latter

270

large enough to serve as harbours. Both shores of the strait are lined with hills, none of them very high, but on the upper Bosphorus these eminences seem higher than they really are because of the way in which they plunge down to the sea in precipitous cliffs. Despite the rapidly increasing urbanization of the Bosphorus shores, particularly on the European side, they are still well-wooded, especially with cypresses, umbrella pines, plane trees, horse-chestnuts, terebinths and judas trees. The magenta to pink blossoms of the judas trees in spring, mingled with the mauve flowers of the wisteria and the red and white candles of the chestnuts, make the Bosphorus most beautiful at that season, particularly in late May, when nightingales begin serenading one another in the blossoming hills and valleys along the strait.

The Bosphorus flows in the general direction north-northeast to south-southwest, but it changes its course half-a-dozen times as it flows from the Black Sea to the Marmara. Its maximum width is 3.5 kilometres, measured along a line between Rumeli Feneri and Anaduli Feneri, the Lighthouses of Europe and Asia, the beacons that mark the entrance to the strait from the Black Sea. The narrowest stretch of the strait is between Rumeli Hisarî and Anadolu Hisarî, the Castles of Europe and Asia, where the facing continental shores are only 700 metres apart. The depth of the Bosphorus at the centre of its channel generally varies from 50 to 75 metres, but at two points near its narrowest stretch it reaches a depth of over 100 metres. The predominant current flows at two to five knots from the Black Sea to the Sea of Marmara, but at a depth of about 40 metres there is a reverse current known as the *kanal*. When the winds blow from the south, the dreaded *lodos*, both currents can change directions for a few hours, one of several reasons why people in Istanbul tend to go mad at such times.

The casual visitor to İstanbul, particularly if one comes in summer, might find it difficult to believe that the Bosphorus can be a perverse and dangerous body of water. Seen from the hills along its shores as it curves and widens and narrows, it often looks like a great lake or a series of lakes, while its rapid flow from the Black Sea to the Marmara give it somewhat the character of a river. Yet anyone who has observe its erratic currents and counter-currents, the various winds that encourage or hinder navigation, the impenetrable fogs that envelop it, even occasionally the icebergs that choke it, will realize that it is indeed part of the ungovernable sea. Here Belisarius fought the invincible whale Porphyry, that Moby Dick that wrecked all shipping for months; and here Gyllius observed the largest shark he had ever seen. Since it is an international waterway, the Bosphorus is busy day and night with a heavy traffic of oil-tankers and cargo ships, as well as occasional ocean-liners and warships, along with ferries and fishing-boats. The numerous sharp and unexpected bends in the strait, along with the occasional storms and dense fogs, can make the passage quite difficult at times. Often ships collide with one another on the Bosphorus or run aground on its banks, smashing into the houses or roadways along its shores. Old Bosphorus-dwellers will tell you stories of having been awakened from their slumbers by a terrific crash, to find their front parlour in ruins and the rusty prow of a tramp steamer protruding into the library, or of how a quiet supper was suddenly disrupted when the yard-arm of a passing schooner smashed through the dining-room window and swept the table clear.

But most often the Bosphorus is serene, though even on the calmest of days one can feel its power as it surges between the continents. It is beautiful at all times of day and night and in all seasons, but particularly under a full moon, which rises out of the hills of Asia and casts a silver path across the strait to the European shore, a phenomenon that the Turks call *mehtap*. The first full moon in autumn usually marks the beginning of the season for the fishermen of the Bosphorus, for it is then that great schools of *lüfer*, a small bluefish, make their way down the Bosphorus. The fishermen use a type of rowboat called a *sandal*, derived from the Venetian *sandalino*, most of them now equipped with outboard motors, each of them with a brilliant lamp that shines down into the depths to attract the dazzled fish. Watching from the shore you can see the *sandals* coming out from the villages along the strait, together looking like a swarm of fireflies drifting down the dark blue stream between the invisible continents, the night sky a lighter blue above them, crowded in luminous clusters down all the bays and coves of the Bosphorus, marine galaxies rivalling the stars in their beauty and luminosity.

The various itineraries of the Bosphorus ferries take them to the transpontine villages on both sides of the straits, with some schedules remaining mostly on one side of the strait and some on the other, occasionally darting back and forth between the continents. The description that follows will be an idealized one, which will take us up the Bosphorus to the villages on the European shore, than on returning we will stop at those on the Asian side.

As the Bosphorus ferry heads up the European shore it passes the docks at Galata, after which we see about 200 metres in from the shore a group of monuments in the quarter known as **Tophane**. The quarter takes its name from Tophane, the Cannon House, a large rectangular building with eight great domes supported by three lofty piers. The original Ottoman cannon foundry on this site was built by Mehmet the Conqueror soon after the conquest. It was completely rebuilt by Süleyman, who replaced it with a larger and more modern establishment in preparation for his campaigns of conquest. Süleyman's foundry has long since disappeared; the present structure was built in 1803 by Selim III, doubtless in connection with his attempt to reform and modernise the Ottoman navy. The building has been restored in recent years and there are plans to reopen it as an exhibition gallery.

Across the highway to the south of Tophane is **Kîlîç Ali Pasha Camii**, one of Sinan's later works. Sinan built this mosque in 1580 for Kîlîç (the Sword) Ali Pasha, one of the great admirals in Ottoman history, the only hero to emerge on the Turkish side at the battle of Lepanto in 1571.

The mosque is preceded by a very picturesque double porch. The outer porch has a deeply sloping penthouse roof, supported by 12 columns on the west façade and three on each side, all with lozenge capitals. In the centre of this porch is a monumental marble portal, and there are bronze grilles between the columns. The inner porch is of the usual type, with five domed bays supported by columns capped with stalactite capitals. Above the entrance portal is the historical inscription, giving the date of foundation of the mosque, and above this is a text from the Koran in a fascinating calligraphy.

Sinan designed Kîlîç Ali Pasha Camii as a near replica of Haghia Sophia on a reduced scale. His main departures from the plan of Haghia Sophia are: the provision of only two columns instead of four between each of the piers to north and south, and the suppression of the exedrae at the east and west ends. Both of these departures seem to have been dictated by the reduced scale. Nevertheless, the absence of the exedrae deprives the mosque of what in Haghia Sophia is one of its main beauties. The *mihrab* is in a square projecting apse, where there are some Iznik tiles of the best period. At the west there is a kind of pseudo-narthex of five cross-vaulted bays separated from the prayer-hall by four rectangular pillars.

The *külliye* of Kîlîç Ali Pasha Camii is extensive, including a *medrese*, a *hamam*, and the *türbe* of the founder. The *medrese*, opposite the southeast corner of the mosque may not be by Sinan since it does not appear in the definitive list of his works. The *hamam* is just in front of the *medrese*; it is a single bath for men, recently restored. Ali Pasha's *türbe* is in the pretty graveyard behind the mosque; it is a plain but elegant octagonal building with alternately one and two windows in each façade, in two tiers. Ali Pasha was buried here in 1587, the circumstances of his death described thus by the historian Josef von Hammer: 'Although ninety years of age, he had not been able to renounce the pleasures of the harem, and he died in the arms of a concubine.'

Directly across the avenue from Kîlîç Ali Pasha Camii is a small mosque known as **Karabaş Camii**. This was founded by Karabaş Mustafa Ağa, who was Chief Black Eunuch under Süleyman the Magnificent and died in 1530. The mosque is of the simple rectangular type with a hipped wooden roof.

Across the side street north of Kîlîç Ali Pasha Camii is one of the most famous of the baroque street-fountains of the city, the **Tophane Çeşmesi**. Built in 1732 by Mahmut I, its marble walls are decorated with arabesques and floral designs carved in low relief that were originally painted and gilded, covered by a charming domed roof with widely overhanging eaves.

Two hundred metres up the shore beyond Kîlîç Ali Pasha Camii we come to **Nusretiye Camii, the Mosque of Victory**. This was completed in 1826 for Mahmut II, who named it in commemoration of his great victory over the Janissaries, whom the troops of his New Army annihilated on 26 June of that year in a battle in Beyazit Square. The architect was Kirkor Balyan, the founder of a large family of Armenian architects who built several imperial mosques and palaces along the Bosphorus for the sultans in the mid-nineteenth century.

Kirkor Balyan had studied in Paris and his mosque shows a curious blend of baroque and *Empire* motifs, highly un-Turkish but not without a certain charm. This mosque abandons the traditional arrangement of a monumental courtyard and substitutes for it, as it were, an elaborate series of palatial apartments in two storeys that forms the western façade of the building, a plan that became a regular feature of all Balyan mosques. Notice the bulbous weight towers, the jutting dome arches so strongly emphasized on the exterior, the overly-slender minarets (they fell down soon after construction and had to be re-erected), the ornate gilded bronze grilles, the interior decoration dripping with marble and *Empire* garlands, and the marvelous baroque *mimber.*

Some 700 metres beyond Nusretiye Camii we come to **Molla Çelebi Camii**, a handsome seaside mosque built by Sinan in 1560–61. The founder was Kadaster (Chief Justice) Mehmet Efendi, a savant and poet in the reign of Süleyman the Magnificent. The building is of the hexagonal type, but here the pillars are actually engaged in the walls; between them to north and south are four small semidomes, and another covers the rectangular projecting apse in which stands the mihrab.

Two hundred metres beyond Molla Çelebi Camii we come to Kabataş, from whose *iskele* ferries leave for Üsküdar and the Princes' Isles. Between Molla Çelebi Camii and the Kabataş *iskele* there are two fountains of considerable interest, and 400 metres farther on there is another one; all three of these were removed from their original places when the shore highway was widened and have been re-erected on their present sites.

Beside the Bosphorus 100 metres north of Molla Çelebi Camii stands the square **street-fountain of Hekimoğlu Ali Pasha**, erected in 1732; it is of marble, beautifully carved, with *çeşmes* on its two faces, but unfortunately it has lost its overhanging domed roof. Across the shore highway from this we see a beautiful rococo *sebil* built in 1787 by **Koca Yusuf Pasha**, Grand Vizier of Abdül Hamit I. It has a magnificent *çeşme* in the centre, flanked on each side by two grilled windows of the *sebil*, and a door beyond; it is elaborately carved and has incrustations of various marbles, while its long calligraphic inscription forms a frieze. The *sebil* has now been converted into a very pleasant café.

The third of the three fountains is across the shore highway from the Dolmabahçe mosque at the bottom of the Ayaspaşa road. This is a *sebil* that was part of a little *külliye* built in 1741 by the *sipahi*, or cavalry knight, **Mehmet Emin Ağa**. The five-windowed *sebil* is flanked symmetrically on one side by a door, and the other by a *çeşme*; there follow three grilled winows opening into a small graveyard built for the founder and his family, his own tomb being, most unusually, within the *sebil* itself. The *sebil*, which was restored in the 1970s, is handsomely carved and decorated with various marbles.

Dolmabahçe Camii was built in 1853 for the Valide Sultan Bezmialem, mother of Abdül Mecit; the architect was Nikoğos Balyan, grandson of Kirkor Balyan. The great cartwheel-like arches are unattractive, and the only agreeable features on the exterior are the two very slender Corinthian minarets, one at each end of the little palace-like structure that precedes the mosque. The baroque clock-

275

tower to the north of the mosque was built by Nikoğos Balyan in 1854; it is made of cut stone and has a height of 27 metres, making it one of the most prominent landmarks on the European shore of the lower Bosphorus.

After passing the clock-tower we come to **Dolmabahçe Sarayî**, by far the largest and grandest of the imperial Ottoman palaces on the Bosphorus.

The site of Dolmabahçe, which means 'the filled-in garden', was a small inlet and harbour on the Bosphorus in Byzantine times. During the final siege of Constantinople in 1453 Mehmet the Conqueror anchored 70 ships of his fleet here in preparation for a stratagem that turned the tide of battle in his favour. After sunset on 22 April 1453 he had his ships placed on wheeled platforms and hauled by oxen, pulling them over the heights of Pera and down to the present site of the Tershane on the Golden Horn, thus bypassing the chain which the Byzantines had strung between the Castle of Galata and the sea-walls below the acropolis. This gave the Turks control of the Golden Horn and set the stage for their final capture of the city on 29 May of that year. Shortly afterwards Mehmet the Conqueror filled in the inlet on the Bosphorus here and laid out a royal garden on the site, hence the name Dolmabahçe. Ahmet I extended the gardens by filling in the little harbour, a project that was completed by his son Osman II. By the beginning of the nineteenth century there was a large imperial seaside pavilion at Dolmabahçe, which Mahmut II used as his summer residence. Then in 1842 Abdül Mecit decided to build a colossal new palace on the site, appointing as chief architects Karabet Balyan (son of Kirkor Balyan) and his son Nikoğos. The palace was completed in 1856, whereupon Abdül Mecit abandoned Topkapî Sarayî and took up residence in Dolmabahçe, which thenceforth served as the principal imperial residence for the remaining years of the Ottoman Empire. After the establishment of the Turkish Republic in 1923, Dolmabahçe served as the presidential residence in Istanbul, and Atatürk stayed there whenever he was in the city. Atatürk died in Dolmabahçe on 10 November 1938, in a seaside bedroom that is still furnished as it was at the time of his death. The palace was restored in the 1960s and is now open to the public as a museum.

The main entrance to Dolmabahçe Sarayî is through the gardens at its southern end. The palace faces the Bosphorus, and its gleaming white marble façade on that side is 248 metres long, with a quay some 600 metres in length. The core of the palace is a great hall flanked by two main wings containing the state rooms and the royal apartments, with the *selamlîk* on the south side and the harem on the north. The apartment of the Valide Sultan is in a separate wing linked to the Sultan's harem through the apartment of the Crown Prince. In addition there was another harem for the women of the younger princes, and still another residence at the northwest corner of the palace for the Chief Black Eunuch. The complex also included rooms for those of the palace staff who lived within Dolmabahçe Sarayî, as well as the royal kitchens, an *imaret* to feed the staff, an infirmary, stables, carriage houses, and barracks for the halberdiers who guarded the imperial residence. All in all, there were 285 rooms, including 43 large salons and six *hamams*, with the Sultan's private bath containing an alabaster bath tub.

The palace interior was the work of the French decorator Sechan, who designed the Paris Opera. A number of European artists were commissioned to adorn the palace with paintings, including Boulanger, Gerome, Fromentin, Ayvazovski and Zonaro. The opulent furnishings of the palace include nearly 4,500 square metres of hand-woven Hereke carpets; the fireplaces and chandeliers are of Bohemian glass and Baccarat crystal; and the world's largest chandelier hangs in the State Room, made from four and-one-half tons of Bohemian glass with 750 lights. The greatest showpiece is the ornate stairway that leads up from the Salon of the Ambassadors, its balusters made of Baccarat crystal and its upper level framed with monolithic columns of variegated marble. Two-thirds of the palace is taken up by the Harem, the most impressive chambers of which are the Valide Sultan's apartment, the Mavi (Blue) Salon, the Pembe (Pink) Salon, the apartment of Abdül Aziz, Atatürk's apartment, and the School Room. Behind the palace there is a secluded garden retreat known as the Aviary, with a little pavilion on a pond and another housing caged birds. Occasional shows of the works of the European paintings in the palace collection are held in the Exhibition Hall, which has a separate entrance approached from the shore highway.

About 300 metres beyond Dolmabahçe Sarayî the ferry stops at the **Beşiktaş** *iskele*. The park behind the *iskele* has a statue of the famous Ottoman admiral **Hayrettin Pasha**, known in the West as **Barbarossa**. The statue, a vivid work by the Turkish sculptor Zühtü Müridoğlu, was erected in 1946 on the fourth centenary of Barbarossa's death. Barbarossa's *türbe* is at the southernmost corner of the park, directly opposite his statue. This is the earliest *türbe* built by

Sinan, dated by an inscription over the door to 1541–42. The structure is octagonal, with two rows of windows, the upper row filled
with stained-glass, modern imitations of the originals.

Directly across the shore highway, beside Barbaros Bulvarî, we
see a well-built **mosque** constructed in alternate courses of brick and
stone. This is another work of Sinan, built in 1555–56 for the
Ottoman admiral **Sinan Pasha**, brother of the Grand Vizier Rüstem
Pasha, who died two years before his *külliye* was completed. The
mosque is preceded by a colonnaded courtyard, with the cells of the
medrese occupying three sides. Within, on the west side, there is a
sort of narthex of five bays, four with domes, the central one cross-
vaulted. The main area of the prayer-hall is surmounted by the
central dome, which rests on six arches, one incorporated in the east
wall, the others supported by four hexagonal pillars, two on the west,
one each to north and south; beyond the latter are side aisles each
with two domed bays.

A short distance south of the Beşiktaş *iskele* we see the **Naval
Museum** (Deniz Müzesi), in whose garden there are arrayed a
number of Ottoman naval guns, cannon balls, torpedoes, and other
mementoes of maritime warfare past. The most famous exhibit in the
museum is a chart of the Atlantic coast of North America done in the
sixteenth century by Piri Reis, the great Ottoman navigator. A separate building houses the museum's collection of *pazar caiques*, the
beautiful rowing barges that the sultans used in travelling to and
from their palaces and pavilions on the Bosphorus and the Golden
Horn.

Some 500 metres beyond the Besiktas *iskele* the ferry passes
Çîrağan Sarayî, recently rebuilt as a casino attached to the new
Çîrağan Hotel. Çîrağan Sarayî was built for Abdül Aziz by Sergis
Balyan and was completed in 1874, two years before the Sultan was
deposed. Abdül Aziz died in Çîrağan on 4 June 1876, five days after
he was removed from the throne; his death was officially declared to
be a suicide, but many believed that he was murdered. He was succeeded by his nephew Murat V (1876), who was deposed later that
year because of severe mental illness, to be replaced by his younger
brother, Abdül Hamit II. (Turks for long afterwards referred to this as
'the year of the three Sultans'.) During the first three decades of
Abdül Hamit's oppressive reign the deposed Sultan Murat and his
family were confined as virtual prisoners in Çîrağan, living in condi-
tions of deplorable squalor and degradation. Murat died in 1905, after
which the palace was restored and used to house the new Parliament

in 1908, the year before Abdül Hamit was deposed and exiled to Thessalonika. Then in 1910 Çırağan was destroyed by fire, with only the smoke-blackened shell of the façade along the Bosphorus standing until the recent reconstruction of the building.

A short distance beyond Çırağan Sarayî on the shore highway is the entrance to **Yîldîz Park**, in which are the various pavilions of **Yîldîz Sarayî**. On the right of the entrance stands **Mecidiye Camii**, built in 1848 for Abdül Mecit.

Yîldîz Park was originally known as the Gardens of Çırağan. These gardens first became famous during the reign of Ahmet III, the Tulip King, who gave them to his son-in-law, the Grand Vizier Nevşchirli Damat Ibrahim Pasha. Ibrahim Pasha hosted the Sultan and his court in some of the fetes that were held each year to celebrate the blossoming of the tulip gardens here and in the Fourth Court of Topkapî Sarayî. These festivals gave their name to the reign of Ahmet III, an era known in Turkish as Lale Devrisi, the Tulip Period, which ended in 1730 when the Sultan was deposed and his Grand Vizier assassinated by the Janissaries. Yîldîz Sarayî, the Palace of the Star, first began to take form during the reign of Mahmut II, and the buildings that one sees today date from his reign to that of Abdül Hamit II, who preferred to live here rather than at Dolmabahçe because of the greater seclusion provided by the walled-in woods of the Çırağan gardens. The pavilions of Yîldîz Sarayî were restored in the 1970s by the Turkish Touring and Automobile Club, and they are now open to the public, with the **Malta Köskü** and several other kiosks serving as cafés embowered in the gardens. The grandest structure at Yîldîz Sarayî is the **Şale**. This consists of two buildings, the first erected in 1889 and the second in 1898, the latter apparently the work of the Italian architect Raimondo D'Aronco, who brought Art Nouveau architecture to Istanbul under the name of the Stile Floreal. The Şale has some fifty rooms, the largest and grandest being the magnificent Reception Hall, with its ceiling decorated in gold leaf, other splendid chambers being the Hall of Mother-of-Pearl and the Yellow Parlour.

A few metres beyond the entrance to Yîîdîz Park a steep but very short lane leads up to the charming little *külliye* of **Yahya Efendi**. Yahya Efendi, one of the most famous Muslim saints in Istanbul, was born in Trabzon at the same time as Suleyman the Magnificent, and his mother served as wet-nurse for the future Sultan. When Süleyman succeeeded to the throne in 1520 Yahya Efendi accompanied him to Istanbul, where he becamed one of the most renowned divines of his time. The little *külliye*, which was built by Sinan shortly before Yahya Efendi's death in 1570, consists of a *medrese* and the saint's *türbe*, which communicates by a large grilled opening with a small wooden mosque covered by a baroque dome, the latter structure apparently a nineteenth-century addition. The setting is very picturesque, with the various buildings of the *külliye* and its ancient graveyard surrounded by a copse of trees on a knoll above the Bosphorus. The *külliye* is a very popular shrine, and there is a constant stream of pilgrims coming to pray in the *türbe*. According to Evliya Çelebi, the shade of Yahya Efendi communicates from his tomb with the spirit of Hîzîrilyas, the great Muslim saint who is probably the Islamic reincarnation of the Prophet Elias. As Evliya describes the shrine, it is 'in a deep shaded recess of the hills, luxuriant with plane, cypress, willow, fir, and nut-trees. Yahya Efendi is buried on top of a hill overlooking the sea; the four walls of his *türbe* are covered with the inscriptions of a hundred thousand divine lovers breathing out their feelings in verse. Even now he converses every Friday night with Hîzîrilyas, taking from him lessons in mysticism.'

The next ferry stop is **Ortaköy**, the **Middle Village**. The village has become a centre for arts and crafts, as well as of night life, and a number of its old houses have been restored as restaurants, cafés, bars, and boutiques. There are numerous restaurants and cafés around the ferry-landing, where in summer artisans and sellers of secondhand books set up their stalls.

On the promontory beyond the *iskele* is the charming **Mecidiye Camii**, built in 1854 for Abdül Mecit by Nikoğos Balyan. Within the village a synagogue of the early twentieth century and a nineteenth-century Greek Orthodox church stand on the right side of the main road, and on the left side is a ***hamam*** dating from c.1570. The *hamam*, which is currently being restored, was built by Sinan for Hüsrev Kethüda, who was Chief Steward for the Grand Vizier Sokollu Mehmet Pasha.

Just beyond Ortaköy the ferry passes under **Boğaziçi Köprü**, the **Bosphorus Bridge**, whose graceful span arcs across to the hills south of the village of Beylerbey on the Asian shore. The bridge opened on 27 October 1973, the fiftieth anniversary of the founding of the Turkish Republic. It is 1,074 metres in length between the two great piers on the opposing continental shores, its roadway 64 metres above the water at the centre of its span. Just above the bridge on the Asian side we see Beylerbey Sarayî, which we will examine in more detail on our return voyage down the Bosphorus.

Ortaköy Mosque with the First Bosphorus Bridge in the background

Yalîs and fortress at Anadolu Hisarî

The next ferry-stop on the European shore is **Arnavutköy**, the **Albanian Village**. Arnavutköy has one of the most colourful harbours along the Bosphorus, with a row of pretty yalîs, or seaside houses, lining the shore south of the *iskele*. The inner village is one of the most picturesque on the Bosphorus, its streets flanked by old wooden houses festooned with vines, a scene reminiscent of Ottoman times. Arnavutköy still has fifty Greek families, who worship in the large nineteenth-century church of Profitis Elias in the village square.

The promontory at the northern end of the village, **Akinti Burnu**, forms the boundary between the bays of Arnavutköy and Bebek, the next village to the north. The current off Akinti Burnu is the strongest of any point on the European side, reaching a speed of over five knots when the prevailing north wind is blowing. This made it very difficult for sailing vessels to round Akinti Burnu on their way up the Bosphorus, and they had to be pulled around the point by porters on shore. Apparently crabs also found it difficult, as Gyllius writes in his book on the Bosphorus: 'I myself saw there stones worn down by the long procession of crabs. And even if I had not seen it I would not have thought it far from the truth that stones should be worn down by the hard claws of crabs, since we see that ants can dig down furrows and make a path by the continuous attrition of their feet.'

Rounding Akinti Burnu, the ferry enters the calm waters of **Bebek Bay**. This is one of the most beautiful bays on the Bosphorus, the hillside above the southern arc of its crescent still retaining its original woods, mainly umbrella pines and columnar cypresses. Just before reaching the *iskele* the ferry passes the old **Egyptian Embassy**, an Art Nouveau palace built in 1912 by Raimondo D'Aronco. Just beyond the *iskele* there is a pretty little mosque built in 1913 by the Turkish architect Kemalettin Bey.

A few hundred metres beyond the *iskele* the shore road passes the lower entrance to the **University of the Bosphorus (Boğaziçi Universitesi)**, whose campus occupies a hilltop site between Bebek and Rumeli Hisari, the next village to the north. This Turkish university was established in 1971, occupying the buildings and grounds of the old **Robert College**. Robert College, which in its time was the finest institute of higher learning in Turkey, was founded in 1863 by Cyrus Hamlin, an American missionary who had baked bread and washed clothes for Florence Nightingale in Üsküdar during the Crimean War. The College was named after Christopher Robert, an

American philanthropist who had priovided the initial funds to build and operate the institution. During the 108 years of its existence the College numbered among its faculty and graduates many important figures, including several who played leading roles in the cultural and political life of Turkey, as well as of Bulgaria.

At the northern end of Bebek Bay the ferry passes a huge Turkish cemetery that dates back to the time of the conquest. The promontory below the cemetery marks the beginning of the Narrows for ships going up the Bosphorus, with the opposing continental shores only 700 metres apart. It was here that the Persian king Darius crossed the strait at the outset of his campaign against the Scythians in 512 BC, leading an army that Herodotus estimated to number 700,000 troops. This crossing was accomplished on a bridge of boats built by the famous Greek engineer Mandrocles of Samos. Darius commemorated this historic event by erecting two columns on the hilltop above the European shore, one in Greek and the other in Assyrian, listing the many nations that contributed contingents for his campaign.

The Narrows are flanked by the Ottoman fortresses of **Rumeli Hisarî** and **Anadolu Hisarî**, the Castles of Europe and Asia, both of which are surrounded by picturesque old villages, whose waterfronts have now been spoiled by the shore highways. Anadolu Hisarî was built c.1394 by Beyazit I, who put Constantinople under siege from then until 1402, when he was defeated by Tamerlane at the battle of Ankara. Constantinople thus gained a reprieve until 1452, when Mehmet II built the great fortress of Rumeli Hisarî directly opposite Anadolu Hisarî on the European shore. This cut off Constantinople from its grain supplies on the Black Sea, an important step in Mehmet the Conqueror's preparation for his siege of the city the following year. After the conquest the two fortresses lost their military importance; Anadolu Hisarî was allowed to fall into ruins, while Rumeli Hisarî was used principally to incarcerate prisoners of war and ambassadors of unfriendly powers. Rumeli Hisarî was restored in 1953 for the celebration of the five-hundredth anniversary of the Turkish conquest; since then it has been open to the public as a museum, and on summer evenings it is used for theatrical performances in the Istanbul Festival. The fortress spans a deep valley with two tall and massive towers on opposite hills and a third at the bottom of the valley on the shore of the Bosphorus, where there is a sea-gate protected by a barbican. A curtain wall, defended by three smaller towers, joins the three major ones, forming an irregular figure 250 metres long by 125 broad at its maximum. Over the gateway to the south tower an Arabic inscription records the date of completion of the fortress as the month of Recep AH 856, or July–August 1452, which is just four months after it was begun. The ferry no longer stops at the **village of Rumeli Hisarî**, one of the most picturesque on the Bosphorus, with its houses clustering around the north side of the Castle of Europe. Up until 1953 part of the village was inside the fortress, the inhabitants supposedly being the descendants of the original garrison stationed there by Mehmet the Conqueror, but these houses were demolished during the restoration.

Just beyond the village the ferry passes under the new **Bosphorus bridge, Fatih (Mehmet the Conqueror) Sultan Mehmet Köprüsü,** which crosses the strait between the hills above Rumeli Hisarî and Anadolu Hisarî, a span ten metres greater than that of the bridge between Ortaköy and Beylerbey. Fatih Köprüsü opened in the summer of 1988, exactly 2,500 years after Mandrocles built his bridge of boats for Darius across this same stretch of the Bosphorus.

The next village on the European shore is **Emirgan,** whose *iskele* is no longer in use. Emirgan takes its name from the Persian prince Emirgüne, who in 1638 surrendered the city of Erivan to Murat IV without a struggle. Emirgüne accompanied Murat back to Istanbul and became one of the Sultan's favourites, for which he was rewarded with the gift of a seaside palace in this village. On the left side of the shore road south of the *iskele* there is a seaside mansion named **Şerifler Yalîsî** which is believed to stand on the site of Emirgüne's palace; most of the present structure dates to the nineteenth century, when a *yalî* was erected here by a Şerif of Mecca named Abdullah Pasha. The village square of Emirgan is very pleasant, shaded by plane trees beneath which throngs of people are continually drinking tea, which the excellence of the local water makes particularly delicious. Beside the square on its southern side is a quaint baroque **mosque,** erected in 1781–82 by **Abdül Hamit I.** The prayer hall is a large almost square room that is curiously unsymmetrical; its decor is quite elegant in its baroque way. Just above the village are the famous tulip gardens of Emirgan, well worth a visit in spring. The Turkish Touring and Automobile Club has restored a number of Ottoman pavilions and kiosks in the gardens; one of them, the **Beyaz (White) Köşk,** has been converted into a concert hall, while the others now serve as cafés.

The next village above Emirgan on the European side is **Istiniye,** which has a deeply-indented bay that up until 1990 contained large

284

dry-docks. Its Turkish name is a corruption of the ancient Sosthenion, which Gyllius identifed as one of the places where Jason and the Argonauts stopped on their voyage up the Bosphorus. Gyllius wrote of Istiniye that 'after the Golden Horn it must be acknowledged the largest bay and safest port of the entire Bosphorus, rich as this is in bays and ports'. Istiniye is still an active fishing-port, and the local fishermen sell their catch at a colourful market along the quay.

The ferry now stops at the *iskele* at **Yeniköy**. This was known in Byzantine times as Neapolis, the New Town, which is what its Turkish name means, despite the great antiquity of the village. Yeniköy is a very attractive village, with some handsome neo-Renaissance *yalîs* along the seafront around the *iskele*. There are more churches in Yeniköy than in any other village on the Bosphorus, three of them Greek Orthodox, one Armenian Catholic, and one Roman Catholic, but their congregations here as elsewhere are much smaller than they were in times past. At the northern extremity of the village there is a stone mansion that once served as the summer embassy of Austria-Hungary, and which is now the Austrian summer consulate. Beyond that is the hamlet of Kalender, named after the order of mendicant dervishes who had a *tekke* there in Ottoman times. A little way beyond Kalender there is a huge wooden *yali* that serves as the summer embassy of Germany.

The next village on the European shore is **Tarabya**, which has long beeen celebrated for the beauty of its crescent bay. The village retains in a slightly modified form its Greek name Therapia, which means 'cure' or 'healing'. This name was given to it in the first quarter of the fifth century by the Patriarch Atticus, ostensibly because of its salubrious climate. But he actually did this to rid the village of its ancient name – Pharmakeus, the Poisoner – which stemmed from the legend that Medea had here thrown away the poison which she had brought with her when she fled from Colchis with Jason after he took the Golden Fleece. During the last two centuries of the Ottoman era Tarabya was a favourite resort of prominent Greeks from the Fener as well as other affuent people from Pera, drawn there by the beauty of the setting and the sophisticated Western atmosphere created by the presence of the summer embassies of the European powers. Just beyond the hotel is the handsome red wooden *yalî* that serves as the summer embassy of Italy. Beyond that are the gardens of the former British and French Embassies, whose mansions burned down in 1911 and were never rebuilt.

The next ferry-stop on the European shore is **Büyükdere**. Its Turkish name means Great Valley, while in Byzantine times it was known as Kalos Agros, the Beautiful Meadow. It was here that the knights of the First Crusade camped in 1096, before they crossed the Bosphorus on their long march across Asia Minor to the Holy Land. There are a number of handsome old *yalîs* along the shore between Büyükdere and Sarîyer, the next village to the north. One of these, the Azaryan Yalîsî, was built in the late nineteenth century by Manuk Azaryan Efendi, who served in the Turkish foreign service during the last years of the Ottoman Empire. Today the *yalî* houses the **Sadberk Hanîm Museum**, a rich collection of antiquities ranging from the Bronze Age up to the Graeco-Roman era, along with Ottoman arts, crafts and costumes, all beautifully displayed. The museum is dedicated to the memory of Sadberk Hanîm, wife of the late Vehbi Koç, who was one of Turkey's leading industrialists.

At **Büyükdere** the Bosphorus is some 3.5 kilometres wide, the greatest width of the strait other than at its entrance on the Black Sea. Above Büyükdere the European shore bends back sharply to the northeast toward the Asian shore, creating a stretch only about a kilometre in width before the strait opens out again between the lighthouses on the Black Sea.

Roads lead inland from both Büyükdere and Sarîyer, the next village on the Bosphorus, passing through the **Belgrade Forest** to **Kilyos**, a village on the Black Sea where there is an excellent sand beach, along with hotels, pensions and restaurants. The road from Büyükdere pases through one of the arches of **Eğrikemer**, the **Bent Aqueduct**, built by Mahmut I and completed in 1732.

Sarîyer is the largest village on the European shore of the upper Bosphorus, and it is also the principal fishing-port on the strait. The port and the fish-market around it are extremely colourful, particularly when the fishermen of Sarîyer return to the port after voyages that take them not only to the upper Bosphorus and the Black Sea but also to the Marmara, the Dardanelles and the Aegean. Some of their catch is served in restaurants around the port, with tables set out on the quay in good weather.

On the coast north of Sarîyer there is a little roadside shrine atop the cliff. This is the *türbe* of a Muslim saint named **Telli Baba**, who is reputed to have the power of finding suitable husbands for young women who come there to pray for his help. Immediately after their wedding ceremony the brides come here in their gowns to fasten talismanic coils of gold and silver wire around Telli Baba's tomb and to thank him for his help.

The last ferry-stop on the European shore is **Rumeli Kavaǧî**. From there most ferries cross the strait to Anadolu Kavagî, the last *iskele* on the Asian side, and from there start their return journey down the Bosphorus. There are numerous fish restaurants around the *iskeles* in both villages, which are very popular places to stop and have lunch during an outing on the Bosphorus.

The shore highway ends at Rumeli Kavaǧî. From here a secondary road leads to an inland highway that runs along the ridge above the Bosphorus out to **Rumeli Feneri**, the last village on the European side of the strait, where it opens into the Black Sea.

The only way to explore the Bosphorus beyond the last ferry-stops is by boat, for the shore roads do not extend much beyond the two villages. An excursion by boat along the upper Bosphorus can be exhilarating, for both shores are wild, rugged and desolate, but quite beautiful. At several places on both shores one finds sandy beaches hidden away in secluded coves; grey herons haunt the cliffs, black cormorants dive into the limpid water, flights of the shearwaters called kîrlangîç skim along the surface in mid channel, and schools of dolphins occasionally gambol by on their way up and down the strait, always a sign of good luck to mariners on the Bosphorus. Among the flights of migratory birds that can best be seen on the upper Bosphorus the most notable is that of the storks, who, according to the *Turkish Almanac*, arrive on 28 February and depart on 28 August, forming great spirals in soaring from and to the heavens.

Three nautical miles beyond Rumeli Kavaǧî we pass a very craggy promontory on the European shore named **Garipçe**, meaning 'strange', or 'curious', probably because of its very contorted topography. Gyllius identified this as Gyropolis, the City of Vultures, one of the places where Jason and the Argonauts stopped on their voyage up the Bosphorus This bizarre name stems from its association with the myth of King Phineus and the Harpies, the winged creatures who seized his food and befouled his table until he wasted away to a wraith. At last the Argonauts arrived and King Phineus was saved by Zetes and Kalais, the winged sons of Boreas, god of the north wind, who drove away the Harpies. Phineus, who was a prophet, expressed his gratitude to the Argonauts by advising them on how to pass through the **Symplegades**, the fearful clashing rocks at the entrance to the Bosphorus. Phineus told the Argonauts to let loose a dove which would fly between the rocks; if it was caught they were to give up their journey, but if it got through safely they were to wait until the Symplegades opened once more and then row their hardest. The Symplegades just shaved off the tail-feathers of the dove, and when the Argonauts rowed through the clashing rocks only slightly damaged the stern-works of *Argo*, fulfilling the King's prophecy.

The Symplegades were also called Cynean, the Blue Rocks, and Gyllius identified them with a striking feature at the very mouth of the Bosphorus on the European side, about a hundred metres off shore at **Rumeli Feneri**, the **Lighthouse of Europe**. This huge rock, which is now joined to the shore by a concrete mole, is about 20 metres high and is divided by deep fissures into several parts. According to Gyllius, 'The ascent to this peak is not open except by one approach, and this is extremely narrow, so that one must climb up on all fours'. The approach is just as difficult today, and the climb to the top is not for the faint-hearted. On the peak of the rock there is a monument known as **Pompey's Column**. It is not really a column but an ancient altar, decorated with a garlanded ram's head and other reliefs now much worn; it once had a Latin inscription, now illegible, the transcription and interpretation of which are matters of discussion. Certainly neither altar nor column had anything to do with Pompey, and no one seems to know why this name was given to the monument. Gyllius thought the altar was probably a remnant of a shrine to Apollo which Dionysius of Byzantium says the Romans erected on one of the Cynean Rocks. The column itself, with its Corinthian capital, toppled down in April 1680 and had utterly disappeared by 1800.

At Rumeli Feneri there are the remains of a fort built in 1769 by a Greek military engineer in the Ottoman service. There was a similar fort in **Anadolu Feneri**, the **Lighthouse of Asia**, but this seems to have vanished, probably worn away by the pounding waves of the Black Sea, which the Greeks called Hospitable only to placate it.

We now cross the Bosphorus and return down the Asian coast of the strait. The most prominent monument on the Asian shore of the upper Bosphorus is the great fortress whose dramatic ruins we see on the heights north of Anadulu Kavağî, from which it is accessible by road. This is popularly known as the **Genoese Castle**, though it was probably built by the Byzantines and then taken over by Genoa in the fourteenth century. The fortress is by far the largest on the Bosphorus, enclosing an area twice as great as that of Rumeli Hisarî, and though mostly in ruins it is very impressive and makes a very romantic sight set high on its promontory above the Bosphorus. Gyllius identified the promontory as the site of two ancient temples, one of them dedicated to the Twelve Olympian Gods and the other to Zeus of the Favourable Winds, and he thought that the latter may have been founded by Jason on his return from Colchis with the Golden Fleece.

The journey by ferry back down the Bosphorus begins at Anadolu Kavagî, with the first stop at **Beykoz**. Opposite Sarîyer we pass the second highest peak along the Bosphorus; this is **Yuşa Tepesi**, the **Hill of Joshua**, whose summit, marked by a power-line pylon, is 201 metres above sea level, surpassed only by Büyük Çamlîca. On the summit there is a shrine of a Muslim saint named Yusa Baba, whose grave, marked by green pillars at his head and feet, is twelve metres long. His tomb, which Europeans call the **Giant's Grave**, was known in antiquity as the Bed of Hercules. This is the place of which Byron wrote these memorable lines in one of the cantos of *Don Juan:*

> The wind swept down the Euxine, and the wave
> Broke foaming o'er the Blue Symplegades,
> 'Tis a grand sight from off the Giant's Grave
> To watch the progress of these rolling seas
> Between the Bosphorus, as they lash and lave
> Europe and Asia, you being quite at ease:
> There's not a sea the passenger e'er pukes in,
> Turns up more dangerous breakers than the Euxine.

Opposite Büyükdere the coast forms a long shallow bay with a rugged and inhospitable coast-line At **Selvi Burnu, Poplar Point**, the coast turns east to the charming valley of **Tokat Deresi**. Here Mehmet the Conqueror built a kiosk, and so later did Süleyman, a place described by Gyllius as a 'royal villa shaded by woods of various trees, especially planes'; he goes on to mention the landing-stairs, 'by which the King, crossing the shallow shore of the sea, disembarks into his gardens'. It is from these landing-stairs that the place gets its modern name, **Hünkâr Iskelesi**, the Emperor's Landing-Place, which in turn gave its name to the historic treaty that was signed here in 1833 between Russia and the Sublime Porte. The present **palace of Hünkâr Iskelesi** was built in the mid-nineteenth century for Abdül Mecit by Sarkis Balyan, brother of Nikoğos Balyan. The palace, which is still shaded by a lovely grove of plane trees, it is now used as a hospital.

The ferry now brings us to **Beykoz**, the largest village on the

Asian shore of the Bosphorus above Üsküdar. The principal monument in Beykoz is a very beautiful **street-fountain** in the village
square. It forms a sort of domed and columned loggia, quite unlike
any other fountain in the city. The fountain was built in 1746 for
Ishak Ağa, inspector of the customs under Mahmut I.

A road leads from Beykoz to the picturesque village of **Şile** on the
Black Sea, where there is a splendid sand beach, with hotels,
pensions and restaurants. The Kumbaba Motel, which is on the
beach west of Şile, occupies the site of ancient **Calpe**, as evidenced
by the architectural fragments found and arrayed there.

Gyllius identified Beykoz as the home of the terrible Amycus,
king of the savage Bebryces. Amycus insisted on boxing with any
stranger who landed on his coast, using the nail-studded gloves
known as *cestus*, and, since he was the son of Poseidon and the best
boxer in the world, he always killed his opponent. But at last he met
his match in one of the Argonauts, Polydeuces (Pollox), son of Zeus
and Leda, who outboxed the King and killed him. The grave of King
Amycus was identified in antiquity with the Bed of Hercules on
Yuşa Tepesi. On the spot where King Amycus was killed there grew
up an *insana laurus*, the insane bay-tree, which resembled Banquo's
'insane root which takes the reason prisoner.'

South of Beykoz at **Incir Köyü**, **Figtree Village**, is the charming
valley of **Sultaniye Deresi** where Beyazit II established extensive
gardens. A little farther on the ferry stops at **Paşabahçe**, the **Pasha's
Garden**, so called from the palace and garden established here by
Hezarpara Ahmet Pasha, Grand Vizier under Murat IV. Hezarpara
means 'a thousand pieces', a name that was given to Ahmet Pasha
when he was killed in 1631 in an uprising by the Janissaries, who
hacked him to bits in the Hippodrome. The village mosque in
Paşabahçe was built in 1763 by Mustafa III. Paşabahçe is renowned
for its glass works, which produces the finest glassware in Turkey.
Paşabahçe also has a large *rakî* factory, which has a cascade fountain
through which flows not water but *raki*, a monument to the
intellect-deading national drink.

The ferry stops next at **Çubuklu**, about whose name, which
means 'with a cane' (in Turkish, *çubuk*), Evliya Çelebi tells an
amusing story:

Beyazit II, having brought his son Selim [the future Selim I] from
Trebizond to Constantinople, gave him in this place in a fit of anger
eight strokes with a cane, which eight strokes were prophetic of
the years of his reign. At the same time, he said to him, 'Boy,

don't be angry, these eight strokes shall fructify during the eight years of your reign. Selim stuck the dry cane into the ground, praying to heaven that it might strike root and bear fruit. The Şeyh Kara Şemseddin and Beyazit himself said, 'Amen'; after which the cane began to grow and even now bears cornels, five of which weigh a drachma.

The village was known in Byzantine times as Eirenaion, or Peaceful, a name that could still be applied to it today. It had a very famous monastery founded in 420 by St Alexander for the order of Akoimetai, the Unsleeping, who prayed in relays around the clock. After the monastery of St John of Studius was built later that century in Constantinople, the Akoimetai moved there and continued their unceasing prayers for a thousand years more, until the Studion was closed at the end of the fifteenth century.

On a hilltop between Çubuklu and Kanlîca, the next village along the Bosphorus, is the former **palace of the Khedive** (Viceroy) of Egypt with its distinctive tower, one of the most prominent landmarks on this stretch of the strait. It was built c.1900 by Abbas Hilmi Pasha, the last Khedive, and for a palace of that date it has considerable charm. Its western façade overlooking the Bosphorus is semicircular, with a handsome marble-columned porch and a semicircular hall within. The upper floor, especially the tower room and a charming loggia on the roof, command some of the finest views on the Bosphorus. The Turkish Touring and Automobile Club has restored the palace and redecorated it superbly in its original Art Nouveau style; it now serves as a deluxe hotel and restaurant.

The ferry next stops at **Kanlîca**. The village has long been famous for its delicious yogurt, which is served in restaurants around the *iskele* and the little square behind it. The **mosque** at the rear of the square was built by Sinan in 1559–60 for **İskender Pasha**, a Vizier of Süleyman the Magnificent. The mosque is of the very simplest type, with a wooden porch and a prayer room covered by a flat ceiling. The porch and roof are clearly modern additions, for Evliya tells us that the prayer room was originally covered by a wooden dome.

Between Kanlîca and Anadolu Hisarî, the next ferry-stop, we pass once again under Mehmet the Conqueror Köprüsü, the upper Bosphorus bridge. As we do so we see on the Asian shore the oldest of all the surviving *yalîs* on the Bosphorus, a rose-red wooden ruin suspended over the water on rotting stilts and corbels. The yalî was built in 1698 by **Amcazade Hüseyin Pasha Köprülü**, Grand Vizier under Mustafa II. The Peace of Carlowitz was signed in this *yalî* on 26 January 1699, ending a war between Russia and the Ottoman Empire.

The ferry now stops at **Anadolu Hisarî**, whose *iskele* is just upstream from the Ottoman fortress of the same name. The fortress is a small one, consisting of a keep and its surrounding wall with a barbican, now partly demolished, guarded by three towers. The French scholar Gabriel has suggested that only the keep and its wall were built by Beyazit II, the barbican and towers being added later by Mehmet the Conqueror when he was building the fortress of Rumeli Hisarî across the strait. The **fortress of Anadolu Hisarî** is a charming little castle and well deserves the name of Güzelce, the Pretty One, by which it was originally known. The village that surrounds it is very picturesque, with its old wooden houses clustered around the castle on its promontory, where the Bosphorus is joined by a little river known as **Göksu**, the **Heavenly Stream**.

Göksu is one of two streams that together make up the **Sweet Waters of Asia**; the other one, a few hundred metres to the south, is **Küçüksu**, the **Little Stream**, where the ferry stops next after Anadolu Hisarî. The Sweet Waters of Asia were a favourite summer resort in Ottoman times, and the sultans often came here in their *pazar caiques* for a day's outing. Several of the sultans built kiosks and other structures here, of which there now remain a small palace and a fountain, both named Küçüksu.

The **Palace of Küçüksu**, a pretty little rococo edifice on the Bosphorus, was built for Abdül Mecit in 1856–57 by Nikoğos Balyan. The palace was used by the last sultans as a pied-à-terre when they visited the Sweet Waters; then in the first half-century of the Republic it was used as a Presidential residence and also to house visiting dignitaries. It was restored in the 1970s and is now open as a museum.

Beside the palace to its south is the **Küçüksu Çeşmesi**, one of the most beautiful baroque fountains in the city, built for Selim III in 1806. The Sultan's name and the date of construction are given in a long calligraphic chronogram of 32 lines inscribed across the four sides of the fountain. The text is by the poet Hatîf, who in the last four lines of the chronogram refers to the *çeşme* as a 'soul-caressing fountain . . . a fragile beauty in the meadow'.

Just south of the *iskele* at Küçüksu we see two of the oldest inhabited *yalîs* on the Bophorus. The one next to the beach at Küçüksu is the **Kîbrîslî (of Cyprus) Mustafa Emin Pasha Yalîsî**, built originally c.1760 but added to and redecorated later on. It is still inhabited by the descendants of Mustafa Emin Pasha. A little farther down-stream we see the **Ostrorog Yalîsî**, a very handsome wooden mansion painted rust-red. This dates from c.1790 and was the residence of the Counts Ostrorog, Polish aristocrats who were ennobled by the French and enlisted in the Ottoman service in the late eighteenth century. The last Count Ostrorog died in the 1970s, but the house is still occupied by his heirs. Pierre Loti was a guest here during his stay in Istanbul, and his room has been preserved as it was at that time.

The ferry stops next at **Kandilli**, next to the promontory opposite Bebek Bay. The waters off the Kandilli promontory are known as the Devil's Current, the strongest on the Asian side of the strait, with a speed of over five knots when the prevailing north wind is blowing. The deepest point in the Bosphorus is 300 metres off the Kandilli promontory, with a depth of 110 metres.

The next ferry-stop is at **Vaniköy**, opposite Arnavutköy. On the hilltop above Vaniköy we see the tower and telescope-dome of the **Istanbul Rasatname**, a meteorological station and astronomical observatory. The Rasatname preserves the astronomical instruments of the great Turkish astronomer Takiuddin, who flourished in the third quarter of the sixteenth century.

The ferry then goes on to Çengelköy, some 1,500 metres farther down the strait. About halfway between Vaniköy and Çengelköy we pass the **Kuleli Military College**, a large building flanked by conical-capped towers. The original training school and barracks here were built c.1800 by Selim III, part of his attempted reform of the Ottoman armed forces. The present structure dates from an extensive rebuilding and enlargement by Abdül Mecit, completed in 1860. The original building served as a military hospital in 1855–56, during the Crimean War. This was one of two hospitals in Istanbul directed by Florence Nightingale, the other being in the much larger Selimiye Barracks in Üsküdar.

The Kuleli College occupies the site of a famous hospice founded c.530 by the Empress Theodora, Justinian's wife; it was called Metanoia, or Repentance, and it was used to house supposedly reformed prostitutes. Procopius writes of this with bitter irony in his *Secret History*, where earlier he gives a lurid description of Theodora's career as a courtesan before she reformed and met Justinian:

> Theodora also devoted considerable attention to the punishment of women caught in carnal sin. She picked up more than five hundred harlots in the Forum, who earned a miserable living by

selling themselves there for three obols, and sent them to the opposite mainland, where they were locked up in a convent called Repentance to force them to reform their way of life. Some of them, however, threw themselves from the parapets at night and thus freed themselves from an undesired salvation.

The ferry now stops at **Çengelköy**, the **Village of the Hooks**. According to Evliya, the village is so-called because after the conquest a store of Byzantine anchors (in Turkish, *çengel*) were found here. The village is very pretty, and around the *iskele* there are a number of seaside restaurants with a view of the lower Bosphorus and the skyline of the old city. Just downstream from the *iskele* we see the **Sadullah Pasha Yalîsî**, a handsome seaside mansion dated c.1790.

The next ferry-stop is at **Beylerbey**, known in Byzantine times as Stavros, or the Cross. Next to the *iskele* there is an imperial mosque known locally as **Beylerbey Camii**. According to its dedicatory inscription, this was built in 1778 by Abdül Hamit I as part of a very extensive *külliye*; the other buildings of the complex, however, are not grouped around the mosque, but are near Yeni Cami in the old city, where we saw the *türbe*, *medrese* and *sebil* on our first itinerary. The mosque, a work of the architect Mehmet Tahir Ağa, is an attractive example of the baroque style, its dome arches arranged in an octagon, vigorously emphasized within and without, its *mihrab* in a projecting apse, richly decorated with an assortment of tiles of different periods ranging from the sixteenth century to the eighteenth. The *mimber* and Koran *kursu* are unusually elegant and beautiful works, both of them of wood inlaid with ivory. The mosque has two minarets, the second added later by Mahmut II.

Beyond the villlage we come to **Beylerbey Sarayî**, whose far end is almost underneath the Bosphorus Bridge. The village and the palace were named after a Beylerbey, or Provincial Governor; this was Mehmet Pasha, who governed Rumelia in the reign of Murat III. Mehmet Pasha built a mansion on this site in the last quarter of the sixteenth century, and though it eventually vanished the name lived on. The present Beylerbey Sarayî was built for Abdül Aziz in 1861–65 by Sarkis Balyan. Beylerbey was used mainly as a summer lodge and as a residence for visiting royalty, the first of whom was the Empress Eugénie of France. Abdül Hamit II was confined in Beylerbey after his return from exile in Thessalonica, and he died here in 1918. The palace was splendidly restored in the 1970s and is now open to the public as a museum.

The palace is in three storeys and is divided into the usual *selamlîk* and harem. The ground floor contains the kitchens, store-rooms and other service facilities, with the state rooms and the imperial apartments on the two upper floors, where there are a total of 26 elegantly furnished chambers, including six grand salons. The grandest of the salons are the Yellow Pavilion and the Marble Pavilion, the latter focused on a large pool with an elaborate cascade fountain. Beylerbey is as sumptuously furnished and decorated as Dolmabahçe, with Hereke carpets; chandeliers of Bohemian crystal; French clocks; vases fron China, Japan, France, and the imperial Ottoman workshops at Yîldîz; and it is adorned with murals by European painters, most notably Ayvazovski. The Royal Stables and their mews have also been restored; these occupy the building to the right of the palace as one looks at it from the sea. The palace is extremely attractive when seen from the deck of a passing ferry, with its two little marble pavilions at either end of the long quay, bordered by gardens that give one a glimpse of what the shores of the Bosphorus must have been like in Ottoman times.

We now pass under the lower Bosphorus bridge once again, after which the ferry stops at **Kuzguncuk**, a very pretty village that has somehow managed to remain unspoiled despite its close proximity to the expanding urban mass of Üsküdar. The next top is **Üsküdar**, after which the ferry crosses the strait to the terminus on the shore of Eminönü on the Golden Horn, where we complete our voyage up and down the Bosphorus.

This also completes our exploration of Istanbul, at which point we might recall the words that Petrus Gyllius wrote of this imperial city more than four centuries ago: 'It seems to me that while other cities are mortal, this one will remain as long as there are men on earth.'

PART II: AROUND THE MARMARA

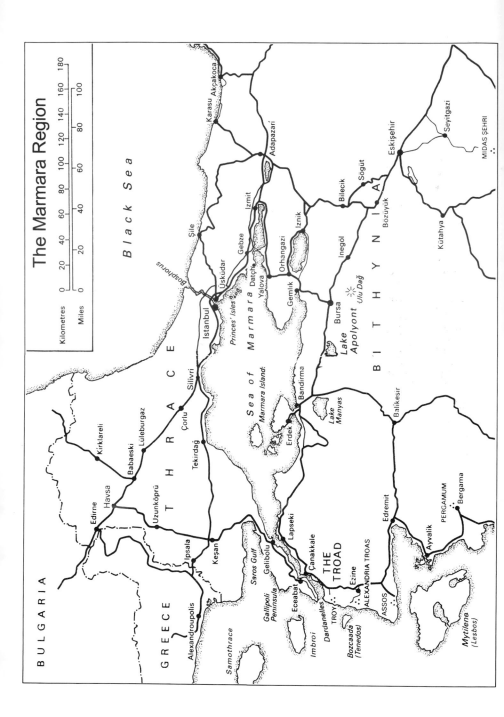

The Marmara Region

21

Istanbul to Edirne

OUR NEXT ITINERARY will take us from Istanbul to Edirne, the first phase of our tour around the Sea of Marmara. This itinerary and the next one will take us through Thrace, the European region of Turkey, which is separated from the Asian part of the country by the Bosphorus, the Sea of Marmara and the Dardanelles.

Thrace is a region with a long and interesting history, and it is rich in monuments of Ottoman architecture ranging from the fourteenth century through the seventeenth. This is particularly true in Edirne, the most historic city in the region. But many of the seemingly insignificant towns one passes on the highway between Istanbul and Edirne have historical associations that go back to antiquity, and some even to the little known prehistoric period of Thrace, whose people and their curious customs are first described in the Histories of Herodotus.

> The population of Thrace is greater than that of any country in the world except India. If the Thracians could be united under a single ruler, or combined, they would be the most powerful nation on earth, and no one could cope with them – that, at any rate, is my own opinion; but in point of fact it is impossible – there is no way of its ever being realized, and the result is that they are weak . . . When a baby is born the family sits around and mourns at the thought of the sufferings that the infant must endure now that it has entered the world, and goes through the whole catalogue of human sorrows; but when somebody dies, they bury him with merriment and rejoicing, and point out how happy he is and how many miseries he has at last escaped.

Not long after Herodotus wrote these lines the Thracian tribes united under Teres, King of the Odrysae, beginning a dynasty that was to last for three generations, continuing through the reigns of his son Sitalces and his grandson Seuthes. The region over which they ruled was vast, for ancient Thrace stretched from the Aegean to the Danube and from the Euxine to the River Strymon in what is now northern Greece. In 429 BC Sitalces was able to raise an army of 150,000 men for an invasion of Macedonia, but the characteristic disunity of the Thracian tribes under his command aborted the campaign within a month with nothing to show for the enormous effort. After the reign of Seuthes the Thracians once again split up along ancient tribal lines, and thenceforth Thrace became a march-land for invading armies: Macedonians, Romans, Byzantines, Bulgars, Byzantines again, and then the Ottoman Turks, who conquered the whole of the region by the end of the fourteenth century. The Turks held all of Thrace up until the last half of the nineteenth century, but the rise of the modern Greek and Bulgarian nations reduced their territory to the region known as Eastern Thrace, which was awarded to the Turkish Republic by the Treaty of Lausanne in 1923. The towns of Turkish Thrace reflect the history of the region, some of them originating as ancient Thracian camps, others as Greek colonies in the archaic period, a number as Roman garrison towns, but all of them now as typically Turkish as any region of Anatolia. Nevertheless one still sees numerous examples of the ancient Thracian type so aptly described by Xenophanes of Colophon in the late sixth century BC: 'Men create gods in their own image, so that when the Thracians make an idol of a god, he has blue eyes, red hair and freckles.'

We will drive from Istanbul to Edirne on superhighway 555, which bypasses all of the towns ennroute, so that one can complete the journey in less than three hours. Those with time to spare can turn off at the various exits for these towns, some of which have interesting and seldom-visited monuments.

The first part of the drive takes us along the Marmara shore past the turn-off to Silivri. **Silivri** is the ancient **Selymbria,** founded by Megarian settlers in 677 BC, nineteen years before the traditional date for the founding of Byzantium. Archaeological finds indicate that the site was inhabited as far back as the Chalcolithic Age (c.5500–3000 BC), and there is reason to believe that before the coming of the Greeks this was an important Thracian city. Like Byzantium, Selymbria remained an independent Greek city throughout most of antiquity, though in 479 BC the local Thracian tribes took control of the city until 408 BC, when it was captured by Alcibiades. In the third century BC Selymbria was amalgamated with Byzantium, and thenceforth it ceased to have an independent history.

About 15 kilometres beyond Silivri the superhighway turns away from the Marmara shore and heads inland across Thrace towards Edirne. Our route follows the course of the ancient **Via Egnatia,**

which was completed by the Romans soon after they established
their Province of Asia in 129 BC. This takes us across the monoto-
nous landscape of the Thracian downs, whose skyline of low rolling
hills is punctuated here and there with tumuli marking ancient
graves, some of which have been excavated and found to be the
tombs of Thracian chieftains. Herodotus writes of these tumuli in his
description of the Thracians and their funerary customs.

> With the Thracians . . . it is customary for a man to have a number
> of wives; and when a husband dies, his wives enter into a keen
> competition, in which his friends play a vigorous part on one side
> or the other, to decide which of them was most loved. The one on
> whom the honour of the verdict falls is first praised by both men
> and women, and then slaughtered over the grave by her next of kin
> and buried by her husband's side . . . When a rich Thracian is bur-
> ied, the custom is to lay out the body for three days, during which,
> after a preliminary period of mourning, a feast is held of all sorts
> of animals slaughtered for that purpose; then the body is buried,
> with or without cremation, a mound is raised over it, and elaborate
> games set on foot. The most valuable prizes in the games are
> awarded for single combat.

The towns that we pass along the Edirne highway were garrison
posts throughout the Ottoman Empire, for they were on the route
along which Turkish armies marched in their numerous invasions of
Europe. These invasions were particularly frequent in Süleyman's
time, and consequently all of these towns on the Edirne road have
mosques and caravansarais and other structures dating from his reign
or those of his immediate successors, most of them works of Sinan.

The first exit that we pass is for **Çerkezköy** and **Saray**, from
which a secondary road goes out to the Black Sea coast at **Kîyîköy**.
Near Çerkezköy there is a well-preserved stretch of the **Long Walls
of Anastasius I**. These were erected by the Byzantines in the late
fifth century, stretching in a great arc of some forty Roman miles
from the Black Sea to the Marmara. Gibbon called these walls
Byzantium's 'Last Frontier', providing an effective outer defence for
Constantinople as long as they were maintained and sufficiently
manned, but when these conditions were not met they were overrun
by powerful invaders, in the first instance by the barbarian Avars in
626. The archaeologist J. G. Crow, in an article on the Long Walls,
says that 'As it survives, it is the most monumental linear fortification dating from antiquity in continental Europe, comparable with
Hadrian's Wall in its complexity and preservation.'

The principal monument in Saray is **Ayas Pasha Camii**, built c.1536 and recently restored. The founder, Ayas Pasha, became Grand Vizier under Süleyman in 1536, replacing the famous Ibrahim Pasha and serving until his death three years later.

Kîyîköy is a picturesque fishing port with a beautiful beach on either side of a river that flows into the Black Sea. Formerly it was known as Midiye, and was predominately Greek up until the population exchange sanctioned by the Treaty of Lausanne in 1923. The village is still surrounded by large sections of its Byzantine walls, whose oldest sections date back to the sixth century AD. On the bank of the river below the village there is a well-preserved rock-hewn church of the medieval Byzantine period, part of a monastic complex that may have been founded as early as the sixth century.

The village stands on the site of ancient **Salmydessos**, a Greek colony founded early in the seventh century BC, probably around the same time as Byzantium. The people of Salmydessos were infamous as wreckers, luring ships ashore with beacons to give them the impression that this was the mouth of the Bosphorus. Salmydessos is mentioned in one of the surviving works of the great lyric poet Archilochus of Paros, who flourished in the mid-seventh century BC. The poem, given here in Richmond Lattimore's translation, is entitled 'The Wreckers and a Former Friend'.

> Slammed by the surf on the beach
> naked at Salmydessos, where the screw-haired men
> of Thrace, taking him in
> will entertain him (he will have much to undergo,
> chewing on slavery's bread)
> stiffened with cold, and loops of seaweed from the slime,
> tangling his body about,
> teeth chattering as he lies in abject helplessness
> flat on his face like a dog
> beside the beach-break where the waves come shattering in.
> And let me be there to watch;
> for he did me wrong and set his heel on our good faith.
> He had once been my friend.

The next exit from the superhighway after Çatalca is for **Çorlu**. Çorlu is the ancient Roman **Cenopurio**, where the Emperor Aurelian was murdered in 275. Çorlu was taken from the Byzantines in 1359 by Murat I, who in the following two years would capture all of the other towns along this road. Beyazit II was deposed here by his son Selim I on 13 May 1512. Beyazit died thirteen days later on the

302

road to his place of retirement in Edirne, with general opinion then and now being that he was poisoned by his son and successor. Eight years later Selim himself died in Çorlu, but news of his death was not released until his son Süleyman had time to rush to Istanbul to take control of the capital and ensure his own succession to the throne. Süleyman later commissioned Sinan to built a *külliye* for him in Çorlu, but this has disappeared. The principal monument in the town is the **Süleymaniye Camii**, built for Süleyman in 1521 by the architect known as Mimar Kasîm.

There was also a small imperial Ottoman palace in Çorlu, but this has long vanished. The palace is mentioned by Lady Mary Wortley Montagu in a letter dated 29 May 1717, describing her journey from Edirne to Istanbul, where her husband was English ambassador to the Sublime Porte. As she writes, referring to Ahmet III as the 'Grand Signior':

> I have had the advantage of very fine weather all my journey, and the summer now being in its beauty I enjoyed the pleasure of fine prospects; and the meadows being full of all sorts of garden flowers and sweet herbs, my berlin perfumed the air as it pressed 'em. The Grand Signior furnished us thirty covered wagons for our baggage and five coaches of the country for my women. We found the road full of the great spahi [*sipahi*, or Ottoman cavalry] horsemen and their equipages, coming out of Asia to the war. They always travel in tents, but I chose to lie in houses along the way. I will not trouble you with the names of the villages we passed in which there was nothing remarkable, but at Chorlu we were lodged in a konak or little seraglio, built for the Grand Signior when he goes this road. I had the curiosity to view all the apartments destined for the ladies of the court. They were in the midst of thick groves of trees, made fresh by fountains, but I was surprised to see the walls almost coverd with little distiches of Turkish verse writ with pencils. I made my interpreter explain them to me and I found several of them well turned, though I easily believed that they lost much of their beauty in the translation. One runs literally thus in English: 'We come into this world, we lodge, and we depart/ He never goes that's lodged within my heart.'

We next pass the exit for **Lüleburgaz**, ancient **Bergula**. Theodosius the Great changed the name of the town to **Arcadiopolis** in honour of his son and eventual successor, Arcadius. The principal monument in Lüleburgaz is the Sokollu Mehmet Pasha *külliye*, built by Sinan for Selim II in the years 1569–71.

The next exit is for **Babaeski**, where excavations have revealed evidence of human habitation dating back to the Bronze Age (c.3000–1200 BC). The principal monument in Babaeski is **Cedit Ali Pasha Camii**, built by Sinan in 1572. Near the mosque there is a beautiful Ottoman **bridge**, built for Murat IV in 1633 by the architect Çoban (the Shepherd) Kasîm Ağa.

The last exit before before Edirne is for **Havsa**, which we will pass through on our next itinerary. We then come to the exit for Edirne, as the superhighway continues on to Bulgaria. The last stretch of the way takes us along highway E-80, the old 'Londra Asfalt'.

We now come to **Edirne**, ancient Hadrianopolis or Adrianople, which is situated near the confluence of the **Meriç** and **Tunca Rivers**, the ancient **Hebrus** and **Tonsus**, respectively. The Greek border crossing is just five kilometres to the west and the Bulgarian check-point 18 kilometres to the northwest.

Once into Edirne the highway leads us along Midhat Pasha Caddesi to Cumhuriyet Meydanî, the centre of the town. As we enter the town we can see three of Edirne's historic mosques: straight ahead is Üç Şerefeli Camii, on the left is Eski Cami, and some distance off to the right is the Selimiye, the principal monument in Edirne.

The original settlement on this site was a Thracian market town founded in the seventh century BC at the confluence of the Hebrus and Tonsus rivers. The original name of the town was Odrysia, the city of the Odrys, referring to the local Thracian tribe that settled there. Later a Hellenic tribe from Epirus known as the Orestes founded a settlement adjacent to Odrysia and called it Orestia, a name that is still borne by the first village beyond the border-crossing in Greece. Then in AD 125 Hadrian combined the two towns into a single city – Hadrianopolis – which in Greek became Adrianopolis and in English Adrianople. Hadrian developed the city into a large military base and centre for the manufacture of armaments. Under Diocletian (284–305) Adrianople became capital of one of the four provinces into which the Emperor divided Thrace. Then after Constantine transferred his capital to the new city of Constantinople, Adrianople developed rapidly and became the most prosperous and populous city in Thrace, a status that it continued to hold throughout the Byzantine period.

During Byzantine times Adrianople appears in history principally in connection with the great battles that were fought in its vicinity.

Edirne

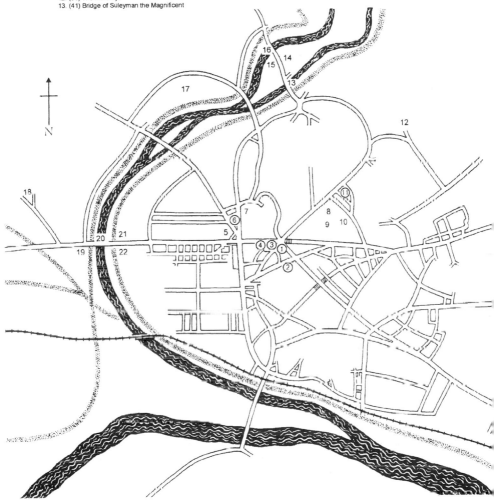

Constantine the Great defeated Licinius on the plain outside Adrianople in 323, setting the stage for his final victory over his rival the following year across the Bosphorus from Byzantium. The Emperor Valens was killed here in battle against the Goths in 378, and in 811 Nicephorus I (802–11) lost his life at Adrianople fighting against Krum of the Bulgars, who fashioned the emperor's skull into a goblet from which he served beer to his officers at the victory feast.

During the following five-and-one-half centuries Adrianople was fought over and captured in turn by the Byzantines, Avars, Bulgars, Latins and Turks, finally falling to Murat I in 1361, after which it came to be called Edirne. Edirne soon afterwards became capital of the rapidly expanding Ottoman Empire, a position it held until a few months after the conquest of Constantinople.

Edirne retained its prominence long after Istanbul became the capital, for several of the sultans and their pashas looked upon the city as their second home, continuing to adorn it with splendid buildings. But in the later Ottoman period the decay of the Empire brought about a decline in the fortunes of Edirne. During the last Ottoman century the city suffered terribly at the hands of invading armies, occupied by the Russians in 1829 and 1878, the Bulgars in 1913, and the Greeks in 1919–23, after which it was formally awarded to Turkey by the Lausanne Treaty in 1923. The wounds of war have healed in the years since then, and today Edirne is a lively and cheerful market town, distinguished by its many imperial Ottoman monuments.

Eski Cami, the **Old Mosque**, was begun by the Emir Süleyman Çelebi, son of Beyazit I, shortly after his father's defeat at the battle of Ankara in 1402. Construction of the mosque was halted while Süleyman fought a war of succession with his brothers Musa Çelebi and Mehmet Çelebi. Süleyman was defeated and killed in 1411 by Musa. Then two years later Musa himself was defeated and killed by the only surviving brother, who thus became sole ruler of the Ottoman Empire as Mehmet I. That same year Mehmet completed work on Eski Cami, as recorded by the dedicatory inscription on the mosque, which also identifies the builder as Ömer ibn Ibrahim and the architect as Hacî Alaeddin of Konya. The mosque was damaged by fire in 1749 and by earthquake in 1752; it was repaired by Mahmut I and was most recently restored in 1932–44.

The building is a perfect square 49.5 metres on a side, divided into nine equal sections covered by nine domes supported internally by four massive piers. The first bay inside the entryway has an open-topped dome, originally with an open oculus that is now covered with a lantern. This bay was probably originally an open court, which the faithful would enter from the main gateway or from the two side portals at the ends of the first bays on either side.

Before crossing the square to see Üç Şerefcli Camii we might explore the market quarter around Eski Cami, where there are three interesting old Ottoman buildings.

Just to the south of Eski Cami is the **Caravansarai of Rüstem Pasha**, built by Sinan in 1560–61. The caravansarai is in two sections, each with a different plan and function. The much larger one on the left, known as the Büyük Han, was designed as an urban *han* for the merchants of Edirne, while the one on the right, the Küçük Han, was built as a caravansarai for travellers. Both *hans* have been restored and now serve as a luxury hotel, the Rüstem Pasha Kervansaray. The restoration received international recognition in 1980, when it was awarded an Aga Khan award in architecture, but unfortunately in recent years the hotel has been neglected and is no longer up to standards.

Just beside Eski Cami we see the **Edirne Bedesten**, built by Mehmet I just after the completion of the mosque. The income from the Bedesten was used for the upkeep of the mosque and the salaries of its staff. Here, as elsewhere, the Bedesten was the commercial centre of the city and not merely a market; its function was to be a secure storage-space and display area for those dealing in the most valuable goods, just as gold-merchants, jewellers, armourers, brocade-dealers, and sellers of expensive carpets. The Edirne Bedesten has been restored in recent years and is now in excellent repair.

Another old Ottoman market flanks the west side of Saraçlar Caddesi, the first main street to the west of Eski Cami. This is the **Semiz Ali Pasha Arasta**, built by Sinan in 1568–69; that was four years after the death of the Grand Vizier, so it must have been founded by one of his heirs in his memory. The Arasta is a long (300 metres) and narrow structure with vaulted shops on either side, 126 in all, really a covered market street rather than a market building like the Edirne Bedesten.

South of the Semiz Ali Pasha Arasta is the old quarter known as **Kale Iç**, or 'Inside the Castle'. The quarter is so called because in Byzantine times it was within the citadel of Adrianople. The streets of the quarter, which is roughly bounded by Saraçlar Caddesi, Talat Pasha Caddesi, and the Tunca, form a rectangular grid pattern, with fragments of the Byzantine walls still visible down by the river.

Across Talat Pasha Caddesi from the Semiz Ali Pasha Arasta we see the ancient tower known as **Kule Kapîsî**, or **Tower Gate**. This is the remnant of a defence tower that once guarded the main gate of the Adrianople citadel. The tower is part of the defence-walls erected by Hadrian, which were rebuilt in 1123 by John II Comnenus when faced by an invasion by the Pechenegs, a barbarian tribe from the Russian steppes.

At the northwest corner of Talat Pasha Caddesi and Hükümet Caddesi, the continuation of Saraçlar, we come to the **Sokollu Mehmet Pasha Hamamî**, built by Sinan in 1568–69. This has been restored in recent years but with its original beauty diminished, for all of its tiles have been lost, though its marble revetment remains.

We now cross Hükümet Caddesi to the western side of Cumhuriyet Meydanî to visit **Üç Şerefeli Camii**. Built by Murat II in the years 1437–47, this was the most monumental edifice erected in the Ottoman Empire before the conquest of Constantinople. Historians of architecture, most notably Aptullah Koran, consider it to be a turning-point in the history of Ottoman architecture, the first step in the creation of the centrally-planned imperial mosques of the fifteenth century. Like Eski Cami, the mosque was restored by Mahmut I after being severely damaged by fire and earthquake in the mid-eighteenth century. The mosque takes its name from the fact that there are three (*üç*) *şerefes* on one of its four minarets, the one at the southeast corner. This minaret is 67.65 metres high, and at the time of its erection it was the tallest in the Ottoman Empire, a record since surpassed by the minarets of the Edirne Selimiye. The central dome of the mosque was the largest one built in the Ottoman Empire up to that time; it was first surpassed by the original mosque of Mehmet the Conqueror, whose dome is believed to have been some 26 metres in diameter. The great dome is supported to north and south by the exterior walls, and on the east and west by two huge hexagonal piers, six metres in diameter, which are the only obstructions within the mosque, so that the faithful have from almost everywhere in the interior a clear view of the *mihrab* and the *mimber*. This was a great advance towards the centrally-planned classical mosques of the latter sixteenth century, when Ottoman architecture reached the pinnacle of its greatness with Sinan.

The culmination of classical architecture came with the **Selimiye**, which stands only a few hundred metres away down Mimar Sinan Caddesi, named after the great architect who designed and built this

The Selimiye, Edirne

magnificent mosque complex. Sinan built the Selimiye for Selim II during the years 1569–75, completing it when he was in his seventy-ninth year, at least, and to the end of his days he held that it was the masterwork of his career, surpassing even the Süleymaniye in its grandeur.

The Selimiye dominates Edirne from an eminence on the east side of town, built on a platform called Kavak Meydanî, the Square of the Poplar, where Beyazit I had erected a palace in the last quarter of the fourteenth century. The mosque and its *avlu*, which are identical rectangles in form, each of them 66 metres wide by 44 metres long, are situated toward the northern end of this platform, with the *medrese* of the *külliye* occupying the southeast corner of the precinct and the *dar-ül hadis* the southwest corner. The western side of the precinct is completely taken up with a commercial building called the **Kavaflar Arasta**, or Cobblers' Arcade, whose 124 shops were once occupied by the guild of shoemakers, with a *dar-ül kura* projecting from the middle of its outer side. The Kavaflar Arasta and the *dar-ül kura* are believed to be additions founded by Murat III, built for him by the architect Davut Ağa. Even counting these two institutions, the number of elements in Selim's *külliye* is surprisingly small, given the size and grandeur of the Selimiye itself, the most magnificent mosque ever erected in the Ottoman Empire.

The Selimiye is surmounted by its great dome, ringed round with eight turreted weight towers and framed by its four slender minarets, the tallest in Islam, 70.89 metres high. The weight towers are the projections of the eight octagonal piers that supply the main internal support for the great dome, which is flanked at the corners by semi-circular exedrae, with a circular apse on the south containing the *mihrab*. The poet Mustafa Sa'i, in his inscription on the wall of Sinan's *türbe* at the Süleymaniye, quotes the architect's boast that his great dome here at the Selimiye surpassed that of Haghia Sophia:

> Those who consider themselves architects among the Christians say that in the realm of Islam no Islamic architect would be able to build such a large dome. In this mosque, with the help of Allah and the support of Sultan Selim Khan, I erected a dome six cubits [a cubit is about 0.5 metres] higher and four cubits wider than the dome of Haghia Sophia.

But Sinan's claim is not quite valid, for the slightly elliptical dome of Haghia Sophia has an average diameter of 31.35 metres, whereas that of the Selimiye is 31.28 metres. Also, the dome of the Selimiye measures 43.50 metres from the floor to its crown, whereas that of Haghia Sophia is 55.60 metres high. But the important thing is not whether Sinan could build a dome higher and wider than that erected by Justinian's architects, but that in developing classical Ottoman architecture to its logical conclusion he could design and construct an edifice that compares in grandeur with the Great Church.

Two of the huge dome piers flank the main entryway from the *avlu* and two others flank the *mihrab*, which is recessed from the nave under a conch. The *müezzins'* tribune is in the centre of the prayer hall, directly under the great dome; this is a marble platform carried on rectangular piers and surmounting a marble patio with a pretty fountain at the centre, an arrangement unique in Ottoman architecture. The *mihrab* is also of marble, as is the *mimber*, perhaps the finest in all of Turkey, with its sides carved in a striking open-work design. The lower walls of the *mihrab* apse are revetted in beautiful Iznik tiles above which there is a calligraphic inscription with flowing white letters on a blue ground. In the southwest corner the imperial loge is carried out from the east gallery on a portico with four arches. This is one of the most gorgeous chambers in all of Turkey, for its tile decoration is unsurpassed anywhere in the country. The *mihrab* in the imperial loge is extraordinary too, for at its centre two superb wooden shutters open to reveal a window looking out over Edirne and its surrounding countryside.

The *medrese* and the *dar-ül hadis* are mirror images of one another. Each has 13 *hücres* forming an ell on two sides of a square portico, with the *dershane* on the third side and the entrance on the fourth, the two buildings having their lecture-halls back-to-back. The *medrese* now serves as the **Museum of Turkish and Islamic Art**, whose exhibits include inscriptions from demolished Ottoman monuments, kitchen utensils from old Edirne houses, Turkish tiles, hand-written copies of the Koran, embroideries, Ottoman glassware, antique weapons, photographs of the Edirne wrestling festivals and a collection of objects that once belonged to a local *tekke* of Bektaşi dervishes, including medallions, healing cups, and inscriptions written by famous dervish calligraphers. In the central garden of the courtyard there is a collection of old Ottoman tombstones, including several that marked the graves of Janissaries, distinguished by the long fold hanging behind the headdress.

The **Archaeology and Ethnographical Museum** is located a short way to the north of the Selimiye, approached by the courtyard gate on that side of the complex. The archaeological collection includes ancient jewellery, pottery, ceramics, coins, architectural fragments and sculpture, most of it from Thrace and some from Anatolia. The ethnographic collection includes Turkish embroideries, kilims, household items, antique ornaments, Ottoman coins, and beautiful Thracian folk-costumes.

The other imperial mosques of Edirne are all located in outlying areas of the city, in keeping with the early Ottoman practice of building royal foundations away from the crowded town centres.

The first of these imperial mosques that we will visit is the **Muradiye**, which stands on a hill to the northeast of town, best approached along Mimar Sinan Caddesi. This edifice was founded by Murat II in 1435 as a *zaviye*, or hostel, for Mevlevi dervishes, whose founder, Celalettin Rumi, appeared to the Sultan one night in a dream and asked him to build a hospice for his brotherhood. Later in his reign Murat converted the *zaviye* into a mosque, rehousing the dervishes in a separate *tekke* in the garden.

The mosque is of the cross-eyvan type; comprising a five-bayed porch, a minaret, and four interior units. The largest unit is the one just inside the entryway, its dome resting on a zone of Turkish triangles and with a lantern on top of its original open oculus. The main eyvan, which contains the *mihrab*, is richly decorated with ceramic tiles and frescoes. The *mihrab* is decorated with some of the finest surviving examples of early Iznik tiles.

The remaining imperial mosques are on the other side of the Tunca, one of the two rivers that nearly encircle Edirne. We approach them by returning to Mimar Sinan Caddesi and following its continuation as it winds to the northeast towards the river. The Tunca here divides into two branches, the first of which we cross on the **Bridge of Süleyman the Magnificent**, built by Sinan in 1554.

This brings us to **Sarayiçi**, an island in the Tunca where once stood the famous **Edirne Sarayî**, begun by Murat II in 1450 and completed by Mehmet the Conqueror. Unfortunately, the palace was destroyed by fire during the Russian occupation in 1878 and most of it has vanished. The principal surviving structure is a tower known as **Adalet Sarayî**, the **Palace of Justice**, because trials were held there during the reigns of Süleyman and his immediate successors. The tower has been splendidly restored, surmounted by a replica of its original upper section with a quaint pyramidal roof.

Since the early years of the Turkish Republic Sarayiçi has been the site of the **Kîrkpînar (Forty Springs) Wrestling Matches**, an annual festival held in mid-June. The origins of this festival go back

to the mid-fourteenth century, when the Ottoman Turks first penetrated into Thrace under Süleyman Pasha, son of Orhan Gazi.
According to tradition, the festival commemorate the wrestling
matches organized by Süleyman Pasha among his forty favourite
companions, so that they could amuse themselves in their camp
between campaigns. When the heroes died in battle each of them
gave rise to a spring, hence the name Kîrkpînar, according to the
legend. As many as a hundred thousand people attend the matches
each year, and for a week Edirne is jammed with rowdy spectators as
well as the wrestlers and their handlers and supporters, along with
pedlars, beggars, musicians, singers, and sellers of food and drink,
the fields around filled with gypsy encampments, giving the whole
scene the atmosphere of a medieval carnival.

After leaving Sarayiçi we cross the second branch of the Tunca on
the **Bridge of the Conqueror**, built by Mehmet the Conqueror
c.1453 to provide access to the countryside from Edirne Sarayî.
Once across we turn left and follow the road that runs parallel to the
river. This eventually brings us to the *külliye* of **Beyazit II**, the most
extensive of the imperial mosque complexes in Edirne, built for the
Sultan by the architect Hayrettin in the years 1484–88.

The pious foundations of the *külliye* line the vast outer courtyard
of the mosque precinct, where once were tethered the horses and
camels of the caravans that stopped there. Along the east side of the
courtyard stand the *imaret* and the food-store; these served the needs
of the travellers who put up there and also supplied food for the
patients and staff of the hospital. The various branches of the
hospital are on the west side of the courtyard. Just beside the mosque
is the domed structure that served as the hospital proper. Adjoining
that is the *timarhane*, or asylum for the insane, and set back at the
end of that is the *tip medrese*, or medical school.

The oldest of Edirne's imperial mosques stands to the southwest
of the *külliye* of Beyazit II. Formerly this mosque was attributed to
Beyazit I and dated to the period of his reign, but now it has been
shown to be a foundation of Murat I, probably erected soon after his
capture of Adrianople in 1361. The mosque was undoubtedly built
on and from the ruins of a Greek church, for the foundations and the
lower courses of the walls are obviously of Byzantine construction.
This is the oldest mosque in Turkey's European region, and though
badly in need of repair it is still serving the faithful of Edirne.

Leaving the mosque, we head back to town along the road that
connects Edirne with **Kapîkule**, the Bulgarian border-crossing.

When we reach the Tunca we see on our right **Mihal Gazi Camii**, built in 1421 by a Greek nobleman who became a Muslim and a Warrior for the Faith. The bridge across the Tunca at this point is also named after **Mihal Gazi**; it was originally built by the Byzantines in the second half of the thirteenth century. The Bridge of Mihal Gazi was repaired on several occasions by the Ottomans, most extensively by Kara Mustafa Pasha, Grand Vizier under Mehmet IV.

On the far side of the bridge, we see on our left a ruined *hamam* named for **Mihal Gazi**, and on our right the little Şahmelek Pasha Camii, built in 1428. We now continue east on Talat Pasha Caddesi, which brings us back to Cumhuriyet Meydanî and the centre of town, having completed our tour of the principal monuments of Edirne. But for those with time to spare there is much more to see in Edirne, some fifty additional historical monuments, including Ottoman mosques, *medreses*, *hamams*, caravansarais, *hans*, fountains and bridges, as well as the scattered remnants of Roman and Byzantine walls, and also an old synagogue still used by the much-diminished Jewish community.

There is a good restaurant at the northwest corner of Cumhuriyet Meydanî, and around the square there are a number of pleasant cafés. This is the centre of Edirne, an ideal place to relax after our tour of the town.

22

Edirne to the Dardanelles

OUR NEXT ITINERARY will take us from Edirne to the Dardanelles, the second stage of our journey through Thrace. Most of the countryside through which we will pass is unspoiled, but numerous ugly holiday villages have in recent years developed along the shores of the Dardanelles, marring its natural beauty.

We begin by driving back along highway E-80 to **Havsa**; there we turn right on highway E-87, which heads southwards parallel to the Turkish-Greek border. Havsa's principal monument is **Kasîm Pasha Camii**, built by Sinan in 1566–67 for Sokollu Mehmet Pasha, who dedicated it to the memory of his son Kasîm.

Forty kilometres from the turn-off we come to **Uzunköprü**, the ancient **Plotinopolis**. This was originally a Thracian settlement that was raised to the status of a city when Thrace was reorganized by Trajan (89–117), who renamed it Plotinopolis after his wife, Pompeia Plotina. The Turkish name of the town, which means 'Long Bridge', comes from the exceptionally long **bridge** that crosses the Ergene river at the approach to the town from the Havsa road. The bridge, which was built for Murat II in 1444 by Hacî Ivaz Pasha, is 1,392 metres long and is carried on 173 arches, some of which have been covered up by silt at the end nearest the town.

Forty kilometres farther along we come to an intersection with highway E-84, which runs from the Greek-Turkish border-post near Ipsala to Tekirdağ on the Marmara, where it connects with highway 100 to Istanbul.

Ipsala stands on the site of ancient **Cypsela**, whose name it preserves almost unchanged. Cypsela was an ancient fortress town that guarded an important ford of the river Hebrus, where a bridge now carries the highway across the border between Turkey and Greece. After their annexation of Macedon in 149 BC, the Romans built the **Via Egnatia** from the Adriatic coast as far as Cypsela, so that they could march into Thrace if the tribes there rose against them. After the organization of the Province of Asia in 129 BC, the Romans extended the Via Egnatia across eastern Thrace from Cypsela via Adrianople to Byzantium.

315

Companion Guide to Istanbul

Here we drive straight through the intersection and continue in the same direction on highway E-87, signposted for Gelibolu on the Dardanelles.

Three kilometes beyond the intersection we come to **Keşan**, a lively town that has been a garrison post since Roman times and is still today, being the headquarters for the Turkish army in Thrace. Keşan stands on the site of ancient **Rhusion**, also known in one era of its history as Risae. The town has one Ottoman monument: **Hersekzade Ahmet Pasha Camii**, dated 1511, a single-unit mosque with a three-bay porch.

At Keşan a secondary road on the right, highway 22–11, is signposted for Enez, a drive of 62 kilometres. **Enez** is on the Aegean coast at the mouth of the Meriç, the ancient River Hebrus, which from Edirne south forms the border between Turkey and Greece. Enez stands on the site of ancient **Ainos**, whose name it preserves in only slightly altered form. Ainos is one of the oldest towns in Thrace, as evidenced by the fact that it is mentioned by Homer in the *Iliad*, as well as by Herodotus and Thucydides. There is still another reference to Ainos in a poem by Alcaeus of Lesbos, who flourished in the sixth century BC. Here again the translation is by Richmond Lattimore:

> Hebros, loveliest of rivers, you issue
> hard by Ainos into the dark blue waters
> of the sea where, passing by Thrace, you end your turbulent
>   passage;
> there where young girls come in their crowds and, bathing
> with light hands their ravishing thighs, enjoy you
> all as if some magical salve were in your wonderful waters.

Archaeological excavations have unearthed some remnants of the ancient city of Ainos. The principal remains of Byzantine Ainos are its impressive defence walls, which have built into them a number of ancient tombstones with funerary reliefs, as well as Latin coats-of-arms from the period 1355–1456, when the city was held by the Genoese family of the Gattilusi. There is also a Byzantine church known as Fatih Camii, converted into a mosque by Mehmet II after he captured the city in 1456, after which it came to be called Enez.

After passing Keşan, highway E-87 takes us over the pine-clad foothills of **Kuru Dağ**, the **Dry Mountain**. The road then winds its way down to the plain at the head of the **Saros Körfezi**, whose usually placid waters we now see gleaming ahead to the south and west. This is the deeply-indented gulf that cuts into Thrace between the delta of the Meriç and the northern coast of the **Gallipoli Penin-sula**, the ancient **Thracian Chersonese**. Then, as we drive around the head of the gulf and up into the hilly neck of the peninsula, we catch our first glimpse of the **Dardanelles**, the Greek **Hellespont**.

The Dardanelles, known to the Turks as Çanakkale Boğazî, is about 62 kilometres long and varies in width from 1,250 metres to eight kilometres, the latter being the distance between its European and Asian shores near the western end of the Sea of Marmara. It flows in the general direction northeast to southwest, its maximum current ranging from 2.5 to 3 knots, which under abnormal condi-tions can increase to as much as 5 knots. The currents are strongest at the Narrows, which for mariners sailing from the Marmara to the Aegean begins at Cape Nagara on the Asian shore and extends to a line between Kilidülbahir and Çanakkale. Çanakkale is the biggest town and port on the Asian shore, while on the European side the largest is Gelibolu, better known in the West as Gallipoli.

There are numerous myths associated with the strait, one being that of Phrixus and Helle, children of Nephele, goddess of the clouds. Their father, King Athamas of Boeotia, was about to sacri-fice Phrixus and Helle to propitiate the gods during a time of drought, having been persuaded to do so by his children's evil step-mother Ino. When Nephele learned of this she flew down from the clouds to save her children, sending them off on a golden-fleeced ram given to her by Hermes. The ram carried them eastward through the heavens, but as they soared over the first of the two straits sepa-rating Europe from Asia Helle fell off and was drowned. Thereafter the strait came to be known as the Hellespont in her memory, and to her also the Greek people owe their name of Hellenes. Phrixus managed to hang on as the ram carried him to the land of Colchis at the eastern end of the Euxine, where he was received with honour by King Areetes and wedded to the Princess Chalciope. As a token of gratitude for his safe arrival, Phrixus sacrificed the ram to Zeus; he then gave the golden fleece to Areetes, who hung it in a grove of trees sacred to Ares. This was the golden fleece that led Jason on his legendary quest in the ship *Argo*.

Another myth tells the story of Dardanos, a son of Zeus who was one of the ancestors of Aeneas, the mythical founder of Rome. According to tradition, Dardanos founded a city bearing his name on the Asian side of the strait, which, as Homer writes, 'was peopled first, ere Ilion [Troy] with its teeming crowds, was settled in the plain.' During the Renaissance the popularity of Homer's epics revived the myth of Dardanos, so that in western Europe the strait came to be called the Dardanelles, although the Greeks continue to call it the Hellespont.

At the neck of the peninsula there is a turn-off on the left for **Bolayîr**. Bolayîr is on the spine of the peninsula at its neck, which is so narrow here we can see the **Saros Gulf** on one side and on the other the entrance to the Dardanelles from the Sea of Marmara.

At the west end of the village a large *türbe* stands in a copse of cypresses high above the plain below. This is the **tomb of Süleyman Pasha**, eldest son of Orhan Gazi, who died here in 1358, killed when he fell from his horse while falconing. Four years earlier Süleyman had led an Ottoman force across the Dardanelles and captured the Byzantine forts of Tzympe and Gallipoli, after which he established a Thracian colony on the Thracian Chersonese. This was the first Turkish foothold in Europe,and within the following half-century Ottoman armies conquered all of Thrace and swept on through the Balkans and up into central Europe.

Buried in the garden beside Süleyman Pasha's *türbe* is the celebrated poet Namîk Kemal (1840–88), one of the leading spirits of the Young Ottomans, the liberals who preceded the Young Turks. It was Namîk Kemal's dying wish to be buried here beside Süleyman Pasha, who personified to him all of the exemplary qualities of the earlier and more heroic Osmanlî spirit that he had hoped to revive in the decadent Ottoman Empire of his time.

Bolayîr has been identified as ancient **Pactye**, whose acropolis is believed to have been on the hill where Süleyman Pasha and Namîk Kemal are buried. Pactye was one of about a dozen Greek cities that were founded on the Thracian Chersonese in the archaic period (700–480 BC), some of them incorporating, as here, previously settled Thracian communities that may in some cases date back to the Bronze Age. Pactye is mentioned by Herodotus in connection with the conquest of the Thracian Chersonese by the Athenian Miltiades, son of Kypselos and uncle of the famous Miltiades, son of Kimon, who led the Greek forces to victory over the Persians at Marathon in 490 BC. After he took control of the Thracian Chersones, the older Miltiades built a wall, the Hexamilion, across the neck of the peninsula to protect it from attacks mounted from the mainland by the Thracian tribes. Traces of this wall have been unearthed by archaeologists in the general vicinity of Bolayîr.

There were three other Greek cities in the vicinity of Pactye, namely **Cardia**, **Aphrodisias** and **Lysimachea**. The latter had been founded in the late fourth century BC by Lysimachus, one of the Diadochi, the former generals of Alexander who after his death in 323 BC fought one another for the vast empire he had conquered. Lysimachus conquered Thrace, founding Lysimachea as his capital and resettling there the people of other cities in the Thracian Chersonese. Then in 281 BC Lysimachus was defeated and killed at the battle of Corupedium by Seleucus, another of the Diadochi, who founded the Seleucid dynasty that ruled over much of western Asia. After his victory at Corupedium Seleucus landed at Lysimachea and set out to conquer Thrace, but soon after his arrival in the city he was assassinated by Ptolemy Keraunos, son of Ptolemy I, another of the Diadochi, who founded the Ptolemaic dynasty in Egypt. The younger Ptolemy claimed that he killed Seleucus to avenge the death of Lysimachus, whose Thracian kingdom he then claimed for his own, but his rule lasted for only a few years.

From Bolayîr we continue along highway E-87 to Gelibolu, where the exit eventually leads us to the shore road and the town centre at its little port. There is a ferry-service from Gelibolu to Lapseki, the ancient Lampsacus, a village on the Asian shore of the Dardanelles. This is a good point to break the journey, for there are a number of restaurants around the port where one can have lunch before continuing down along the peninsula.

Gelibolu was known to the Greeks as **Callipolis**, the 'Good City'. In antiquity it was much less important than its transpontine neighbour Lampsacus, but the positions were reversed in the medieval Byzantine era, when Callipolis became the stronghold of the Hellespont. Justinian built the first fortress here, which was restored and strengthened by the Emperor Philippicus Bardanes (711–13). Thenceforth the main crossing-point on the strait was between Callipolis and Lampsacus, whereas in antiquity it had been at the Narrows between Abydos and Sestos, a Greek city on the Thracian Chersonese. One historic crossing between Callipolis and Lampsacus took place in 1190, when the German Emperor Frederick Barbarossa led his army across the strait here at the beginning of the Third Crusade.

The Castle of Callipolis was the key to the Hellespont throughout the Middle Ages, and as long as the Byzantines held it they controlled the western maritime approaches to Constantinople. But in 1303 Callipolis was occupied by the Grand Army of Catalonia, a wild band of mercenaries hired by Andronicus II to help the Byzantines fight against the Turks. The Catalans, under the leadership of

Roger de Flor, used the castle as a base to ravage Thrace, holding out there for seven years against repeated attacks by the Byzantines and their Genoese allies. The Catalans finally abandoned Callipolis in 1310, moving south to conquer Athens, after which the Byzantines regained the castle. Then in 1354 the castles at Callipolis and the nearby town of Tzympe were captured by Süleyman Pasha. The Byzantines were able to regain Callipolis for brief intervals after Christian naval forces made their way through the Hellespont in wars against the Turks, the first being a crusade led by Amadeo of Savoy in 1366, followed by a campaign led by the French Marshal Boucicault in 1416, and then a Venetian war against the Ottomans in 1444. When Mehmet II came to the throne in 1451, he built a number of forts on the Dardanelles in order to cut off Constantinople from the West, erecting the fortresses of Kalei Sultaniye on the Asian shore of the Narrows and Kilidülbahir on the European side. A century later, during another war between Venice and the Ottoman Empire, the Turks built two more fortresses at the Aegean end of the strait: Kumkale on the Asian side and Sedülbahir on the European. More forts were built along the Dardanelles in the third quarter of the eighteenth century, during a war between the Ottoman Empire and the Russians.

After the Turkish conquest of Constantinople, Gelibolu, as it was known to the Turks, became a major port-of-call for the Ottoman navy, whose warships always stopped here on their way to and from their campaigns in the Mediterranean. A number of Turkish commanders seem to have stayed on to live in Gelibolu after their retirement, for in the old Turkish cemetery on the outskirts of town there are several *türbes* built by Ottoman captain-pashas. The most renowned of these is Piri Reis (1465–1554), the Ottoman navigator whose *Katibe Bahriye*, or *Book of the Sea*, is the earliest extant Turkish nautical compendium. There is a **statue of Piri Reis** on the waterfront in Gelibolu, and in the castle there is a small **museum** with exhibits concerning his life and career, including his famous chart of the North American coast. Other notable tombs in the cemetery are those of Karaca Bey, standard-bearer of Süleyman Pasha when he captured Callipolis; Sarîca Pasha, a fifteenth-century governor of Gelibolu; and Sinan Pasha, a sixteenth-century Ottoman admiral. The most interesting monument in the cemetery is a *namazgah*, or open-air *mescit*, dated by an inscription to 1407. This is constructed of marble blocks and panels re-used from an ancient structure; it is unique in that its *mihrab* is flanked by a pair of *mimbers*.

The principal monument in Gelibolu is its **Byzantine castle**, the ruins of which form part of the inner harbour. During Ottoman times the castle was used as a prison, principally for those captured by the Ottoman navy in Mediterranean campaigns. One civilian prisoner of note was Shabbetai Sevi, a young Jewish rabbi from Izmir who in 1666 proclaimed that he was the long-awaited Messiah, a claim that was believed by multitudes of Jews all over the Ottoman Empire and even in western Europe. Shabbetai was imprisoned in the castle at Gelibolu for six months in the fall and winter of 1666–67. He was then taken to Edirne for a hearing before Mehmet IV, at which time he denied his faith and became a Muslim. Shabbetai persuaded tens of thousands of his followers to convert to Islam, promising that one day he would return as their Messiah. This gave rise to the strange sect known to the Turks as Dönme, or Turncoats, ethnic Jews who became Muslims but retained many of their Jewish customs and beliefs. There are several thousand Dönme still living in Turkey, almost all of them in Istanbul and Izmir, though it would seem that few of them still await the second coming of their lost messiah.

The principal Ottoman building in Gelibolu is its **Bedesten**, a more modest structure than those we have seen in Istanbul and Edirne, with six domes in two rows of three each, supported internally by a pair of columns.

The forts on the Dardanelles were modernized and new gun emplacements were built along the strait at the beginning of World War I, after the Ottoman Empire entered the conflict as an ally of Germany. This led to the Gallipoli campaign, starting on 18 March 1915, when the Allied Navy tried to force its way through the Narrows. The attempt was a catastrophe for the Allies, for three of their battleships were sunk by shore batteries and mines and two more were put out of action, with 2,750 British and French sailors losing their lives. The Allied command had already decided that the strait could not be forced by the fleet alone, and so they began planning for an amphibious landing on the Gallipoli peninsula. The initial landings took place on 25 April 1915 at Cape Helles, the promontory at the Aegean end of the peninsula, followed soon after by landings farther up the coast at Suvla Bay and the bay that would come to be known as Anzac Cove, named for the Australian and New Zealand troops who predominated in the landing there. This was the beginning of a nine month battle in which 110,000 men of the Allied and Turkish forces lost their lives fighting over a few square miles of barren ground at the southwestern end of the

321

Thracian Chersonese. Due to the stubborn resistance of the Turks, led brilliantly by Atatürk, then known as Mustafa Kemal Pasha, the Allies were unable to break out of the Gallipoli peninsula, and they were finally forced to withdraw early in 1916.

We now leave Gelibolu and begin driving down the European shore of the Dardanelles. About 13 kilometres beyond Gelibolu the road crosses the Cumalî Çayî, which empties into the Dardanelles at a little cove known as Ince Limanî, the Port of the Pearl. The stream was known to the Greeks as **Aegospotami**, or Goat's River. This gave its name to the battle of Aegospotami, which was fought here in the summer of 405 BC, with the Athenians under Conon being utterly defeated by the Spartans and their allies led by Lysander. This was the last battle of the Peloponnesian War, for when the news of their crushing defeat reached Athens it was clear to the Athenians that they had no choice but submission to their enemies.

About 18 kilometres farther along we come to the site of ancient **Sestos**; this is on a bay at the beginning of the Narrows opposite Cape Nagara, the site of ancient **Abydos**. Both were Greek colonies founded in the seventh century BC, Sestos by Aeolians from the northern Aegean coast of Asia Minor and Abydos by Ionians from Miletus. All that is left of Sestos are some remnants of its medieval defence-walls, while the few fragments that remain of Abydos are in a military zone and off-limits to civilians.

Sestos and Abydos were the two most important cities on the Hellespont in classical times, when the main crossing-point of the strait was here at the Narrows. The Persian king Darius crossed from Sestos to Abydos in 511 BC, on the way back from his campaign in Scythia. His son Xerxes crossed at the same point at the outset of his invasion of Greece in 480 BC, marching his army from Abydos to Sestos on a bridge of boats made for him by his engineers. As Herodotus describes the scene, Xerxes reviewed his forces while seated on a marble throne on the cliff-top at Abydos. 'And when he saw the whole of the Hellespont hidden by ships, and all the beaches and plains filled by men, he congratulated himself – and a moment later burst into tears.' When his uncle Artabanus asked him why he wept, Xerxes replied, 'I was thinking, and it came to my mind how pitifully short life is – for of all those thousands of men not one will be alive in a hundred years' time.'

Another momentous crossing of the strait took place here in 334 BC, when Alexander the Great began his campaign to conquer Asia. When the Macedonians reached the Hellespont, Alexander himself crossed at the Aegean end of the strait to make a pilgrimage to Troy, leaving Parmenio to lead his army across from Sestos to Abydos. A few days later Alexander rejoined his army and led them to victory at the battle of the Granicus, which was fought a day's march from Lampsacus near the shores of the Propontis, his first victory over the Persians in his invasion of Asia.

The crossing between Sestos and Abydos is the site of the romantic legend of Hero and Leander. Leander, a youth of Abydos, fell in love with Hero, a priestess of Aphrodite in Sestos, and each night he swam the Hellespont to see her, guided by a lamp that she placed on the European shore. But one night the lamp was extinguished in a gale and Leander lost his way, drowning in the Hellespont. When his body was washed ashore in Sestos, Hero threw herself into the water in despair and lost her life too. The oldest account of this myth is the epic *Hero and Leander*, written in the late fifth century AD by the Greek poet Musaeus Grammaticus, which was first translated into English in the early seventeenth century by George Chapman.

> Two townes there were that with one sea were wald;
> Built neere, and opposite: this, Sestus cald;
> Abydus that: then love his bow bent high,
> And at both cities, let one arrow fly.
> That two (a virgin and a youth) inflam'd:
> The youth was sweetly grac'd Leander nam'd;
> The virgin, Hero. Sestus, she renownes,
> Abydus hee, in birth: of both which townes
> Both were the beauty-circled stars; and both,
> Grac'd with like lookes, as with one love and troth.
> If that way lye thy course, seeke for my sake,
> A tower, that Sestian Hero once did make
> Her watch-tower: and a torch holding there,
> By which, Leander his sea-course did steere.
> Seeke likewise, of Abydus ancient towers,
> The roaring sea lamenting to these houres,
> Leander's love, and death.

The legend of Hero and Leander inspired Byron to swim the Hellespont at the Narrows, a feat he accomplished on 3 May 1810, when he was passing through the strait on the British frigate *Salsette*. Six days later Byron commemorated this feat in his poem, 'Written After Swimming from Sestus to Abydus'.

> If, in the month of dark December
> Leander, who was nightly wont

323

(What maid will not the tale remember?)
To cross they stream, broad Hellespont!

If, when the wintry tempest roared,
He sped to Hero, nothing loth,
And thus of old thy current pour'd,
Fair Venus! how I pity both!

For me, degenerate modern wretch,
Though in the genial month of May,
My dripping limbs I faintly stretch,
And think I've done a feat today.

But since he cross'd the rapid tide,
According to the doubtful story,
To woo, – and – Lord knows what beside,
And swam for Love, as I for Glory;
'Twere hard to say who fared the best:
Sad mortals! thus the gods still plague you!
He lost his labour, I my jest:
For he was drown'd, and I've the ague.

Byron returned to the legend in his *Bride of Abydos*, referring to the doomed lovers at the end of the second canto:

The wind are high on Helle's wave
As on that night of stormy weather
When love, who sent, forgot to save
The young – the beautiful – the brave
The lonely hope of Sestus' daughter.

We now come to a turn-off to the right for **Kabatepe**, a landing stage on the Aegean side of the peninsula, where there is a ferry-service out to the island of **Gökçeada**, the Greek **Imbros**. Imbros and **Tenedos**, the Turkish **Bozcaada**, were given to Turkey by the Lausanne Treaty, because their proximity to the Aegean end of the Dardanelles makes them strategically essential for the defence of the strait. The two islands still have a small number of Greeks among their population, but many more return for the summer holidays, for both Gökçeada and Bozcaada are now becoming popular resorts.

The Kabatepe turn-off is one of the two main approaches to the Gallipoli battlefield sites, leading to **Anzac Cove** and a number of Allied and Turkish military cemeteries and war memorials. The Australian memorial is at **Lone Pine**, that of New Zealand is at **Çunuk Bayîr**, and there is a monumnt commemorating the Turkish dead at the **Nek (Cesaret Tepe)**. There is another Turkish memorial at **Arî Burnu** on Anzac Cove, and also a war museum at Kabatepe with photographs and memorabilia of the battle. The monument at Arî Burnu is inscribed with the words that Atatürk spoke in 1934, when he greeted the Anzac visitors who came to dedicate their war memorial at Lone Pine:

> These heroes that shed their blood and lost their lives. . . You are now lying in the soil of a friendly country. Therefore rest in peace. There is no difference between the Johnnies and the Mehmets to us where they lay side-by-side in this country of ours. . . You, the mothers who sent their sons to far-away countries wipe away your tears; your sons are lying in our bosoms and are in peace. Having lost their lives in this land they will be our sons as well.

Continuing along highway E-87 past the Kabatepe turn-off, at the far end of the bay we come to **Eceabat**, where there is a ferry service across the strait to **Çanakkale**. Eceabat, known to the Greeks as **Madytos**, was founded in the seventh century BC by Aeolian Greeks from the Aegean coast of Asia Minor. Madytos was one of the more important towns in the Thracian Chersonese in the fifth century BC, mentioned by both Herodotus and Thucydides, but by the early Byzantine period it had declined to the status of a mere village.

Five kilometres farther down the strait we come to **Kilidülbahir**, where there is also a ferry service across to Çanakkale. The village takes its name from the picturesque Ottoman fortress around which it clusters. Kilidülbahir and the fortress of **Kalei Sultaniye** opposite on the Asian coast were built by Mehmet II just prior to his conquest of Constantinople in 1453. Kilidülbahir, the Lock of the Sea, consists of two defence towers connected by massive curtain walls, its outline forming a heart-shaped enclosure facing out across the sea toward Kalei Sultaniye. During the Gallipoli campaign these were known as the Inner Castles, while the fortresses of Sedülbahir and Kumkale were called the Outer Castles.

The promontory just beyond the port of Kilidülbahir was known in antiquity as **Cynossema**, the Dog's Grave. The curious name stemmed from a legend that Hecuba, wife of King Priam and mother of Hector, was transformed into a dog and buried there after the fall of Troy. Cynossema gave its name to a battle that was fought off the promontory in 411 BC, when the Athenians defeated the Spartans. The battle of Cynossema was the last major action recorded by Thucydides in his *History of the Peloponnesian War*, for shortly afterwards the narrative breaks off abruptly. He writes of how supremely confident the Athenians were after the battle, for it seemed to them that they would at last emerge victorious in their long struggle against the Spartans. But six years later they would go down to final defeat at the battle of Aegospotami, just six miles up the Hellespont from Cynossema.

The second approach to the Gallipoli battlefield sites is the road that continues down the coast from Kilidülbahir, passing several memorials to Turkish soldiers who died at their guns during the campaign. The road veers inland and up into the hills through a pine forest before heading down along the spine of the narrowing peninsula to **Alçîtepe**, the Greek **Krithia**. Signposts at the crossroads here indicate the directions to the various war cemeteries and memorials on this part of the peninsula. Off to the right are the cemeteries at **Twelve Tree Copse**, **Pink Farm** and **Lancaster Landing**; and to the left are the **Beach Cemetery**, the **Redoubt**, **Skew Bridge** and **Cape Helles**.

The main road turns left at Alçîtepe and goes out to the end of the peninsula, where we find the British and Commonwealth War Memorial at **Cape Helles** and the Turkish monument known as **Mehmetcik Anîtî**. (Mehmet is the nickname of common soldiers in the Turkish Army, the equivalent of the British Tommy.) British and Commonwealth (principally Anzacs) dead in the Gallipoli campaign numbered 34,000, while the Turks lost 66,000. Nearby is the French War Memorial, the last resting-place of most of the 9,000 French soldiers who died in the battle, including the 500 black Senegalese troops who were killed in a diversionary attack at Kumkale on the Asian side of the strait. The Senegalese and the Turks fought on the same ground, the banks of the Skamandros river on the windy plain of Troy, where the Achaians and the Trojans had battled during the siege of Troy more than three thousand years before, as described by Homer in the *Iliad*. Before the Senegalese were withdrawn, they buried their dead on the Trojan plain, and after the Turks reoccupied Kumkale and they interred their own fallen on the same ground. This incident is a haunting reminder of a scene in Book II of the *Iliad*, where the Trojans and Achaians agree on a brief truce to bury their dead, 'whose dark blood has been scattered beside the fair waters of the Skamandros'. (Here and elsewhere the translations from Homer are by Richmond Lattimore.) King Priam of Troy led the Trojans in their grim task, after which the Achaians performed theirs, as they 'piled their slain upon a pyre, with their hearts in sorrow/ and burned them upon the fire, and went back to their hollow vessels'.

The Turkish war memorial on Cape Helles stands above **Morto Bay**, another landing-point in the Gallipoli campaign. Looking down on the bay we see on its right side the ruins of the Ottoman fortress of **Sedülbahir**, one of the two **Outer Castles**, the other one barely visible across the strait at Kumkale. The Outer Castles were erected in 1659 by Mehmet Köprülü Pasha, Grand Vizier of Mehmet IV; they were rebuilt in 1773–75 by Baron Francois de Tott, a Hungarian military engineer in the service of Abdül Hamit I.

The promontory that forms the left horn of Morto Bay is known in Turkish as **Eski Hisarlîk**, the **Old Fortress**. This name stems from the scattered ruins of ancient **Elaeus**, the westernmost city on the Thracian Chersonese, virtually all traces of which were destroyed during the Gallipoli campaign. Elaeus was founded in the sixth century BC by settlers from Athens, and its citizens fought as allies of the Athenians throughout the Peloponnesian War. The site of Elaeus was excavated by Heinrich Schliemann, the discoverer of Troy. At Elaeus Schliemann excavated a tumulus that he identified as the tomb of Protesilaos, the first Achaian to be killed in the Trojan War. Homer writes of Protesilaos in Book II of the *Iliad*, in the so-called Catalogue of Ships, where he lists the contingents that fought in Agamemnon's army at the siege of Troy.

> Those who hold Phylake and Pyrasos of the flowers,
> the precinct of Demeter, and Iton, mother of sheepflocks,
> Antron by the sea-shore, and Pteleos deep in the meadows,
> of these in turn Protesilaos was the leader
> while he lived; but now the black earth has closed him under,
> whose wife, cheeks torn with grief, was left behind in Phylake
> and a marriage half completed; a Dardanian man killed him
> as he leapt from his ship, far the first of all the Achaians.

The tumulus of Protesilaos is mentioned by both Herodotus and Thucydides, and it had a renowned oracular shrine that was always visited by Greek mariners who passed through the Hellespont. Alexander himself offered sacrifice here just before he crossed the Hellespont at the beginning of his invasion of Asia. According to his ancient biographer Arrian, 'Alexander's purpose in performing this ceremony was to ensure better luck for himself than Protesilaos had'. After visiting the tomb, Alexander crossed from Elaeus to the beach on the Asian shore of the Hellespont where the Achaians were supposed to have landed at the beginning of the Trojan War, and from there he went to make his pilgrimage at Troy. 'It is generally believed,' Arrian writes, 'that Alexander sailed from Elaeus to the Achaian Harbour, himself at the helm of the admiral's ship, and that half way over he slaughtered a bull as an offering to Poseidon and poured wine from a golden cup into the sea to propitiate the Nereids.'

We now walk out to **Cape Helles**, the site of one of the two lighthouses that mark the entrance to the Dardanelles, the other being at Kum Kale. There were probably beacons on these capes in ancient times, for Aeschylus, in his tragedy *Agamemnon*, writes that Clytemnestra received news of the fall of Troy through a series of fire signals that were flashed from tower to tower all the way from the Hellespont to Mycenae.

Cape Helles was the central point in the first landings of the Gallipoli campign on 25 April 1915, with V Beach and S Beach to the right, and to the left W Beach and X Beach, from the point of view of the Allied soldiers who came ashore under fire from the Turkish machine gunners and riflemen on the cliffs above. Most of the Irish troops were in the 1st Battalion, Royal Dublin Fusiliers, who approached V Beach on a converted collier named the *River Clyde*, running aground near the eastern side of the bay, from where they were ferried in long lifeboats until they reached the shallows, making their way up the strand through underwater barbed wire under a hail of bullets. One of their surviving officers, Lieutenant-Colonel H. E. Tizard, describes the scene that he witnessed from the *River Clyde*:

> I don't think that of about 240 who were in the boats more than 40 got ashore without being hit; most of them were killed outright. I saw many cases just then who had just jumped out of the boats having to wade ashore got hit and fell face downward in the water; a chum, who had got ashore, seeing this, would come back and pull him out of the water, so that he would not be drowned. In nearly every case the men who did this were killed. Men in the boats who were hit tried to get away from the hail of lead by getting out of the boats on the far side in order to keep out of sight, thus getting the boat between them and the shore. There were four or five boats along the shore at intervals broadside to it, and behind each of them four or five men who had been hit. Some were holding on to the gunwhales and others were hanging on with their arms through the ropes which were looped round the boats to prevent themselves sinking in the water which was up to their waists. After a time I noticed these men sunk from exhaustion and loss of blood were drowned. The water by this time all along the shore and especially round the boats was red with blood.

The men who died that day coming ashore from the *River Clyde* are now buried in a cemetery above the centre of V Beach, midway between Sedülbahir and Cape Helles, where on anniversaries of the landings visitors and a dwindling number of their surviving comrades come to pay their respects. A part of Allied veterans landed once again at Cape Helles on 25 April 1975, just sixty years to the day after they had fought their way ashore from the *River Clyde*. This time they found waiting for them on the shore only a handful of white-haired Turkish veterans, and the old men embraced and wept on the same beach where they had tried to kill one another in the flower of their youth. Every anniversary since then has seen fewer and fewer veterans return, for time has taken its inexorable toll. And soon they will all be gone, as the living memory of Gallipoli passes into what Homer calls 'the country of dreams', just as did that of Homeric Troy.

23

Çanakkale to Troy

WE NOW TAKE the ferry across from either Kilidülbahir or Eceabat to **Çanakkale**, a lively town that for the past two centuries has been the principal port on the Dardanelles. During early Ottoman times the town was known as Kalei Sultaniye, after the fortress that we see to the south of the quay; it then had a considerable number of Greeks, Armenians and Jews among its population, which is now almost completely Turkish. Around 1740 the town became a noted centre for the making of earthenware pottery (in Turkish, *çanak*), so that it came to be called Çanakkale, the Pottery Castle.

Kalei Sultaniye, now known as **Çimenlik Kale**, is still occupied by the Turkish military, and so it is off-limits except for its inner courtyard, which serves as the **Military Museum**, with most of the exhibits associated with the Gallipoli Campaign. Its most notable exhibit is a replica of the minelayer *Nusret*, which dropped mines in the path of the Allied fleet in the Narrows on the eve of 18 March 1915, sinking or disabling five battleships, a remarkable exploit that turned the tide of battle in favour of the Turks.

Çanakkale's other museum is on the outskirts of town beside the Izmir highway. This is the **Archaeological Museum**, which has exhibits from Troy and other sites in the Troad, the region south of the Dardanelles along the northern Aegean coast. There are a few interesting objects from the collection of Frank Calvert, the man who led Schliemann to the site of Troy. One room in the museum is devoted to antiquities found in the **Dardanos Tumulus**, an ancient grave mound on the Asian side of the Dardanelles west of Çanakkale. The objects found in the tumulus, which was excavated in 1974, include bronze utensils, household goods and other objects of daily life, terracotta pottery, and jewellery, all of it dating from the fourth to first century BC. This is all that remains of the ancient city of Dardanos, whose eponymous founder gave his name to the Dardanelles. Pottery sherds found elsewhere on the site of Dardanos range in date from the early Bronze Age to the Hellenistic period.

Using Çanakkale as our base, we will now drive southwest along the Dardanelles to visit the site of Troy. Heading out of town on highway E-87, the road to Izmir, we pass **Güzclynli**, where the road veers inland away from the strait, climbing uphill through a forest of pine and valonia oak. The highway continues its ascent until it reaches the crest of the coastal ridge at Intepe, from where we command a panoramic view of the Trojan plain. The highway then descends to the **Dümrek Su**, the **Simois** of Homer, and thence to the turn-off for **Hisarlîk**, the site of ancient **Troy**.

That Hisarlîk is in fact the site of Homer's Troy is now established almost beyond doubt. The first archaeological investigation at Hisarlîk was made by Frank Calvert, who in the latter half of the nineteenth century served as both American and British consul in Çanakkale, while he and his two brothers also operated a farm in the Troad. The farm included the mound at Hisarlîk, where Frank Calvert had made an exploratory dig in 1865 which indicated to him that this might be the site of an ancient city. The mound at Hisarlîk had long been pointed out as as the site of Ilium, the city that had flourished here during the Hellenistic and Roman eras and to which Xerxes, Alexander the Great, Julius Caesar and Constantine the Great came when they made pilgrimages to Troy. And scholars in both ancient and modern times believed that Ilium was built on the ruins of Homeric Troy, which seems to have been destroyed along with all of the other great fortress-cities of the Bronze Age in the late thirteenth century BC. But proof that Hisarlîk was in fact the site of ancient Troy was not provided until Heinrich Schliemann carried out his pioneering researches, which have now led most scholars to believe that the *Iliad* was based on Greek folk-memories concerning the siege of a great Bronze Age fortress at the Asian end of the Hellespont, with the epic itself having been written some five centuries later by a poet who was familiar with the topography of the site. Calvert guided Schliemann around the mound at Hisarlîk in the summer of 1868, showing him the finds he had made and convincing him that this was the site of ancient Troy. As Schliemann wrote the following year, the site 'fully agrees with the description that Homer gives of Ilium and I will add, that as soon as one sets foot on the Trojan plain, the view of the beautiful hill at Hisarlîk grips one with astonishment. The hill seems designed by nature to carry a great city . . . there is no other place in the region to compare with it.'

When Schliemann made his preliminary excavations at Hisarlîk in 1870, he found that the debris of millennia had accumulated on the hill to a depth of fifty feet. Since he assumed that the Troy he was looking for was at the bottom of this mass, he set out to clear away this debris in one slice, and in three annual campaigns, from 1871 to 1873, employing an average of 150 workmen daily, he cut right through the mound in a great north-south trench some 130 feet wide. While digging the trench he noticed that the excavated earth did not form a homogeneous mass, but was stratified in superimposed layers that he correctly assumed represented the successive settlements on the site. The lowermost, and presumably the earliest, he called Troy I. Schliemann thought that he could discern seven distinct layers, of which he believed Troy II to be the Homeric city because of the wealth of jewellery and gold objects he found there, a hoard that he called 'Priam's Treasure'. Schliemann continued his excavations at Hisarlîk, and in 1882 he was joined there by the young German archaeologist Wilhelm Dörpfeld. Eight years later Schliemann and Dörpfeld made an important discovery in the southern sector of the mound, in the level later to be called Troy VIIa, unearthing a palatial structure known as a *megaron*, whose central hall was supported internally by two pillars. This *megaron* was so similar to the royal halls he had discovered at Mycenae and Tiryns that Schliemann was forced to change his mind about the dating of the various strata, and he decided that the sixth layer from the bottom, and not the second, was the Homeric city for which he was searching. This view is still generally held by archaeologists, though the numbering and dating of the layers has subsequently been changed. Schliemann continued to dig at Hisarlîk until a few months before his death on 26 December 1890. Dörpfeld then took charge of the project, and in 1893–94 he unearthed the massive fortifications of Troy VII, dramatic evidence that this was in fact the city that Homer had described in the *Iliad*.

Dörpfeld concluded his excavations at Hisarlîk in the summer of 1894, convinced that he and Schliemann had discovered the Homeric city. The site was then untouched until 1932, when a team of archaeologists from the University of Cincinnati in the USA began excavating under the direction of Carl W. Blegen. Blegen's group continued excavating at Troy until 1938, but the outbreak of World War II the following year ended their project and delayed the publication of their findings until 1950. During the next four decades there were only sporadic excavations at Hisarlîk. Excavations began again in 1988 under the German archaeologist Manfred Korfmann, supervising a joint team from the universities of Tübingen and Cincinnati. The project continues to the present day, using more scientifically advanced techniques and methods of analysis than were available to the previous excavators. One of its aims is to study the economic and social life of the ancient city in the various periods of its existence, another related goal being to identify the successive waves of humanity that passed betwen Europe and Asia as they crossed the Hellespont within sight of Troy.

What emerges from the archaeological work of the past century and more is a stratigraphical picture, an historical palimpsest as it were, of a site inhabited more or less continuously from the early Bronze Age up until late antiquity, with each successive settlement resting on the rubble and ashes of the city that came before it, some destroyed by fire, some by earthquake, some by besieging armies. Even an amateur can detect the discontinuities from one level to another, and although to an untrained eye the picture is a confused one, archaeological evidence has established nine main levels, most of which have several sub-strata. The publications of Blegen's group lists 46 levels in all, grouped among nine major chronological strata. The currently accepted dates for the various strata are as follows: Troy I (3000–2500 BC), Troy II (2500–2300 BC), Troy III (2300–1700 BC), Troy IV, V, VI (1700–1250 BC), Troy VIIa (1250–1180 BC), Troy VIIb (1180–1000 BC), Troy VIII (1000–85 BC), Troy IX (85 BC–AD 400 to 600).

The modern excavations have substantiated Schliemann's belief that **Troy I** was the original settlement on the Hisarlîk hill, the earliest finds dated c.3000 BC. The excavations unearthed the walls of several houses in this stratum, all of them of the *megaron* type. Schliemann discovered the defence walls of Troy I when he dug his trench through the mound at the beginning of his excavations; these can be distinguished from subsequent fortifications by the fact that they are made from piles of field stones as contrasted with the carefully worked defences of later periods. The main gate of Troy I was on the south side of the circuit, as would be the case in all of the succeeding settlements at Hisarlîk, for this is where the terrain permits the easiest approach to the city fom the Trojan plain.

Troy II was rebuilt on the same site after the original settlement had been destroyed by fire. By this time the population of the city seem to have increased, for the walls of **Troy II** enclosed a somewhat larger area than the fortifications of the original settlement. As in the first settlement, the main gate of Troy II was on the south side, somewhat to the southeast of the other gateway. There were other portals as well, including a ***propylon***, or **monumental entryway**, on the southeast arc of the fortifications, from which a well-paved ramp of limestone leads down to the Trojan plain. Troy II seems to have been one of the first cities to have been built on a regular plan, for the houses of this period unearthed within the fortifications appear to have been laid out on a rectangular grid pattern, centered on a large *megaron* that may have been a royal residence. Unfortunately, a large part of this structure was destroyed when Schliemann dug his trench. Most of the golden jewellery and other precious objects discovered by Schliemann, including the hoard known as 'Priam's Treasure' (so called because he thought that it belonged to the ruler of Homeric Troy), were found in and around this ***megaron***, which he called the **House of the City King**. It was the imperial scale of this *megaron*, together with the treasure, that led Schliemann to his original identification of Troy II as the Homeric city. But he and Dörpfeld later determined that Troy II was destroyed by fire c.2200 BC, about a thousand years before the fall of Troy and the other great cities of the late Bronze Age, and so it was far too early to be the city of which Homer wrote.

There was little of note disovered in the next three levels at Hisarlîk, **Troy III, IV and V**, the only easily identifiable structures being a few house walls. Dörpfeld contemptuously referred to the settlements in these three levels as 'miserable villages', which were not fortified until the period of Troy V, when the area was enclosed within a defence wall much inferior to that of Troy II.

The most clear-cut discontinuity in the mound comes with Troy VI, which Blegen divided into three major periods, futher divided between them into eight sub-strata. The archaeological findings clearly indicate that Troy VI emerged in the middle of the Bronze Age, as evidenced by the large number of swords and other objects of bronze found in that level. These bronze objects and the pottery and other finds in Troy VI differed markedly from those of other levels, evidence of the arrival at Hisarlîk of people of a quite different culture from those who had lived there before. A unique find establishing this difference of cultures was the skeleton of a horse, indicating that the newcomers were warriors who not only used bronze weapons but also fought from horseback or from horse-drawn chariots. This would have given them a great advantage over the indigenous people of the Troad. The most striking evidence of the militant character of the new settlers is the splendid circuit of **defence walls** with which they ringed Troy VI, for these fortifications show a much more advanced knowledge of military engineering and architecture than do the earlier walls at Hisarlîk.

The Muradiye, Edirne

The walls of Homeric Troy

According to Blegen, Troy VI was destroyed c.1300 BC in a very sudden catastrophe, probably an earthquake, as evidenced by the toppling of whole sections of the defence walls of that period. (Current opinion dates this catastrophe to c.1250 BC) The next level at Hisarlîk, Troy VII, was divided by Blegen into three substrata, of which the first, VIIa, shows no cultural discontinuity whatsoever with Troy VI. The archaeological evidence indicates that the people who inhabited Troy VIIa rebuilt the city immediately after the catastrophe, but less than half a century later the city was destroyed again. Blegen found evidence that this second catastrophe was preceded by the erection of crude and hastily-built structures just inside the defence walls, as if a shanty town was created to house people from the surrounding countryside at a time of siege. This and other evidence led Blegen to identify Troy VIIa as the city described by Homer in the *Iliad*, a conclusion that is still being debated in archaeological circles. Blegen concluded that Troy VIIa was destroyed in the mid-thirteenth century BC, at about the same time as Mycenae, Tiryns, Pylos and other great fortress cities of the Late Bronze Age, those places that Homer mentions in the Catalogue of Ships in Book II of the *Iliad*.

The designations assigned by Blegen to the two later substrata of Troy VII are Troy VIIb1 and Troy VIIb2. According to Blegen, many of the inhabitants of Troy VIIa apparently survived the catastrophe that destroyed their city, and soon afterwards they built a new settlement on the ruins of the old one. The archaeological evidence indicates that the new defence circuit followed the same course as the previous one, with the south gate located at the same place as the earlier entryway. There is no evidence of any cultural discontinuity between the second phase of Troy VII and the first one, but at the beginning of the third phase a different type of pottery made its appearance at Hisarlîk, which Blegen and other scholars have attributed to a new population settling on the mound early in the twelfth century BC. These new settlers, it is believed, came from the Balkans and, after crossing the Hellespont, seized control of Troy before some of them moved more deeply into Anatolia. This third phase of Troy VII came to a close c.1100 BC, when the settlement at Hisarlîk was devastated by fire, part of a wave of destruction that brought an end to the civilization of the Bronze Age all over the Aegean and in Anatolia, marking the beginning of the Dark Ages of the ancient world.

After this catastrophe the site seems to have been only sparsely inhabited for about four centuries, until it was settled again by

Aeolian colonists from Tenedos and Lesbos c.700 BC. The city founded by the Aeolians was known in Greek as Ilion and in Latin as Ilium, identified by Blegen as Troy VIII, while Troy IX is the **Ilium Novum** of Hellenistic and Roman times, venerated throughout the Graeco-Roman world as the successor of Homeric Troy.

The most important monument of Ilium is the **Temple of Athena**, whose ruins were found in the northeast quarter of the mound. This temple is mentioned by both Homer and Herodotus. In Book VII of his *Histories* Herodotus writes that Xerxes made a pilgrimage here just before he crossed the Hellespont, sacrificing a thousand oxen as an offering to 'the Trojan Athena'. Alexander also made a pilgrimage to Athena's temple when he crossed the Hellespont to visit Troy, as Arrian writes:

> Once ashore he travelled inland to Troy and offered sacrifice to Athena, patron goddess of the city; here he made a gift of his armour to the temple, and took in exchange, from where they hung on the temple walls, some weapons which were still preserved from the Trojan War. These are supposed to have been carried before him by his bodyguard when he went into battle.

Strabo writes that Alexander vowed to rebuild the Temple of Athena. But the lightning pace of his campaign made it impossible for him to do so himself, and so his promise was fulfilled by his successor Lysimachus when he became ruler of Thrace and northwestern Asia Minor after Alexander's death in 323 BC. The new temple of Athena built by Lysimachus was of the Doric order, as evidenced by the architectural fragments that Schliemann found in the northeastern sector of the Hisarlîk mound, where its site is identified by a signpost. This temple, described by Homer as being on the 'peak of the citadel', is the setting for one of the most moving scenes in the *Iliad*, where the priestess Theano leads the Trojan women in prayer, imploring Athena to help them and promising that they will 'instantly dedicate within your shrine twelve heifers,/ yearlings never broken, if only you will have pity/ on the town of Troy, and the Trojan women, and their innocent children'.

Troy was also a place of pilgrimage for the Romans, because of the legend that Rome had been founded by Aeneas, the only Trojan leader who survived the fall of Troy. Julius Caesar, who believed himself to be a direct descendant of Aeneas, visited Ilium in 48 BC and gave the city immunity from taxes. Ilium had been badly damaged c.82 BC during the First Mithridatic War, but the Romans

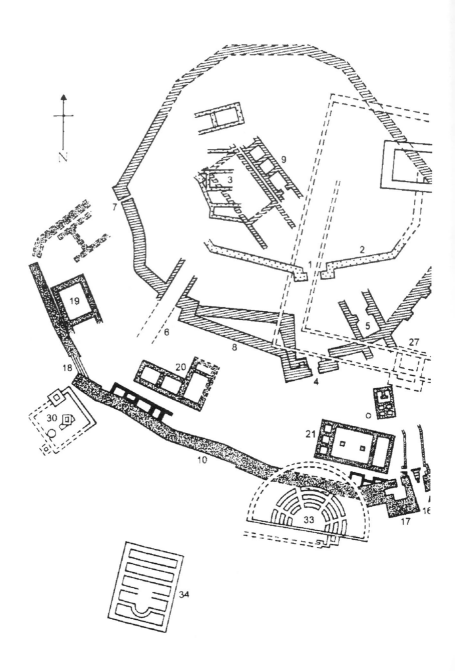

Troy

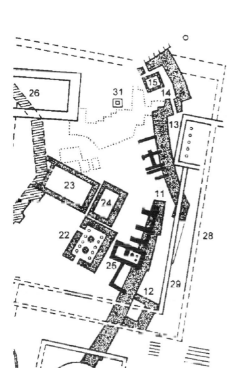

1. Gate
2. City Wall
3. Megarons
4. Gate
5. Gate
6. Gate and Ramp
7. Gate
8. City Wall
9. Megarons
10. City Wall
11. Gate
12. Tower
13. Gate
14. Tower
15. Well-Cistern
16. Dardanos Gate (Skaian Gate)
17. Tower (the Great Tower of Ilium)
18. Gate
19. House
20. Palace - Storage House
21. Pillar House (Palace of Priam)
22. House with Columns
23. House
24. House
25. Storage
26. Temple of Athena
27. Entryway to Temple of Athena
28. Outer Court Wall

29. Inner Court wall
30. Shrine
31. Waterwork
32. Senate house
33. Odeion
34. Roman baths

339

completely rebuilt it during the reign of Augustus (27 BC to AD 14). At that time the entire top of the mound was levelled to enlarge the sacred enclosure of Athena's temple, which was then completely rebuilt once again, using many architectural elements from the Hellenistic structure. Other edifices dating from this Roman rebuilding are the *odeion*, the **theatre**, and the *bouleuterion*, or **council house**, all of which are in the southeastern sectior of the site.

The city of Ilium Novum lasted on into Byzantine times, becoming an episcopal see in the fourth century. Thenceforth it went into decline, and by the beginning of the Ottoman era it seems to have disappeared altogether. When Cyriacus of Ancona visited the site in 1444 he found it completely deserted. After Byron came here in May 1810 he wrote to Henry Drury: 'The only vestiges of Troy, or her destroyers, are the barrows supposed to contain the carcases of Achilles, Patroclus, Antilochus, Ajax, etc., but Mt Ida is still in high feather, though the Shepherds are not much like Ganymede.'

Archaeologists have discovered that the main gates of Troy were on the south side of the city, giving access from the citadel to the plain below. Schliemann thought that he had discovered the Homeric Skaian Gate in the impressive entryway to the southeast, where a ramp with huge limestone slabs leads up to the citadel, and in a *megaron* inside the gate he unearthed a treasure trove that convinced him that he had discovered the **Palace of Priam** (also known as the Pillar House) and beside it the **Great Tower of Ilium**. As he wrote enthusiastically at the time:

> There is not a more sublime situation in the area of Troy than this, and I therefore presumed that it was the Great Tower of Ilium which Andromache ascended because 'she had heard that the Trojans were hard-pressed and that the power of the Achaeans was great.' May this sacred and sublime monument of Greek heroism forever attract the eyes of those who sail through the Hellespont!

Modern scholarship has shown that the structure unearthed by Schliemann at that spot belonged to Troy II, destroyed a thousand years before the fall of Priam's city. The excavations by the Cincinnati group in the area farther south and west of the acropolis unearthed the impressive structures that Blegen has assigned to Troy VIIa, the Homeric city. This city was surrounded by a powerful defence-wall with several massive towers and two large entryways, the largest being the **Southern Gate**, which today is still the principal means of access to the plain below. Just inside the Southern

Gate is the largest and most impressive of the dwelling-places unearthed at Troy, the so-called **Pillar House**, which by Mycenaean standards is a building of monumental proportions. This probably occupies the same site as Homer's **Palace of Priam**, while the Southern Gate would seem to be where the **Skaian Gates** were located, for that was the principal entryway to the city from the plain below, with the Great Tower of Ilion just beside it. This would be the site of a poignant scene in Book III of the *Iliad*, where Priam and the city elders, sitting atop the Great Tower, look out over the plain to where the Trojan and Achaian armies are facing one another, as Paris and Menelaus prepare to engage one another in single combat. Helen is told of the impending battle by the goddess Iris and rushes to the tower to watch. The old men, who have been chattering away like cicadas, lower their voices at her approach, one of them murmuring that the Trojans and Achaians could not be blamed for fighting over such a beautiful woman, for 'terrible is her face to the likeness of immortal goddeses'. Priam calls out to Helen, telling her to sit beside him on the tower, 'to look at your husband of time past, your friends and your people'. Then he comforts her by saying that 'I am not blaming you: to me the gods are blameworthy/ who drove upon me this sorrowful war against the Achaians'.

Helen's role in the ruination of Troy has inspired poets since Homer's time, among them Edmund Spenser, who refelects upon it in this stanza from *The Faerie Queen*:

> Fayre Helen, flowre of beautie excellent
> And girlond of the mighty Conquerors,
> That madest many Ladies deare lament
> The heavy losse of their brave Paramours,
> which they far off beheld from Trojan toures,
> And saw the fields of faire Scamander strowne
> with carcases of noble warrioures
> Whose fruitless lives were under furrow sowne,
> And Xanthus sandy bankes with blood all overflowne.

From the peak of the Hisarlîk mound we command a view of the entire Trojan plain and the background of the *Iliad*. On a clear day one can see far off to the southeast the peaks of Mount Ida, where Zeus sat enthroned as a spectator during the siege of Troy. Out in the Aegean we see the islands of Tenedos and Imbros, between which, according to Homer, there was a deep underwater cave where Poseidon stabled his horses. Behind Imbros we can see the peaks of the island of Samothrace, from where Poseidon watched the battle.

The principal landmarks on the Trojan plain itself are the so-called **Heroic Tumuli**, the grave-mounds that since antiquity have been identified with Achaian heroes of the siege of Troy. Homer mentions these tumuli in Book III of the *Odyssey*, where King Nestor of Pylos describes the Trojan plain to Telemachus, son of Odysseus:

> . . . all who were our best men were killed in that place;
> there Aias lies, a man of battles, there lies Achilleus,
> there lies Patroklos, who was like the gods for counsel,
> and there lies my own beloved son, both strong and stately,
> Antilochus, surpassingly swift to run, and a fighter. . . .

The tumuli mentioned by Nestor have been identified with four mounds on the coastal periphery of the Trojan plain, one of them on the shore of the Dardanelles and the other three near the Aegean close to the mouth of the strait.

The tumulus on the shore of the Dardanelles has long been identified as the **tomb of Telamonian Aias**, known in English as the Greater Ajax, to distinguish him from Lokrian Aias, the Lesser Ajax. Telamonian Aias was so called because he was the son of Telamon, King of Salamis, who a generation earlier had sailed with Jason on the ship *Argo* in search of the Golden Fleece. Aias was a giant of a man, by far the largest in stature of the Achaians, and in prowess he rivalled Achilles and Odysseus. After Achilles died Aias thought that the fallen hero's armour would be awarded to him, but instead it was presented to Odysseus. This drove Aias out of his mind and he committed suicide, whereupon the Achaians buried him on the shore of the Hellespont and built a tumulus of earth as a memorial to him. This story is the theme of Sophocles's tragedy, *Aias*. There was a sanctuary dedicated to Aias here in antiquity, with a huge cult-statue of the hero that was carried off by Mark Antony and presented to Cleopatra. The statue was returned to its rightful place by Augustus after his victory over Antony and Cleopatra at the battle of Actium in 31 BC. Hadrian made a pilgrimage to the sanctuary of Aias during his tour of Asia Minor in 123. He found that the sea had worn away part of the tumulus, exposing the whitened bones of a giant of a man, which he kissed reverentially and reburied in a new tumulus on higher ground, the one we see today. The tumulus was excavated in 1879 by Schliemann, who dated it to the reign of Hadrian, but he found evidence that the mound was probably erected on the site of an older *heroon*, a shrine dedicated to a hero. Close to the tumulus Schliemann discovered 'a mutilated marble statue of a warrior, draped and of a colossal size' This was undoubtedly the cult statue of Telamonian Aias, the one removed by Antony and returned by Augustus. The statue has long since disappeared, along with the bones of the hero whom Helen of Troy in the *Iliad* describes as 'gigantic Aias, wall of the Achaians'.

The three **tumuli** at the Aegean end of the plain near the mouth of the Dardanelles have long been identified as those of **Patroklos, Achilles** and **Antilochus**. As we look at them from the Hisarlîk mound, the tumulus of Patroklos is on the right; close beside it to the left is that of Achilles, and some distance farther away to the left is that of Antilochus, the three of them so identified by travellers both ancient and modern. Schliemann dug exploratory shafts into the tumuli of Patroklos and Achilles, but though he discovered pottery and other objects of some antiquity, including an iron sword, he did not find any evidence of a Mycenaean burial. Nevertheless, he concluded from his reading of Homer that both heroes were buried in the same tomb, the tumulus of Achilles, and that the so called Tumulus of Patroklos must have been the burial-place of some other warrior chieftain. Schliemann's belief that Patroklos and Achilles were buried in the same tomb was based on two passages from Homer, one in the *Iliad* and the other in the *Odyssey*. The first passage is in Book XXIII of the *Iliad*, where the ghost of Patroklos appears to Achilles in a dream, saying to him, 'Therefore, let one single vessel, the golden two-handled/ urn the lady your mother gave you, hold both our ashes'. The second passage is in the last book of the *Odyssey*, where the ghosts of Agamemnon and Achilles meet together with the shades of other departed Achaians in 'the meadow of Asphodel . . . the dwelling-place of souls, the images of dead men'. There Agamemnon tells Achilles about the circumstances of his death on the Trojan plain and of how he and the other Achaian warriors had mourned for him 'for ten and seven days, alike in the day and night time', until 'on the eighteenth day we gave you to the fire, and around you slaughtered a great number of fat sheep and horn-curved cattle.' Then Agamemnon tells Achilles that they gathered his white bones at dawn, 'together with unmixed wine and ungents', and placed them in the golden urn his mother Thetis had given him, mixing them 'with the bones of the dead Patroklos'. Finally Agamemnon describes to Achilles the tumulus that he and his army erected as a memorial to him and his beloved friend:

Around them, then, we the chosen host of the Argive
    spearmen, piled
up a grave mound that was both great and perfect,
on a jutting promontory by the wide Hellespont,
so that it could be seen from far out on the water
by men now alive and those to be born in the future.

Out on the **Trojan plain** itself, crimson with poppies in the spring, we can see the undulating stream of the Skamandros flowing into the Dardanelles beside the Harbour of the Achaians, where Agamemnon marshalled his army for the siege of Troy, as Homer describes them in Book II of the *Iliad*: 'They take up position on the blossoming meadow of the Skamandros, thousands of them, as leaves and flowers appear in season.' And somewhere down on the Trojan plain below the Hisarlîk mound is the site of Hektor's tumulus, now vanished, but which was still pointed out to travellers as late as the seventeenth century, along with those of Aias, Patroklos, Achilles and Antilochus. The burial of Hektor, eldest son of King Priam, is the last scene in the *Iliad* and one inevitably recalls it when looking out over the Trojan plain at the end of a visit to Troy.

they carried out bold Hektor, weeping, and set the body
aloft a towering pyre for burning. And set fire to it . . .
. . . thereafter
the brothers and companions of Hektor gathered the white bones
up, mourning, as the tears swelled and rolled down their cheeks.
Then they laid up what they had gathered in a golden casket
and wrapped this about with soft robes of purple, and presently
put it away in the hollow of the grave, and over it
placed huge stones laid close together. Lightly and quickly
they piled up the grave barrow, and on all sides were set up
    watchmen
for fear the strong-greaved Achaians might too soon set upon them.
They piled up the grave barrow and went away, and thereafter
assembled in a fair gathering and held a glorious
feast within the house of Priam, king under God's hand.
Such was their burial of Hektor, breaker of horses.

24

Çanakkale to Bursa

OUR NEXT ITINERARY will take us from Çanakkale to Bursa, first heading back along the Asian shore of the Dardanelles and then going around south of the Sea of Marmara, the ancient Propontis The first part of this journey will take us through the region known in antiquity as **Mysia**, that part of northwestern Asia Minor east of the Troad, while the second part will be in ancient **Bithynia**, the region around the eastern end of the Propontis on to the Bosphorus. According to the geographer Strabo, both the Mysians and Bithynians were Thracians, the two peoples having crossed over from Europe in their migrations. The region around the common border of Mysia and Bithynia was also called Hellespontine Phrygia, the westernmost extension of the region in west-central Anatolia known anciently as Phrygia.

The first stage of our journey takes us along highway E-90 into the hills east of Çanakkale, passing on our right a road that leads inland to the region north of Mount Ida. The highway then winds down toward the shore of the Dardanelles, passing **Yapîldak**, a village on a stream of the same name. Yapîldak has been identified as **Arisbe** and its stream as the **River Selleeis**, both of which are mentioned by Homer in Book II of the *Iliad*; they appear there in the so-called Catalogue of the Trojans, those who fought as allies of King Priam of Troy:

They who dwelt in the places about Perkote and Praktion,
who held Sestos and Abydos and brilliant Arisbe,
their leader was Asios, Hyrtakos' son, a prince of the people,
Asios, son of Hyrtakos, whom huge and shining
horses carried from Arisbe and the river Selleeis.

Arisbe is where Alexander rejoined his army after crossing the Hellespont, as his biographer Arrian notes:

From Troy, Alexander marched to Arisbe, where his entire force had taken up position after crossing the Hellespont; next day he proceeded to Perkote, and the day after passed Lampsacus and

halted by the river Practius, which has its sources in Mount Ida
and flows into the sea [the Marmara] which connects the Black
Sea with the Hellespont.

Twenty-five kilometres out of Çanakkale we come to **Lapseki**,
the Asian terminus of the ferry from Gelibolu. We might pause here
for a drink at one of the cafés around the ferry-landing from where
there is a good view of the inner end of the Dardanelles.

As we have noted, Lapseki is the ancient **Lampsacus**, founded in
654 BC by Ionian Greeks from Miletus and Phocaea on the Aegean
coast of Asia Minor. During the Graeco-Roman period Lampsacus
was one of two cities that controlled maritime trade through the
Hellespont, the other being Abydos, the reason being their good
harbours. Strabo describes Lampsacus as 'a notable city with a good
harbour, and still flourishing like Abydos'. Lampsacus was famous
for its wine, which its citizens claimed to be worthy of the gods.
Only a few architectural fragments and sarcophagi remain of the
ancient city, one of three places given by King Xerxes of Persia to
the Athenian turncoat Themistocles for his services, presenting him
'Magnesia for his bread, Myus for his meat, and Lampsacus for his
wine'.

Lampsacus was the last home of Anaxagoras, the first great
philosopher to reside in Athens, where his most famous student was
Pericles. Anaxagoras was born c.500 BC in the Ionian city of
Clazomenae on the Aegean coast of Asia Minor. He moved to
Athens when he was twenty and remained there until he was
banished in 459 BC, after his conviction on charges of impiety and
Medesism (being pro-Persian). Anxagoras then settled in Lampsacus
and founded a school of philosophy there, directing it until his death
in 428 BC. After his death the people of Lampsacus erected an altar
in memory of Anaxagoras in their market square, dedicating it to
Mind and Truth, which were at the core of his philosophy. The anniversary of the death of Anaxagoras was for long afterwards celebrated in Lampsacus, and by his dying request the students of the
city were given a holiday on that day.

Lampsacus was also noted as the birthplace of the fertility god
Priapus, who appeared on the city's coins with his gigantic phallus.
His cult here is mentioned by the traveller Pausanias in his *Guide to
Greece*, written in the mid-second century AD; as he observes: 'This
god receives honours wherever goats or sheep graze and bees swarm;
but in Lampsacus they believe in Priapus more than anyone; they say
he is the son of Dionysus and Aphrodite.'

During the sixth and fifth centuries BC Lampsacus passed successively under the control of the Lydians, Persians, Athenians and
Spartans. The city was exceedingly prosperous, its importance as a
port enhanced by its lucrative trade in the gold and silver objects that
its artisans made and shipped far afield. Its wealth in the classical
period is evidenced by the fact that it was assessed twelve talents in
the Delian Confederacy, one of the largest contributions of any city
in Asia Minor. Lampsacus continued to be a prosperous city
throughout the Hellenistic period, when it was an ally of Pergamum,
and on into the Roman era, when it was the second city in Asia to
ally itself with Rome, the first being Ilium, the name by which Troy
was then known. During the Byzantine era Lampsacus was
surpassed as a port by Callipolis, Turkish Gelibolu. It was taken by
the Ottomans in the mid-fourteenth century, after which it was
known in Turkish as Lapseki. The town has one monument from the
early Ottoman era, Süleyman Pasha Camii, which dates from the
mid-fourteenth century, though completely rebuilt in recent times.

We now continue on our way, as the highway takes us along the
inner end of the Dardanelles, then veering to the right to follow the
shore as it curves around at the western end of the Sea of Marmara.
A few kilometres farther along the highway curves inland for a long
stretch to pass across the base of a huge peninsula.

Halfway along this stretch we pass a turn-off on the left for
Karabiga, a port-town on the promontory of the peninsula.
Karabiga has been identified as the site of ancient **Priapus**, named
after the fertility god. Strabo describes the city thus in Book XIII of
his *Geography*: 'Priapus is a city on the sea, and also a harbour.
Some say it was founded by the Milesians, who at the same time also
colonized Abydos and Proconnesos, whereas others say it was
founded by Cyziceni [people from Cyzicus]. It was named after
Priapus, who was worshipped there.'

A short way beyond the Karabiga turn-off we cross the main
branch of the **Biga Çayî**, the ancient **River Granicus**. This river
gave its name to the battle of the Granicus, fought here in early June
of 334 BC. The Macedonians, some 50,000 strong, had crossed the
Hellespont a few days before under the command of Parmenio, and
Alexander had rejoined them after his pilgrimage to Troy, marching
them up the strait past Lampsacus and around the southern shore of
the Propontis toward the ford across the Granicus. As he did so his
scouts reported that the Persians had taken up positions on the opposite bank of the Granicus. Parmenio advised that they wait until the

following morning to make the crossing, but Alexander gave orders to attack as soon as the Macedonians had formed their line of battlle. The events that followed are described by Arrian, who first sets the scene of the battle:

> The Persians had about 20,000 cavalry and nearly the same number of foreign mercenaries fighting on foot. Back from the river the ground rose steeply, and they took up a position with their mounted troops along the bank on a very broad front with the infantry in the rear. At one point on the river-bank they had massed their squadron in strength – for it was here that, threatening their left, they could see Alexander himslf, an unmistakable figure in magnificent armour, attended by his suite with an almost ecstatic reverence.
>
> There was a profound hush, as both armies stood for a while motionless on the brink of the river, as if in awe of what was to come. Then Alexander, while the Persians still waited for the crossing to begin, that they might fall on his men as they were struggling up the farther bank, leapt upon his horse and called upon his bodyguard to follow and play the man . . . then he himself at the head of the right wing of the army, with trumpets blaring and the shout going up to the God of Battle, moved forward into the river . . .

Alexander was in the thick of the fighting, killing Mithridates, son-in-law of King Darius III. Immediately afterwards one of the Persians struck at Alexander with his scimitar and sliced off part of his helmet. But Alexander quickly speared him through the breast, and when another Persian raised his scimitar against him the man was killed by one of the Companions, the elite cavalry of the Macedonians. After recounting this episode, Arrian then describes the final phase of the battle.

> The Persians were now in a bad way: there was no escape for horse and rider from the thrust of the Macedonian spears; they were being forced back from their position and, in addition to the main weight of the attack, they were suffering considerable damage from the lightly-armed troops who had forced their way in among the cavalry. They began to break just at the point where Alexander in person was bearing the brunt of things.
>
> Once the centre failed to hold, both wings of the Persian cavalry broke too, and the route was complete. About 1,000 were killed – no more – because Alexander soon checked the pursuit of them in order to turn his attention to the foreign mercenaries, who had remained in their original position, shoulder to shoulder – not,

indeed from any deliberate intention of proving their courage, but simply because the suddenness of the disaster had deprived them of their wits. Ordering a combined assault by infantry, Alexander quickly had them surrounded and butchered to a man, though one or two might have escaped notice among the heaps of dead. About 2,000 were taken prisoner.

Arrian then concludes his account by describing the aftermath of the historic battle, the initial Macedonian victory in Alexander's invasion of Asia:

The Macedonian losses were small: about twenty-five of the Companion cavalry were killed during the first assault. . . Rather more than sixty of the other mounted troops were killed, and about thirty of the infantrymen. By the order of Alexander all the dead were buried with their arms and equipment on the day after the battle, and their parents and children were granted immunity from local taxes and all forms either of personal service or dues payable upon property. For the wounded he showed great concern; he visited them all and examined their wounds, asking each man how and in what circumstances his wound was recived, and allowing him to tell his story and exaggerate as much as he pleased. He also gave rites of burial to the Persian commanders who fell fighting in the enemies' ranks; the Greek prisoners of war he sent in chains to hard labour in Macedonia, as a punishment for contravening the resolution of the League of Corinth by fighting in a foreign army against their own countrymen. As an offering to the goddess Athena, he sent to Athens 300 full suits of Persian armour, with the following inscription: 'Alexander, son of Philip, and the Greeks (except the Lacedaemonians) dedicate these spoils, taken from the Persians who dwell in Asia.

Alexander then headed south with most of the army through Mysia and Phrygia toward Sardis, the Persian capital of western Asia Minor, while he sent a detachment eastward under Parmenio to take Daskyleion, capital of the province of Hellespontine Phrygia.

Four kilometres farther along we pass on our right a turn-off for **Biga**, the town for which the Biga Çayî is named. Biga has been identified as ancient **Sidene**, which is mentioned by Strabo in Volume XIII of his *Geography*: 'And on the Granicus was situated the city Sidene, with a large territory of the same name, but it is now in ruins.'

Continuing along the highway, we come out to the shore of the Marmara again at Denizli, and a few kilometres farther along we cross the **Gönen Çayî**, another river that has its source on Mount

Ida. This has been identified as the ancient **River Aesepus** mentioned in the *Iliad* by Homer, who places its source on the eastern slope of Ida. The Aesepus was generally taken to be the boundary between Hellespontine Phrygia and the Troad.

We continue along the E-90 as far as the turn-off on the left for Edincek and Erdek. After passing Edincek the road takes us on to the narrow isthmus that links the mainland with the huge Kapîdağ peninsula. At the isthmus a secondary road on the right leads around the southeastern side of the peninsula, while the main highway veers left to go around the southwestern side of the peninsula to Erdek. Between these two roads, at the northern end of the isthmus we find the seldom-visited ruins of ancient Cyzicus, once the most important city in Hellespontine Phrygia. (The ruins have never been excavated and are heavily overgrown with vegetation, so that it takes some effort to find them, particularly since they are widely scattered.)

The **Kapidağ peninsula** was in antiquity known variously as **Arctonoros (Bear Mountain)** or **Arctonissos (Bear Island)**. It was then indeed an island, which its early settlers linked to the mainland by bridges that could be removed when enemies appeared; in later times alluvial deposits created the isthmus that we see today. The Turkish name of the peninsula comes from its central peak, **Kapî Dağ**, which has an altitude of 782 metres. This was known in antiquity as **Mount Dindymus**, taking its name from Meter Dindymene, known to the Greeks as Rhea and the Phrygians as Cybele. There was a temple of the Mother Goddess on Mount Dindymus which, according to Strabo, was founded by Jason and the Argonauts when they landed on the peninsula during their voyage aboard *Argo*.

Cyzicus was a Greek colony founded by Miletos in 756 BC and refounded in 656 BC, according to tradition, with pottery finds generally corroborating these dates. The indigeneous people of the area at the time of the first foundation of Cyzicus are referred to by Strabo as the Doliones. The Doliones are mentioned by Apollonius Rhodius in his *Argonautica*, where he describes how the Argonauts fought both the aborigines and the civilized inhabitants of Cyzicus when they landed on the peninsula, the battle with the Cyziceni being due to mistaken identity.

Cyzicus became an important banking centre through its electrum (an alloy of gold and silver) coins, the famous Cyziceni 'staters' which were issued from c.600 BC onwards and became an international medium of exchange. Athens made an agreement with

Column drum from Temple of Hadrian at Cyzicus, Erdek

351

Cyzicus for the minting of gold staters to be used in the Athenian maritime empire, the confederation established by Athens after the Greek victory over the Persians at Plataea in 479 BC.

Cyzicus submitted to Persian hegemony after the conquest of northwestern Asia Minor by Cyrus the Great in 546 BC. The Cyziceni refrained from joining the other Greek cities in Asia Minor in their revolt against Persia in 499 BC, and so when the uprising was crushed five years later Cyzicus was spared the destruction visited upon the rebels by the vengeful Persians. Cyzius became one of the leading cities in northwestern Asia Minor during the classical period, rivalling Byzantium in importance and in the extent of its possessions. During the fifth century BC it was a member of the Delian Confederacy, its annual tribute being the largest of all the cities in Hellespontine Phrygia. During the Hellenistic period Cyzicus was an ally of Pergamum, which was then the most important state in western Asia Minor. This alliance was cemented in the third quarter of the third century BC, when Attalus I of Pergamum married Apollonis, daughter of a prominent citizen of Cyzicus, Their sons, who succeeded to the Pergamene throne in turn as Eumenes III and Attalus II, built a magnificent temple in Cyzicus c.160 BC dedicated to the deified Queen Apollonis. Cyzicus continued to prosper on into the Roman period, as evidenced by Strabo's description of the city in his time, which spanned the reign of Augustus (27 BC – AD 14).

> Cyzicus is an island in the Propontis, being connected to the mainland by two bridges; and it is not only the most excellent in the fertility of its soil, but in size it has a perimeter of about five hundred stadia [95 kilometres]. It has a city of the same name near the bridges themselves, and two harbours that can be closed, and more than two hundred shipyards. One part of the city is on level ground and the other is near a mountain called Arctoros. . . This city rivals the foremost cities of Asia in size, in beauty, and in the excellent administration of affairs both in peace and in war. And its adornment appears to be a type similar to that of Rhodes and Massalia [modern Marseilles] and ancient Carthage . . . the Romans honoured the city; and it is free to this day, and holds a large territory, not only that which it has held from ancient times, but also other territory presented to it by the Romans . . .

Hadrian commissioned a temple in Cyzicus at the time of his visit in 124, when he honoured the city by giving it the title of Metropolis and Neocorus, or Temple Warden. The temple, dedicated to the deified Hadrian, was not completed until 167, in the reign of Marcus Aurelius. It was a colossal edifice of the Corinthian order, measuring 76.9 by 40.5 metres on its *stylobate*, the upper step of its platform, and its 62 peripheral columns were 21.3 metres tall, with a lower diameter of 2.13 metres, making it the largest temple in Asia Minor. In fact, its dimensions were so awe-inspiring that in late antiquity it supplanted the Artemisium at Ephesus in lists of the Seven Wonders of the World.

Cyzicus was looted and destroyed in 673 by the Arabs, who for five years afterwards used the city as a base for their attacks on Constantinople. The city was further ruined by several earthquakes, most notably in 1063, fifteen years before it was taken by the Selcuks. By the end of the Byzantine era the city was an abandoned ruin, never again to be occupied.

The earliest European traveller known to have visited Cyzicus was Cyriacus of Ancona, who came here first in 1431 and again in 1444. At the time of his first visit Cyriacus found that a large part of the temple of Hadrian was still standing, although he mistakenly identified it as a sanctuary of Persephone because of an inscription he copied from a nearby altar. At the time he noted that 33 columns of its peripteral colonnade were still standing, along with its pedimental sculpture, which was 'undamaged and intact, almost in its original splendour'. When Cyriacus returned in 1444 he found that two of its columns had disappeared, having been toppled and used as building material by the locals. This quarrying of the buildings of Cyzicus continued until the entire colonnade of Hadrian's temple had vanished, leaving only its substructure and some architectural fragments, along with the ruins of other edifices scattered around the area at the northern end of the isthmus.

The road around the southeastern side of the peninsula passes a section of the ancient defence walls of Cyzicus, which extended across the narrow neck of the present isthmus. These walls are believed to date to the fifth century BC. The fragmentary stretch of wall beside the road here is known as Demir Kapî, the Iron Gate. This is probably the site of the gateway that led out to the harbour of the city, where the stone blocks of quays and moles can still be seen. A short way farther along we come to Asağî Yapîcî, where we turn left and drive uphill to Hamamlî, a village built on and from the ruins of Cyzicus. The acropolis of the ancient city is just to the southwest of the village, situated on a spur of Mount Dindymus, which rises above it to the north. The theatre was on the south slope of the acropolis, where one can still barely discern the outline of its *cavea*. Below the acropolis to the west are the impressive ruins of the Roman amphitheatre, dating from the late second century AD, built astride a stream whose water was used to flood the arena for a *naumachia*, or mock naval battle. The villagers in Hamamlî refer to the amphitheatre as Belkis Sarayî, or the Palace of Belkis, the Queen of Sheba.

Returning to the main road, we now drive around the southwest end of the peninsula toward Erdek. After crossing the stream that flows down through the amphitheatre we pass on our left the ruins of an hexagonal tower dating from the sixth century AD, probably from the reign of Justinian. A short distance beyond that we see on our right the vaulted substructures of Hadrian's temple. largely covered with earth and overgrown with shrubbery. The locals refer to these substructures as Mağalar, or the Caves, and consider them to be the haunts of demons.

We now drive on to **Erdek**, a port town just beyond the southwesternmost promontory of the peninsula. Erdek has been identified as the ancient **Artace**, a Greek colony founded by Miletos in the mid-eighth century BC, probably at the same time as Cyzicus. Unlike Cyzicus, Artace joined the Ionian revolt in 499 BC, and five years later the victorious Persians took their revenge by burning the city to the ground. The city was subsequently rebuilt, but it was destroyed again during the Mithridatic Wars in the first century BC. Artace revived during the medieval Byzantine era, but it never again achieved the status of a city.

The present town of Erdek is a relatively modern foundation. All that remains of ancient Artace are some architectural fragments displayed in the town park, along with others from Cyzicus. One notable exhibit is a fragment of a column from the temple of Hadrian at Cyzicus, its surface beautifully carved with the relief of a vine bearing clusters of pendant grapes.

Erdek is the port of embarkation for the **Marmara Islands**, a small archipelago near the western end of the Sea of Marmara. The largest island of the group by far is **Marmara Adasî**, the ancient **Proconnesos**. This island has been famous since antiquity for its beautiful marble (in Greek marble is '*marmara*', in Turkish '*mermer*'), from which the archipelago and the Sea of Marmara take their name. Strabo writes of Proconnesos in Book XIII of his *Geography*, where he notes that it has a city of the same name 'and also a great quarry of white marble that is highly recommended; at any rate the most beautiful works of art in the cities in that part of the world, and especially those in Cyzicus, are made of this marble.'

We now retrace our route from Erdek to the isthmus, where at the junction we take the road that is signposted for **Bandîrma**. Bandîrma is the ancient Panormus, later known to the Greeks as Panderma. Today it is a small port from which there is a car-ferry to Istanbul, and it is also the northern terminus of the railway line to Izmir.

From Bandîrma we once again head eastward on highway E-90, signposted for Bursa. Thirteen kilometres out of Bandîrma we come to a Y-junction, where we continue on the E-90 toward Bursa, while the road to the right leads to Balîkesir.

At the junction we pass the northeastern corner of **Manyas Gölü**, the ancient **Lake Daskylitis**, also known in Turkish as **Kuş Gölü**, or **Bird Lake**. The lake is the site of **Kuş Cenneti**, or **Bird Paradise**, a bird sanctuary and national park. Since time immemorial this has been a stopping-place on the migratory route of birds flying between Europe and Africa. Among the species one sees here in great number are the spoonbill, cormorant, pelican, grey common heron, white and grey night herons, egret, grebe, wild duck, goose, swan and stork, the latter arriving and departing in their appointed seasons in great spirals that can be seen above the lake from miles away.

The ancient name of the lake comes from that of **Daskyleion**, whose site has been excavated by Profssor Ekrem Akurgal at the village of Egili near the southeastern corner of Kuş Gölü. Professor Akurgal identified the site from Strabo's statement that 'near Lake Daskylitis is the city Daskyleion'. Daskyleion is believed to have been founded by the Lydians early in the seventh century BC. During the achaic period it was the capital of the Persian satrapy, or province, of Hellespontine Phrygia. After Alexander's victory at the battle of the Granicus, he sent Parmenio with part of the army to take Daskyleion, which was captured without bloodshed when the Persian garrison fled. The excavations revealed a small section of the city walls as well as a variety of objects dating from the classical and Hellenistic period, some of which are exhibited in the Istanbul Archaeological Museum. The most notable of these are three funerary stelae with reliefs in the Graeco-Achaemenid style, dated c.400 BC.

Twenty-two kilometres beyond the junction along the E-90 we come to **Karacabey**. The town is named for Karaca Pasha, who served as Vizier under both Murat II and Mehmet II. He was killed at the second Ottoman siege of Belgrade in 1455, after his body was brought back for burial here, in the *türbe* of a mosque founded by his heirs in his memory. The mosque, which is of the cross-axial eyvan type, was badly damaged in 1922 and has recently been restored.

A few kilometres beyond Karacabey we pass on our right another road to Balîkesir, after which we continue on the E-90 toward Bursa. After another few kilometres we come to **Ulubat**, a village at the western end of a lake of the same name, Ulubat Gölü. A large modern monument in the village commemorates the local hero Ulubatlî Hasan, a giant Janissary who died in the Ottoman capture of Constantinople in 1453, killed as he headed the charge in which the Turks first broke into the city.

The village is just to the west of the site of ancient **Lopadion**, a city at the western end of Ulubat Gölü, which is also known as **Apolyont Gölü**. The latter name is a corruption of that of ancient **Lake Apolloniatis**. This shallow lake attracts fishermen and hunters from far afield, for its waters are teeming with carp, perch, pike, sturgeon and crayfish, its shores abounding in wild geese, pheasants and woodcock, as as well as in protected herons, cranes, pelicans and swans.

A short way beyond Ulubat we see off to the right a huge ruin of an Ottoman structure near the lake shore. This is the **Issîz Han**, an early Ottoman caravansarai. An inscription over the gateway records that the caravansarai was founded by the Emir Celaleddin in 1394, during the reign of Beyazit I. The building is 44 metres long and 22 metres wide, with two rectangular chambers flanking its entryway. The interior is divided into three barrel-vaulted aisles separated by two rows of five pillars each, the middle vault higher than those on the sides, all covered by a gable roof. The Issîz Han is a smaller verion of the great Selcuk caravansarais that are still to be seen along the old highroads of central Anatolia, hostels where traders and their caravans could put up for the night in their journeys across Turkey.

At the eastern end of the lake a turn-off to the right leads to **Gölyazî**. This is a picturesque fishing-village on a peninsula extending southward at the end of the lake. The village extends out on to an islet, which used to be connected to the end of the peninsula by a narrow isthmus that is submerged at times of high water, though a bridge now links it to the mainland.

Gölyazî is the site of ancient **Apollonia ad Rhyndacum**. The second part of the city's name came from the **Rhyndacus**, a river now known as the **Mustafakemalpaşa**, which flows into the southern side of the lake. This river formed part of the boundary between Mysia and Bithynia. Apollonia ad Rhyndacum was founded by Miletos c.700 BC, one of several cities that the Milesians established in this region. An inscription found at Miletos records that in the second century BC the people of Apollonia, the Apolloniates, reafirmed their bonds with their mother city. As the inscription reads, the Apolloniates 'having examined the histories of this subject and other documents answered that Apollonia was in reality a colony of the Milesians, their ancestors having created it at the time when they sent an expedition into the Hellespontic and Propontic regions, and having subdued the local barbarians with the spear, founded various Greek cities like our own, having been conducted under the auspices of Apollo of Didyma.'

Some ruins of ancient Apollonia are still visible; these include a number of large stone blocks from the defence wall that once ringed the islet and extended across the isthmus to connect it with the fortifications on the peninsula. The little mosque on the highest point of the islet is believed to stand on the site of an ancient temple, probably one dedicated to Apollo, the patron deity of the city. Fragments of the temple can be seen here and there in the vicinity of the mosque, as well as in the walls of the surounding houses. There are also remains of the necropolis of Apollonia on the eastern side of the peninsula between the road and the lake, the most notable funerary monunment being a large sarcophagus. Toward the southern end of the peninsula one can still discern the concave form of the *cavea* of the ancient theatre. One relic from the more recent past is the shell of a Greek Orthodox church. This was abandoned by its congregation in 1923, at the time of the population exchange that followed the Turkish War of Independence.

There are more ruins on a nearby islet known as **Kîz Adasî**, the **Maiden's Island**, where there are remains of an ancient structure that may have been another temple of Apollo.

Returning to the main highway, we continue driving eastward, as we now enter the region that in antiquity was known as **Bithynia**. The greatly increased traffic is evidence that we are now approaching Bursa. As we enter the outer suburbs we see some of the Ottoman houses and monuments of the city known to the Turks as Yeşil (Green) **Bursa**, and looming above it to the southeast the massed peaks of **Ulu Dağ**, the **Great Mountain**.

25

Bursa

THE OLD TOWN of **Bursa**, the Greek **Prusa**, lies below the northwestern slope of **Ulu Dağ**, the ancient **Mount Olympus** of **Bithynia**. (Apparently 'Olympus' is a pre-Hellenic name meaning 'mountain'; there was also a Mount Olympus in Lycia, in southern Asia Minor, as well as the famous mountain in Thessaly that was believed to be the home of Zeus and the other Olympian deities.)

The original name of the city was **Prusias ad Olympum**, founded in 183 BC by King Prusias I of Bithynia. The kingdom of Bithynia had been established in 297 BC by Zipoetes, who had defeated both Lysimachus and the Seleucid king Antiochus I to create his realm. He was succeeded in 279 BC by his son Nicomedes I, who fourteen years later founded the city of Nicomedeia (Izmit) as capital of Bithynia. Bithynia, which by then was completely Hellenized, reached its greatest extent under Nicomedes' grandson, Prusias I, who founded several other cities beside Prusias ad Olympum. The Bithynian kingdom finally came to an end in 74 BC, when Nicomedes IV bequeathed his realm to Rome. The city prospered under Roman rule, according to Pliny the Younger, who notes that it had a number of impressive temples and other splendid edifices. All that remains of the ancient city are some massive fragments of the defence wall that encirled its Byzantine citadel, known in Turkish as Hisar, or the Fortress, on the eminence that towers above the centre of modern Bursa.

Prusa, as it was known to the Greeks, remained an important city in the Byzantine era. Then in 1326 it was captured by the Ottoman Turks under Osman Gazi, two years after he succeeded his father Orhan Gazi, when he took the title of sultan. The city, known to the Turks as Bursa, thereupon became the first capital of the rapidly-expanding Ottoman realm. Bursa remained the capital until Orhan Gazi was succeeded in 1359 by his son Murat I, who shifted the centre of government to the newly-captured city of Edirne. But Bursa retained pride of place even after the government moved to Edirne, for it was revered as the first capital of the Ottoman state, the burial place of Osman Gazi and the first five sultans. Their imperial mosques and mausoleums still adorn the town, once one of the love-liest in Anatolia.

The town has lost some of its renowned beauty in recent years because of the mass construction of ugly modern buildings, which replace the venerable Ottoman houses that once clustered pictur-esquely under Bithynian Olympus, embowered in the trees that led it to be called Bursa the Green. We must refer to travellers in late Ottoman times to evoke a picture of what Bursa was like in the days of its glory. William Hamilton, in his *Researches in Asia Minor, Pontus and Armenia*, describes the town as it was in 1836, referring to it as Brusa, mistakingly thinking that its Byzantine fortress was early Ottoman:

> No town in Asiatic Turkey is more celebrated or more justly so, for its picturesque situation and appearance than Brusa. Situated at the southern edge of a rich and well cultivated plain, covered with gardens and mulberry plantations, its buildings extend some way up the steep and rocky hills which rise immediately behind it. Thick overhanging woods begin to rise directly above the town, while many trees, particularly the tall cypresses, rise in and about it, interspersed with numerous graceful minarets and glittering domes. To complete the picture, a flat table-land, standing out a little in advance of the hills, rises up in the middle of the town, the precipitous cliffs of which are surmounted by the ivy-clad walls and towers of a castle of an early date, dating probably from the time when Brusa was the capital of the Turkish empire. Such a scene, on a sunny day, when every tree and flower was putting forth its first shoots and buds, backed by the range of Olympus, whose deep and snowy valleys reflected every variety of tint, was the most welcome sight that could greet a traveller on his first ap-pearance in the East.

Cumhuriyet Meydanî is the city centre of Bursa, and we will begin our tour of the city there by walking westward along Atatürk Caddesi. This soon brings us to **Ulu Cami**, the **Great Mosque**, which dominates the recently restored Ottoman market quarter of old Bursa.

Ulu Cami was built in the years 1396–99 by Beyazit I, known to the Turks as Yîldîrîm, or Lightning, because of the speed with which he moved his armies back and forth between campaigns in Europe and Asia. The Sultan financed the construction of Bursa's Ulu Cami with the loot from his victory at the battle of Nicopolis on 24 September 1396, when he routed a Crusader army led by King Sigis-mund of Hungary. This is the grandest of all the Great Mosques

Bursa

N

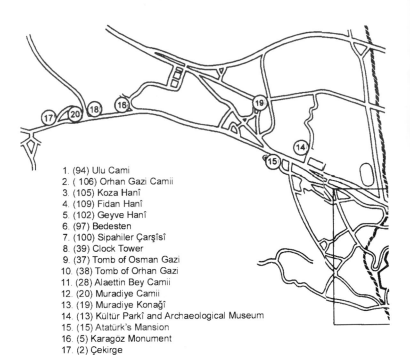

1. (94) Ulu Cami
2. (106) Orhan Gazi Camii
3. (105) Koza Hanî
4. (109) Fidan Hanî
5. (102) Geyve Hanî
6. (97) Bedesten
7. (100) Sipahiler Çarşîsî
8. (39) Clock Tower
9. (37) Tomb of Osman Gazi
10. (38) Tomb of Orhan Gazi
11. (28) Alaettin Bey Camii
12. (20) Muradiye Camii
13. (19) Muradiye Konağî
14. (13) Kültür Parkî and Archaeological Museum
15. (15) Atatürk's Mansion
16. (5) Karagöz Monument
17. (2) Çekirge
18. (4) Eski Kaplîca Hamam
19. (10) Yeni Kaplîca Hamamî
20. (3) Külliye of the Hudavendigàr
21. (133) Yeşil Cami and Türbe
22. (130) Külliye of Beyazit I

erected in Anatolia during the two centuries preceding the Turkish conquest of Constantinople, demonstrating the ascendancy of the Ottomans over their rivals among the Türkmen *beyliks*, or emirates.

The exterior of Ulu Cami is particularly handsome, with its façade of honey-coloured limestone from Mount Olympus. The two minarets rise from the northwest and northeast corners of the building; an inscription on the first of these records that it was erected by Beyazit I; the second, which stands free of the building, was probably built by Mehmet I, who succeeded to the throne after an eleven-year war of succession that followed the death of Yîldîrîm after he was defeated by Tamerlane at Ankara in 1402.

Twelve great piers divide the vast interior of the mosque into twenty domed areas. One of these areas, the second in from the main door, contains a *şadîrvan* pool with a cascade fountain at its centre, the latter being a nineteenth-century replacement of the original *selsebil*. The crown of the dome was originally left open to the elements, a feature of early Ottoman mosques in Bursa, but in a modern restoration this oculus has been glassed in. Nevertheless, the effect remains most attractive, for the *şadîrvan* court is still filled with light, sparkling on the water pouring from the cascade fountain for the ablutions of the faithful. This court is the off-centre focal point of the mosque, for there the longitudinal axis from the front entryway to the *mihrab* is intersected by the transverse axis defined by the two side entrances. The *mimber* is a superb work in carved walnut, one of the finest in Turkey. The twenty domes rest on pendentives, and on the exterior they are carried by octagonal drums. The domes along the longitudinal axis are higher than those on either side, which diminish in height progressively. The impressive main gateway is apparently not part of the original structure; it has been suggested that it was built by Tamerlane during his occupation of Bursa in 1402–03, although local authorities vehemently deny this. During that time Beyazit was suffering through his last days as Tamerlane's captive, after having been defeated by the Mongols at the battle of Ankara in mid-August of 1402. As wrote Arabshah, the chronicler of Tamerlane's bloody career: 'The son of Osman fell into a hunter's snare, and became confined like a bird in a cage.'

We now walk eastward parallel to Atatürk Caddesi through the new and attractive plaza that has been created outside the old Ottoman market quarter.

At the far end of the plaza we come to the oldest of Bursa's imperial mosques – **Orhan Gazi Cami** – erected in 1339. The mosque

Interior of Ulu Cami, Bursa

was destroyed twice, first by the Karamanid Türkmen tribe in the interregnum that followed the battle of Ankara, and then by an earthquake in 1855; it was repaired after both catastrophes, presumably with some changes in structure. Nevertheless, the essential plan of the mosque is the same as the original, which was the earliest example of the cross-axial *eyvan* type. Its five-bay porch is supported on the façade by six piers, with a slender column separating the two arches at either end, and with the three central bays domed and those at the ends flat-topped cross-vaults. We pass through a domed antechamber to the central hall, a rectangle with a deep arch on the north that creates a square base on the upper level for the hemispherical dome. The main *eyvan* is raised by three steps from the central chamber; it is rectangular in plan at both lower and upper levels so that its dome is ellipsoidal rather than spherical, with a niche in its southern wall containing the *mihrab*. Two more rectangular *eyvans* flank the central hall, with deep arches to north and south so that they are square at the upper level to provide a base for their hemispherical domes; here as elsewhere these were used as *zaviyes* for wandering dervishes. The central hall and the three *eyvans* differ in their dome heights and in the manner in which the transition is made from the square base to the circular or elliptical cornice, though all of them have drums that are octagonal on the exterior.

The principal market area of Bursa lies behind the two mosques we have just visited, approached from the inner side of the plaza. Many of the old *hans* in this quarter were well restored in the same project that created the plaza. Something of the quarter's former oriental armosphere has been lost in the process, but one still has the feeling here of being in an old Ottoman market town, where one could easily spend the day wandering through the labyrinthian arcades in search of a bargain.

The huge market building that takes up most of that side of the plaza is the **Koza (Silk Cocoon) Hanî**. This was built in 1490 by Beyazit II for the silk trade. Like most of the other *hans* in the market it is square in plan, with a porticoed courtyard surrounded on all sides by shops on two storeys, the upper ones opening off a gallery. At the centre of its porticoed courtyard an octagonal *şadîrvan* is surmounted by a *mescit*, a feature derived from the imperial Selcuk caravansarais of the thirteenth century.

A short distance to the north is the equally huge **Fidan (Sapling) Hanî**, built c.1470 by Mahmut Pasha, Mehmet the Conqueror's

Grand Vizier. West of the Fidan Hanî is the smaller **Geyve Hanî,** built in the second decade of the fifteenth century by Hacî Ivaz Pasha, who served as the imperial architect under Mehmet I. South of that is a bath known as **Bey Hamamî,** to the west of which is the Bey Hanî; both of these were built in 1339 as part of the *külliye* of Orhan Gazi Camii. The Bey Hamamî, recently restored, is the oldest Turkish bath in existence.

North of Bey Hanî is the Bedesten, a rectangular building covered with fourteen domes in two rows of seven each, supported internally by seven piers The **Bursa Bedesten,** built during the reign of Beyazit I, was used to store and display only the most valuable goods, such as brocades, jewellery and objects of gold and silver. North of the Bedesten is the **Sipahilar (Cavalry Knights) Carşîsî,** a covered bazaar built by Mehmet I. It is rectangular in plan, covered by a single row of four domes.

West of Ulu Cami the avenue divides into two branches, with Orhan Gazi Caddesi on the left and Altîparmak Caddesi, the main highway, on the right. We cross the intersection to take Orhan Gazi Caddesi, which leads to the hilltop quarter known as Hisar, the citadel of the town from antiquity through the Byzantine era. Along the first steep stretch of Orhan Gazi Caddesi we see the massive remnants of the citadel's ancient defence-wall, originally constructed in the Hellenistic era and rebuilt during both the Byzantine and Ottoman periods. This is virtually all that remains of the ancient Greek city of Prusa, the rest of which is buried under Ottoman Bursa.

At the top of the acropolis we come to the **Clock Tower,** which rises from the northeast corner of the citadel. Here we find the tombs of **Osman Gazi** and **Orhan Gazi,** which stand in a park on the site of the first Ottoman royal palace, erected here after the capture of Bursa in 1326. Osman Gazi died in the nearby town of Soğut in 1324, and his body was reinterred here after the capture of Bursa. His burial-place had formerly been the baptistry of the Byzantine church of St Prophitis Elias which Orhan Gazi converted into a mosque after capturing the city. When Orhan Gazi died in 1359 he was buried in what had been the nave of the church. The building has been destroyed and rebuilt several times, and the royal tombs one sees today are the result of a complete reconstruction commissioned in 1868 by Sultan Abdül Aziz. All that remains of the original church are some fragments of mosaic pavement around the catafalque of Orhan Gazi.

Behind the tombs there is a broad esplanade that commands a sweeping view out over the lower town of Bursa and its surrounding hills. Before we leave the citadel we might stroll along its picturesque back streets, where a few old Ottoman houses still survive, though they are fast disappearing. At the southwestern corner of the citadel we find the oldest mosque in Bursa, Alaettin Bey Camii, built in 1335. This was erected by Orhan Gazi in memory of his younger brother Alaettin, who died in 1331 after having served as First Vizier and commander of the Ottoman army. It is a single-unit mosque preceded by a porch of three bays, whose facade is supported by four columns with Byzantine capitals. The interior is a square room 8.2 metres on a side, surmounted by a hemispherical dome carried on a sixteen-sided belt of large triangular planes, an arrangement known as 'Turkish triangles'. The minaret is part of the original structure, though the upper section is a modern replacement. Aptullah Kuran, the Turkish architectural historian, reckons that this is the earliest extant minaret in Ottoman architecture.

The street that goes down from the southwestern corner of the Kale leads to Kaplîca Caddesi, which brings us northwestward to the Muradiye, the imperial mosque complex that gave its name to the surrounding neighbourhood.

The **Muradiye mosque complex** was built in the years 1424–26 by Murat II, father of Mehmet the Conqueror. This was the last imperial mosque complex to be erected in Bursa. Besides the mosque itself, it included a *medrese*, an *imaret*, the *türbe* of the founder, and numerous other tombs, some of which were built in later times.

The **mosque** is of the cross-axial *evyan* type with a five-bay porch, similar to Orhan Gazi Camii, and it too has a pair of *zaviyes* flanking its main chamber. The main difference is that here the two domes are of the same height and look identical from the outside, though they differ in their interior.

The **medrese** of the Muradiye complex is the most beautiful in Bursa. The courtyard forms a perfect square with five *hücres* each on the east and west sides, larger cells in the corners, and a pair of rooms on either side of the entryway; the little *dershane* opposite the entrance is noted for its brilliant tile decoration. The *medrese* serves as a dispensary, its courtyard converted into a pretty garden with a fountain at its centre. Little now remains of the *imaret* that once served food to the students and the staff of the *külliye*.

The *türbe* of **Murat II** stands in the garden beside his mosque and *medrese*, surrounded by a dozen other tombs. The great warrior died in Edirne on 3 February 1451 and was brought back to be interred in his *külliye*, the last Ottoman sultan to be buried in the old capital of Bursa. His tomb has a simple grandeur about it, with his earth-filled mable catafalque lying alone under the open oculus of the dome, whose octagonal drum is carried on four piers and four columns with Byzantine capitals from which spring eight pointed arches. Murat's tomb was left open to the elements according to the terms of his last will and testament: 'Bury me in Bursa near my son Alaettin. Do not raise a sumptuous mausoleum over my grave . . . but bury me directly in the ground. May the rain, sign of the bendiction of God, fall upon me.'

Those buried in the tombs around Murat's *türbe* include a number of royal princes and princesses, along with the mothers and wives of several sultans and members of their households. Two of the tombs are of particular interest in the history of the imperial Ottoman line.

The *türbe* just to the west of Murat's is that of Prince Mustafa, eldest son of Süleyman the Magnificent. Mustafa was heir-apparent until he was executed in 1551 by Süleyman, who had been persuaded by Roxelana that his son was plotting to usurp the throne. Thereby Roxelana's son Selim II, the Sot, succeeded to the throne when Süleyman died in 1566, and with his reign began the long and inexorable decline of the Ottoman Empire.

The next *türbe* to the southwest contains the graves of two sons of Mehmet the Conqueror, Princes Mustafa and Cem. Mustafa was killed in action in 1474 at the age of twenty-five while on campaign in Konya, and Mehmet the Conqueror brought him back to Bursa to be buried next to his grandfather Murat. Cem died in 1495 in Italy, having spent fourteen years in exile after being defeated by his brother Beyazit II in a war of succession after their father Mehmet the Conqueror's death. Cem's body was not brought back to Bursa for burial until 1499, for even after his death he continued to be the subject of negotiations between Beyazit and the European powers that had held him captive. Evliya Çelebi, in his *Seyahatname*, tells a fabulous tale concerning the return of Cem's remains to Bursa:

> The corpse of Cem, together with his property, amongst which was an enchanted cup, which became brimful when delivered empty into the cup-bearer's hand, a white parrot, and some thousands of splendid books, were delivered up to Said Çelebi and Haydar Çelebi that they might be conveyed to the Sultan . . .

While they were digging the grave there was such a thunderclap and tumult in the sepulchral chapel, that all who were present fled, and not a soul of them was able to pas its threshold till ten days had passed, when this having been represented to the Sultan, the corpse of Cem was buried by his order near to that of his grandfather. . . .

Just to the west of the *külliye* we see a beautiful old Ottoman mansion known as the **Muradiye Konak**. The *konak*, which dates from the early eighteenth century, has been been superbly restored and furnished in the style of late Ottoman times. It is now open as a museum.

We now continue to the end of Kaplîca Caddesi, turning left on Besikçiler Caddesi and continuing in the same direction on Çekirge Caddesi, the extension of Altîparmak Caddesi. On the right side of Çekirge Caddesi we pass **Kültür Parkî**, where the people of Bursa come in summer to enjoy themselves at outdoor cafés and an amusement park. Within the park is the **Archaeological Museum**, which has on exhibition antquities found in Bursa and the surrounding region, including a large number of funerary stelae from the late Roman and early Byzantine eras. On the left side of the avenue we see a mansion where Atatürk stayed whenever he visited Bursa, and which is now a museum dedicated to his memory.

At the second intersection beyond the park we see on our right the **Karagöz Monument**. This is a modern memorial to the two principals of the ancient Turkish shadow-theatre, Karagöz and Hacîvat, who, according to tradition, were two Greeks who worked on the construction of Orhan Gazi Camii in Bursa. The first Karagöz plays in which they appeared as characters were written in the fourteenth century by Şeyh Kusteri of Horosan. The Karagöz puppet-theatre, which spread all across Asia and even into Greece, is still very much alive in Turkey, part of the rich tradition inherited from the Ottoman era.

The avenue finally brings us to **Çekirge**, a suburb in the hills west of the town centre of Bursa renowned for its thermal baths. There are a number of good hotels here that originally catered to those who came to bathe at these baths, whose waters come from hot springs that have been used since Roman times. The oldest of the baths is the **Eski Kaplîca Hamamî**, which is supposed to have been founded by Justinian and Theodora, though the present baths were erected by Murat I. Another renowned baths is the **Yeni Kaplîca Hamamî**. According to Evliya Çelebi the Yeni Kaplîca baths were built for Süleyman the Magnificent after he was cured of his gout by bathing in the hot springs there. Evliya describes the delights of bathing in the Yeni Kaplîca baths, which he compares with the Eski Kaplîca Hamamî:

> Though this hot bath is not in such good repute as the former, yet it is a pleasant place, where lovers delight with their beloved, especially in the long winter nights; when these baths are lighted with candles, a thousand tricks are played by the bathers, swelling their aprons into sails, others joining hands and imitating the cries of boatmen, 'Tira Mola!', drive the water around like a whirlpool, which forces all of those who are in the water to follow the quick rotation of it.

On the brow of the hill near the main square in Çekirge we find the oldest of Bursa's imperial mosque complexes, the **Hüdavendiğâr**, founded by Murat I. (Hüdavendiğâr is a pompous imperial title, used only by Murat I, meaning 'Creator of the Universe'.)

The *külliye* was erected during the years 1365–85. The long delay in its completion was due to the fact that Murat spent most of his reign on campaign in the Balkans, leaving him little time to supervise the construction of his *külliye*. It was completed four years before his death at the first battle of Kossovo, 27 August 1389, when he was struck down by a Serbian assassin at the moment of his greatest victory. Murat's remains were then brought back for burial in the *türbe* of his mosque complex in Bursa.

The Hüdavendiğâr is a two-storeyed building with a mosque-hospice on the ground floor and a *medrese* above. The mosque is preceded by a five-bay porch with a gallery of five bays above, the two floors connected by a pair of stairways flanking the vestibule. The interior of the ground floor comprises four *eyvans* around a central fountain court, as well as six other rooms, three on either side. The two storeyed central hall is a square surmounted by a dome eleven metres in diameter and 22 metres high, with an oculus in its crown. A flight of steps leads up from there to the prayer-hall, a rectangular room covered by a barrel-vault, with the *mihrab* placed inside a niche that forms a pentagonal protrusion at the back of the building. The *medrese* on the second floor has a large room between the staircases, eight cells on either side of the central hall and the prayer hall, and a small room above the *mihrab*. The Hüdavendiğâr is altogether an extraordinary building, and nothing like it would ever again be built by the Ottomans. Murat I is buried in a türbe in front of his *külliye*.

Two other imperial mosque complexes stand on the hillside to the southeast of the city centre. The best approach is to return to

Cumhuriyet Meydanî and head east along Ataturk Caddesi. This crosses a bridge over Gok Dere, the Stream of the Sky, which flows down from Ulu Dağ. Once across the bridge we take the second left into Yeşil Caddesi, which soon brings us to **Yeşil Cami, the Green Mosque.**

Yeşil Cami was commissioned by Mehmet I in 1412, the year before he finally became Sultan after the long civil war that followed the death of his father Yîldîrîm Beyazit. The architect was Hacî Ivaz Pasha, whose Geyve Hanî in the market area we saw earlier on this tour. The mosque was not finished when Mehmet died in 1421, and although work continued for another three years afterwards it was never completed, lacking its entrance portico. Nevertheless, Yeşil Cami is the grandest and most beautiful of the imperial mosques in Bursa, both in the harmony of its design and the richness of its interior decoration.

The design is yet another variation of the cross-axial *eyvan* type. Beyond the vestibule we pass through a small barrel-vaulted *eyvan* into the central court, in the centre of which there is a *şadîrvan* pool. On the left and right there are side *eyvans* elevated by a single step above the central court, while the main eyvan – the prayer hall – is raised by four steps. Each of the side *eyvans* is flanked by a pair of rooms of comparable size, all four of them originally serving as *zaviyes* for itinerant dervishes. The dome over the central court, which is slightly higher than the one over the prayer hall, is surmounted by a lantern, a replacement of the original open oculus. Looking backwards from the central court, we see above the entrance *eyvan* the beautifully-tiled imperial loge, and to either side of it the screened balconies that were reserved for the royal family. This is surely the most beautiful mosque interior in Bursa, with the magnificent *mihrab* framed in the great arch of the prayer-hall *eyvan*, and the still water of the *şadîrvan* pool mirroring the brilliant warm colours of the stained-glass windows in the *kible* wall, the one oriented toward Mecca.

Yeşil Türbe, the mausoleum of Mehmet I, stands at the top of the hill across the street from the mosque. Originally its exterior walls were revetted in the turquoise tiles from which the *türbe* and the mosque took their names, but these were destroyed by the 1855 earthquake and replaced by modern Kütahya tiles. The interior decoration of the *türbe* rivals that of the mosque itself, particularly the finely-carved doors, the tile revetment of the walls, the beautifully-decorated *mihrab*, and the sultan's sarcophagus, with its ornate epitaph in golden calligraphy on a blue ground.

Bursa

The mosque complex of Mehmet I also included a *medrese*, an *imaret*, and a *hamam*, but of these only the *imaret* has survived. The *imaret* now houses the Museum of Turkish and Islamic Art, whose collections include Ottoman weapons, kitchen utensils, jewellery, calligraphy, and antique Islamic books.

The fourth of Bursa's imperial mosque complexes is that of Beyazit I, which stands on a hilltop site to the northeast of Yeşil Cami. The best approach is to sight on it from the outer courtyard of Yeşil Cami and then follow the streets which lead in that general direction.

The **mosque complex of Yîldîrîm Beyazit** was begun in 1390 and completed in 1395. It too was badly damaged in the 1855 earthquake; since then it has been restored twice, once in 1878 and again in 1948, yet it seems to have retained its original form and character. The original *külliye* consisted of the mosque with its dervish hospice, along with two *medreses*, a hospital, a palace, and the *türbe* of the founder. Today all that remains are the mosque, the *türbe*, and one of the *medreses*, which now serves as a dispensary.

The mosque is preceded by a five bay porch, through which we pass via a domed vestibule into the central hall. The interior plan is of the familiar cross axial *eyvan* type, with pairs of *zaviyes* flanking each of the side *eyvans*. The three *eyvans* are raised three steps higher than the central hall; they are all domed, with the cupola of the main *eyvan* being only slightly higher than that of the central court, while those of the side *eyvans* are considerable lower. The two minarets were destroyed, one of them in 1855 and the other in 1949, and they have never been reconstructed. The exterior of the mosque is particularly handsome, with its strong portico of five arches and its shining façade of marble and cut stone.

The best time to visit Bursa is in spring, when the broad plain below Ulu Dağ turns a virginal green and the hillsides are bright with wild flowers and blossoming trees. And of course no visit to Bursa is complete without an ascent of the great mountain itself, which in winter beomes a popular ski resort. One approach is to take the cable car which starts from the hillside east of town, not far from Yeşil Cami, another is to drive up the mountain road that ascends from Çekirge. This takes one to the area that is used as a ski resort in winter, and from there it is a three-hour walk to the summit, 2,543 metres above sea-level, by far the highest peak in northwestern Turkey. The mountain is now the **Ulu Dağ National Park**, more than 11,000 hectares of woodland that includes olive groves and

371

stands of bay, chestnut, elm, oak, plane, beech, pine, juniper and aspen. The view from the summit is awesome, with all of Bursa and central Bithynia spread out below.

26

Bursa to Istanbul via Iznik

OUR FINAL ITINERARY will take us from Bursa to Istanbul, stopping en route at Iznik. The first stage of this last route will take us north from Bursa on highway 238, which brings us down through the tree-clad Bithynian hills to the Marmara shore. We reach the sea at Gemlik, a port at the head of the gulf of the same name, an extension of the southeastern end of the Sea of Marmara.

Gemlik is the ancient **Cius**, one of the places where Jason and the Argonauts stopped on their voyage through the Propontis, enroute to the land of Colchis. Heracles, one of the Argonauts, went ashore with his friend Polyphemus and his servant Hylas, the beautiful young son of King Theiodamas of the Droypes, whom he had kidnapped after killing the youth's father. Hylas was sent to draw water from a spring to cook the evening meal, while Heracles went with Polyphemus to cut a tree, for he wanted to make an oar to replace the one he had broken. The nymphs who inhabited the spring were so taken by the beauty of Hylas that they drew him down into its waters, promising him immortality. Polyphemus heard Hylas cry out and went back to look for him with Heracles, but though they searched throughout the night they failed to find the lost youth, while in the meanwhile the other Argonauts eventually lost patience and set sail without them. Heracles, suspecting that the locals had kidnapped Hylas, took several of them hostage and ordered them to go in search of the lost youth. He then continued on his wanderings, leaving Polyphemus behind to found the city of Cius, where once a year the priests would set out in procession to the spring where Hylas had disappeared, thrice calling out his name, answered only by an echo from the surrounding forest.

Miletos founded a Greek colony at Cius in the eighth century BC, probably on the site of a Bithynian settlement. Cius remained an independent city until the end of the fourth century BC, ruled by a series of local tyrants. Mithridates, the last of these, was executed by Antigonus when he took control of the region in 302 BC. His nephew, also named Mithridates, escaped and fled to Amaseia in the Pontus. There he founded the Kingdom of the Pontus, one of his descendants being the famous Mithridates VI Eupator, who fought the Romans in three wars during the first half of the first century BC. Cius was captured and sacked in 205 BC by Philip V of Macedon. Philip then presented the city to his ally Prusias I of Bithynia, who renamed it Prusa ad Mare. It served as the port of Prusa ad Olympum, just as Gemlik does today for Bursa.

After passing Gemlik the highway heads inland to the east and then northeast. Then, ten kilometres from Gemlik, it brings us to **Orhangazi**, a large village at the western end of **Iznik Gölü**, the largest lake in northwestern Turkey. Orhangazi is near the site of ancient Basilinopolis, which was founded by the Emperor Julian the Apostate c.361 in honour of his mother Basilina.

At Orhangazi we turn right on to highway 150, which takes us around the northern shore of Iznik Gölü, the ancient **Lake Ascania**. The lake is set in a beautiful plain ringed round by the blue Bithynian hills, with lush farmland, orchards and groves of trees coming right down to the reeds at the water's edge. Then, forty kilometres from Orhangazi, the road rounds the eastern end of the lake and brings us to **Iznik**, the ancient **Nicaea**.

The first view of Iznik is very impressive, as we emerge from a grove of trees at the lake's end and suddenly see a magnificent circuit of ancient defence-walls. Raymond of Aguilers first saw these walls in June 1097, approaching Nicaea with the army of the First Crusade; in his chronicle he describes it as 'A town strongly defended, both by nature and skill . . . encircled by walls that need fear no assault of man nor shock of machines.'

The defence walls of Nicaea were first erected in the Hellenistic period during the wars of the Diadochi, the successors of Alexander the Great. The city itself was founded in 316 BC by Antigonus I, who named it Antigoneia. Around 300 BC the city came under the control of Lysimachus, who named it Nicaea after his deceased first wife, a daughter of Antipater, who served as Regent of Macedonia during Alexander's invasion of Asia. Soon after the death of Lysimachus in 281 BC Nicaea was captured by Nicomedes I of Bithynia, and it served as the capital of his kingdom until he founded Nicomedia in 265 BC. After Nicomedes IV bequeathed his kingdom to Rome in 74 BC, Nicaea became capital of the Roman province of Bithynium, which was organized by Pompey. During the medieval Byzantine era Nicaea was capital of the *theme*, or military province, of the Opsikon, which included all of northwestern Asia Minor south of the Propontis. Diocletian resided here for a time, as did

Iznik

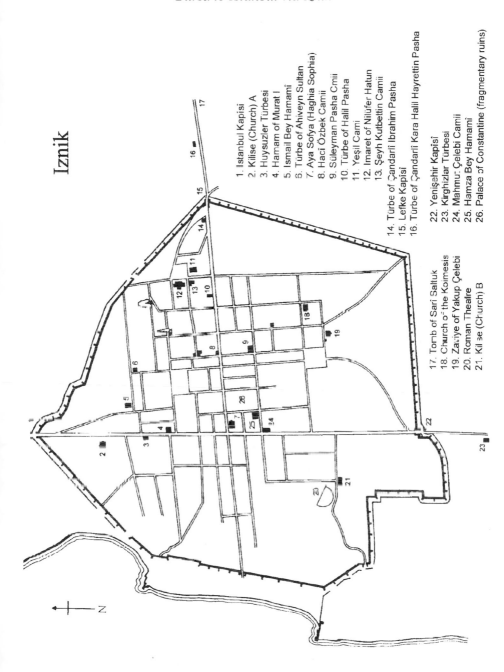

1. Istanbul Kapısı
2. Kilise (Church) A
3. Huysuzler Türbesi
4. Hamam of Murat I
5. Ismail Bey Hamami
6. Türbe of Ahiveyn Sultan
7. Aya Sofya (Haghia Sophia)
8. Hacı Özbek Camii
9. Süleyman Pasha Cmii
10. Türbe of Halil Pasha
11. Yeşil Cami
12. Imaret of Nilüfer Hatun
13. Şeyh Kutbettin Camii
14. Türbe of Çandarli Ibrahim Pasha
15. Lefke Kapisi
16. Türbe of Çandarli Kara Halil Hayrettin Pasha

17. Tomb of Sari Saltuk
18. Church of the Koimesis
19. Zaviye of Yakup Çelebi
20. Roman Theatre
21. Kilise (Church) B

22. Yenişehir Kapisi
23. Kirghizlar Türbesi
24. Mahmut Çelebi Camii
25. Hamza Bey Hamami
26. Palace of Constantine (fragmentary ruins)

Constantine the Great and Justinian. The First Ecumenical Council of the Church was convened in Nicaea by Constantine in 325, and its statement on the nature of Christ came to be known as the Nicene Creed.

During the medieval era Nicaea was captured in turn by the Goths, Arabs, Persians, Selcuks, Crusaders, Byzantines, Ottomans, Mongols, and then again by the Ottomans. Nicaea was taken by the Selcuk Turks in 1081, after which it became capital of the Sultanate of Rum, a realm that included most of Anatolia. Alexius I Comnenus succeeded in recapturing Nicaea from the Selcuks in 1097 with the aid of the knights of the First Crusade. After the capture of Constantinople by the Latins in 1204, Nicaea became the capital of one of the surviving fragments of the Byzantine Empire under Theodore I Lascaris (1204–22). The Lascarid dynasty ruled brilliantly in Nicaea for more than half a century, paving the way for the recapture of Constantinople in 1261, and beginning the cultural renaissance that flowered in Byzantium during its last two centuries.

A new age in the history of the city began in 1331, when it was captured by the Ottoman Turks under Orhan Gazi, after which it was known as Iznik. Iznik was sacked by Tamerlane shortly after his victory over Beyazit I at Ankara in 1402, as were all of the other cities in Anatolia that had the misfortune to be in the path of the Mongol horde. But Iznik recovered quickly after the Mongols departed, and under the revived Ottoman Empire it became one of the leading cities in western Anatolia.

During the next three centuries Iznik was celebrated for its beautiful ceramic tiles, which were used to adorn the palaces, mosques, tombs and other edifices of the Ottoman Empire, and which remain as its greatest contribution to Islamic art. Iznik tiles reached the peak of their perfection in the latter part of the sixteenth century, when they were used to adorn all of Sinan's great buildings. The quality of Iznik tiles declined sharply after 1620, when the potters here seem to have lost the mastery of their art, and though the kilns continued to be worked on into the mid-eighteenth century their products never again came close to their earlier perfection. By that time Iznik itself had declined to the status of an Anatolian farming village, surrounded by the monuments of its illustrious past. Then in 1922 Iznik was devastated during the fighting that took place during the last days of the Graeco-Turkish War, leaving it in ruins as the Ottoman Empire came to an end. The town has revived considerably since then, helped by the income from the flow of visitors who come to see its historic monuments. The most impressive of these are its ancient defence-walls, which though partially in ruins still almost completely encircle the town, giving it an aura of romantic grandeur.

The original Hellenistic walls of Nicaea were still standing in Strabo's time but not a trace of these now remains. The present walls were begun by the Emperor Gallienus (253–68) after the Goths sacked the city in 256. Inscriptions still visible over the Yenişehir and Lefke gates record that the walls were completed by Claudius II Gothicus in 268–69. Numerous other inscriptions record an extensive rebuilding of the walls by Michael III in 858, perhaps after one of the numerous earthquakes that shook the city. The worst of these hit Nicaea in 1065 and destroyed a large part of the city, causing considerable damage to the defence-walls, which were soon afterwards rebuilt. The last extensive restoration of the walls was by John III Vatatzes (1222–54), who added an outer wall and raised the height of the inner wall and its towers. This restoration produced the walls as we see them today, one of the most impressive Byzantine fortifications in Anatolia.

The main circuit of walls was 4,427 metres in circumference, its height ranging from 10 to 13 metres, strengthened by 114 defence towers, round or square in cross-section and 17 metres high. The outer wall added by John III extended around all sides of the city except the one facing the lake. The outer circuit was guarded by defence towers that were spaced in the intervals between the towers of the inner wall, and outside of the external curtain wall there was a ditch that at times of siege was filled with water so as to form a moat. There were originally four main gates, one at each of the cardinal points of the compass. The western gate, facing the lake, has vanished, but those on the other three sides have survived, though only part of the one on the south is still standing. In addition, there is a gate in the southwestern part of the circuit, giving access to the theatre, and also eleven smaller entryways at other points in the walls. The main gateways in the north, east and south sides were the principal entryways into Iznik up until the 1960s, when breaches were made in the walls beside each of them to facilitate the flow of traffic.

The road from Orhangazi enters the town through a breach in the walls beside **Istanbul Kapîsî**, one of the four main gateways in the defence-walls. This is the best-preserved and most impressive of the three surviving main gateways. It is a triple gate, with entryways in both the outer and inner walls and a third portal leading into the city from an oval courtyard inside the walls. The middle gate is actually a triumphal arch with a triple arcade, erected to commemorate Hadrian's visit to Nicaea in 124. The lintels of the innermost gate are surmounted by ancient theatrical masques, undoubtedly taken from Nicaea's Roman theatre.

Like most Hellenistic cities, Nicaea was laid out and built by city-planners, and its streets form a rectangular grid oriented along the cardinal directions. Atatürk Caddesi, the main avenue of the town, leads south from Istanbul Kapîsî to Yenişehir Kapîsî, while Kîlîçaslan Caddesi forms the east-west axis between Lefke Kapîsî and Göl Kapîsî.

About 220 metres south on Atatürk Caddesi, on the right side of the avenue, we come to an archaeological site known as Kilise (Church) A. The church was founded c.1254 by Theodore II, along with a school of philosophy, and dedicated to St Tryphon, whom the Emperor believed had saved his life.

Walking south from Istanbul Kapîsî along Atatürk Caddesi, just beyond the first turning on the right we come to a burial-place known as **Huysuzlar Türbesi**, the **Tomb of the Bad-Tempered Ones**. Locals believe that a Muslim saint named Uma is buried here, and that he has the power to turn naughty children into well behaved ones, if they are left by his tomb for a while.

On the left side of the next block there is a *hamam* built by **Murat I**, one of the oldest Ottoman baths in existence. There is another old bath nearby on the street that leads off to the left from Istanbul Kapîsî; this is the **Ismail Bey Hamamî**, also known as **Selcuk Hamamî**, but despite the latter name it is not Selcuk but early Ottoman. Although extremely dilapidated, the latter *hamam* is a unique masterpiece; each of its four domes, two of which have fallen in, are decorated in a different style, the most beautiful consisting of a dozen spiral arms extending from the crown to the uppermost of a series of honeycomb bands that extend far down the walls.

Continuing along in the same direction, we turn right at the next corner. As we do so we pass on our left the fourteenth-century *türbe* **of Ahiveyn Sultan**, the sainted head of a local brotherhead called the Ahi. They were known as the Ahi Brotherhood of Virtue, a religious and fraternal society formed by the craft guilds throughout Turkey in the Selcuk era and continuing through the early Ottoman period. The fourteenth-century Muslim traveller Ibn Battuta, who was received by Orhan Gazi at Bursa and also visited Iznik, praises the hospitality that he received from the Ahi brotherhood at one of their lodges:

Nowhere in the world are there to be found any to compare with them in solicitude for strangers, and in ardour to serve food to satisfy wants, to restrain the hand of the tyrannous, and to kill the agents of [unjust] policy and those who join them. An *akhi*, in their idiom, is one whom the assembled members of his trade, together with others of the young unmarried men and boys who have adopted their celibate life, choose to be their leader. . . When we had taken our place among them, they brought in a great banquet with fruits and sweetmeats, after which they began their singing and dancing. Everything about them filled us with admiration and we were greatly astonished at their generosity and innate nobility.

After passing the *türbe* we continue straight ahead as far as the second corner on the right, where we turn into a street that takes us back to Atatürk Caddesi. There we turn left and continue to the centre of town, where Atatürk Caddesi crosses Kîlîçaslan Caddesi.

At the southeast corner of the intersection we see the ruins of an ancient basilica below street level. This is the former church of **Haghia Sophia**, the principal monument of Byzantine Nicaea, known in Turkish as Aya Sofya. From Strabo's description of Nicaea, the basilica would appear to occupy the site of the Roman gymnasium which stood at the exact centre of the city, where the streets from the four main gateways intersected, just as they do today.

Excavations in 1935 revealed that the first church of Haghia Sophia on this site was probably built during the reign of Justinian. The Seventh Ecumenical Council met in this church for seven sessions in September and October 787, and in the final meeting the assembled bishops voted to restore icons to the churches of Byzantium. The excavations also revealed that this first church was destroyed by the earthquake of 1065, and that it was replaced by the present basilica, which was also dedicated to Haghia Sophia.

When Orhan Gazi captured Nicaea in 1331 he immediately converted Haghia Sophia into an Islamic house of worship, renamed Ulu Cami, the Great Mosque. The building was wrecked by Tamerlane in 1402 and was badly damaged again in the mid-sixteenth century, probably by an earthquake, after which it was repaired by Sinan on Süleyman's orders. The structure fell into disrepair in late Ottoman times, and then in 1922 it was destroyed in the fighting between the Greeks and the Turks. Part of the structure has since been restored, principally the apse, the pair of domed side-chapels flanking it, and the side walls. A glass covering protects what remains of the mosaic pavement of the nave. All that survives of the church's frescoes is under an arch on the north side of the nave; this represents a Deesis, in which Christ is flanked by the Virgin and St John the Baptist. In the apse, which is part of the Justinianic church, there is a *synthronon*, or semicircular tier of seats for the clergy.

The principal Ottoman monuments of Iznik are on the eastern side of town, which we approach by walking along Kîlîçaslan Caddesi toward Lefke Kapîsî At the fourth turning on the left we come to the oldest mosque in Iznik, **Hacî Özbek Camii**, erected in 1333, just two years after Orhan Gazi captured Nicaea. This is in fact the oldest Ottoman mosque in existence, its date of foundation recorded in the dedicatory inscription still in place on the building. The brick dome is covered with terracotta tiles, many of them original; these are curved to fit a spherical surface, a typical feature of early Ottoman mosques. The mosque is unusual in that it never had a minaret. The building originally had a three-bay porch whose arches were carried by two marble columns with Byzantine capitals, but this was demolished when the street was widened in 1939. The porch was replaced by a very ugly vestibule, which mars the external appearance of the mosque. Fortunately the interior has largely retained its original appearance, except for a gallery and some minor renovations done in 1959. The mosque is of the single-unit type: a square room, some eight metres on a side, covered by a hemispherical dome resting on a belt of Turkish triangles. There are three niches in the south or *kible* (the direction of Mecca) wall, the central one containing the plain and unattractive *mihrab*, part of the modern restoration.

We now make a short detour southward on Süleyman Sokağî, the side street opposite Hacî Özbek Camii. At the end of the block we come on our left to the **Süleyman Pasha Medresesi**, built by Orhan Gazi's eldest son a few years after the conquest of Nicaea. This was the first building to be designed specifically as a *medrese* by the Osmanlî Turks, and thus it is of particular interest in the history of Ottoman architecture. Its three-sided porticoed courtyard is now open on the north side, but originally this was almost certainly walled in. The *dershane* is off-centre on the south side, with one *hücre* to its east and two to its west, while there are four cells each on the other sides. The portico in front of the *hücres* has three bays on the south side and two each on the east and west. There was also a pool with a cascade fountain in the middle of the courtyard, but this has vanished.

Interior of the Tomb of Prince Mustafa in the Muradiye, Bursa

Yesil Camii, the Green Mosque, in Iznik

We now return to Kîlîçaslan Caddesi and continue walking eastward, and on the third block beyond Hacî Özbek Camii we come on our left to the *türbe* **of Çandarlî Halil Pasha**. Halil Pasha was a member of the famous Çandarlî family that gave five Grand Viziers to the Ottoman Empire during the fourteenth and fifteenth centuries. Halil Pasha was the fourth in that line, serving as Grand Vizier under both Murat II and Mehmet II. But Halil Pasha incurred Mehmet the Conqueror's wrath, and soon after the conquest of Constantinople he was beheaded, the first Ottoman Grand Vizier to be executed.

At the next corner we turn left on Müze Sokağî. On the right side of the street we come to **Yeşil Cami, the Green Mosque**, so named because of the colour of the tiles that revet its minaret; these were originally from the Iznik kilns, but they have since been replaced by much inferior Kütahya tiles. This interesting mosque was built between 1378 and 1392 for Çandarlî Kara Halil Hayrettin Pasha. The dedicatory inscription records that the mosque was designed and built by the otherwise unknown Hacî ben Musa, the first Ottoman architect to be identified by name. The founder was originally known as Kara Halil, but he was given the name Hayrettin by Murat I. Under Orhan Gazi he had served as Chief Justice and commander of the army, which he had led in the capture of Iznik, and then under Murat he became Grand Vizier, the first to hold that post in the Ottoman Empire. Hayrettin Pasha served as Grand Vizier until the time of his death in 1386, when he was on campaign in Macedonia. It was he who founded the Janissary Corps and staffed it with the *devşirme*, the levy of Christian youths who were converted to Islam and trained for a life in the Sultan's service.

Yeşil Cami has a porch of three bays, with two arches on the open ends. The three bays are covered by flat-topped cross-vaults, the middle one also surmounted by a fluted dome carried on a high octagonal drum; internally the dome rests on a belt of Turkish triangles. The main prayer-hall, a typical domed square, is preceded by a narthex-like antechamber of three bays, with its arches supported by two massive columns. The side bays are covered by flat-topped cross-vaults, while the central one supports a dome, much lower than that in the porch, with a closed lantern on top. The main dome is a hemisphere eleven metres in diameter and with its crown 17.5 metres above the floor, resting on a belt of Turkish triangles very much like those in Hacî Özbek Camii.

Continuing along Müze Sokağî, at the next corner we come to the **Imaret of Nilüfer Hatun**. This was built in 1388 by Murat I, who dedicated it to his mother Nilüfer Hatun, wife of Orhan Gazi. It was originally built as a *zaviye*, or hostel, for members of the Ahi Brotherhood of Virtue; later it became an *imaret*, serving free food to the poor of Iznik.

The *imaret* is built of single courses of stone alternating with four courses of brick, its vaults and domes covered with ceramic tiles. The building is preceded by an open-ended porch of five bays, with the central one surmounted by a small dome. The main hall is a square surmounted by a lofty dome carried on a belt of Turkish triangles. On either side there are two large rooms with much lower domes; each of these has a large *ocak*, or hearth, and were used as both kitchens and dormitories. In front of the main hall is another chamber of similar size divided into two lateral sections by a great arch, with each half covered by a small dome; this served as a *mescit*, as evidenced by the *mihrab* niche in the south wall.

The *imaret* now serves as the **Iznik Museum**, whose archaeological and ethnographical collections include objects from the Hellenistic, Roman, Byzantine, Selcuk and Ottoman periods. One exhibit of particular interest is devoted to the famous Iznik kilns, which have been excavated in recent years. (The museum keeper has the keys to a **Roman tomb** with frescoes outside Istanbul Kapîsî; apply to him if you wish to see the site, known as **Yeraltî Mezar**.)

Before leaving the *imaret* we might reflect upon the remarkable woman to whom this building was dedicated. Born into a noble Byzantine family, she was only a very young girl when she was captured in 1299 during a raid by Osman Gazi, the founder of the Osmanlî dynasty. Osman Gazi then gave her to his son Orhan Gazi, who made her his Birinci Kadin, or First Wife, wherupon she took the name Nilüfer Hatun. Although Orhan Gazi eventually acquired three other wives, including a daughter of John VI Cantacuzenus (1341–54), Nilüfer was apparently always first in his affections. She gave birth to his first two sons, Süleyman Pasha and Murat I, who succeeded his father in 1359. When Orhan Gazi was off on campaign Nilüfer Hatun acted as his Regent, the only woman in Ottoman history to serve in this role, which she did with great success. She also exercised power as Valide Sultan during Murat's reign, the first to hold that title.

Just beside the *imaret* we see the ruined **Şeyh Kutbettin Camii**, built in 1492 and destroyed in 1922 during the Graeco-Turkish War. The mosque was built by Çandarlî Ibrahim Pasha in honour of Şeyh Kutbettin, a renowned teacher at one of Iznik's *medreses* in the late fourteenth and early fifteenth centuries. After Tamerlane sacked Iznik in 1402 Şeyh Kutbettin confronted the fearsome Mongol leader and rebuked him, saying 'You kill and are proud of your reputation as a devil!' The rebuke stung, but Tamerlane uncharacteristically restrained his rage and spared Şeyh Kutbettin, who was thereafter revered as a saint.

We now retrace our steps along Müze Sokağî and then turn left on Kîlîçaslan Caddesi, walking towards Lefke Kapîsî. As we approach the gate we see on our left the *türbe* of **Çandarlî Ibrahim Pasha**. Ibrahim Pasha was Grand Vizier for twenty years, first under Mehmet I and then under Murat II, serving until his death in 1428. He was the third in the Çandarlî family to serve as Grand Vizier, following in the steps of his brother Ali Pasha and their father Kara Halil Hayrettin Pasha.

Like Istanbul Kapîsî, **Lefke Kapîsî** has a triumphal arch between its inner and outer gates, also erected to mark Hadrian's visit in 124. An inscription on the archway records that it was erected by the Proconsul Plancius Varus. Two panels of ancient reliefs have been built into the front façade of the outer gate; they show Roman centurions in battle against tribesmen, perhaps the Goths who were defeated by Claudius II Gothicus.

There are a number of interesting tombs in the old Turkish graveyard outside Lefke Kapîsî, where the Adapazarî road is paralleled on its right by an ancient aqueduct, a work of Justinian.

About 400 metres outside the gate, on the left side of the road, we see the very impressive *türbe* of **Çandarlî Kara Halil Hayrettin Pasha**, dated 1387. The *türbe* consists of two domed chambers, with the dome over the front hall much higher than the one to the rear, which has an oculus. The front chamber is merely the anteroom, and the inner hall is the tomb proper, containing the marble sarcophagi of Hayrettin Pasha and his son Ali Pasha. Ali Pasha succeeded his father as Grand Vizier, serving first under Murat I and then under Beyazit I; he died in 1407, during the interregnum that followed the Ottoman defeat at Ankara in 1402.

A little farther along we see another *türbe* on the other side of the road, just to the right of the aqueduct. This is the **tomb of Şarî (Blond) Saltuk**, a thirteenth-century Selcuk saint who was one of the first followers of Hacî Bektaş Veli, founder of the Bektaşi order of dervishes.

Returning through Lefke Kapîsî and retracing our steps along Kîlîçaslan Caddesi, we now take the first turning on the left, Istiklal

Lefke Kapîsî, Iznik

Caddesi. At the end of the fourth block on the right we see the exigious ruins of a Byzantine church, of which there remains only some traces of its mosaic pavement and a few sculptural and architectural fragments. This is the **Church of the Koimisis**, the Dormition of the Virgin, dated to the seventh or eighth century. It was used as the royal chapel by the first Byzantine Emperor of Nicaea, Theodore I Lascaris, who was buried here in 1222. The church continued in use up until 1922, when it was destroyed in the Graeco-Turkish War. A short distance to the east there are the pathetic remains of a Byzantine fountain-house, which may have been the baptistry of the Church of the Dormition. One of the stones enclosing the fountain has a faint relief showing a Jewish *menorah*, or candlestick, along with an inscription in Hebrew. This has led to the suggestion that there was an ancient synagogue nearby, for Nicaea did have a sizeable Jewish population in late Roman and Byzantine times.

We now walk back past the church along Yakup Sokağî, which at the next corner on the left brings us to the **Zaviye of Yakup Çelebi**, now converted into a mosque. The founder of this hospice, a smaller version of the Imaret of Nilüfer Hatun, was a younger brother of

Beyazit I. Yakup and Beyazit were the only surviving sons of Murat I at the time of the Sultan's death immediately after the battle of Kosova in 1389, when he was killed by a captive Christian on the battlefield. Yakup had distinguished himself by his bravery in the battle, but as soon as Beyazit succeeded to the throne he had his brother executed, the first instance of the code of fraticide that was to be practiced in the imperial Ottoman line for the next two centuries. Beyazit justified the killing of his brother by stating that he had acted to avoid a possible war of succession, quoting the appropriate words of the Koran: 'Death is better than disquiet'. Yakup Çelebi's *türbe* stands in front of his *zaviye* to the west. It is a domed structure with arches springing from huge piers at the corners of the building, one of the earliest examples of an open *türbe* in Ottoman architecture.

We now resume our walk along Yakup Sokağî, after which we cross Atatürk Caddesi and continue for about 300 metres along the street that leads in the same direction on the other side. This brings us to the site of the **Roman theatre** of Nicaea, a vast site that is now being excavated. The excavations have uncovered parts of the stage building and its side exits, as well as the proscenium, orchestra, *cavea* and *diazoma*. It can now be estimated that the theatre had a capacity of some 15,000. Fragments of a Byzantine church (Kilise B) of the thirteenth century and a large burial-ground have been found above the *cavea*. Excavation of the stage-building uncovered numerous ancient architectural and sculptural fragments, including a relief showing Roman charioteers in action. Elsewhere on the site archaeologists have uncovered large quantities of pottery from the Roman, Byzantine, Selcuk and Ottoman periods.

The theatre and a gymnasium at the centre of the city were built by Pliny the Younger, a project that he carried out while he was the Roman governor of Bithynium during the years 111–13. It proved to be a very frustrating task, as Pliny writes in a letter to Trajan (98–117), complaining that the theatre remained unfinished because a number of wealthy citizens of Nicaea had not come up with the funds they had pledged to the project, and noting also that work on the gymnasium had been halted because of the incompetence of the architect.

Returning to Atatürk Caddesi, we now turn right and walk south to **Yenişehir Kapîsî**. This too is a double gate, with an inscription recording that it was built in 268 by Claudius II Gothicus. The ruinous condition of this gate is due to the fact that it bore the brunt of two attacks on the city, by the Selcuks in 1081 and the Ottomans in 1331. Through this gate Alexius I Comnenus passed in triumph in

1097, after the Byzantines and their Crusader allies recaptured Nicaea from the Selcuks, as did Orhan Gazi in 1331 after Çandarlî Kara Halil Pasha had taken the city from the Byzantines. The modern road to Yenişehir and Bursa bypasses this historic gateway, and today it is used only by the villagers who have farms outside the walls in its vicinity.

About 200 metres outside Yenişehir Kapîsî, on the right side of the road, there is a tomb known as **Kîrghîzlar Türbesi**. According to tradition, it was built as the burial-place for the Kîrghiz warriors who died fighting as allies of the Ottomans during the siege of Nicaea in 1331. The tomb, which dates from the early Ottoman period, has two chambers, one barrel-vaulted and the other with a hemispherical dome on a high octagonal drum.

Returning to Yenişehir Kapîsî, we now walk back along Atatürk Caddesi toward the centre of Iznik. Three blocks before the town centre we see on our right an old mosque whose entrance is on the side street, Millet Caddesi. This is **Mahmut Çelebi Camii**, built in 1442 for a brother-in-law of Murat II. It is a single-unit mosque with a porch of three bays, a smaller and less ambitious version of Yeşil Cami, but its original character has been marred by a poor restoration. One block down Millet Caddesi and on the other side of the street we see the **Hamza Bay Hamamî**, a bath built in the reign of Murat II that is still functioning.

Turning to the left on the street beside the mosque, we see across the way a large archaeological site. This excavation, begun in 1981 by Professor Oktay Aslanapa, uncovered a building of the fourth century AD, which from the fifteenth century through the seventeenth was used for manufacturing the famed **Iznik tiles**, with some of the kilns having survived.

Continuing past the archaological site, we take the second turning on the left, which brings us back to Kîlîçaslan Caddesi. We pass Haghia Sophia and cross the intersection, continuing westward along Kiliçaslan Caddesi to **Göl Kapîsî**, the **Lake Gate**. The ancient entryway here is the only one of the four main gates of Nicaea that has not survived, though its name remains. The Lake Gate was still standing when the French traveller Charles Texier visited Iznik in 1833, and he writes that it was a very impressive portal, finer than the other three, with an inscription recording its dedication by Claudius II Gothicus.

The transverse wall that protected the Lake Gate to the south has survived, and on the shore where it ends we can still some huge squared stones half-submerged in the waters of the lake. This is all that remains of a palace that Constantine the Great built in Nicaea, and where he convened the First Ecumenical Council of the Church. There are restaurants and picnic grounds down on the shore outside the Lake Gate. There is no more pleasant spot to conclude a visit to Iznik than here, looking out over the lake and the lovely Bithynian countryside around it, with the mighty walls of the once-great city of Nicaea providing a dramatic backdrop to the scene.

Before leaving Iznik we will visit the Roman tomb known as **Yeraltî Mezar**, having first obtained the keys from the curator at the museum. The tomb is some five kilometres north of Iznik, approached via the secondary road that branches off to the right from highway 150 toward the village of Elbeyli. This is an early Christian tomb, probably of the fourth century, discovered accidentally in 1967. The tomb has since suffered considerable damage from thieves, but it still preserves most of its original paintings; these depict plates of fruit and vases of flowers, along with quail, pheasant, partridge and four magnificent peacocks, the Byzantine symbol of incorruptibility and eternal life.

We leave Iznik via Yenişehir Kapîsî, and then at the first main intersection we turn right on highway 16–09, which leads along the south side of Lake Iznik to Orhangazi. There we turn right on highway 575, heading north toward Yalova.

The highway winds down steeply through the Bithynian hills toward the shore of the Marmara, whose blue waters we soon see ahead. We finlly reach the sea at **Yalova**, a small port at the head of the deeply indented **Izmit Körfezi**, the ancient **Gulf of Nicomedeia**. Yalova was devastated in the earthquake of 17 August 1999, with considerable loss of life.

Here we will make an excursion to **Termal**, 11 kilometres to the southwest of Yalova. Termal was known to the Greeks as **Thermae Pythia**, because of its hot springs and its shrine of Apollo Pythia. This has been a famous spa since Roman times, and both the early Byzantine emperors and the late Ottoman sultans came here to take the waters, as did Atatürk, who re-established it as a resort in the early years of the Turkish Republic.

The present baths and the open-air swimming pool cluster around Hamam Deresi, a stream that is fed by hot springs. The oldest of the baths is the **Kurşunlu Hamam**, whose foundations are early Byzantine; the Hellenistic and Roman funerary stelae embedded in its exterior walls were excavated in 1932 from a site behind the old cinema building at the top of the hillside park.

Immediately behind the cinema is an archaeological site known as the **Rotunda of Justin II**, dated to the period of his reign (565–78). The Rotunda was part of a palace that Justin built in Thermae Pythia, as evidenced by a capital found there with his monogram and that of his wife Sophia. The excavations also unearthed the remains of a church dedicated to the Archangels Michael and Gabriel, built by Constantine the Great and restored by Justinian. Constantine came to the baths here during his last illness, and he was headed here on his final journey when he died at Ankyron, on the north shore of the Gulf of Nicomedeia. Justinian also came here frequently with his wife Theodora, who sought relief from her last illness in the baths of Thermae Pythia.

After returning to Yalova we head eastward on highway 130, which takes us along the southern shore of the Gulf of Izmit. Twelve kilometres from Yalova we turn left for the pier at Topçular, where there is a ferry-service across the gulf to Darîca. This spares one the long drive around the gulf via **Izmit**, the ancient **Nicomedeia**, where what little remains of the ancient Bithynian capital is buried beneath the characterless modern town.

As the ferry approches the pier at **Darîca** we see on the hillside along the shore to the right the impressive ruins of a medieval fortress. Known in Turkish as **Eskihisar**, this has been identified as **Dakibyze**, a Byzantine fortress that guarded the entrance to the Gulf of Nicomedeia. When Michael VIII Palaeologus usurped the throne in 1259, he blinded his predecessor, the young John IV Lascaris (1258–59), and imprisoned him in the fortress of Dakibyze. John spent the rest of his days in Dakibyze, outliving Michael, who died in 1281.

After landing from the ferry we make our way through a confusing series of chaotic intersections to the E-80 superhighway, following the signs for **Fatih Sultan Mehmet Köprüsü**, the upper Bosphorus bridge. The highway takes us across the northwestern-most peninsula of Bithynia, and after passing through the Asian suburbs of Istanbul we cross the Bosphorus over the upper bridge. Down below to the left is the great Turkish fortress of Rumeli Hisarî on the European shore of the Bosphorus, and on the skyline to the south we see the domes and spires of Istanbul, the imperial city, to which we now return after having traveled completely around the Sea of Marmara.

Glossary

The following are some Turkish words and technical terms that are used frequently in the text. Turkish words in parentheses are the form that they take when they are modified by a preceding noun; e.g. Yeni Cami = the New Mosque, whereas Sultan Ahmet Camii = the Mosque of Sultan Ahmet I.

ada (adasî): island
ağa (ağasî): high Ottoman official or officer
ambulatory: a covered walkway
anta (pl. antae): slightly projecting pilaster of a wall; columns placed between *antae* are said to be *in antis*.
arasta: a Turkish market street
architrave: a lintel carried from the top of one column to another, the lowest element of an entablature
archivolt: molding or other ornaments around the sides and top of a curved opening, as an arch
arcosolia: burial niches
avlu: the forecourt of a mosque
avli: the forecourt of a church
ayazma: holy well or spring
baş: head or chief
barbican: an outer defence work of a city or castle, especially around a tower, gate or bridge
basilica: a church with a central nave and side aisles of lower height
bayram: Turkish holiday
bedesten (bedesteni): a multi-domed building, usually in the centre of a Turkish market, where valuable goods are stored and sold
bema: a raised platform reserved for the clergy in a Byzantine church
beylik: Türkmen principality
birinci: first
birinci kadîn: first wife of a sultan
bulvar (bulvarî): boulevard

391

büyük: big
cadde (caddesi): avenue
caique: wooden sailboat or rowed barge
camekan: the reception or dressing-room of a Turkish bath.
cami (camii): mosque
capital: the topmost member of a column
caravanserai (in Turkish, kervanserai): an inn for travellers
çarşî (çarşîsî): market or bazaar
cavea: the auditorium of a Greek theatre
çeşme (çeşmesi): Turkish fountain
ciborium: a canopy supported by columns over an altar
conch: in architecture, the plain semidome of an apse
cornice: the upper member of the entablature
counterscarp: battlement outside moat of the Theodosian walls
cross-axial eyvan type: a mosque or medrese with eyvans on both of
    its axes
cuerda seca: a technique in which the colours in a tile are prevented
    from running into one another by a hair-like dividing line of
    permanganate of potash
curtain wall: a defence wall linking towers in a fortress
dağ (dağî): mountain
darülhadis: school of Islamic tradition
darülkura: school for learning to read and recite the Koran
darüşşifa: Islamic hospital
dershane: lecture hall of a medrese
devşirme: periodic levy of Christian youths into the Janissaries
diazoma: aisle in a Greek theatre
divan: couch; imperial Ottoman council; a collection of poems
entablature: the superstructure carried by a colonnade, comprising
    architrave, frieze and cornice
epistyle: the Greek word for the architrave
eski: old
exedra (pl. exedrae): a semicircular niche
exonarthex: outer vestibule of a Greek church
extrados: the outer curve of an arch
eyvan: vaulted alcove open at outer end
fayton: horse-drawn carriage
firman: Ottaman decree
frieze: the middle element of an entablature; also any horizontal
    zone decorated with reliefs
Gazi: warrior for the Islamic faith

Glossary

göbektaş: the central heated platform in the steam room of a Turkish bath
göl (gölü): lake
hamam (hamamî): Turkish bath
han (hanî): Ottoman commercial building or inner-city caravanserai
hararet: steam room of a Turkish bath
harem: women's section of a Turkish home or palace
hünkâr kasrî: imperial pavilion
hünkâr mahfili: imperial loge
hisar (hisarî): castle
hücre: students' cell in a medrese
hypocaust: a series of small chambers and flues through which the heat of a fire is distributed
icon: holy picture
iconostasis: the screen between the nave and chancel of a Greek church; invariably hung with icons
imam: the Muslim cleric who presides over prayers at a mosque
imaret: the public kitchen in a mosque complex
impost: in architecture, the top member of a column, pier or wall, upon which the weight of an arch will rest
intrados: the inner curve of an arch
iskele (iskelesi): ferry-landing
Janissaries: elite corps of the Ottoman army
kadîn: woman; wife
kafes: cage; the apartment in the harem of Topkapî Sarayî where the younger brothers of the sultan were confined
kale (kalesi): fortress
kapi (kapîsî): door or gate
kapî ağasî: the Chief White Eunuch in Topkapî Sarayî
kasîr (kasrî): royal pavilion
kervanserai: caravanserai
kible: direction of Mecca
kilim: flat-weave carpet
kilise: church
kîz: girl
kîzlar ağasî: the Chief White Eunuch in Topkapî Sarayî
konak (konağî): an Ottoman mansion
köprü (köprüsü): bridge
köşk (köşkü): kiosk
köy (köyü): village
küçük: little

kule (kulesi): tower
külliye (külliyesi): Ottoman religious complex, usually comprising a
 mosque and its associated buildings
kuran kürsü: throne on which the imam sits when he is reading the
 Koran
kütüphane (kütüphanesi): library
lokanta (lokantasî): restaurant
lunette: in architecure, that surface at the upper part of a wall which
 is partly surrounded by a vault which the wall intersects
martyrium: shrine of a Christian martyr
medrese (medresesi): Islamic school of theology
megaron: the principal hall of a Bronze Age Greek palace
mektep: Ottoman primary school
mescit (mescidi): small mosque
meydan (meydanî): a village square or town centre
meyhane: tavern
mihrab: niche in a mosque indicating the direction of Mecca
mimar: architect
mimber: the pulpit in a mosque
minaret: the tower beside a mosque from which the müezzin gives
 the call to prayer
müezzin: Islamic cleric who gives the call to prayer and chants the
 responses to the prayers of the imam
müezzin mahfili: the raised platform in a mosque from which the
 müezzin chants the responses to the prayers of the imam
müneccim: the mosque astronomer
muvakithane: house of the mosque astronomer
müze (müzesi): museum
narthex: vestibule of a Greek church
namagzah: outdoor place of Islamic prayer
ocak: a Turkish fireplace or hearth
oculus: circular opening in a roof
oda (odasî): room or chamber
ogive: pointed arch
opus Alexandrinium: mosaic pavement consisting of circular stones
 of various colours
opus sectile: a mosaic pavement inlaid in stone or marble in geometric patterns
parateichion: outer terrace of the Theodosian walls
parecclesion: side chamber in a Byzantine church, often used as a
 funerary chapel

Glossary

pasha: one of the highest-ranking Ottoman official, the equivalent of a general

pazar (pazarî): bazaar or market

pazar caique: imperial rowed barge

pendentive: triangular curved overhanging surface which springs from the corners of a square or rectangular base to the cornice of a circular or polygonal dome

penetralia: in architecture, the innermost parts of a palace or temple

plinth: a block serving as a base for a statue, or, the lowest member of a base

peribolos: terrace between the inner and outer walls of the Theodosian walls

protichisma: outer wall of the Theodosian walls

reveal: the side of an opening for a window or doorway, between the frame and the outer surface of the wall

roundel: a circular pane, recess or window

şadîrvan: ablution fountain

sandal: small boat

saray (sarayî): palace

sarnîç: cistern

sebil: fountain-house used to distribute water free to passers-by

selamlîk: the men's section of a Turkish home or palace

selsebil: cascade fountain

şerefe: balcony of a minaret

Şeyh: head of a Muslim religious order

Şeyhülislam: the head of the Ottoman religious hierarchy in the Ottoman Empire

sibyan mektebi: Ottoman primary school, sometimes simply called a mektep

soffit: the underside of an arch or cornice

soğukluk: the chamber of intermediate temperature in a Turkish bath

sokak (sokağî): street

sphendone: curved end of a hippodrome

spina: central axis of a hippodrome

squinches: an arch, lintel, corbeling or the like, carried across the corner of a room to support a superimposed mass

suterazi: Ottoman water-control tower

synthronon: tiers of seats for the clergy around the periphery of the apse

tabhane: a hospice for travelling dervishes

tekke (tekkesi): a dervish lodge

tepe (tepesi): hill
timarhane: Ottoman insane asylum
tip medrese: Ottoman medical school
top: cannon
tuğra: imperial Ottoman monogram
tumulus (pl. tumuli): earth mound
türbe (türbesi): mausoleum
Turkish triangles: a curved surface of triangles that performs the
    same function as a pendentive
ulema: ruling body of Islamic clerics
tympanum (pl. tympana): in architecture, the space within an arch,
    and above a lintel or subordinate arch
Valide Sultan: mother of a reigning sultan
vakfiye: Ottoman deed of foundation
Vizier: high-ranking Ottoman official, member of the imperial
    council
volute: in architecture, a spiral or scroll-like conformation
voussoir: truncated wedge-shaped block forming part of an arch
weight-turret: same as a weight-tower
yalî (yalîsî): waterfront mansion
yeni: new
yokuş (yokuşu): steep path
yol (yolu): road
zaviye: side chamber in a mosque used as a hostel for dervishes

Food

Turkish cuisine is one of the most renowned in the world, and in Istanbul and its environs around the Marmara you can enjoy it in all of its abundance and variety. Istanbul has restaurants (*lokanta*) catering to every taste and social class, ranging from humble cookshops for workers to deluxe restaurants with elaborate Turkish and international menus.

Turks usually begin their meal with cold hors d'ouevres (*soğuk meze*), which are brought to the table on a huge tray (*tepsi*) from which you can select anything your heart desires. You can then order various hot hors d'oeuvres (*sîcak meze*). After that comes the main course, either meat (*et*) or fish (*balîk*), which may be followed by a sweet (*tatlî*) or fruit (*meyva*) and Turkish coffee (*kahve*).

Many restaurants serve only kebabs, and in some of these, known as *ocakbaşî lokanta*, you can cook the meat yourself on a grille. The cookshops frequented by workers have a much simpler approach, displaying their dishes in the refrigerator or in pots and pans so you can just point out your choices to the waiter.

The menu below includes most of the popular dishes that are served in Istanbul restaurants.

So uk Meze (cold hors d'oeuvres)
ahtapot: octopus
beyaz penir: white goat cheese
biber dolmasî: green peppers stuffed with *pilav*, or cooked rice
cacik: chopped cucumbers with yoghurt and garlic
çig köfte: steak tartar Turkish style
çiroz: dried salted thin mackerel
domates dolmasî: tomatoes stuffed with *pilav*
fava: mashed broad beans with dill weed
haydari. thickened yoghurt with garlic and dill weed
humus: mashed chick peas with sesame seed oil
imam bayîldî: (literally, 'The Imam Fainted') aubergines with
    parsley

lahana dolmasî: cabbage stuffed with *pilav*
lakerda: salted bonito
midye pilakîsî: mussels cooked with olive oil and served cold
patlîcan dolmasî: stuffed aubergines cooked in olive oil
pilaki: white or red beans cooked in olive oil
tarama: carp roe
yaprak dolmasî: green peppers stuffed with *pilav*
zeytin: olives

Salata (salads)
çoban salata: (Shepherd's Salad) chopped peppers, tomatoes,
    lettuce, cucumbers and celery
fasulye ezmesi: dried kidney bean salad
ispanakoku salatasî: spinach root salad
karides: shrimp
marul: Romaine lettuce
pancar salatasî: beet salad
patates ezmesi: mashed potato salad
patlîcan salatasî: aubergine salad
piyaz: dried white kidney bean salad
salatalîk salatasî: cucumber salad
yeşil salata: green salad
yoğurtlu kabak salatasî: zucchini salad with yoghurt

Sîcak Meze (hot hors d'oeuvres)
Among the most popular hot *meze* dishes are the various types of
    börek, thin layers of pastry with various fillings, such as the
    following:
etli börek: *borek* with minced meat filling
ispanaklî börek: *borek* with spinach filling
pastîrmalî börek: *börek* filled with dried spiced beef
peynerli börek: *börek* with cheese filling

Other popular hot *meze* dishes are the following:
arnavut ciğer: chopped liver and onions
et saute: thin slices of meat sautéed in tomato and pepper sauce
izgara köfte: grilled meatballs
kabak kîzartmasî: fried zucchini
kokoreç: charcoal-grilled stuffed mutton intestines
menemen: eggs scrambled with green and red peppers and white
    cheese
midye dolmasî: fried mussels served in the shell and stuffed with *pilav*

midye tavasî: fried mussels
patates köftesi: potato croquettes

Çorba (soup)
domateslî çorba: tomato soup
domates pirinç çorbasî: tomato and rice soup
düğün çorbasî (Wedding Soup): soup with meat, vegetables, egg and
  paprika
işkembe çorbasî: tripe soup
mercimek çorbasî: lentil soup
sebze çorbasî: vegetable soup
tavuk çorbasî: chicken soup
yayla çorbasî: beef soup with yoghurt

Etler (meat dishes)
Meat (and fish) may be prepared in several ways: grilled (*izgara*),
  fried (*tava*), roasted (*kîzartma*), in casserole (*güveç*), or grilled on
  a skewer (*şış*). The general types of meat are the following:
bonfil: steak fillet
ciğer: liver
dana: veal
kiyma: minced meat
kuzu: lamb
pirzola: lamb chops
sîğîr: beef

Among the most popular meat dishes are the various types of kebabs:
bahçevan kebab: meat cooked with all of the vegetables one would
  find in a typical kitchen garden
Beyti kebab: wrapped lamb cutlet
Bursa kebab: döner kebab served with yoghurt and tomato sauce,
  also called Iskender kebab
çöp kebab: same ingredients as in *tas kebab*, but cooked in a wax-
  paper envelope
döner kebab: pressed lamb cooked on a rotating spit over a charcoal
  fire and carved off in thin slices
islim kebab: meat and vegetables cooked in a covered casserole
kağît kebab: meat, vegetables and herbs in a wine sauce, cooked in a
  wax-paper envelope
şiş kebab: lamb skewered on a spit with tomatoes and onions and
  grilled over a charcoal fire
tas kebab: lamb stew with rice and vegetables

Other popular meat dishes are:

cîzbîz köfte: grilled meatballs
eksiki köfte: meatballs with rice in thick creamy sauce
güveç: meat or poultry baked together with vegetables in a casserole
hünkâr beğendi ('The Sultan's Favourite'): puréed aubergine served
  with meat or chicken
Izmir köfte: meatballs and potato slices cooked in tomato sauce
kadîn budu ('The Lady's Thigh'): ground meat and rice formed into
  oval patties and then dipped into beaten eggs and fried
karnîyarîk ('Belly Split Open'): ground meat cooked together with
  aubergines
kîş türlüsü: a winter (*kîş*) dish cooked with meat, carrots, celery,
  potatoes and leeks
karîşîk izgara: mixed grill
kuzu çevirme: stuffed lamb grilled on a charcoal fire
kuzu fîrîn: roast leg of lamb
kuzu şaşlik: grilled lamb
kuzu tandir: oven roast lamb
şatobriand: Chateaubriand
şnitzel: schnitzel
türlü: lamb stew with vegetables

Balîk (Fish)
alabalîk: trout
balîk buğulama: fish stew
balîk köftesi: ground fish patties
barbunya: red mullet
çinakok: a species of small bluefish
dil: sole
hamsi: anchovy (fresh)
istavrit: horse mackerel
kalkan: turbot
karagöz: black bream
kîlîç: swordfish
kîlîç şişte: swordfish skewered on a spit and cooked over a charcoal fire
lüfer: bluefish
levrek: bass
mercan: bream
palamut: bonito
tekir: small red mullet
üskümrü: mackerel

Food

Tavuk (Poultry)
tavuk: chicken (it also means poultry)
çerkez tavuk (Circassian chicken): chicken with walnut sauce
pîlîç: young chicken
pîlîç dolmasî: stuffed chicken
pîlîç kağîta: chicken cooked in a wax-paper envelope
tavuklu beğendi: chicken in egg purée
tavuklu güveç: chicken casserole
bîldîrçîn: quail
hindi dolmasî: stuffed turkey
kaz: goose
keklik: partridge
ördek: duck
sülün: pheasant

Hamur Isleri ve Pilav (breads/pasta and rice pilaf)
bazlama: small, thick pita bread
beyaz pilav: cooked rice
bulgur pilavî: cracked wheat pilaf
domatesli pilav: cooked rice with tomatoes
ekmek: bread
kîzarmîş ekmek: toasted bread
etli pide: Turkish meat pide
iç pilav: rice with raisins, pine nuts and diced chicken liver
lahmacun: spicy Turkish pizza with meat and onions
mantî: Turkish ravioli
puf boreği: deep fried wafer thin dough with cheese or meat
su boreği: flaky pastry pie with white cheese

Sebze (vegetables)
bezelye: peas
bamya: okra
biber: green peppers
çalî fasuliye: green string beans
domates: tomatoes
enginar: artichoke
fasulye: green beans
havuç: carrots
hîyar: cucumber (also called *salatalîk*)
ispanak: spinach
kabak: zucchini

karnîbahar: cauliflower
kereviz: root celery
kuskonmaz: asparagus
lahana: cabbage
mantar: mushrooms
maydonoz: parsley
pancar: beets
patates: potatoes
patlîcan: aubergine
pirasa: leeks
pirinç: rice (*pilav* when cooked)
soğan: onion

Meyva (fruit)
çilek: strawberry
elma: apple
erik: plum
grepfrut: grapefruit
incir: fig
karpuz: watermelon
kavun: melon
kiraz: cherry
limon: lemon
muz: banana
portakal: orange
şeftali: peach
üzüm: grapes
vişne: sour cherry

Tatlî (sweets and puddings)
aşure ('Noah's Pudding'): sweet pudding with walnuts, raisins and peas
ayva: quince
ayva kompostu: stewed quince
baklava: many-layered pastry filled with walnuts, baked and soaked in syrup
bal kabağî tatlîsî: pumpkin dessert
bülbül yuvasî ('The Nightingale's Nest'): shredded wheat with pistachios and syrup
dondurma: ice cream
ekmek kadayîfî: crumpet in syrup

helva: dessert made with farina and flour mixed with nuts and served with cinnamon
kadîn göbeğî ('The Lady's Navel'): doughnut soaked in syrup
lokma: flour dessert fried in oil and soaked in syrup
muhallebi: pudding made from milk, rice and rose-water
sutlaç: rice pudding

İçkiler (drinks)
rakî: a strong (87 proof) anise-flavoured drink, usually mixed half-and-half with water
bira: beer
şerap: wine
beyaz şerap: white wine
kîrmîzî şerap: red wine
meyva suyu: fruit juice
kola: Coca Cola or Pepsi Cola
su: water
maden suyu: mineral water
süt: milk
ayran: a kind of liquid yoghurt
boza: a drink made from millet
çay: tea
kahve: Turkish coffee; with no sugar (*sade*); little sugar (*az şekerli*); medium sweet (*orta şekerli*); sweet (*şekerli*)

Miscellaneous
biber: pepper
buz: ice
kîzarmîş patates: chips
tuz: salt
omlet: omlette
peynir: cheese
şeker: sugar
sirke: vinegar
tereyağ: butter
yag: oil
yoğurt: yoghurt
yumurta: egg
zeytinyağî: olive oil

Emperors and Sultans

Byzantine Emperors
(*ruled in Nicaea only)

Constantine the Great, 324–37
Constantius, 337–61
Julian, 361–63
Jovian, 363–64
Valens, 364–78
Theodosius I, 379–95
Arcadius, 395–408
Theodosius II, 408–50
Marcian, 450–57
Leo I, 457–74
Leo II, 474
Zeno, 474–91
Anastasius I, 491–518
Justin I, 518–27
Justinian I, 527–65
Justin II, 565–78
Tiberius II, 578–82
Maurice, 582–602
Phocas, 602–10
Heraclius, 610–41
Constantine II, 641
Heraclonas, 641
Constantine III, 641–68
Constantine IV, 668–85
Justinian II, 685–95
Leontius, 695–98
Tiberius III, 698–705
Justinian II (2nd reign), 705–11
Philippicus Vardan, 711–14
Anastasius II, 714–15
Theodosius III, 715–17
Leo III, 717–41
Constantine V, 741–75
Leo IV, 775–80
Constantine VI, 780–97
Eirene, 797–802
Nicephorus I, 802–11
Stauracius, 811
Michael I, 811–13

Leo V, 813–20
Michael II, 820–29
Theophilus, 829–42
Michael III, 842–67
Basil I, 867–86
Leo VI, 886–912
Alexander, 912–13
Constantine VII Porphyrogenitus, 913–59
Romanus I Lecapenus, 919–44
Romanus II, 959–63
Nicephorus II Phocas, 963–69
John I Tzimisces, 969–76
Basil II, 976–1025
Constantine VIII, 1025–28
Romanus III Argyrus, 1028–34
Michael IV, 1034–41
Michael V, 1041–42
Theodora and Zoe, 1042
Constantine IX, 1042–55
Theodora (2nd reign), 1055–56
Michael VI, 1056–57
Isaac I Comnenus, 1057–59
Constantine X Doucas, 1059–67
Eudocia Macrembolittisa, 1067
Romanus IV Diogenes, 1068–71
Michael VII Doucas, 1071–78
Nicephorus III Botaneiates, 1078–81
Alexius I Comnenus, 1081–1118
John II Comnenus, 1118–43
Manuel I Comnenus, 1143–80
Alexius II Comnenus, 1180–83
Andronicus I Comnenus, 1183–85
Isaac II Angelus, 1185–95
Alexius III Angelus, 1195–1203
Isaac II Angelus (2nd reign), 1203–04
Alexius IV Angelus, 1203–04
Alexius V Doucas Mourtzouphlos, 1204
*Theodore I Lascaris, 1204–22

*John III Vatatzes, 1222–54
*Theodore II Lascaris, 1254–58
*John IV Lascaris, 1258–59
Michael VIII Palaeologus, 1259–82
Andronicus II Palaeologus, 1282–1328
Michael IX Palaeologus, 1294–1320
Andronicus III Palaeologus, 1328–41
John V Palaeologus, 1341–91
John VI Cantacuzenus, 1347–54
Andronicus IV Palaeologus, 1376–79
John VII Palaeologus, 1391–1425
John VIII Palaeologus, 1425–48
Constantine XI Dragases, 1449–53

Latin Emperors of Constantinople

Baldwin I of Flanders, 1204–05
Henry of Hainault, 1206–16
Peter of Courtenay, 1217–18
Yolanda, 1218–19
Robert of Courtenay, 1221–28
Baldwin II, 1228–61
John of Brienne, 1231–37

Ottoman Sultans
(*ruled before the Turkish capture of Constantinople)

*Osman Gazi, c.1282–1326
*Orhan Gazi, 1326–59
*Murat I, 1359–89
*Beyazit I, 1389–1402
(Interregnum)
*Mehmet I, 1413–21
*Murat II, 1421–51
Mehmet II (Fatih), 1451–81

Beyazit II, 1481–1512
Selim I, 1512–20
Süleyman I, the Magnificent, 1520–66
Selim II, 1566–74
Murat III, 1574–95
Mehmet III, 1595–1603
Ahmet I, 1603–17
Mustafa I, 1617–18
Osman II, 1618–22
Mustafa I (2nd reign), 1622–23
Murat IV, 1623–40
Ibrahim, 1640–48
Mehmet IV, 1648–87
Süleyman II, 1687–91
Ahmet II, 1691–95
Mustafa II, 1695–1703
Ahmet III, 1703–30
Mahmut I, 1730–54
Osman III, 1754–57
Mustafa III, 1757–74
Abdül Hamit I, 1774–89
Selim III, 1789–1807
Mustafa IV, 1807–08
Mahmut II, 1808–39
Abdül Mecit I, 1839–61
Abdül Aziz, 1861–76
Murat V, 1876
Abdül Hamit II, 1876–1909
Mehmet V Reşat, 1909–18
Mehmet VI Vahidettin, 1918–22
Abdül Mecit (II) (caliph only), 1922–24

Kings of Bithynia

Zipoetes, c.297–279 BC
Nicomedes I, c.279–255 BC
Ziaelas, c.255–228 BC
Prusias I, 228–185 BC
Prusias II, 185–149 BC
Nicomedes II, 149–128 BC
Nicomedes III, 128–94 BC
Nicomedes IV, 94–74 BC

Museums, Monuments
and Archaeological Sites:
Opening Hours

The list below gives the hours of admission to the various museums, monuments and archaeological sites covered in this guide. Mosques are not included on this list; they are open during the five occasions of daily prayer, and often at other times as well. The larger mosques are open throughout the day. The smaller ones may be closed between the hours of prayer, but if you stand patiently by the front door someone will usually fetch the caretaker to open the mosque. Shoes must be taken off at the door and placed on a shelf, usually inside the mosque. Shorts should not be worn when visiting a mosque, and women should wear a head-scarf and cover their arms.

Most of the Greek, Armenian and Roman Catholic churches in Istanbul are accessible during the day, although you will have to ring the bell and wait for the caretaker to admit you.

Archaeological sites and local museums outside Istanbul are usually open 9.00–17.00, although the hours may be extended in summer.

The opening hours listed below for the museums and monuments in Istanbul may vary by half-an-hour or an hour according to the season. All museums, monuments and fenced-in archaeological sites are closed on the following national holidays: 23 April, 1 May, 19 May, 27 May, 30 August, 29 October. They are also closed during the religious holidays of Şeker Bayram and Kurban Bayram, whose dates are regulated by the Islamic calendar and thus change from year to year.

Opening Hours

HOURS OF ADMISSION TO THE MUSEUMS
AND MONUMENTS OF ISTANBUL

Akrida Synagogue, Kurkçu Çeşme Sok. 15, Balat (tel. 521–5710); permission to visit can be obtained from the Chief Rabbinate (Hahambaşîlîğî, Yemenici Sok. Tünel (tel. 244–8794)

Archaeological Museums (Arkeologi Müzeleri), Sultan Ahmet, tel. 520–7740). Archaeological Museum: open 9.30–16.30; some of the galleries are at present closed for restoration, while others are open on a rotating basis, so one should check the listing at the ticket desk, which also gives the opening times for the Çinili Köşk and the Museum of the Ancient Orient (Eski Şark Müzesi). The latter museum is currently closed for restoration. All sections of the museums are closed Mondays.

Atatürk Museum (Atatürk Müzesi), Halaskargazi Cad. 250, Şişli, tel. 240–6309: open 9.30–16.30; closed Thursdays, Sundays.

Aynalîkavak Kasrî, Kasîmpaşa-Hasköy Yolu, Hasköy, tel. 256–9750: open 9.00–17.00; closed Mondays, Thursdays.

Basilica Cistern (Yerebatansaray), Yerebatan Cad., Sultanahmet, tel. 522–1259: open 9.00–17.00 daily.

Beylerbey Palace (Beylerbey Sarayî), Beylerbey, tel. 0216-321–9320: open 9.30–16.00; closed Mondays, Thursdays.

Calligraphy Museum (Hat Sanatlar Müzesi), Beyazit Square, tel. 527–5851: open 9.00–16.00; closed Sundays, Mondays.

Caricature Museum (Karikatür Müzesi), Karacîlar Cad., Barbaros Bulvarî, tel. 521–1264: open 9.00–17.00 daily.

Carpet and Kilim Museums (Halî ve Kilim Müzesi), Sultanahmet, tel. 518 1330: open 9.30 12.00, 13.00–16.00; closed Sundays, Mondays. Dolmabahçe Palace (Dolmabahçe Sarayî), Beşiktaş, tel. 258–5544: open 9.00–16.00; closed Mondays, Thursdays.

Fethiye Camii (Church of the Pammakaristos), Fener, tel. 522–1750: permission to visit must be obtained from the Director of the Haghia Sophia Museum.

Fire Brigade Museum (Itfaiye Müzesi), Itfaiye Cad. 9, Fatih, tel. 524 1126: open 9.30–14.30; closed Mondays.

Galata Mevlevi Dervish Monastery and Museum of Divan Literature (Divan Edebiyatî Müzesi), Galip Dede Cad. 15, Tünel, tel. 245–4141: open 9.30–16.30.

Galata Tower (Galata Kulesi), Büyükhendek Sok., Şişhane, tel. 245–1160: open 8.00–21.00 daily.

407

Haghia Eirene (Aya Ireni), Topkapî Sarayî: open only during recitals and exhibitions.

Haghia Sophia (Aya Sofya), Sultanahmet, tel. 522–1750: open 9.30–16.30; closed Mondays.

Ibrahim Pasha Palace and the Museum of Turkish and Islamic Art (Türk ve Islam Eserleri Müzesi), At Meydanî 46, Sultanahmet, tel. 518–1385): open 10.00–17.00; closed Mondays.

Istanbul Library (Çelik Gülersoy Foundation), Soğukçeşme Sok., Sultanahmet, tel. 512–5730: open 10.00–12.00, 13.00–16.30; open Mondays, Wednesdays, Fridays.

Kariye Camii (Church of St Saviour in Chora), Kariye Camii Sok., Edirnekapî, tel. 631–9241: open 9.30–16.30; closed Tuesdays.

Rahmi M. Koç Industrial Museum (Koç Endüstrial Müzesi), Hasköy Cad. 27, Sütluce, tel. 265–7153: open 10.00–17.00; closed Mondays.

Küçüksu Palace (Küçüksu Kasrî): open 9.00–16.00; closed Mondays, Thursdays.

Military Museum (Askeri Müze), Harbiye, tel. 233–7115: open 9.00–17.00; closed Mondays, Tuesdays.

Mosaic Museum (Mozayik Müzesi), Arasta Sok., Sultanahmet, tel. 518–1205: open 9.00–17.00; closed Tuesdays.

Naval Museum (Deniz Müzesi), Beşiktaş, tel. 261–0040: open 9.30–17.00; closed Mondays, Tuesdays.

Rumeli Hisarî Fortress, Rumell Hisarî, tel. 263–5305: open 9.30–17.00: closed Mondays.

Sadberk Hanîm Museum, Büyükdere Cad. 27–29, Sarîyer, tel. 242–3813: open 10.30–17.00; closed Wednesdays.

Topkapî Sarayî, Sultanahmet, tel. 512–0480: open 9.30–17.00; Harem open 10.00–16.00; closed Tuesdays.

Yedikule (Castle of the Seven Towers), Yedikule, tel. 585–8933: open 9.30–17.00; closed Mondays.

Yîldîz Palace, Beşiktaş, tel. 258–3080, ext. 380: Şale Köşk & Marangozhane open 10.00–16.00; closed Mondays, Tuesdays.

Select Bibliography

Oktay Aslanapa. *Turkish Art and Architecture*, London, 1971

Apollonius of Rhodes. *The Argonautica*, translated by E. V. Rieu, London, 1959

Arrian. *The Campaigns of Alexander*, translated by Aubrey de Sélincourt, New York, 1971

Esin Atîl. *The Age of Süleyman the Magnificent*, Washington and New York, 1987

Franz Babinger. *Mehmed the Conqueror and His Time*, translated by Ralph Manheim, edited by William Hickman, Princeton, 1978

Patrick Balfour (Lord Kinross). *Atatürk, The Rebirth of a Nation*, London, 1964; *The Ottoman Centuries*, London, 1987

Carl. W. Blegen. *Troy and the Trojans*, London, 1963

Ottaviano Bon. *The Sultan's Seraglio: An Intimate Portrait of Life in the Ottoman Court*, edited by Godfrey Goodwin, London, 1996

Evliya Çelebi. *Seyahatname (Narrative of Travels)*, translated by Joseph von Hammer, London, 1834; reprinted (2 volumes) New York, 1968

Fanny Davis. *The Palace of Topkapî*, New York, 1970

Glanville Downey. *Constantinople in the Age of Justinian*, Norman, Oklahoma, 1960

John Freely. *Stamboul Sketches*, Istanbul, 1974; *Istanbul, The Imperial City*, London, 1996

John Freely and Augusto Romano Burelli, photographs by Ara Güler. *Sinan, The Architect of Süleyman the Magnificent*, Paris, 1992

Godfrey Goodwin. *A History of Ottoman Architecture*, London, 1971; *The Janissaries*, London, 1994; *The Private World of Ottoman Women*, London, 1997

Peter Green. *Alexander of Macedon*, London, 1970

N. G. L. Hammond. *A History of Greece to 322 BC*, Oxford, 1967

Herodotus, *The Histories*, translated by Aubrey De Sélincourt, New York, 1954

Joan Haslip. *The Sultan; the Private Life of Abdül Hamit II*, London, 1958

Homer. *The Iliad*, translated by Richmond Lattimore, Chicago, 1951

Colin Imber. *The Ottoman Empire, 1300–1481*, Istanbul, 1990

Halil Inalcîk. *The Ottoman Empire; The Classical Age, 1300–600*, London, 1973; *The Ottoman Empire: conquest, organization and economy*, London, 1978

Romilly Jenkins. *Byzantium, The Imperial Centuries, A.D. 610–1071*, London, 1966

Richard Krautheimer. *Early Christian and Byzantine Architecture*, revised by the author and Slobodan Curcic, New Haven, 1986

Aptullah Kuran. *Sinan, The Grand Old Man of Ottoman Architecture*, Washington, 1986

Michael Levey. *The World of Ottoman Art*, London, 1971

Bernard Lewis. *The Emergence of Modern Turkey*, Oxford, 1961; *Istanbul and the Civilization of the Ottoman Empire*, Norman, Oklahoma, 1963

Raphaela Lewis. *Everyday Life in the Ottoman Empire*, London, 1971

Cyril A. Mango. *Byzantine Architecture*, New York, 1976; *Byzantium, The Empire of the New Rome*, London, 1980

Philip Mansel. *Constantinople, City of the World's Desire, 1453–1924*, London, 1995

Gülrü Necipoğlu. *Architecture, Ceremonial and Power; the Topkapî Palace in the Fifteenth and Sixteenth Centuries*, Cambridge, Massachusetts, 1991

Donald M. Nicol. *The Last Centuries of Byzantium, 1261–1453*, Cambridge, 1972

John Julius Norwich. *Byzantium, The Early Centuries*, London, 1988; *Byzantium, The Apogee*, London, 1991; *Byzantium, The Decline and Fall*, London, 1995

George Ostrogorsky. *History of the Byzantine State*, translated by Joan Hussey, Oxford, 1956

Alan Palmer. *The Decline and Fall of the Ottoman Empire*, London, 1992

Leslie P. Peirce, *The Imperial Harem; Women and Sovereignty in the Ottoman Empire*, Oxford, 1993

N. M. Penzer. *The Harem*, London, 1965

F. E. Peters. *The Harvest of Hellenism*, New York, 1970

Nicole and Hugh Pope. *Turkey Unveiled*, London, 1997

Michael Psellus. *Chronographia*, translated by E. R. A. Sewter, London, 1953

David Talbot Rice, *The Art of Byzantium*, London, 1959

Select Bibliography

Tamara Talbot Rice. *Everyday Life in Byzantium*, New York, 1967

Lyn Rodley. *Byzantine Art and Architecture: An Introduction*, Cambridge, 1994

Steven Runciman. *Byzantine Civilization*, London, 1933; *The Fall of Constantinople, 1453*, Cambridge, 1965; *The Last Byzantine Renaissance*, Cambridge, 1971

Sanford Shaw and Ezel Kural Shaw. *History of the Ottoman Empire and Modern Turkey.* Vol. I: *Empire of the Gazis; The Rise and Decline of the Ottoman Empire, 1280–1808*, Cambridge, 1976. Vol. II: *Reform, Revolution and Republic: The Rise of Modern Turkey*, Cambridge, 1977

Thucydides. *The Peloponnesian War*, translated by Rex Warner, Harmondsworth, 1954

Paul A. Underwood. *The Kariye Djami* (3 volumes), Princeton, 1966

411

Index

Index

Index

Index

Index

Index

Index